Managing Information Across the Enterprise

❖ ❖ ❖

Robert K. Wysocki, Ph.D.
Director
Career Management Systems
Computerworld
Framingham, Massachusetts

Robert L. DeMichiell, Ph.D.
Professor, Information Systems
School of Business
Fairfield University
Fairfield, Connecticut

JOHN WILEY & SONS, INC.
New York   Chichester   Brisbane   Toronto   Singapore   Weinheim

ACQUISITIONS EDITOR	Beth Lang Golub
ASSISTANT EDITOR	David B. Kear
MARKETING MANAGER	Leslie Hines
SENIOR PRODUCTION EDITOR	Jeanine Furino
TEXTBOOK DESIGNER	Nancy Field
ASSISTANT MANUFACTURING MANAGER	Dorothy Sinclair
FREELANCE ILLUSTRATION COORDINATOR	Gene Aiello

This book was set in ITC Garamond Light by Carlisle Communications and printed and bound by R.R. DONNELLEY & SONS INC. The cover was printed by PHOENIX COLOR.

Recognizing the importance of preserving what has been written, it is a policy of John Wiley & Sons, Inc. to have books of enduring value published in the United States printed on acid-free paper, and we exert our best efforts to that end.

Copyright © 1997, by John Wiley & Sons, Inc.

All rights reserved. Published simultaneously in Canada.

Reproduction or translation of any part of
this work beyond that permitted by Sections
107 and 108 of the 1976 United States Copyright
Act without the permission of the copyright
owner is unlawful. Requests for permission
or further information should be addressed to
the Permissions Department, John Wiley & Sons, Inc.

Library of Congress Cataloging in Publication Data:

Wysocki, Robert K.
    Managing information across the enterprise / Robert K. Wysocki,
Robert L. DeMichiell.
      p. cm.
    Includes bibliographical references.
    ISBN 0-471-12719-1 (cloth : alk. paper)
    1. Information technology—Management. 2. Management information
systems. I. DeMichiell, Robert L. II. Title.
HD30.2.W97   1997
658.4'038—dc20
                                         96-30257
                                                        CIP

CIPPrinted in the United States of America
10 9 8 7 6 5 4 3 2 1

Prologue

◆ ◆ ◆

◆ NEW LEARNING CHALLENGE

The pace of change in information technologies and their applications in business is staggering. It is impossible for any one individual to keep up. As a result, many managers have found that they must make choices in technologies that they will track. Because of this rapid change, the business community should begin to appreciate the difficulty of providing students with an education that prepares them for their life's work. The learning challenge is further exacerbated by the constant battle to understand the line that separates education from training.

Because of this accelerated rate of change in technology and its application to the enterprise, the educational task is formidable. Additional problems arise when one considers the business opportunities that have been created as a result of those very same changes in technology. Who, for example, could have envisioned the feeding frenzy that the Internet has created? To plan an effective marketing strategy one must now consider how the immediate access to vast stores of information on the Net and the World Wide Web affects the way customers discover products and services. If the Internet is not incorporated in the business plan, it may mean relinquishing market share to the competition with little promise of regaining it. To incorporate the Internet is to court a confusing and bewildering array of possibilities with no guidelines or experiences to draw upon for counsel or advice.

◆ THE NEED FOR A NEW BUSINESS AND TECHNOLOGY PROFESSIONAL

In 1990 *Information Systems: Management Principles in Action* (Wysocki and Young, 1990) was published. It has been widely adopted and met with success. We have received many comments and praise for having written a text that appeals to the practitioner but has not ignored established research tradition. The fast pace of technological change has necessitated a revision of the book to incorporate the emerging partnership between business and technology professionals. Reviewing the book we realized that massive change in the form of a complete reorientation of our thinking was needed. As a result we decided to offer a new text rather than a revision of the previous work. In fact, we estimate about an 80% change in content between the first book and this new first edition. Rather than continue the same organization of the book (corporate, functional, and end-user) we have chosen another approach that parallels the changes in corporate organizational structure. That is, we focus on enterprise, process, function, and end-user. At the same time we introduce a new corporate citizen, the information-enabled practitioner. This is a professional whose role in the enterprise includes information technology as an essential component of the skills profile. Many authors have written of the need for this new professional. Their models assumed a working partnership between the technology professional and the business professional. Our more contemporary model addresses the need for a single professional who possesses skills in both technology and business.

◆ WHY AND HOW WE WROTE THIS TEXT

The purpose of this book is to provide a solid foundation for the student in the concepts and principles of managing information across the enterprise. In doing so we bring to the student the basic premise that information is a corporate resource and is the simultaneous responsibility of everyone in the enterprise. The technology belongs to everyone and everyone has a role in exploiting it for business value.

It is clear that major and accelerated changes are occurring in business, government, education, and information technology. This text captures the essence of all of these elements, establishes a taxonomy for planning the future, and prepares students to be information-enabled managers (IEMgrs) for the world of work and life. The world-enterprise-people-information technology taxonomy is reshaped and reconfigured to uncover the issues in a sequence more meaningful to the aspiring executive of tomorrow. Early chapters of the text lay the foundation for a world view of the changing nature of the workplace. More detailed information follows on new roles of IEMgrs within this emerging enterprise scenario. Later chapters extend general operating functions and processes into development of appropriate systems methodologies needed to incorporate information technology into corporate activity. All aspects of end-user computing and the problems associated with new vendor relationships culminate the material.

◆ ORGANIZATION

Text

Our text is divided into three parts: enterprise, process, and function. If we insist on viewing the organization as a hierarchy, it must be done using these three terms. This concept is not new. As organizations began to realize the importance of focusing on customer service, the structural evolution soon followed. The enterprise is seen as a collection of value chains (a.k.a. processes) that serve customers (internal as well as external). The value chains are supported by any number of the traditional business functions. That is, business functions support value chains and value chains enable the enterprise to realize its vision.

The chapters that comprise each section follow the same general structure. Following each chapter, we have a section titled *Reflections*. *Reflections* are food for thought, discussion topics, issues, and problems. They are designed to force the student to extend thinking beyond the obvious, to depict the real world, and to consider several solutions and opportunities.

Reflections

The section on *Reflections* consists of four types of student investigations. The *STEP Model Reflections* relate directly to the model described extensively in Chapter 1. The other three **Reflections** are described in concept in the following segments and require more information (see the *Reflections* segment at the end of the *Prologue*).

General Concepts

Issues and discussion points suggested by the content of the text are given to the student for consideration. These are not "List the 10 causes of the Civil War" type questions. Rather, they are posed to the student to stimulate thinking and generate lively discussion. They are excellent topics for discussion in small groups or the class as a whole. Some of them suggest project work outside of class by individuals or teams. Others require further research in the literature for more in-depth treatment of the concepts.

STEP Model

In Chapter 1, we introduce the *STEP Model* as an explanation of the linkages between technology, process, and people. These *Reflections* are designed to refine the use of the model and highlight the major issues and concerns.

Ethics

Rather than write a separate chapter on ethics, we have integrated ethics throughout the text as appropriate. This approach provides a more meaningful examination of the ethics issues that permeate several areas of information management. Generally, students will tend to dismiss non-technical factors as unimportant and comment on issues in a cursory or obvious way. We strive to force students to look beyond the obvious and for that reason, they will have difficulty answering the questions based solely on the material in the chapter.

Integrating Case Study

Several recent consulting engagements provide a basis for a comprehensive case study of most of the concepts and principles discussed. We decided to incorporate this integrating case study depicting a fictitious wholesale industrial supplies firm (ISI) throughout the text. In addition to the usual case evaluations and problem-solving exercises, we have included several experiential exercises. These exercises engage the entire class in role playing exercises and have proven to be excellent opportunities for students to practice professional roles. Although some information for organizing the case study for student investigation is provided as an integral part of the material presented, the Instructor's Manual gives extensive detail on how to teach the case effectively.

◆ ASSUMPTIONS AND AUDIENCE

Because this book is dedicated to the exploration of the sophisticated and yet inadequately developed area of information management, it proceeds on the assumption that the reader is well-versed in the basics of information systems. Specifically, students' familiarity with the fundamental terminology is assumed, as is a basic understanding of essential management practices. This knowledge should be obtainable through industry experience or introductory courses in management principles, organizational behavior, and IS required in undergraduate and graduate business programs.

The text has been prepared for upper-division undergraduate and graduate students of management and information systems programs interested in the evolving issues and challenges of information management. Furthermore, the text is not intended for a course on managing the information systems department. Our basic premise is that information is managed by all professionals in the enterprise. Therefore the title *Managing Information Across the Enterprise* reflects that corporate-wide focus. The text is applicable both to the technical professional aspiring to more managerial duties and to the general management student preparing to practice management in organizations in which the strategic use of information is pervasive. The text will be valuable to the student in disciplines other than management and information systems who can foresee that familiarity with major issues in both of these disciplines will be invaluable in work and life.

Prologue　　　　　　　　　　　　　　　　　　　　　　　　　　　　　　vii

◆ ACKNOWLEDGMENTS

We would like to thank the reviewers for their suggestions and ideas for improving the qualtity of the content and presentation of this book:

William H. DeLone, American University
Mary Giovannini, Northeast Missouri State University
Varun Grover, University of South Carolina
Thomas Harris, Ball State University
Deepak Khazanchi, Northern Kentucky University
Stephen E. Lunce, Texas A&M International University
Ian McKillop, Wilfrid Laurier University
Linda Salchenberger, Loyola University—Chicago
Bharat Shah, Ryerson Polytechnic University
Robert D. Wilson, California State University—San Bernardino
Dale Young, Miami Univesity

◆ ANOTHER THOUGHT

We believe that our efforts are missionary. Information is a strategic resource that belongs to everyone in the organization. But we must not forget the role of people and process in completing that strategy. We are issuing a "wake-up call" to both practitioners and academics. We introduce a new way of viewing the enterprise—through the eyes of information-enabled professionals. In so doing, we hope to encourage further exploration of the seminal ideas presented.

If our aims are realized, this text will help its readers and students deal with important information management issues effectively and creatively. Nowhere do we dignify proprietary or parochial interests by their inclusion; each area is included because it is important enough to affect the enterprise in its use of information. We have included topics not traditionally found in books on information management and have excluded some that are normally included. It is our contention that information-enabled professionals should possess a skills profile that extends beyond the technical or business areas. That skill set is treated comprehensively in what follows.

Robert K. Wysocki
Robert L. DeMichiell
May 1996

Reflections

ETHICS

Rationale

In order to remain competitive in the business world today, there is a continuous need for increased productivity, satisfied workers, and the appropriate application of computer technology. Tradeoffs of cost, organizational disruptiveness, and ease of use of the technology are examined to some extent in the development process. However, socio-ethical issues may very well not receive equal treatment in the planning, design, and implementation stages of development.

The same scenario can describe university information systems education. Students have to produce and be satisfied customers of the educational process or they dropout. They are taught planning and design of information systems with the primary emphasis on technical aspects. Generally, socio-ethical factors are not integrated in all courses in information systems undergraduate or graduate curricula. As a result, students receive segmented instruction on human affairs in information processing and identify technical and economic factors as most important in the application of information technology to the enterprise. Social, cultural, moral, and ethical aspects of computing are difficult to address for the following reasons:

a. The very nature of the topic requires expertise in a variety of disciplines, such as management, computer systems, philosophy, social sciences, and psychology;

b. It is debatable whether or not value systems (ethics) can be taught;

c. Any inclusion of socio-ethical factors in systems development courses raises additional questions concerning why, when, and how they should be included;

d. The methodology may include team-teaching, and as such presents the usual difficulties in faculty agreement on course focus, scope, content, and case-studies; and,

e. Students prefer technical and economic solutions because they are tangible and measurable; they don't like ambiguity and complexity of solution introduced by worker retraining, power end-users and decentralized control, and organizational impact.

The problem with establishing educational scenarios in systems courses which do not consider fully these non-technical issues is that students will be unaware of their importance in life after school. One solution is to integrate socio-ethical concepts in systems development courses with certain objectives focused on student exploration of all automation feasibility concerns.

Approach

The general approach suggested in this text is to require students to explore information technology from a totally unstructured perspective at the outset. In each of chapters 11-14, a scenario is presented to commence the learning process. A limited number of facts are provided. There are neither predetermined rules of investigation nor given assumptions. Leading statements, issues, comments, questions, and/or conversations are given only to provoke informal discussions and further research. The sessions uncover human dilemmas related to specific problems and not just information data flow diagrams, processing bottlenecks, and faulty data integrity. The semi-structured case "starters" provide problem-centered or event-driven scenarios.

The underlying philosophy of this approach is that there is no single solution. There are only alternatives and a best solution, based on tangible and intangible tradeoffs. Students are encouraged to develop independent solutions in small discussion group format, justify their findings and conclusions, and report their results orally to the rest of the class.

Student Deliverables

a. Student notes—case "starter," general class discussion, small group discussion, oral and written reports

b. Analysis of case—facts, issues, key words, requirements, key players, decision-makers, semantics

c. Database issues (if any)—general specifications, inputs, outputs, conceptual design, security

d. Simulation models—type of model, scope and purpose, analysis, randomness, application

e. Synthesis of concepts—impact of ethics issues on "process" of design/use and other factors

Reflections

GENERAL CONCEPTS

Discussion questions at the end of each chapter are designed to be thought-provoking and not just an application of concepts. The experience of the reader is drawn into a discussion of issues, problems, and solutions with focus on special areas related to the major topics introduced in the chapter. Options are allowed for the non-experienced reader to gain that experience in the form of work projects at a client site. The purpose of this approach is to add a "hands-on" dimension to learning through example.

In some cases, the discussion questions suggest research areas for more of an in-depth investigation of material in the literature. Questions/projects can be addressed individually or by self-directed work teams with oral and written reporting responsibilities. Response to the questions cannot be found simply by reviewing the material in the chapter; the student must go beyond the obvious and reach for answers which may be argumentative, controversial, and not right or wrong. In writing the questions, the authors have used their extensive experience in business, government, and education to lead the student in a particular direction for solution without providing too many assumptions, constraints, and facts. Most of the burden of proof is placed on the student to justify his/her comments.

Reflections

INTEGRATING CASE STUDY

A single case study is continued throughout Chapters 6–14. When the focus of the text is shifted to the acquisition and management of computer resources, a single case study not only integrates the discipline areas, but also suggests the team approach to the introduction of information technology in the most prudent and effective manner. Although the framework for analyzing and solving the myriad of problems related to managing information technology commences with technical considerations (defining system requirements and meeting them by competing student teams), other factors are brought into the scenario in later chapters. In this way, students can "prototype" the process by delivering a solution according to a standard framework and reiterate the process as new variables enter the scenario. The delivery and rapid modification of solutions is consistent with timely customer response and a comprehensive, or total systems, view of strategies for effective use of information technology across the enterprise.

The selected case study is Industrial Supplies, Incorporated (ISI), a regional wholesale industrial supplies firm with three independent product distribution centers, some centralized control of operations, and some automation. ISI is a composite of several real companies which offers a scenario conducive to a wide range of topics in all aspects of feasibility (technical, economic, operational, and political). We enter the scenario at a time when additional computing is necessary to retain current customers and to grasp opportunities in both buying and reselling products. A small company of several million dollars of revenue is selected because it has limited resources to devote to solving a major survival problem. How can automation be most effective in guaranteeing that survival?

In addition to the relationship of the ISI case to text content, the case reinforces our approach to learning. We believe that students learn best by doing. The teams are comprised according to specific roles and responsibilities. This role-playing requirement adds realism to the process and allows students to investigate problems from a certain perspective. During general discussion of the case, the mix of roles from different students presents an interesting and informative format. In small group discussions (within and outside of class), interpersonal skill development is nurtured. A more detailed description of this methodology is included in the instructor's manual. Several options are suggested for a range of investigation from individuals and selected topics to teams and a complex scenario. The element of role-playing can be varied and the case need not be addressed in all chapters subsequent to Chapter 6, where it is introduced. In each later chapter, the case can be examined or not depending on the interest of the instructor.

Contents

♦ ♦ ♦

PART I: ♦ Enabling the Enterprise — 1

Chapter 1: Strategies for Technology-Enablement through People: STEP Model — 3

- ♦ CYBERSPACE: A GLOBAL VIEW — 3
  - Control Systems in Human Affairs 3 / Changing Nature of the Workplace 5
- ♦ BUSINESS PROFESSIONALS IN THE INFORMATION AGE — 6
  - Strategic Opportunity and Information Technology 6 / The Information Superhighway 6 / Electronic Commerce 9 / The Virtual Corporation 9 / The International Dimension 12 / Changing Roles 14 / Career Planning: Who Is in Charge? 16
- ♦ EMERGENCE OF AN INFORMATION AGE PROFESSIONAL — 17
  - Need for the Marriage of Business and Technology Professionals 17 / A Taxonomy for Planning the Future 19
- ♦ A NEW MODEL—STEP: Strategies for Technology-Enablement through People — 19
  - Lack of Attention to People 21 / Lack of Attention to Process 21 / Lack of Attention to Technology 21 / Getting There from Here 22
- ♦ REFLECTIONS — 23
  - General Concepts 23 / STEP Model 25

Chapter 2: The Information-Enabled Manager — 26

- ♦ THE GLOBAL VILLAGE — 26
- ♦ THE LEARNING ORGANIZATION — 29
- ♦ WILL THE NEW INFORMATION-AGE PLEASE STAND UP? — 29
  - Definition the Information-Enabled Manager (IEMgr) 30
- ♦ EDUCATION AND TRAINING OF THE IEMgr — 33
  - Planning and Implementing Professional Development 33
- ♦ REFLECTIONS — 38
  - General Concepts 38 / STEP Model 38

xii Contents

Chapter 3: ***Information-Enabled Management Across the Enterprise*** 39
- ◆ MODELS OF INFORMATION MANAGEMENT 39

  Nolan's Six Stages Model 42 / The Strategic Grid 47 /
  Benefit/Beneficiary Matrix 50
- ◆ ENTERPRISE WIDE RESPONSIBILITY OF THE IEMgmt TEAM 52

  The Support Category 55 / Turnaround Category 56 / The Factory
  Category 56 / The Strategic Category 56 / Evolution of the IEMgmt
  Team 57
- ◆ EMERGING PARTNERSHIP: USER MANAGER AND INFORMATION SYSTEMS
  MANAGER 57

  The Support Category 58 / The Turnaround Category 58 /
  The Factory Category 58 / The Strategic Category 58
- ◆ CHANGING NATURE OF THE CHIEF INFORMATION OFFICER (CIO) 59

  IEMgmt Shared Responsibility with the CIO 60 / Strategic
  Direction Setting 60 / Information Technology Exploitation 60 /
  Business Systems Planning 61 / Systems Development and
  Maintenance 61
- ◆ LEGACY SYSTEMS, INTEGRATION, AND CHANGE MANAGEMENT 61

  Developing a Partnership and a Leadership Role 62 / Establishing a
  Collaborative Planning Environment 63 / Systems Integration 63 /
  Change Management: The Risk-Averse Culture 63
- ◆ REFLECTIONS 64

  General Concepts 64 / STEP Model 65

Chapter 4: ***Assessing Strategic Opportunities*** 66
- ◆ INFORMATION TECHNOLOGY AS A COMPONENT OF COMPETITIVE STRATEGY 66
- ◆ PLANNING IS DYNAMIC NOT STATIC 69
- ◆ THINKING OUTSIDE THE BOX 70
- ◆ NEED FOR PLANNING 74
- ◆ THE PLANNING CHALLENGE 75
- ◆ LINKING INFORMATION TECHNOLOGY TO BUSINESS PLANNING 76
- ◆ THREE LEVELS OF PLANNING 78
- ◆ INFORMATION SYSTEMS PLANNING METHODS 80

  Stand alone Planning 80 / Reactive Planning 80 / Linked
  Planning 81 / Integrated Planning 81 / Critical Success Factors 82
- ◆ ENTERPRISE DATA MODELING 84
- ◆ MANAGING THE INFORMATION SYSTEMS PORTFOLIO 85
- ◆ THE BUSINESS SYSTEMS PLANNING METHODOLOGY 85
- ◆ INTEGRATED STRATEGIC INFORMATION SYSTEMS PLANNING 91

  Step 1: Environmental Analysis 91 / Step 2: Business Planning 93 /
  Step 3: Business Unit and Departmental Planning 93 / Step 4:

Contents   xiii

        Development of the Strategic Information Systems Plan   93 /
Step 5: Data Planning   93
- ♦ CHANGING WINDOWS OF OPPORTUNITY   94
- ♦ REFLECTIONS   94

        General Concepts   94 / STEP Model   95

Chapter 5: *Organizational Deployment of the Information Function*   97

- ♦ TRENDS IN INFORMATION SYSTEMS ORGANIZATION   97

        The Initiation Stage   98 / The Contagion Stage   98 / The Control Stage   98 / Integration and Data Administration Stages   99 / The Maturity Stage   99

- ♦ TRENDS IN DEPLOYING THE INFORMATION FUNCTION   100

        Centralized to Decentralized   101 / A Hybrid Structure   103 / Which Structure Is Best?   103 / Function to Process   104 / Cross-Functional and Self-Managed Teams   106 / Mainframe to Client/Server: The Current Situation   106

- ♦ PERVASIVENESS AND DECENTRALIZATION   108

        IEMgr and Power User Relationships   109 / Work Group Computing   109 /

- ♦ ORGANIZATIONAL STRUCTURES: SOME BASIC CHOICES   110

        Functional Structure   110 / Project Structure   110 / Matrix Structure   112 / Task Force and Self-Directed Work Team Structures   114

- ♦ EVOLUTION TO A SUPPORT ORGANIZATION   114

        Internal Considerations   114 / External Considerations   115

- ♦ STEERING COMMITTEES   116
- ♦ REPORTING TO THE CEO   117
- ♦ OUTSOURCING: AN INTRODUCTION   118

        Operations   118 / Network Support   119 / Hot Line   119 / Applications Development   119

- ♦ REFLECTIONS   119

        General Concepts   119

Chapter 6: *Acquiring and Managing Computer Resources*   121

- ♦ GROWING IMPORTANCE OF USER/VENDOR RELATIONSHIPS   121
- ♦ OUTSOURCING ISSUES: PART I REVISITED   123
- ♦ SELECTIVE OUTSOURCING: A FRAMEWORK   126
- ♦ OUTSOURCING PROCESS   128
- ♦ IMPLEMENTING THE COMPUTER RESOURCE MANAGEMENT MODEL   128
- ♦ COLLABORATION STRATEGIES   132
- ♦ DEVELOPING THE REQUEST FOR PROPOSAL (RFP)   134

Contents

♦ NEGOTIATING THE CONTRACT	134
♦ CONCLUDING COMMENTS	134
♦ REFLECTIONS	141
General Concepts 141 / SIS Case Study 141	

PART II: ♦ Redesigning Business Processes — 147

Chapter 7: *Emerging Process View of Organizations* — 149

♦ WHAT IS A BUSINESS PROCESS? — 149

Definitions: Bounding the Process 150 / Components: Personnel, Technology, Process 152

♦ BUSINESS PROCESS CATEGORIES — 154
♦ ROLE PERSPECTIVES — 156

External and Internal Views 156 / Process Owners and Scope of Authority 157

♦ THE QUALITY IMPERATIVE — 157

Lessons Learned 158 / "Progress" and the Enhancement of the Life and Work 160 / What Is Meant by Quality? 161 / What Is Meant by "Value-Added" and Can it Be Measured? 161 / Strategy and Vision: Are They Different? 161 / Productivity: What Is It? 162 / Organizational Integrity 162

♦ QUALITY FUNCTION DEPLOYMENT (QFD) — 163

Stage 1: Organizational Integrity 164 / Stages 2, 3, & 4: Paradigm Shift from Function to Process 165 / Stages 5, 6, & 7: Customer Requirements, Competition, and Corporate Issues 166 / Stage 8: General Design: Requirements and Technical Analysis 168 / Stages 9, 10, 11, & 12: Detailed Design and Implementation 172

♦ APPLICATION OF THE QFD MODEL — 173

Business Example 173 / Higher Education Example 174

♦ REFLECTIONS — 176

General Concepts 176 / STEP Model 177 / ISI Case Study 177

Chapter 8: *Business Process Redesign* — 179

♦ DOWNSIZING AND RIGHTSIZING: REPOSITIONING WORKERS — 179
♦ BUSINESS PROCESS REDESIGN HIERARCHY — 180

Enterprise Level—Business Reengineering 180 / Process Level—Process Quality Management 182 / Activity Level—Continuous Quality Improvement 182

- ♦ BUSINESS REENGINEERING METHODOLOGIES — 182
  - Identify Process 184 / Plan the Reengineering Project 185 / Implement the New Process 186
- ♦ PROCESS QUALITY MANAGEMENT — 187
  - Case Study—O'Neil & Preigh Church Equipment Manufacturers 188 / The Role of IEMgmt in Process Quality Management 192
- ♦ CONTINUOUS QUALITY IMPROVEMENT — 192
  - Identify Quality Improvement Areas 192 / Perform Gap Analysis 193 / Prioritize Quality Gaps 193 / Manage the Activity Improvement Project and Monitor Performance 193 / The Role of IEMgmt Continuous Quality Improvement 193
- ♦ PROJECT MANAGEMENT — 193
  - Introduction 193 / Job Functions and Tasks for Project Management 195 / Definition of a Project 197 / Project Parameters (Cost, Time, and Resources) 198 / Project Management Life Cycle 199 / IEMgr's Role in Managing Projects 201
- ♦ REFLECTIONS — 203
  - General Concepts 203 / STEP ModeL 204 / ISI Case Study 205

Chapter 9: *Human Resource Development* — 206

- ♦ UNDERSTANDING INFORMATION-ENABLED PROFESSIONAL DEVELOPMENT — 207
  - Describing Tasks, People, and Skill Requirements 208 / Building the Information-Enabled Professions Database 209 / Staff Skills Profile Database 209 / Bloom's Taxonomy 210 / Self-assessments 212 / Career Interests Profile 212 / Learning Styles Profile 212 / Job Analysis 219
- ♦ CAREER DEVELOPMENT PLANNING — 223
  - Organizational Culture and Commitment 223 / Individual Responsibility 224 / Manager's Responsibility 224
- ♦ CAREER DEVELOPMENT PLANS — 225
  - Components of a Career Development Plan 225 / The Career Development Planning Process 226
- ♦ ENTERPRISE WIDE CONSIDERATIONS — 229
  - Staff Planning 230 / Planning the Corporate Training Program 230 / Role of the IEMgmt Team 230
- ♦ REFLECTIONS — 231
  - General Concepts 231 / ISI Case Study 232

Chapter 10: ***The Service Role of Information Technology***   233
- ♦ THE TRIPLE ROLE   233
  Reactive Role   234 / Proactive Role   234 / Collaborative Role   235
- ♦ CHANGING FUNCTIONS OF INFORMATION SYSTEMS   235
  Systems and Programming   236 / Operations   236 / Technical and Network Services   237 / Corporate DataBase Access   237 / Training and Education   238 / Help Desks   238 / Technology Gatekeepers   238 / Standards   239
- ♦ ISLANDS OF TECHNOLOGY   239
  Office Automation   239 / Computer-Integrated Manufacturing   240 / Desktop Publishing   241 / Imaging and Document Management   241 / Multimedia   241 / Integration Options   242
- ♦ ORGANIZING FOR CONTROL OF INFORMATION   243
  Command and Control Structures   243 / Non-hierarchical Structures   243
- ♦ MANAGING ORGANIZATIONAL CHANGE   244
- ♦ REFLECTIONS   245
  General Concepts   245 / ISI Case Study   245

PART III: ♦ Enabling Business Functions   247

Chapter 11: ***Linking Information Technology to Business Functions***   249
- ♦ DECISION-MAKING   249
  Decision and Executive Support Systems   249 / Decision-Making Process   250
- ♦ BUSINESS SIMULATION FOR BUSINESS FUNCTIONS   255
  Expectations   255 / Simulation Model Design: A Manager's Perspective   256 / The Simulation Process   258 / Artificial Intelligence and Expert Systems   261 / The Brain, Neural Nets, and Fuzzy Logic   263
- ♦ BUSINESS APPLICATIONS AND INFORMATION TECHNOLOGY   265
  Corporate Planning   265 / Marketing   266 / Manufacturing, Production Scheduling, Inventory   268 / Accounting and Finance   269 / Human Resources   270
- ♦ REFLECTIONS   272
  General Concepts   272 / STEP Model   273 / Ethics   274 / ISI Case Study   274

Contents   xvii

Chapter 12: ***Systems Development Methodology***   276
- ◆ TRADITIONAL PERSPECTIVE   277

  Efficiency   278 / Communications   279 / Control   279 / Documentation   280 / Role Definition   280 / Consistency   280

- ◆ SYSTEMS DEVELOPMENT CONSIDERATIONS FOR THE IEMgr   281

  Enterprise Wide Strategies for Applications Development   285 / From Enterprise to Process to Function Levels   287 / Application Partnerships   289

- ◆ TAXONOMY FOR DEVELOPMENT   289

  Maintenance Projects   289 / Systems Upgrade Projects   290 / New Applications Development   291

- ◆ INCORPORATING A PROJECT MANAGEMENT METHODOLOGY   293

  Sizing the Project   294 / Establishing Project Scope and Detailed Project Planning   294 / Monitoring and Controlling Project Work   295

- ◆ SYSTEMS DEVELOPMENT   295

  A Strategic Approach   295 / Design and Development Strategies   296 / Deployment Strategies   298 / Post Deployment Audits   299

- ◆ DATA MANAGEMENT   299

  The Corporate Data Model: Access, Security   299 / Distributed Data   300 / Data Architecture Alternatives   302 / Relational Data Structures   302 / Entity Relationship Model   303 / Emergence of Object Technology   304

- ◆ REFLECTIONS   305

  General Concepts   305 / STEP Model   306 / Ethics   307 / ISI Case Study   308

Chapter 13: ***Information Technology at the End User Level***   309
- ◆ TYPES OF END USERS   310

  Type III End Users   310 / Nonprogramming End Users   312 / Command-Level End Users   312 / Programming-Level End Users   312 / Functional-Support End Users   313 / End User Computing Support Personnel   313 / Data Processing Programmers   313

- ◆ IMPORTANCE OF END USER COMPUTING   314
- ◆ MANAGEMENT CONCERNS   314

  Senior Managers   314 / IS Management   315 / User Management   315 / IEMgmt Team   316

- ◆ GLOBALIZATION AND INFORMATION TECHNOLOGY   316
- ◆ WORK GROUP COMPUTING   317

  Intradepartmental and Interdepartmental Relationships   318

Contents

♦ ELECTRONIC COMMERCE 319
♦ CONTROL VERSUS AUTONOMY 321

An Anthology of End-User Computer Support Strategies 321

♦ ORGANIZING FOR END-USER SUPPORT 324

The Corporate Model Unit 324 / The Decision Support Systems Unit 325 / The Information Center Unit 325

♦ REFLECTIONS 326

General Concepts 326 / STEP Model 326 / Ethics 327 / Integrating Case Study 328

Chapter 14: *The Support Role of Information Technology* 329

♦ DEVELOPING A SUPPORT SERVICE LEVEL AGREEMENT 329
♦ ROLES AND RESPONSIBILITIES 330

Setting Corporate Policy and Standards 330 / Data Administration 330 / Communications 331 / Technology Research 332 / Training and Education 332

♦ END-USER MANAGEMENT RESPONSIBILITIES 332

Applications Management: Implementation Strategies 332

♦ IMPLEMENTATION POLICIES AND PROCEDURES 333

The Life Cycle of End-User Systems Development 334 / Hard and Soft Controls 335 / Certifying User-Developed Systems 339

♦ REFLECTIONS 341

General Concepts 341 / Ethics 342

Epilog ♦ POSITIONING THE ENTERPRISE FOR THE FUTURE WITH PEOPLE AND TECHNOLOGY 345

APPENDICES ♦

A.1 *Information-Enabled Management (IEMgmt) Curriculum* 347

A.2 *Case Study Research Data for Computer Resource Management Model* 335

References 357
Index 367

PART I

◆ ◆ ◆

Enabling the Enterprise

We are in the midst of a total revolution in the business world! The last five years have brought changes that many could not have foreseen. In less than four years, we will witness the close of the twentieth century. What further changes will have occurred in the remaining years of this decade can only be guessed. One lesson we have learned from the past is that most forecasts regarding technology and information, and their application in business, have traditionally fallen short of the mark. History will undoubtedly repeat itself.

The reason that it is so difficult to look into the future with any certainty is that we are in a very unstable situation. Creativity is driving new product development and customer service enhancements in unpredictable ways. The need to remain competitive has caused the enterprise to focus its efforts on cost reduction that can be passed on to the customer. To do this with any degree of success presents the enterprise with a major challenge. That is, how can we increase efficiency and effectiveness and at the same time increase customer service and improve the marketing mix? Information technology has become the critical component in almost every strategy.

In this, the first of a three-part effort, we concentrate our discussion at the enterprise level—saving business processes and functions for parts two and three. We begin by observing how the assimilation of information technology into every aspect of corporate life has given rise to a new professional. We call these professionals *information enabled* and establish their role as a critical part of every strategic effort. We argue that they are the key to the future if businesses are to compete successfully in the global economy.

Part I sets the stage for an in-depth study of how the information-enabled manager (IEMgr) will further the corporate effort to exploit information technology. The past is evidence that the traditional command-and-control structure will not work in the new world of business. To be successful, the old stovepipe structures must be removed and replaced with a more flexible and adaptive team structure. David I. Cleland discusses this evolution in a just-published book entitled "Strategic Management of Teams." We believe that the IEMgr is the focal point of such efforts and introduce that thesis here.

Chapter 1 develops a conceptual model that describes the evolution to an information-enabled organization that every enterprise will undergo. Our Strategies for Technology Enablement through People (STEP) Model introduces a framework that will be developed throughout the text. The outcome is further described in Chapter 2 and then followed, in Chapter 3, by an in-depth definition of the IEMgr within the information-enabled enterprise. We introduce four types of IEMgrs and show how each has a unique role to play in positioning the enterprise for the future. Chapter 4 continues with a discussion of information technology planning and shows how that activity engages the entire organization with the IEMgr playing a critical role. In Chapter 5, we discuss how information technology management, its organizational structures, and its deployment through the organization have changed and will continue to change as the senior management team learns how to organize for flexibility and maximum use of human resources. Part I closes with an extension of the boundaries of information technology activities into the user and vendor communities. Throughout the discussion, IEMgrs are the focal point of every worthwhile strategy. ◆

Chapter 1

Strategies for Technology Enablement through People: The STEP Model

◆ ◆ ◆

*T*he business world is not what you think it is. There are dynamic forces at play that portend a business world in which information technology must occupy a position of critical importance if the enterprise is to thrive and be successful. What is that business world like? What kinds of professionals are employed in the companies in this new world? How should organizations prepare for the coming changes? How should individuals prepare for the coming changes? These and other equally significant questions will occupy us for the remainder of this book. This chapter sets the stage for what follows. In the remaining chapter, we will drill down into the details from the enterprise to the process to the function to the individual professional and see what their world will be like and how they can best prepare for it.

Understand, however, that we are somewhat speculative in looking ahead. However, we have based our observations on the near term and the best insights that our peers have to offer of what that future holds.

◆ CYBERSPACE: A GLOBAL VIEW

Control Systems in Human Affairs

It is clear that our quest to store, retrieve, manipulate, and present information is transforming us into a cybernetic society :-). If you look at the preceding symbol from the right side of the page, you will see an electronic "smiley," one of the hundreds of symbols circulated on electronic bulletin boards illustrating that a new culture is upon us. As we move into the next century, high technology will have invaded nearly every aspect of work and life. Time and space will have been further compressed, and because information is power, the power brokers will be those individuals who own or have access to the information engine, the computer. These "knowledge workers" will have taken more control of their lives by the increased availability of user-friendly computer systems for personal and organizational productivity. Machine-plus-person will soon become a formidable team in addressing the right issues, defining problems, and making the best decisions to solve those problems.

The process of bringing people and technology together has been difficult for organizations even though ample technical and economic justification exists. Some individuals accelerate their use of computer technology and become power users (perhaps even "cyberpunks") while others actively or passively resist employing technology in their daily work [Hafner and Markoff, 1991]. Still others enjoy the process of discovery and eventually may exert some electronically created control over the life and work of others. In some cases, their intrusions on the Internet have sinister motivations and often result in massive computer failures.

At the other extreme are the "humanists," who view the machine-centered life as a human weakness rather than a strength. For these individuals, the major objective is to ensure that computer feasibility starts with the needs of humans (end-users) and not with technological availability. It is clear that the world is quite complex and some of it can only be organized by humans with the help of machines.

The basic ingredient of the social and business organization is information. Until recently, the trend has been to centralize corporate power in the hands of a few highly placed executives. As information technology has become more pervasive through the organization, this trend has been reversed. A class of "new knowledge elite" is emerging. This group is enabling the organization's response to customer demands for quality products and services and increased productivity. As part of that response, the organization has been restructured. Command-and-control structures are being replaced by flatter, leaner, decentralized, and more customer-focused structures. Workers are empowered to deal with customers on the organization's behalf. For many organizations this means a breath of fresh air as life seems to have been restored.

Control, responsibility, and accountability are being pushed down in the organization—in many cases to individual workers, who are becoming more computer-fluent every day. Decentralization of organizational control is now possible due to the proliferation and distribution of microcomputer technology to every level of the workforce. Workers can do their own word processing, use electronic mail, download data from corporate files, and prepare effective graphical presentations, thereby exercising some direct control over organizational decision making. Somewhere on the spectrum between cyberpunk and humanist extremes are individuals who are prepared to accept responsibility for this local control and assess the worth of both sides on each important issue;

analyze fully the impact on society, the organization, and individual citizens; and manage information with a human-centered and technology-enabled perspective.

Control is relegated to individuals who share information without filtering it, use information and do not abuse it, incorporate key individuals in problem solving and decision making, and integrate information technology into the fabric of business operating functions. Their focus is on the technical, economical, operational, political, and socioethical feasibilities of the introduction of information technology into business environments. They maintain a spirit of inquiry and investigation without risk of demotion, embarrassment, or ridicule.

The goal is to exploit information technology only as it meets human needs. Corporate information systems should reward the activities of reflection, creativity, innovation, and collaboration among multifunctional workers in order to grasp new opportunities and minimize threats. Change is welcomed. The organization is created to respond to irrationality and chaos; hierarchical structures are eliminated in favor of business process alignments. The manager of tomorrow must think about ways that computers add value to the business enterprise as a whole.

Changing Nature of the Workplace

Information technology has dramatically affected the way we live and work. Everything is faster, more complex, global, and electronics driven. The information highway is built and we are learning to navigate it. Businesses incorporate information technology in their strategic planning, daily operations, and, in some cases, into their products and services as well (Davidson, 1995). The quest for quality and responsive customer service has caused some businesses to adopt total quality management procedures, reduce their staffs, and/or rethink corporate goals and objectives in order to compete in the global marketplace.

Workers may react to such strategic moves with apprehension, caution, and withdrawal. Others may see the scenario as one of increased opportunity and look beyond their current job to begin preparing for a new career. Business, industry, government, and higher education environments share more information, form partnerships, encourage creativity and risk, face unstructured problems with enthusiasm, and delegate authority to lower levels in the organization. Worker teams create and implement business projects focused on business processes and search for business value. Workers are liberated in that they report less and less to functional managers and participate on empowered and self-directed teams focused on quality and productivity. They are integrated into the decision-making process with outcome-based performance measures. Corporate success relies on fast, flexible, and friendly teams formed by a new breed of business professional. The new professionals are multidisciplined. In addition to having expertise in the business functions (marketing, finance, production, distribution, human resources, etc.), they range from computer fluent to computer expert. We call these professionals *information enabled* and define them more formally in Chapter 2.

BUSINESS PROFESSIONALS IN THE INFORMATION AGE

Strategic Opportunity and Information Technology

As global competition becomes keener, business and industry must become more adept at exploiting information technology in order to assure the success and even the survival of their organizations. Doing so will require the integration of business planning and information systems management into a comprehensive strategic framework. The emergence of the empowered worker and the decentralization of decision making provide the infrastructure needed in order for this integration to occur.

The "technology gap" (the difference between available technology and assimilated technology) is closing as a new breed of technology-fluent professionals take their place on the management team. They understand the need for a proper balance of technology and humanism (humans managing that technology) in all enterprise activities. During the past decade, we saw the gap widen because the rapid increase of functionality and cost performance of information technology outraced management's ability to manage the technology. Now, however, software has become more *intuitive*—making it easier for the manager to harness this technology to best advantage.

What enterprise strategies can be employed to create synergy between technology and the people who use it so as to maximize personal and organizational productivity? The companies sketched in the sections that follow were able to establish and sustain a competitive advantage in their business planning and execution. The examples are drawn from the personal experiences of the authors and illustrate the need for an enterprise approach to problem analysis and solution. In Chapter 4, this case study research is used to formulate a generic model for effective management of information technology.

The Information Superhighway

The Internet is a network of approximately 15,000 networks. In fact, the Internet is the largest such network in the world with over 30 million subscribers and a growth rate of nearly 10 percent per month. If that growth rate is sustained, there should be about 100 million subscribers in a little more than 10 years. Corporations are rushing to get their Home Page up on the World Wide Web (WWW). What is all this rush about? Have businesses been swept up in the emotion of it all and signed on just because everyone else is doing it or is there some valid business reason behind it all?

There is no question that the successful businesses of the next millennium will be those that are connected to the Internet, although it has not yet reached commercial quality. Security, encryption, and the identification of allowable business transactions are three areas needing some work. There is also some concern that since it is not a managed service, it may not provide the reliability

Exhibit 1-1

A Framework for Examining Internet Business Impact

Business Value	COMPRESSION OF TIME	OVERCOMING GEOGRAPHIC RESTRICTIONS	RESTRUCTURING RELATIONSHIPS
Efficiency	Accelerate Processes	Gain Economies of Scale	Bypass Intermediaries
Effectiveness	Reduce Float Time	Add Global Control	Replicate Scarce Knowledge
Innovation	Provide Service Excellence	Develop New Markets	Build Networks

and consistency required of large-volume users. However, it is the great equalizer. Companies of all sizes can take advantage of the services and expand their market reach. The playing field for small companies has been leveled.

Internet applications occur in four phases: getting connected, establishing a marketing presence, connecting to core business systems, and subscribing to applications running on the Internet. The lack of a safe payment process continues to be an obstacle to commercialization of the Net. In addition, we suggest that the graphical user interfaces (GUIs) need to be upgraded to make browsing the Net a little less frustrating. There is so much information on the Net that unless you know exactly what you are looking for, you may not be able to find it.

The commercial value of the Net can only be guessed at this point. Exhibit 1-1 offers a type of benefit/beneficiary matrix framework for categorizing the business opportunities of the Internet.

Let us examine each of the nine cells in Exhibit 1.1 to see exactly how the impact on business value is realized. First, we note that networks being built by organizations can attach to the Internet and broaden the range of communications within and among organizations. This attachment mechanism is the major advantage and benefit to organizations. Additional advantages are the focus of the next sections.

Efficiency—Compression of Time

The operative technology here is Electronic Data Interchange (EDI). By removing the non–value-added time (i.e., the time that elapses in which no value is added to a product or service, such as moving, storing, counting, inspecting, checking, revising, copying, etc.) and transmitting purchase orders, invoices, and payments electronically, the time between, say, order entry and order fulfillment decreases, thus improving the level of customer service.

Efficiency—Overcoming Geographical Restrictions

The disadvantages of decentralization brought on by geographic distances are mitigated through rapid and easy electronic transactions among plant locations.

Efficiency—Restructuring Relationships

The thinning of organizations has empowered workers at lower levels with decision-making authority and created opportunities for direct contact with the customer without the encumbrance of intermediaries. Organizational flattening has a direct favorable impact on customer service not only in the quality, but also in the efficiency of operations. On-demand access by the worker to data and information makes this possible.

Effectiveness—Compression of Time

Data and information are immediately accessible. Gone is the wait time. Colleagues can share R&D results almost in real time. Customers can have direct access to status information on their order. Managers can summarize data collected from several locations and report same-day results in graphical format.

Effectiveness—Overcoming Geographical Restrictions

Global networks and global positioning satellites have streamlined the communications interface. Information is available any time and any place.

Effectiveness—Restructuring Relationships

With a flatter organizational hierarchy, knowledge is shared throughout the organization. The "Open Book" organization of Jack Stack in *The Great Game of Business* (Stack, 1992) can be a reality.

Innovation—Compression of Time

Anything that can reduce response time to the customer is viewed as a positive impact on market position. Reduced response time could be illustrated by a one-stop-shopping representative for the customer; by screen displays of customer information triggered by the PBX system; by direct customer access into their accounts on the organization's database to check order status and view account information; and by vendor access into the organization's database to check inventory levels for replenishment orders.

Innovation—Overcoming Geographical Restrictions

The cost per inquiry, cost per lead, and cost of sales can be dramatically lowered using electronic communications rather than "snail mail." Electronic mail allows for expanding markets with added benefits far exceeding the incremental costs of providing such services.

Innovation—Restructuring Relationships

Tying customers electronically to a company was demonstrated a number of years ago with such examples as American Hospital Supply. American Hospital Supply put terminals on the desks of their customers so that they could place their orders electronically. This became a barrier to entry for other suppliers doing business with America's customers. Barriers to switching into the electronic mode continue to occur at an even greater rate over the Internet and other value-added networks (VANs).

Electronic Commerce

The perceptive student will have realized by now that the boundaries of the enterprise are changing. We have already seen that EDI links customers and retailers, retailers and distributors, and distributors and manufacturers. These firms all lie along the same value chain and complement one another. But there is more. We are seeing the emergence of "trading partnerships." These are agreements between two or more companies that are mutually beneficial. The agreements can be as simple as repetitions of a single business transaction or as complex as opportunities may dictate. While this may not sound too exciting on the surface, when we consider that these trading partnerships are not limited to companies that are directly linked to one another in the value chain, it becomes more meaningful.

Trading partners may be competitors who have found some mutual benefit from a particular business arrangement. An obvious example is the automatic teller machine (ATM). Small banks can provide better service to their depositors by extending the network of machines into their trading area through alliances with competitor banks. Both the bank and its competitors are thus stronger competition to the very large banks that also provide ATM services in their trading area. Another example from the hotel reservation business places competing hotels in a single database with an online reservation system. The cost of developing and maintaining the database is shared among the member hotels. The system works much like an airline reservation system with the members benefiting from overflow business from their competitors. Such trading partnerships have been shown to increase customer satisfaction and bookings compared to the situation where each was competing individually against the others.

The Virtual Corporation

Information technology has created the global village. The business world is not as big as it used to be. Businesses can now exist in a variety of formats. The need to be physically in a particular place is no longer required. For example, a few years ago IBM decided to mobilize its sales and field support personnel. Their offices were taken away and instead they were allowed to reserve a cubicle when they needed to attach to the network or use any of the office support services. They simply plugged their laptop into the network and their phone number was forwarded to the cubicle they had reserved. We are also seeing the growth of businesses that exist totally on the public access networks. Information is bought and sold over the networks; research data is compiled and stored and available for purchase to any interested party; orders are placed, payments made, and deliveries scheduled. Business can literally be transacted anyplace, anytime, and from anywhere. The traditional physical boundaries are no longer a necessary part of many businesses.

With recognition of global implications, the changing general nature of the workplace and its impact on individual and organizational control systems, and a glimpse of strategies needed to accommodate these new directions, it is necessary to discuss some changes in the way corporations market and deliver products and services. Davidow and Malone [1992] use the term "virtual corporation" to describe how corporations of tomorrow will respond to rapidly changing customer-created specifications for those goods and services. They define the virtual corporation as one that can deliver "cost-effective instantaneous production of mass-customized goods and services." While this is certainly idealistic, there are examples of such organizations that have come very close to meeting the definition. Prescription eyeglass lenses can be ordered, ground, and delivered in less than one hour. Camcorders, polaroid pictures, ATMs, the ten-minute oil change, and other examples abound. The customer has stretched the organization to the limits by insisting on immediate gratification. Old schemes of moving from market research to mass production to competitive advertising are becoming obsolete. Businesses are being reengineered to produce a product or service whenever the customer requests such. At the foundation of this revolution we find information technology. It is the enabler!

This just-in-time production/inventory/purchase cycle continues to be strained as the timeframe within which it operates continuously shrinks. Information technology is most helpful to those corporations with the capability to be flexible, and adapt to changing market demands and new target audiences, and thereby "virtually" create products to meet customer requirements. The objective is to be immediately responsive, to deliver quality, to be cost competitive, and finally, to retain the customer for future purchases.

In order to accomplish this objective, the corporation builds direct links to the customer, perhaps through electronic data interchange (EDI) technology. Suppliers place computer systems on-site for purchasers to browse for needed items, check for costs and special discounts, place the order (electronically), and indicate prearranged payment procedures and schedules. If the browsing process does not clarify requirements, "knowbots" (programs on the network with intelligence) can help to find things. Invoices may or may not be produced to gain signatures and/or approvals. Follow-up visits by suppliers ensure that the system is reliable, secure, and fast, that the product has quality, and that the customer is satisfied.

Middle management positions are disappearing. Their responsibilities are being pushed down to the individual contributor level where the authority to act and be accountable is then vested. Champy (1995) observes that the old chain-of-command, obedience-oriented, procedure-driven approach is quickly disappearing. It is too slow and too bureaucratic, and requires too many levels of management to function effectively. The traditional business functions (production, marketing, sales, distribution, etc.) are being aligned with business processes (new product development, order entry, order fulfillment, customer service, etc.).

Information technology has become a critical component in this new organizational structure. By making data accessible across the organization, information technology makes it possible for businesses to function when defined as a system of interdependent processes rather than a collection of business functions. Work flow analysis, process mapping, and document management are greatly facilitated. This positions the enterprise to capitalize on its strengths and grasp new opportunities. Furthermore, this new structure positions the enterprise closer to the customer—allowing quick response to needed change as well as the ability to initiate changes that will improve customer service.

Clearly the new order is based on the knowledge worker—a technology-enabled professional or manager, who can use their curiosity, imagination, and creativity to enable self-directed work teams to develop strategies and implement actions [Peters, 1992]. The most competitive weapon proves to be the mind. Workers are organized cross-functionally so that they can focus on processes and the customer without the need to create new bureaucracies. It is the "age of the loosely structured organization"—one based more on trust than on chain of command. These new and more fluid organizations define function first, and only then do they choose form. Furthermore, that form remains in place only as long as it adds value to the effort. Johansen and Swigart (1994) have more to say on this organizational strategy, which they call the "fishnet organization." We see, then, that the focus has clearly shifted to "how can we get the job done and better meet customer needs," and only then defining the adaptive structure within which to "get it done."

New organizational infrastructures are emerging as the cost performance ratio of computers improves and data communications technology continues to advance. By the year 2020, the full power of this technology will be realized [Davis and Davenport, 1994]. The problem of meshing people and technology within the fabric of massive networks should be alleviated by that time. Right now, organizations cannot comfortably absorb the influx and change of information technology and the creation of organizational structures to accommodate that rapid change. The decade of the 1990s is one of growth, more complexity regarding the appropriate use of information technology, and, again, finding the balance between people and machines for the most productive use of that technology.

Total quality management practices pervade business and industry, with a mixed bag of successes and failures. Productivity increases, cash flow improves, and cost containment has fallen short of corporate expectations. Tomasko's [1993] description of the "rethinking" corporation suggests that managers become enabled with information technology to resize for strengths, reshape for flexibility, response, and focus, and rethink how the firm is managed.

Champy [1995] reinforces this approach with extensive case study data on corporations of various types, sizes, and objectives. His earlier work with Hammer [Hammer and Champy, 1993] concentrated on reengineering the corporation (total quality management) and this latest book validates the need for a new breed of manager to reengineer the organization. Our experience defines this individual as one who can move easily between strategy and implementation. Not everyone can create novel ideas (strategies) and take action (behaviors) on them. Champy's [1995] "hard" and "soft" approaches indicate that this flexibility is needed in order to neutralize the impact of command-and-control structures and make possible a more pluralistic and cross-functional view of the enterprise.

Another factor of importance is the socialization of the workforce brought upon us by this pluralism. Management-labor relations will become more complex as all workers are encouraged to be strategists and implementers. At the same time, the role of managers changes to coach, mentor, and facilitator. In the scenario suggested here, career planning becomes more important to the individual. Jobs are becoming obsolete; people can no longer expect retirement after thirty years with the same company, and those individuals unwilling to relinquish the spotlight in favor of group recognition will find themselves left behind. There will be a shift from solution finders to question makers, and for some people this transition will not be easy. Penzias [1989], in his reflective text on ideas and information, states that such increase in complexity will give rise to the need for a more cooperative effort among people of diverse backgrounds and experience.

The International Dimension

To conclude this section on business in the information age, we offer some observations on the international scene. Although the United States is a melting pot of cultures, there is some sense of law and order. Media, and more importantly electronic media, play an important role in freely collecting and disseminating information throughout the nation. Almost all inhabitants come in contact with some form of communication about national and international affairs. Hundreds of millions of computers plug into a global information infrastructure and conduct some form of business.

With this extensive distribution of computing comes the opportunity for workers and private citizens to use and misuse information. Standards of conduct for using the Internet have not been formulated by the United States, much less other developed and developing nations of the world. Some international standards exist for hardware and software design; few standards prevail for the use of information technology. Global information sharing takes the form of international conferences. Software piracy is rampant in Asia; it is estimated that 97 percent of all the software in Thailand has been copied and that seven or eight copies of well-known packages exist for every legitimate one sold in Singapore [Forester, 1992]. The United States loses $12 billion a year; Europe loses $4.5 billion per year. Different cultures, laws, and computer-fluency levels create different value systems on global activity.

It has been suggested that reengineering the corporation and its management will tend to democratize the workforce when information technology is harnessed and distributed properly. If a country does not have the technology to realize this potential, it does not provide improvement of goods and services and therefore does not add business value. The authors had the opportunity to conduct a major international symposium in Prague dedicated to assisting the people of Czechoslovakia to pave the way toward a free market economy after 40 years of communist oppression [DeMichiell and Wysocki, 1990]. Although the program proved most beneficial to this group of leading academics, government officials, and business leaders in formulating strategies for the next five years, the country did not have enough information technology in place to develop realistic implementation plans.

For example, privatization of property was an important first step in this process. There was no automated inventory system for the country. The Czechs and the Slovaks at that time were trying to decide whether they would remain unified. More importantly, there is the factor of mindset and the ability of individuals to openly share ideas and offer opinions. Technology had not outraced application; there was little technology. The opportunity to think creatively and openly was a difficult hurdle to overcome at the symposium even for the country's leaders. It was not clear at that time (or even today) whether communism would return to Czechoslovakia. The method of conducting business was government driven and monitored; people did not have to think, they completed only defined tasks.

The major point here is that the stage of development for both technology and people must be known before any model of managing information technology can be applied effectively. When the international dimension is placed on top of the issues of cyberspace, control systems, the changing nature of the workplace, strategies for competition, electronic commerce, and virtual corporations, it becomes clear that the roles of business professionals will change dramatically as we move into the next century. It is incumbent on us to look at complexity, information, and control in our pursuit of the improvement of the quality of work and life. Our sights should abandon the outdated machine-centered view and its inherent focus on human weakness. We must direct our attention to a machine-assisted and human-centered design strategy. To use technology wisely, we need to think more carefully about what we value and how technology can help reach those deeper goals [Malone and Rockart, 1991].

Changing Roles

The business world is becoming more complex; more information is available, and tougher decisions are being made on many options. Even more accelerated change is probable. Computing will continue to proliferate, and users will become more computer-fluent. All of this activity will necessitate more of a need to manage information more effectively (the right information) and efficiently (for the right people at the right time). Further, information must be managed across the enterprise as well as among enterprises. For effective management of information technology, there are a few prerequisites:

1. The organization expects and rewards individuals who are committed to these concepts:
   a. General philosophy of total quality management
   b. Empowerment with accountability at all worker levels
   c. Self-directed work teams and business process reengineering
   d. Management process reengineering; creating change
   e. Customer service, quick response, customer retention
   f. Enablement through information technology
   g. Continuous improvement of work and information flow
   h. Focus on value-added business activity, even when risk is involved
   i. Less importance placed on organizational status, job description, control
   j. Creative and innovative approaches to break open new opportunities
   k. Collaboration with co-workers and information sharing
   l. Working on diverse and cross-functional teams
   m. Team evaluation; individual evaluation by peer group
   n. Lifelong learning; adaptation to changing work requirements
   o. Technology, people, and process factors balanced in every solution
2. Individuals buy into these concepts and conduct themselves accordingly.
3. The organization places function (getting the job done) before form (delineating corporate structures to get it done).
4. In the event of arrangements with other companies (mergers, acquisitions, trading partnerships, sales), every effort will be made to continue this philosophy.

These concepts embody the direction in which progressive corporations are headed. If individual creativity is not nurtured, encouraged, and rewarded, the wrong problems will be addressed in the wrong way with unsuccessful results.

One popular strategy is to provide a learning environment that supports individuals in their quest to acquire knowledge and skills through theory and practice. Theory is presented in education and training programs. Skill is acquired through practice with on-the-job activity. The business objective is to continually improve the product and services portfolio. To accomplish that objective requires a creative mind—constantly working to achieve innovation [Kanter, 1989]. Creativity is necessary because the problems have become more complex and the solutions require that we step out of the traditional mode of thinking. Alter [1996], in an in-depth interview with Rosabeth Moss Kanter, editor of the *Harvard Business Review,* pursues this topic further. Kanter has devoted over 25 years of her professional life examining how innovation is woven into the fabric of an organization. Her research suggests that the generation of ideas (creativity) is not the problem; the difficulty lies in implementation (innovation). Companies will have to change reward systems and the way departments communicate with each other. Bureaucratic inertia will have to be overcome and changed in favor of flexibility and responsiveness. The biggest single mistake they make is underestimating the time and cost of change.

Managers spend much time estimating. Creative and visionary managers make better and more practical estimates. Managers who make information technology–enabled implementation plans with empowered employees expected to think and act are the ones who lead productivity gains. Various approaches have been used to identify, attract, and satisfy potential customers and align such customer-driven activity with productivity for more accurate estimating. In addition to creative approaches to product development, managers must be creative and innovative in the use of information tools.

It can be argued that creativity and innovation cannot be taught. Because of the dire need to incorporate these "soft" topics into the "hard" world of technology, workers (and students) must be given the opportunity not only to tolerate ambiguity and complexity, but also to welcome the intrusion of humanistic attributes into problem solving throughout the enterprise.

What can organizations do to promote creative and innovative approaches supportive of the concepts listed above and set the stage for the contemporary organization? If one takes the view that humans enter the world with brains and not minds, everything that happens from birth is mind development. This transformation is accomplished by formal curricula in our school system, by self-managed learning activity, and by gaining experience through everyday life.

Organizations can help develop creative and innovative minds by changing the emphasis of training, education, and experience from expert, or logical reasoning based on selected facts to liberal (contextual) concepts of knowledge. Specifically, organizations can:

1. Hire individuals with a mindset willing to incorporate soft, imprecise, and impractical kinds of liberal knowledge into technologically sophisticated business solutions.
2. Encourage workers to enroll in education and training programs that go beyond the "professional" realm of direct job-related skill development.
3. Support the concept of lifelong learning and encourage workers to retrain for future tasks and take responsibility for their careers.

4. Promote team-building and interpersonal skill development.
5. Through thought and action, establish reward systems consistent with the precepts of this new enterprise model.
6. Encourage academe-business relationships in order to strengthen the connection between corporate training and higher education.
7. Include liberal courses for technology workers and vice versa.
8. Support guest lecturers on-site to reinforce the case for interdisciplinary thinking as an integral part of business strategies and operations.
9. Support guest lecturers on-site to present views on cultural differences, ethical practice in business, socioeconomic factors, political considerations, and other "soft" and often personal judgments for addressing mission-specific problem areas and permit the open and free exchange of ideas.

Career Planning: Who Is in Charge?

Once total organizational commitment is in place to support the notion of some type of enterprise model comprised of people, process, and technology in proper balance, workers at all levels must take charge of their own professional development and accept responsibility for assessing and grasping opportunities. Trying to identify what is relevant to career planning is elusive [Cheney, 1989]. Cheney states that we are taught throughout our formal education to keep emotion from intruding on scientific investigation. Emotion runs rampant with children up to age eight; then they begin to substitute creative instincts for more socially acceptable scientific approaches based on logic, deduction, and inference, particularly when the problem is mechanical or technological.

Relevance is a relative term. If organizations continue to build information systems around the way they conduct business today, they will not be here tomorrow. Organizations must develop flexible structures so that they can adapt today's business functions to the business processes that will be needed tomorrow. Organizations must nurture professionals who will fit this new paradigm of business behavior. The challenge is to resurrect childhood creative senses and, together with others, develop innovative products and services. In the contemporary corporation, they are the ones who are not afraid to "step out of the box." Such workers are critical to success.

The major difficulty for these workers is how to cope with the continual demand for a changing skill set. It is difficult to know where your career is headed. You must be aware of the impact of technology and society on organizations of the future in order to determine a career and life development strategy. We have become accustomed to a stable corporate environment led by a select few. They act as mentors and provide advice on climbing the corporate ladder through a time-tested regimen of 50- to 60-hour work weeks focused on completing tasks in a timely, complete, and accurate manner. Those days are gone.

Senior managers will have to rethink the skills needed by those workers who aspire to leadership positions. In addition to the changing business picture and complementary comments on an emerging new breed of information-enabled manager, they will need some insight into the future job market. The next 20 years will require more and more knowledge workers who change jobs more often, work on project after project, and view their education as a lifelong activity [Petersen, 1994].

Because of information technology, career paths for information systems (IS) professionals and for general operating managers have become more of a maze. Regardless of current position, academic background, and experience, those workers who are technologically advantaged, business-savvy, and people oriented will be successful. We develop this notion in the next section.

◆ EMERGENCE OF A NEW INFORMATION AGE PROFESSIONAL

Need for the Marriage of Business and Technology Professionals

Information technology is an integral part of business. If business, governmental, and educational organizations are to survive, they must not only have automation, but also have a comprehensive process for the continuous application of information technology to their operating environment. In order for this process to be effective, it must meaningfully engage the entire enterprise. In this way the organization's applications development portfolio can be analyzed and prioritized according to cost, risk, disruptiveness to operation, practicality, impact on other enterprise operating functions, and complexity. Evaluation of these attributes will determine what, when, and how applications should be developed for meeting organizational goals and objectives. The portfolio is dynamic; it will continuously change in response to market conditions and technological advances.

A formal and documented master plan provides the foundation for managing information technology. The two planning documents (enterprise strategic plan and information technology plan) are developed concurrently and interdependently so that an integrated systems and enterprisewide solution emerges. One way to ensure that integrated activity occurs is to develop the enterprisewide plan under the leadership of an information-enabled team. People, process, and technology issues are discussed in the form of a continuum where the mix is determined by market demand, competition, and the need for quick response. The long-term success of the enterprise is best served by achieving a balance between people, process, and technology.

The plan will be dynamic—constantly changing in response to or anticipation of a changing business climate. The enterprise plan must be business driven and technology enabled. It would be a mistake, however, to assume that the IS department, through its manager, is in a reactive role regarding plan formation. The effective IS manager will collaborate with senior management and other business unit managers both in the traditional reactive role as well as in the now strategically important proactive role. We return to this discussion in Chapter 4.

A better scenario will be one in which every member of the planning team has some measure of information technology expertise. To some extent this will happen naturally with the passage of time. There are three reasons for this. First,

Exhibit 1-2

TAXONOMY: Managing Information Across the Enterprise
[Enabling Managers with Information Technology to Meet Societal, Organizational, and Individual Needs]

The World

The Enterprise
[Business, Government, or Education]

PEOPLE	INFORMATION TECHNOLOGY
Information-Enabled Managers (IEM)	*Computers and Telecommunications*
Attributes	**Cyberspace**
Enterprise Systems Knowledge	Systems Development Methodology
Information Technology Knowledge	Systems and Applications Software
Information Technology Capability	Client-Servers, Networks
Human-Centered Strategy for IT	Information Highway
Higher Order Thinking Skills	Data Modeling, Programming
Adaptable to Environment **+**	Microcomputing, Multimedia
Lifelong Learning Motivation	User-Friendly Software
Strong Interpersonal Skills	Electronic Mail, Commerce
Cooperative, Collaborative	End-User Computing
Team-Oriented, Process-Driven	Computer Systems Management
Visionary, Conceptual, Analytical	Decision Support and Expert Systems
Self-Directed in Work and Life+	Executive Support Systems

ENTERPRISE OUTCOMES

Quality
- **Process**: Portfolio of Processes and Applications
  - Philosophy: Short-Term & Long-Range Planning
  - Goals & Objectives: Value-Added Concepts
- **Process Management**: Strategies and Operations
  - Business Systems & Information Technology Planning
- **Empowerment**: Teams and Individuals
  - Self-Directed to Plan, Design, Act, Evaluate
  - Cross-Functionality, Diversity, Creativity
- **Continuous Improvement**: Organization, Processes, & Individuals
  - Learning Organization: Philosophy, Strategies, Action Plans
  - Process Workflow: Managing Information with Collaboration
  - Individuals: Lifelong Learning and Career Planning

Customer Service
- **Competitive Forces**
  - Deliver Product/Service at Lowest Cost
  - Develop Unique, Differentiated Product/Service
  - Meet Specialized Markets
- **Response**
  - Time and Space: Electronic Communication in Global Village
  - Customization of Products (Virtual Products)

an increasing number of managers' education includes computing and information systems. Second, computing is becoming more intuitive and managers are beginning to take the initiative to learn to use and access data from their desktop machines. Third, colleges and universities are beginning to awaken to the shifting business paradigm and are designing curricula that more closely match the needs of the information age manager for an integrated study of information technology, business functions, and business process knowledge and skills.

The conclusions here are obvious. As information and information technology become more pervasive in function, process, product, and service, it is incumbent on the professional stakeholders to become more multidisciplined, with technology being one of the essential disciplines. Similarly, technologists must become more like the business professionals. They must expand their tool kit to include a working knowledge of the functions, processes, products, and services that define their enterprise.

A Taxonomy for Planning the Future

In summary, we have discussed the need for people/process/technology issues to be addressed in an integrated fashion by the enterprise as part of developing a global business strategy. In fact, the three components are inextricably linked. Not only is there the need for a proper balance between technology and people, as we have already discussed, but there must be a balance between technology and process as well as between people and process.

These issues, problems, approaches, and concepts can be organized with a total systems view in the form of a taxonomy [Exhibit 1-2]. This taxonomy is enterprise-outcome driven and indicates that people or information technology alone cannot be effective in achieving those outcomes. Also, it suggests that a new breed of information-enabled manager will be required to lead the enterprise to successful results.

◆ A NEW MODEL: STEP—STRATEGIES FOR TECHNOLOGY-ENABLEMENT THROUGH PEOPLE

The planning taxonomy suggests that enterprise outcomes are a result of the mix of people, process, and information technology trying to be productive in work and life. This mix is shown as a *strategy for technology enablement through people,* or the STEP Model [Exhibit 1-3]. The achievement of the proper mix requires an action-oriented framework, which goes beyond awareness of the issues and problems and focuses on a structured process of directed change.

The first step is to assess the current status of the enterprise. (We discuss this assessment in more detail in Chapter 3.) It could be a startup company making some use of information technology, not yet having established an organizational style and only beginning to define and stabilize the processes that will be the framework for its business activities. Alternatively, the enterprise could be

Exhibit 1-3: The STEP Model

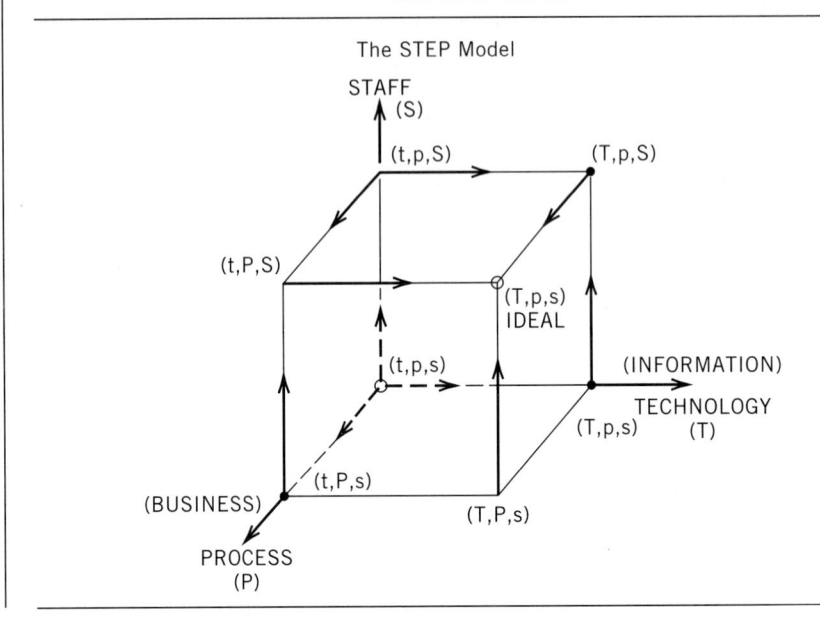

[Diagram: A 3D cube representing the STEP Model with three axes: STAFF (S) vertical, TECHNOLOGY (T) / (INFORMATION) horizontal right, PROCESS (P) / (BUSINESS) horizontal left-front. The eight vertices are labeled:
- *(t,p,s) — origin*
- *(T,p,s)*
- *(t,P,s)*
- *(t,p,S)*
- *(T,P,s)*
- *(T,p,S)*
- *(t,P,S)*
- *(T,P,S) IDEAL]*

established with a comfortable client base and quality products but losing market share and new opportunities because it cannot respond fast enough because it has not deployed its people to the business processes (the corporatewide information system may be outdated and/or its people may not be sufficiently computer literate).

At the other extreme of the people-technology spectrum, the enterprise may have completed an extensive reengineering effort with full deployment of information technology to the new enterprisewide systems and to the individuals who use the system. This type of enterprise must also focus on its people to restore balance to a work environment that has emphasized process and technology.

In order to describe how an enterprise moves from little or no enablement of information technology to extensive and fulfilling enablement, we have introduced the STEP Model. It captures the issues that the enterprise and the individual professional must face in order to make the necessary transitions.

The vertices describe the extreme positions of an enterprise in need of a new business strategy. Trivially, the enterprise cannot function only on process, or technology, or staff. Some mix is required. Conceptually, the edges of the cube represent some mix of the three components. For example, enterprises that focus on technology and process but ignore staff will lie somewhere on the technology-process surface. The closer they lie to the technology vertex, the more emphasis they place on technology over process. As the enterprise moves away from the technology-process surface toward the staff vertex, they place more emphasis on their staff and, consequently, the degree of technology enablement increases. The point (T,P,S) represents the ideal balance of technology, process, and staff that enables the enterprise to maximize its use of technology. Beyond that, any plan to move the enterprise forward with new technology or new processes (reengineering, for example) will upset the equilibrium unless all three components are taken into account. Let us look at a few specific cases and see what actions the enterprise might take.

Lack of Attention to People

These enterprises may be holding onto the command-and-control structures introduced during the Industrial Revolution. There are few defensible reasons to sustain such structures in today's business world. Rather, the enterprise needs to look for ways to empower its workers with more responsibility and authority. This is a natural consequence of putting more focus on improved customer service. Implementing self-directed work teams and professional development programs are strategies that may be employed.

Lack of Attention to Process

These enterprises may be holding onto the functional type of organizational structure. If so, they have discovered that is not the most effective or efficient way to compete. There are at least three alternatives that they should consider: (1) At the strategic level, business process reengineering could be undertaken. This would have a major impact on the way business is conducted and usually results in the enterprise changing from a business function to a business process emphasis; (2) at the operational level, the enterprise might consider work flow analysis of selected areas as a means to reduce the time and improve the quality of an existing business process; and (3) a given business process might be further improved through some form of continuous quality improvement program. Total Quality Management (TQM) programs will be valuable during the transition to a process-oriented business structure.

Lack of Attention to Technology

These enterprises may be holding onto the notion that information systems is a backroom function and not part of the strategic equation. While this notion is certainly disappearing, many organizations are experiencing a leadership void in their IS management area and are struggling to shed the outdated notions of the role of information technology. We will have more to say on this situation in Chapter 3. For now it is sufficient to note that the IS department needs to take a leadership role in folding technology into the strategy set if the enterprise is to take advantage of the information technologies in impacting efficiency, effectiveness, productivity, and competitive position.

There are three approaches available to the IS manager faced with this imbalance. The first is to look at the business environment and identify others who have made good use of information technology in certain parts of their operation. These so-called "best of breed" investigations may excite senior management about the possibilities. Demonstrations and site visits have been effective in many situations. Second, comparative studies, or benchmarking, can engage management in taking an interest in alternative solutions to a business problem that has technology implications. And third, an enterprisewide strategic planning process that integrates information technology and the business units is essential. This process will consider the three components of the STEP Model.

Getting There from Here

So now that we have identified the situation faced by organizations as they plan for full exploitation of the information technologies, a logical question is: "How do we get there from here?" Exhibit 1-3 gives us the roadmap. For example, let us take an organization that is highly dependent upon the latest technologies—say they are information brokers of some kind. They have focused on building a technology infrastructure that makes them the envy of the industry. They have the latest and best hardware environment of anyone in their industry. They have grown rapidly and spent little time on developing processes for handling customer requests and even less time developing their human resources.

Only recently have they realized the value of their people and the fact that turnover has been high primarily because their workers are not as productive as expected or as committed to the business as senior management would like them to be. What should they do? Exhibit 1-3 has the answer. First observe that the company is located at coordinates (T,p,S). The directional arrow suggests that they should first enable their staff. The people-enablement tools listed in Exhibit 1-4 offers several suggestions as to how that process might be undertaken. Once they have reached the coordinates at (T,p,S) they are ready to take the step to move to the ideal point (T,P,S), for which Exhibit 1-4 again offers several process-enablement tools. Some combination of the tool sets might also be employed to move them directly toward the ideal point at (T,P,S). Note that Exhibit 1-3 shows the pathway from any coordinate to the ideal point. The patterns suggest that people enablement supersedes process enablement, which supersedes technology enablement. The STEP Model will be our template for much of the remaining chapters in this text. As appropriate, we will refer to this model to help put into perspective your study of the IEMgr in the context of the information-age enterprise. IEMgrs are defined at the four points of the technology-process surface at the base of the cube. It will be discussed in more detail in Ch. 2.

> **Exhibit 1-4** | **People, Process, Technology Enablement Tools**
>
> **People Enablement Tools**
> - Worker Empowerment
> - Self-Directed Work Teams
> - Professional Development Programs
> - Task Forces
> - Project Management Methodologies
> - Creativity & Problem Solving
>
> **Process Enablement Tools**
> - Business Process Reengineering
> - Process Quality Management
> - Continuous Quality Management
> - Total Quality Management
> - Quality Function Deployment
> - Work Flow Analysis
> - Process Flow Diagramming
>
> **Technology Enablement Tools**
> - Best of Breed
> - Benchmarking
> - Integrated Strategic Information Systems Planning
> - Strengths, Weaknesses, Opportunities, & Threats Analyses
> - Environmental Scans

Reflections

GENERAL CONCEPTS

1. Advances in information technology products far outstrip the enterprise's ability to absorb them. This presents a dilemma. The creative use of technology is a critical success factor, but who has time to understand the technology, let alone determine how it can be used to advantage? The organization that does understand the effective use of information technology will be successful. The organization that doesn't address this topic will be out of business.

   How does an organization position itself to take advantage of technology when the time to do so is limited? What strategy would you recommend? What can the individual worker do to fit into enterprise strategy?

   What advice can you, as a business or information technology manager, give to your staff in preparing to take advantage of information technology for personal and organizational productivity?

2. Information technology makes it possible to access data and do work any time, any place. This means that going to the office is no longer necessary to get work done. In a certain sense, our direct access to information has reduced the need for face-to-face human contact. Are we to become a nation that communicates only through voice mail messages?

If so, what sociological impact would you see?

What measures might be taken to avoid the problems you see?

What are the benefits of fewer personal meetings and your work schedule?

Does information technology help you to separate work and personal life?

What do you think of companies charging to talk to a person (rather than to a voice mail system)? Is this just an economic (efficiency) issue?

3. Describe the ideal information-enabled enterprise.

How would you see yourself working in such an environment?

Are you willing to accept the responsibility that is placed on the individual in such organizations? Why? Why not?

Are you willing to accept accountability for your actions? for team actions?

4. The question of control always arises when worker empowerment and self-directed work teams are considered by the enterprise. Some managers are "command-and-control" persons who have to be in charge of events and/or other people. Without clear control, they are confused and feel that they are not contributing to leadership and are not taking "action."

Is there some credence to the notion that one does not really need to be in control to manage or lead enterprise efforts?

Can one put aside personal status symbolism and career moves and still be productive?

Can one be a hero (in the general concept of the "macho" person) without control?

Will the enterprise recognize and reward a passive but productive hero who is a team player, cooperative, and focused on mission-critical activity?

5. The terms *management, leadership, efficiency,* and *effectiveness* have been used throughout this chapter.

How are they related to each other?

Is there some graphic image you can design to clarify their meanings?

How are the terms *time compression* and *space compression* related to management effectiveness?

6. The concept of a "job" is disappearing. Certainly, this activity will not happen overnight since almost all workers are in jobs and want to remain in them. As organizations begin to place more emphasis on the value-added dimension of hiring people (what you can do for the enterprise, now and in the future), it might be prudent for you to think about your career development rather than your current job.

How can the enterprise help you with career development?

What can you do to help yourself and take charge of your career?

What are the psychological and social implications of job disappearance?

If the movement is more toward self-directed work teams, what changes will the individual have to make in order to function effectively on team projects?

7. *Information technology* has a scientific connotation. It sounds like the "hard" subjects of databases, programming, and systems analysis. On the other hand, the "soft" subjects, like management, humanities, and some business processes, suggest a more laid-back approach to problem-solving through reflection and discussion rather than procedural, quantitative methods.

Do you agree with "hard" and "soft" categories?

If creative approaches are needed in both categories, separately and concurrently, how can innovative actions result if individuals continue to think of them separately?

Can creativity be developed, or is one born with such an attribute? Is it work related?

STEP MODEL

1. A case has been made by the authors to force the enterprise to look at their processes, people, and information technology from a three-dimensional perspective (STEP Model).
    a. How would you determine the starting point for the organization? The model does not have measurable scales in the three directions (axes). Be creative and develop some criteria and "weights" for the criteria that could translate to numbers on each axis.
    b. Is there some survey that could be conducted for an organization to place it somewhere within the "cube"?
    c. Once the starting point is defined, how would you assess the organization to select the right path to follow to the ideal (maximum T, P, and S)?

Chapter 2

The Information-Enabled Manager

◆ ◆ ◆

In Chapter 1 we developed the argument that to be successful an organization needs to develop professionals that are multidisciplined. One of those disciplines needs to be information technology. In this chapter we formally introduce the information-enabled manager (IEMgr). The IEMgr is a professional who

- *Has a command of information technology at the level needed to meet the challenges that will arise in the business unit and in the dynamic business environment in which their enterprise competes*
- *Places the customer first in every aspect of their business activities*
- *Is vested with the responsibility and authority to discharge their duties in an empowered environment*

Such a professional is truly a corporate citizen and has been empowered through the information technologies to fully exploit opportunities that these technologies present. While we may argue about the extent to which such professionals are now in the workplace, there can be no argument about the need for them. In this chapter we explore this new phenomenon and set the stage to further discuss the emerging role of the IEMgr at the process, function, enterprise, business-environment, and global levels.

◆ THE GLOBAL VILLAGE

Computers and telecommunications have changed the electronic landscape from the distribution of information among and between enterprise-specific activities to information exchange with other enterprises throughout the world. Businesses merge, collaborate, form trading partnerships, and share information on market demand and on processes needed to meet that demand. Governments enter into political arrangements to create, maintain, or conclude sanctions on nations under scrutiny for human rights abuse, unfair trading laws, or aggressive military behavior. Institutions of higher education collaborate on student admissions, work with business and government on research and development projects, and create faculty and student exchanges with foreign countries.

According to Drucker [1992], there is a distinct trend toward trading partnerships as a central concept of business practice and that trend has become irreversible. In addition, Drucker identifies four other business trends (not forecasts, but definite conclusions he has reached): (1) a continuing formation of world alliances, (2) more radical enterprise restructuring within this decade, (3) current governance called into question, and (4) domination by international considerations rather than domestic ones during this decade. Information technology (for those nations with the capability) enables the enterprise to respond effectively to these trends.

In order for a country to gain a competitive edge in world markets, the enterprise must restructure and delayer itself, develop business strategies, and maximize the creativity and productivity of its employees. When this approach is planned and implemented across the enterprise, a shift in focus will materialize from thinking global to being global, from domestic markets to global markets, and from global competition to global collaboration [Burrus, 1993]. Windows of opportunity with an emphasis on how much, when, and how value is added by each venture is an important criterion for corporate direction. Faster may not mean better, especially when information technology is involved. Value, like productivity, is an elusive term and cannot be defined simply in terms of input/output, price/performance, or return on investment ratios. Each ratio contains variables which may not be quantifiable and, further, new directions of the enterprise in the global marketplace make those definitions even fuzzier.

Adding to the problems brought on by those fuzzy definitions are factors such as the impact of new technologies, workforce expertise and experience, the synergistic influences of collaborative arrangements, nonstandard global accounting systems, performance evaluations based on process effectiveness, more complex input variables, and deferred, intangible, and serendipitous returns. The more complex and wide-ranging the information systems we create in the future, the more difficult it will be to anticipate the cost of having people interact effectively with the technology [Leebaert, 1991]. Leebaert explores the future of the information age across the entire global front and stresses the concept that idle human capacity and not idle information technology is the major problem in bringing people and technology together.

◆ THE LEARNING ORGANIZATION

Successful enterprises of the future will be those which have both a vision and the discipline to make that vision a reality. This delicate balance of vision and action in the face of resource constraints is a strategy that will allow individuals and teams to excel [Kanter, 1989]. Kanter's text on corporate strategies for success in the 1990s suggests that a new kind of business hero is needed to avoid the excesses of the "corpocrat," one who conserves and protects the status quo, as well as of the corporate "cowboy," one who speculates and promotes new ventures. Her new hero is one who is fast, flexible, focused, and friendly (the four Fs). Information technology is the major enabler that helps establish focused perspectives and plans of action. The need for interpersonal skill development and team building suggests the emergence of an environment of mutual respect and individual empowerment. However, in order to attain such significant behavioral changes additional strategies must be developed.

Individuals continue to learn through a lifetime. Each person has unique motivation and capacity to learn through a variety of formal and informal programs. Peter Senge of MIT [Senge, 1990] defines learning from experience as a delusion. He indicates that we never directly experience the consequences of many decisions and therefore do not gain from the experience. The cycles of feedback stretch over years and "trial and error" learning is ineffective.

Traditionally, organizations cope with major change by assigning functional units to selected parts of the problem or issue—temporarily removing the problem from view. Whatever learning takes place is short term and, like short-term memory, does not provide lasting benefit. For the organization to be a true "learning organization," it must develop an atmosphere conducive to long-term benefits. This means, first of all, that the problem or issue must be perceived from a total systems point-of-view. In the words of Senge [1990], the learning organization is one

> where people continuously expand their capacity to create results they truly desire, where new and expansive patterns of thinking are nurtured, where collective aspiration is set free, and where people are continually learning how to learn together.

Senge identifies five disciplines—new mental models, shared vision, team-building, personal mastery, and systems thinking—to be the foundation for forward-looking organizations of the future. This systems-thinking approach will force workers to let their natural urges for inquisitiveness, creative initiatives, and collaboration with co-workers emerge. Today, the hiring needs of corporate America are for multiskilled individuals who have a sense of the business disciplines, are information enabled, and understand the importance of establishing good interpersonal relations. Furthermore, they must be able to function in a rapidly changing business environment. New hires are either placed on the fast track through more education and diverse learning experiences or are just marking time until the next job.

The learning corporation encourages lifelong learning for all managers who are motivated to create products and services and add value to the enterprise, while knowing that they will probably not be with the company for their entire working lives. As the worker learns how to learn and therefore adapt to change, the organization learns, creates new opportunities, and competes. As a result, technological, social, and economic changes can be effectively addressed by the learned manager [Naisbitt and Aburdene, 1985].

◆ WILL THE NEW INFORMATION-AGE PROFESSIONAL PLEASE STAND UP?

Because of what we have already said, it would seem that this question is out of order. Taking a broad-brush approach we could say that every professional is an information-age professional. For it is true that every professional either already depends on information systems for the practice of his or her profession, will shortly do so, or will be forced to find another line of work. It would seem that no one can escape the computer. It will continue to make greater inroads into how we live and work.

For purposes of further discussion we will partition the enterprise's employees into two groups of workers:

1. Information systems (IS) professionals—those for whom information systems is their primary subject matter expertise and who are organizationally attached to the IS department
2. Non–IS professionals—those for whom information systems is not their primary subject matter expertise and who are not organizationally attached to the IS department

The reason for this partitioning will soon become clear.

Historically, IS professionals have been known for their technical skills and their ability to master rather obscure and arcane languages. More recently, they have broadened their scope and have begun to learn about the business of their organization and about the business disciplines that drive it. Along with this broadening they are beginning to develop skills and relate information systems to the business of the enterprise. The more progressive among them will have even taken on a more proactive role in helping the organization use technology for strategic benefit. To help in your understanding of the dynamics involved, envision a scale running from left to right with the left side of the scale representing technology and the IS professional and the right side representing business functions and the non-IS professional (Exhibit 2-1). The third dimension measures the ability of individuals, with their balance of expertise in information technology and business functions/processes, to exploit IS for the strategic advantage of the enterprise. As IS professionals begin to acquire a better understanding of the business (indicated by movement toward the function/process vertex) they likewise increase their value to the enterprise (indicated by movement along curve A).

On the other hand, non–IS professionals have been known for their business sense and have relied almost totally on IS professionals to bring the computer into their business activities. More recently, they have broadened their scope and, first out of necessity and then out of interest, have learned to communicate with the computer. More progressive users will have taken on a more proactive role with respect to information systems by developing their own application systems apart from any support by IS professionals. In terms of our business-technology

Exhibit 2-1

A Perceptual Map for Exploiting Technology and Business Functions/Processes for Strategic Advantage

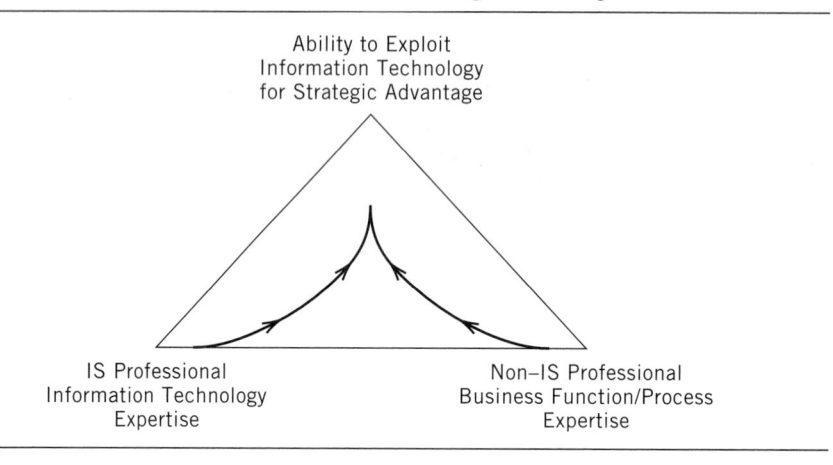

```
                    Ability to Exploit
                  Information Technology
                   for Strategic Advantage


        IS Professional              Non–IS Professional
    Information Technology         Business Function/Process
          Expertise                       Expertise
```

continuum, they have started to move from the right (business functions/processes) to the left (technology enablement). In so doing they simultaneously move toward the strategic advantage vertex.

Will the two groups ever converge at some middle point? In a sense we say they will. Certain members of both groups will become the business technologists. More precisely, we choose to call this new breed *Information-Enabled Managers* (IEMgrs) and define them in the sections that follow.

Definition of Information-Enabled Managers (IEMgrs)

What They Are Not

First, let us be clear that *the IEMgr is not a new position on the organizational chart.* People in such positions are not necessarily managers in the traditional sense that they direct the activities of others under their charge. They do manage information and may manage people. As we will see, they carry out their mission to effectively apply and use information technology from a variety of traditional positions located throughout the enterprise.

What They Are

Information-enabled managers (IEMgrs) are multidisciplined with one discipline in information technology and the other in business processes and functions. One discipline is the primary focus and the other one is secondary. IEMgrs, in general, are capable of

- Understanding the strategic relationship between information technology and the business processes and functions
- Discovering ways to exploit information technologies for strategic benefit
- Combining their primary and secondary subject matter expertise to propose, design, develop, and implement systems that help the enterprise attain and sustain strategic advantage in the marketplace
- Advising senior management on further applications of information technology at the business function and process level
- Leading the enterprise's effort to exploit the information technologies
- Sponsoring and supporting ideas for further use of the information technologies
- Combining business acumen with technical expertise to create innovative products and services
- Applying information technology in response to business unit problems requiring resolution
- Supporting and continuously improving the efficiency and effectiveness of business operations

For more details on these new-breed professionals, see related articles by Wysocki (1990a, 1990b).

While few professionals could claim to be an IEMgr, it is clear that there is a growing demand for such multidisciplined individuals. In fact, a 1990 study published by the British Computer Society announced the need for 10,000 "hybrid managers" (their equivalent of our IEMgr) in the UK by 1995. As is true of many forecasts in the information technology industry, they were probably a bit conservative in their estimate. The IEMgr concept extends to include four different categories of professional as described in Exhibit 2-2. For instance, *an IEMgr (TP—both capital letters) means high-technology and high-process expertise. Lowercase letters indicate a secondary level of expertise.* The technology-process surface of the STEP model cube (Exhibit 1-3) defines the four types of IEMgrs as the four corners of that surface.

IEMgr(Tp)

These managers are found in the IS department. Their primary orientation is technical. They are responsible for designing and implementing the technology infrastructure that supports the needs of the business functions and processes. In order to construct and support this infrastructure, they must be experts in information technology and understand enough of business functions and processes to link them tactically and strategically. Among their managerial responsibilities are technology gatekeeping, strategic planning for information technology, and technology implementation. They might hold such positions as CIO, IS Manager, Technology Services Manager, and other mid-level IS management positions. They interact with senior managers, business unit managers, business function managers, and process owners at a strategic and tactical level.

Exhibit 2-2

The IEMgr Taxonomy

The IEMgmt Team

HI TECHNOLOGY ──────────────────────────── HI PROCESS

	(Tp) hi tech lo proc	(TP) hi tech hi proc	(tp) lo tech lo proc	(tP) lo tech hi proc
Sr. Mgmt.	CIO IS Mgr.	CIO IS Mgr.		CIO VP Bus. Unit
Process Mgmt.	Mgr., Tech. Services	Mgr., Applic. Develop.	Mgr., Bus. Unit	Mgr., Bus. Unit
Project Mgmt.	Dir., Adv. Tech. Gp.	Leader, Quality Team (Reeng.)	Leader, Continuous Improvement Action Team	Leader, Task Force on PI.

One could successfully argue that the natural evolution of senior IS management will be to the IEMgr(Tp). That argument would say that this will come about as IS managers realize that their success (ability to add value) depends on their ability to embrace and understand the business of the enterprise. There is sufficient evidence to suggest that this is already happening.

IEMgr(TP)

These managers are process experts, have the same technical expertise as the IEMgr(Tp), and are attached to a business function or process. Generally, they may report to the IS department but could also report to a function manager or process owner. They are capable of designing and implementing technology applications for their business function or process. Among their managerial responsibilities are business process reengineering, business process improvement, total quality management, technology gatekeeping as it applies to their function or process, best-of-breed investigations and benchmarking, comparable uses of the technologies, and meeting the applications development needs of their function manager or process owner.

These IS professionals will eventually evolve from those (systems analysts, for the most part) who have recently been deployed into the business units as part of a downsizing or reengineering effort. As they serve the needs of the business unit they will necessarily have to improve their information technology, business function, and business process skills.

IEMgr(tp)

These professionals support the business functions and processes and report to the function manager or process owner. They function in a more passive role by performing business activities that are technology based. They do not have technology development and implementation expertise but are able to suggest systems improvements or even new applications. Their role is supportive and operationally based.

IEMgr(tP)

These management professionals are the function managers and process owners. Their primary expertise is in the business function or process for which they are responsible. As managers they also have the capability of identifying technology applications to improve their area of responsibility. Through their IEMgr(TP) they will implement technology solutions. Just as the IEMgr(Tp), these professionals recognize the importance of expanding their information technology skills.

IEMgmt Team

We will have reason to refer to all four types of IEMgrs. For convenience, we will refer to all four types collectively as the IEMgmt Team. Collectively, the team guides the enterprise in its use of information technology at the strategic, tactical, and operational levels. The IEMgmt Team is a new concept and will be developed in subsequent chapters. We believe that this team must evolve as a precondition for success in the information-age enterprise.

IEMgrs are a new paradigm that we are introducing into the evolution of the business model. Other writers have commented on the need for such professionals (Keen, 1991) and a few universities have even introduced courses that address these information-age professionals and the skills that they must possess in order for the enterprise to remain competitive. Through every chapter of this book we will study the changes that can be brought about by IEMgrs and particularly their role in the future of our businesses. Please understand that the paradigm is developing even as we write about it. As such, we are taking you to the edge of the technology-management envelope. Much information remains to be uncovered but some of it has already become clear. An exciting process of discovery awaits us all. As students of information management you will certainly join a work world where more of this paradigm will have become the natural order.

◆ EDUCATION AND TRAINING OF THE IEMgr

Planning and Implementing Professional Development

Today's better-prepared students become tomorrow's better-prepared managers. Many U.S. corporations teach remedial education and skill development at the cost of hundreds of millions dollars per year. Even at this level of expense, corporations are not keeping pace with the need for training and education. The problem has been exacerbated by the downsizing and delayering decisions of recent years. Reducing the workforce has not had a proportional effect on the amount of work to be done. The result is that the remaining workforce has to cover not only their prior responsibilities but also many of those once assigned to the now departed workers. In many cases they are responsible for tasks that they lack the requisite skills to perform. Training programs have not been implemented to provide the newly created need for skills development.

In fact, many of the exact training programs needed were also victims of the downsizing and delayering! Furthermore, workers want such programs so that they can keep their skills up to date and remain employable. Learning organizations should want employees to enter into a lifelong learning contract so the corporation can realize "learning" status and grow more competitive. Once the enterprise decides to make a commitment for the training and education of its workforce, they must decide what programs to support. There are four major steps in planning for such professional development.

Step 1: Be aware of the difference between training and education and act accordingly

Coming to a conclusion about the nature, scope, audience, and cost of any professional development program is to understand the difference between training and education. Usually training is enterprise driven, even though the enterprise may supplement its training programs with those developed and delivered through outsourcing. Training is skill oriented and focuses on knowledge, comprehension, and application. These lower-order thinking skills rely on memory, repetition, and problem-solving. Higher-order thinking skills are more conceptual (analysis, synthesis, and evaluation) and with a liberal arts program define what we associate with the educational enterprise.

The IEMgr for tomorrow's world needs both training and education. IEMgrs should develop a professional development plan and stick to it! Often they are prevented from doing so because of busy and/or incompatible schedules, inappropriate topics offered, cost, and other barriers. Typically, the enterprise's training staff has been downsized, is underbudgeted, and more focused on immediate critical needs than longer-term development plans. Even though business may drastically change in the next decade, it is easier to justify programs to meet departmental needs for lower-order skill development (word processing, project management, use of electronic mail and the Internet, and other specific job-related activity).

Unless you are well versed in the role of education in society and organizations, it may be difficult to justify liberal arts courses (western civilization, music appreciation, literature, etc.) and relate it to everyday management activity, even though everyone might agree that a "well-rounded" education is necessary for societal demands. If the IEMgr is to respond to a global marketplace (new cultures) from the viewpoint of self-directed work teams (diverse workgroups) and grasp new opportunities (using creative and innovative approaches), then it is important to train and educate the information-enabled manager.

Step 2: Allow for the new shift from individual power to team power and integrate the concept in the educational experiences provided

Planning professional development programs by the enterprise and by the individual means to look beyond performance as a measure of effectiveness and into the underlying character of the person [Kaplan, 1991]. If the rules of the game are to change from individualistic and heroic acts to a team structure, it is in the interest of the worker to be aware of this power shift and what it means to him or her. Typically, corporate executives see themselves as hard-working, late-working, work-consumed managers. Work comes before their personal life and is driven by money, rewards, and perks. They are action-oriented, decisive, and born to lead. What happens when chain-of-command structures are replaced by more collaborative models? The new direction means submersion into team-controlled processes where status on the hierarchical organization chart disappears.

Certainly, it is unrealistic to expect individuals to dramatically change their behavior to be consistent with these new enterprise directions. Further, what is needed is a better balance between the two extreme characteristics (action-oriented, decisive hero vs. reflective and interpersonal team member) to be employed as the situation demands [Kaplan, 1991]. The IEMgr should be flexible in moving across the "character" continuum in line with changing organizational goals and objectives. There is no single and correct pathway for the IEMgr to pass through the maze of business complexity, organizational competitiveness, and personal productivity.

What can higher education do to prepare the IEMgr for navigating the maze? It has been implied that a balance of technological, conceptual, and human development skills are needed for a trained and educated IEMgr to be effective in the next century. Kao [1991] verifies that entrepreneurial and intrapreneurial ventures are ongoing for the 1990s and beyond. This spirit of entrepreneurship encourages creativity. If the organization develops a style of doing business conducive to its employees rising to the challenge at the right time with the right information and for the right reasons, these ventures have a high probability of success.

Step 3: Assess the educational climate for quality, response, and customer service and ensure that the philosophy and principles are consistent with the external environment

This step requires institutions of higher education to conduct a self-assessment, not only in terms of content delivered to students but also in how it is delivered. Alignment to societal, business, and governmental activity with imperatives for quality, fast response, and customer service applies to educational institutions as well as the business community. Managerial leadership needed for the next millennium moves from individual to group and from mentor to facilitator. The process of developing and implementing curricula needs revision if educators are to provide students and groups of students with the knowledge and motivation to observe, reflect, imagine, and judge critically. Under the present scheme of curriculum development and governance, faculty design and deliver the academic programs and administrators plan and provide resource support for implementation. Their roles and responsibilities (and power) are separated. The academic model needs to take on more of the process structure of the business world.

Step 4: Develop concurrently a business partnership with higher education for program development and support

This step requires that institutions of higher education develop a business outcome model so there is linkage with the philosophy, policies, and procedures that exist beyond the enterprise, and convert the separation of power between faculty and administration to a single, integrated, and formal collaborative power arrangement within the enterprise. A business outcome model depicting the academe-business linkage is shown in Exhibit 2-3. The model appears to be a sequential portrayal of activity from top to bottom. However, if one examines the model *before* any curriculum design occurs, it is evident that business and learning outcomes are addressed at the outset. The charge to higher education from the business community is to produce students who can perform in the workplace, can adapt to a constantly changing environment, can develop creative solutions, and are "systems thinkers."

In the top half of Exhibit 2-3, the expression "virtual work environment" is used to connote an artificial environment where students take some risks (academic and personal) to meet course requirements. In the actual working environment, the added risk of job performance (retention, career growth) is the incentive to be even more productive than in the virtual environment created in the classroom. Educational learning outcomes based on business requirements are designed for the most effective learning situation. The highlighted segment of the exhibit under "academe" shows learning objectives with an emphasis on higher-order thinking skill development. During international presentations directly related to this topic [DeMichiell & Wysocki, 1990; DeMichiell & Pavlock, 1994; DeMichiell, 1995; Boisjoly & DeMichiell, 1995], world experts generally agreed that the business outcome approach has merit. It creates and strengthens academe-business partnerships at the same time that students are placed on a more defined road leading to managerial positions and the cultivation of a lifelong learning habit.

Next, the integration of classroom methodology is examined for inclusion of higher-order thinking skill development. Effective learners are encouraged to embrace chaos and to reorder it in fresh, creative ways [Sinetar, 1991]. If one takes

Exhibit 2-3

Business Outcome Model

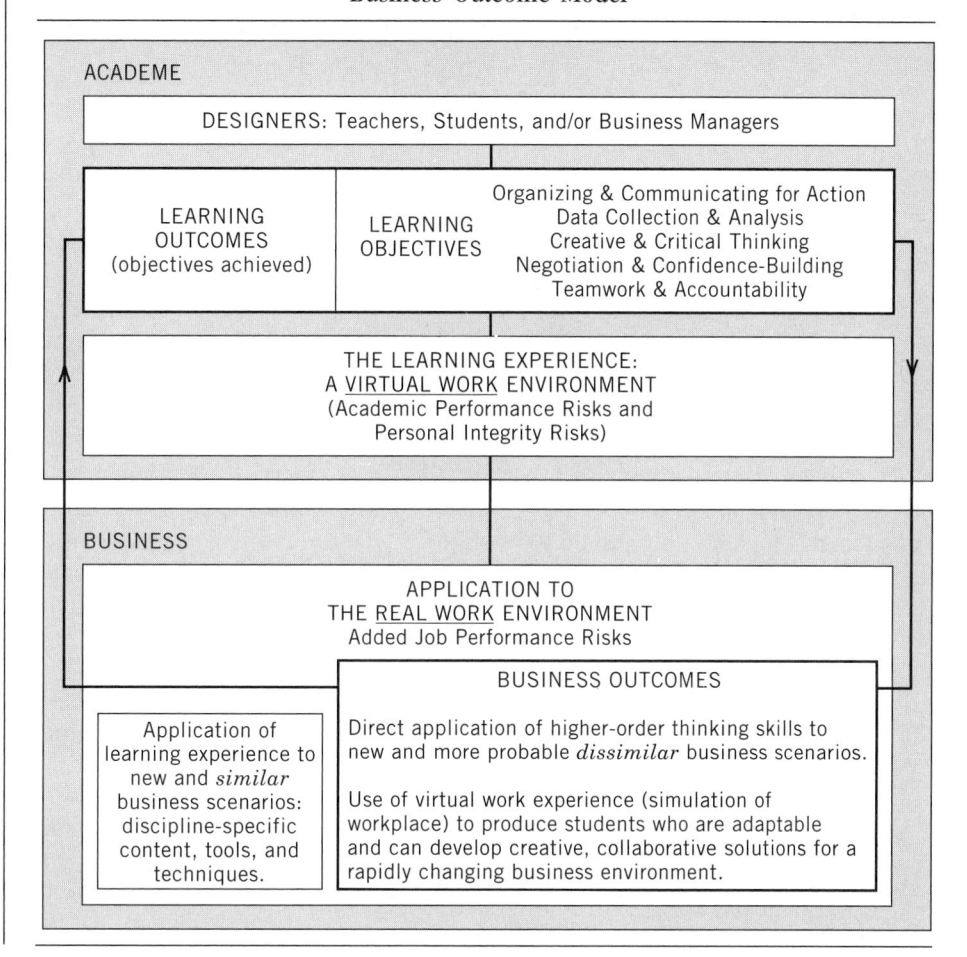

ACADEME

DESIGNERS: Teachers, Students, and/or Business Managers

| LEARNING OUTCOMES (objectives achieved) | LEARNING OBJECTIVES | Organizing & Communicating for Action
Data Collection & Analysis
Creative & Critical Thinking
Negotiation & Confidence-Building
Teamwork & Accountability |

THE LEARNING EXPERIENCE:
A <u>VIRTUAL WORK</u> ENVIRONMENT
(Academic Performance Risks and
Personal Integrity Risks)

BUSINESS

APPLICATION TO
THE <u>REAL WORK</u> ENVIRONMENT
Added Job Performance Risks

BUSINESS OUTCOMES

| Application of learning experience to new and *similar* business scenarios: discipline-specific content, tools, and techniques. | Direct application of higher-order thinking skills to new and more probable *dissimilar* business scenarios.

Use of virtual work experience (simulation of workplace) to produce students who are adaptable and can develop creative, collaborative solutions for a rapidly changing business environment. |

the view that teaching is a transformational activity [Christensen, 1991] aimed at students taking charge of their learning experience (the view of the authors), they are allowed the opportunity to design as well as conduct learning in the classroom. For this opportunity to exist, faculty and administration must collaborate effectively.

Reflections

GENERAL CONCEPTS

1. Will it be easier to develop the IEMgr from those who are technology-oriented or from those who are business-oriented? Why? Include both education and training requirements for this upgrading.

2. Under what circumstances would it make sense for an organization to be technology driven? to be business driven?
    How about an organization that is simultaneously technology and business driven? Is that possible? If yes, why? If not, why not?

3. What can higher education do to promote such approaches?
    Where does the responsibility of education end?
    Do corporate training programs compete with higher education for students? If so, is this cost effective?

4. How would you advise your college or university to prepare students to be IEMgrs? Be creative!

5. Adding value to the enterprise is a phrase that continues to appear in the literature with regard to acquiring information technology, developing business applications, taking training or education courses, corporate acquisitions and mergers, and so on.
    What are the difficulties in developing criteria and measuring value added in these types of activities?

6. Investigate a business, government, or education environment (any department; any program, process, or project) for a clear understanding of how that activity adds value to the enterprise.

7. Information enablement applies to individuals, managers (four types of IEMgrs and IS Staff), and the enterprise.
    What is your definition of information enablement?
    Does the concept of an IEMgmt Team help to focus the enterprise on managing people and technology in a more organized manner?
    What are the problems associated with the differences in motivation for each of these three groups (individuals, managers, enterprise)? What are the commonalities?

STEP MODEL

1. Where is the IEMgr on the STEP Model? What types of IEMgrs would be influential in moving the enterprise along a predetermined path to the ideal mix of process, people, and technology, and how would their impact be most influential?

2. For each of the three dimensions of the STEP Model, how would value added be demonstrated as the enterprise moves from its current position to the ideal situation?

Chapter 3

Information-Enabled Management Across the Enterprise

◆ ◆ ◆

In this chapter we develop a conceptual foundation that will enhance your understanding of the practical limits of IS management. Several classical models describe the evolution of IS and its management. Next, several taxonomies summarize applications systems and briefly trace the evolution of software and hardware

◆ MODELS OF INFORMATION MANAGEMENT

Beginning as early as the late 1950s, we have seen the information systems management model oscillate between centralized and decentralized structures. The rationale underlying these shifts in management approach were sound for their time even though in retrospect it appears that management wasn't sure what it was doing. As time passed, technology became more pervasive, computer literacy increased, and business conditions changed, there was always a rationale for what was done to reorganize and redeploy the IS function. We would like to think that the present changes will be permanent, as we did with the other changes that took place in earlier times. Perhaps they are permanent, but who knows for sure? Does it really make any difference? In the long run we are just trying to make the best business decisions—and that includes organizing and deploying information systems responsibly across the organization.

Information systems seem to be going the way of the telephone. There was a time when even the simplest of phone calls had to be processed by a trained operator. As time moved on and voice communications technology advanced, the user took a more active role in the transaction. Now we seldom have reason to talk to a trained operator. Routine transactions are handled by the user.

A similar pattern is emerging with information technology. At first only a few had the skills to communicate with computers in a mysterious language that used cryptic codes. The user was totally dependent on the computer programmers who understood these languages. Their tools were crude and the results often unpredictable, but users persevered. We have now reached a stage in the development of the technology wherein the tools are useable by any professional willing to invest minimal effort to learn them. As with the telephone, many of the processes required for its use disappeared into the technology. For example, systems development methodology is being imbedded into the end-user tools. We recall that not too many years ago the pundits were predicting the disappearance of the programmer and even the systems analyst and their replacement by sophisticated software under end-user control. As preposterous as that may have seemed, we have learned never to say *never* when it comes to information technology.

Over the nearly 40-year history of commercial computing we have seen the management of information systems undergo as extensive an evolution as the technology itself. Despite the continual swing of the pendulum from centralized to decentralized, one thing seems clear. The responsibility for information systems is separating into three broad groupings: strategy, infrastructure, and application. Strategy is vested in a staff position called chief information officer (CIO), and is of recent vintage. The CIO, who need not be a technology expert, is responsible for the strategic direction of the organization as driven by information technology. The information systems department as we know it today provides and cares for the infrastructure. In general, they are responsible for the timely and reliable deployment of computing resources. The list includes hardware, software, data, communications, technology evaluation, training, and advisement. The user community as we know it today is responsible for applications. In general they are responsible for managing applications development and maintenance. We will discuss the responsibilities of each of these groups in more detail later in Part III.

This environment may seem daunting and even a bit radical to some. Organizations have passed the point of automating routine operations. The business value of information technology lies in the organization's ability to exploit it for strategic advantage. This involves not only the most creative challenges for new information-based products and services, but also improvement of effectiveness and efficiency through business process redesign efforts (business reengineering, process improvement, and quality management). None of these activities involve information systems professionals operating in isolation from the business professionals. In fact, they must be composites of one another. That is, both must possess the technology skills as well as the business skills. This new breed of manager, which we call the IEMgr, must be forthcoming in organizations if he/she is to rise to the challenge of exploiting information technology. This text explores the nature of IEMgrs, where they originate, how they are deployed, and how they relate to one another and the organization. By taking this approach we are preparing students for the immediate and near-term business environment.

In summary, the responsibility of managing the information systems function is a shared responsibility between the information systems manager and the business unit manager, both of whom meet the definition of IEMgr as introduced

Exhibit 3-1

A Taxonomy of the Information-Age Professional

	Type			
	1	2	3	4
MANAGER	Y	N	N	Y
RESPONSIBILITY	Infrastructure Design	Process Improvement	Technology Support	Process Management
REPORTING	IS	IS or Process	IS or Process	Process

in this text. They are both multidisciplined—one is expert in information technology and the other is expert in a business function or process, but each has secondary and significant skills in the other's discipline. Exhibit 3.1 graphically depicts this hybrid professional.

As we can see, business technologist responsibilities range from designing the infrastructure (for which they must have technology expertise and be process literate), to improving business processes (for which they must have technology expertise and be process experts), to supporting business processes (for which they must be process literate and information and technology literate), to managing business processes (for which they must have process expertise and be information and technology literate). Understand clearly that such managers are just beginning to emerge. They are not the product of any college or university degree program, for no such programs currently exist. They are more the product of their environment. Many were displaced information systems analysts and programmers. As information systems departments downsized, or decentralized if you prefer, these professionals were deployed out to the business functions and processes. In many cases, they formed into information systems units that were captive of a business process or function. They became the first information systems professionals assigned outside the information systems department. As they learned through job experience about their assigned function or process they evolved into the first IEMgrs(TP). Those who could adopt a business-first perspective no doubt succeeded in making the transition. Those who could not have found some other profession in which to earn their living.

We should give recognition to another management approach that is finding favor in the more progressive organizations. In this variation, information systems professionals are assigned to a business function or process but do not sever their ties to the information systems department. Their ties are to an information systems manager. Often attached to "centers of excellence" or "core competency areas," they are under the management of a "coach," whose responsibility is development and deployment of information technology skills. While they often take a proactive role in skills development of the professionals in their discipline, they also react to requests for skills development and training. This looks much like the typical matrix organization but is different in that the individual, while permanently assigned to the business process, receives skills training under the direction of the information systems "coach."

Information systems have evolved through several stages since the mid- to late 1950s, when computers were first used commercially. This evolution dramatically affected organizations at all levels. In the functional departments, computers began to be used to automate manual procedures and thus to change departmental structures and operations in radical ways. At first, senior management played little part in computerization other than to concur in and approve hardware and software acquisitions. It was considered a backroom function that impacted the organization at the operational level. The only business value was the expected reduction in the cost of doing business. Eventually, however, senior managers had to step in, impose controls, and resolve disputes that arose between the user and the IS department.

With the rapid and unceasing spread of computer use, IS managers themselves have evolved and their roles and interactions at all levels of the organization are still undergoing continual change as organizations seek to define roles and responsibilities of the IS department. The roles and responsibilities of the IS department over the last decade are being deployed into the IEMgmt team, which is the focus for the next decade. There already are strong indications of this growing migration, as we have discussed.

Nolan's Six Stages Model

Perhaps the most widely known explanation of the evolution of IS is the *stages hypothesis* [Nolan and Gibson, 1974; Nolan, 1979]. Nolan [1979] argued that IS develops in six stages, as shown in Exhibit 3-2. We will describe these stages historically, that is, from the vantage point of a modern IS organization that has experienced the transition from stage to stage.

Stage 1: Initiation

In this stage the computer was introduced into the organization. In the late 1950s, the data processing (DP) unit typically consisted of a supervisor (sometimes called the lead programmer), a data entry clerk, and perhaps an operator. Usually, the department was attached to the accounting or finance area. Not too surprisingly, the first applications were accounting related (for instance, general ledger, accounts payable, accounts receivable, and payroll). Such accounting activities were well-defined, operated with a fixed set of rules, and consisted of a repetitive set of operations. Being labor intensive, they were excellent candidates for the first automated systems.

The initiative for developing such systems came almost exclusively from the DP unit. The analysis, design, and programming tools available to automate manual accounting processes were crude, labor intensive, and cryptic to all but a few. Systems development methodologies were not sophisticated enough to allow reasonable definitions of systems requirements and development. Actual project completion times far exceeded estimated times.

Models of Information Management

Exhibit 3-2 — Six Stages of Data Processing Growth

Growth Processes

	Stage 1 Initiation	Stage 2 Contagion	Stage 3 Control	Stage 4 Integration	Stage 5 Data administration	Stage 6 Maturity
Applications portfolio	Functional cost-reduction applications	Proliferation	Upgrade documentation and restructuring of existing applications	Retrofitting existing applications using database technology	Organization Integration of applications	Application integration "mirroring" information flows
DP organization	Specialization for technological learning	User-oriented programmers	Middle management	Establish computer utility and user account teams	Data administration	Data resource Management
DP planning and control	Lax	More lax	Formalized planning and control	Tailored planning and control systems / Transition point	Shared data and common systems	Data resource strategic planning
User awareness	"Hands off"	Superficially enthusiastic	Arbitrarily held accountable	Accountability learning	Effectively accountable	Acceptance of joint user and data-processing accountabilty

Level of DP expenditures

SOURCE: Reprinted by permission of the *Harvard Business Review*. An exhibit from "Managing the Crises in Data Processing" by Richard L. Nolan (March-April 1979) Copyright © 1979 by the President and Fellows of Harvard College: all rights reserved.

During this stage, both the DP staff and the systems users were learning about the new technology and learning how to work together. It was a rather clumsy and frustrating time! Because users had no concept of what to expect, they had no reason to be dissatisfied with what they received or with the time required to get it. During this stage—a classic case of the blind leading the blind—both user and programmer were initially quite tolerant of the process.

The IS manager (usually called the automation data processor (ADP) or DP supervisor) followed what might be called a hero strategy: Simply rush ahead and secure the needed resources. Taking this approach typically did not represent either a sound management decision or a good business decision, but at the time, the new user community was determined to computerize any corporate activity with high labor costs. Most requests for automation were approved by senior management with little in-depth evaluation. Indeed, senior managers had no alternative but to approve the many requests they received; they did not know what kind of questions to ask and would not have known how to evaluate the answers. Eventually, this pattern would have to come to an end.

Stage 2: Contagion

As information systems were put into operational status, users became increasingly enthusiastic about the possibilities for further uses of these new technologies. As a result, the demand for more computer applications increased rapidly. In some cases, the electronic data processing (EDP) group (by now raised to the status of a department) aggravated the situation by overselling computerization and their ability to deliver results. It was not uncommon to hear EDP personnel promise sophisticated systems that would literally replace the manager with a button. Computers were going to make all the decisions. It is no surprise that such brash statements were not welcomed by the managers who might be affected by such developments.

We now know how unrealistic those promises were, but they did create great excitement among a somewhat naive user community. The contagion stage in the evolution of IS is often characterized as a period of unbridled growth, first in the volume of requests for new systems and then in the volume of requests from the EDP department for more and better hardware and software. Because computing was typically treated as an overhead expense, users felt no need to restrict their requests. There was little in the way of managerial control. During this stage the general perception was that one had to be a mathematician to learn the special languages of the computer and that few people could refute the arguments put forth by the technical wizards for more equipment. The EDP department usually had its way.

Stage 3: Control

The inevitable began to happen: missed deadlines, cost overruns, systems that didn't work, and expectations not met caught the attention of senior management, which had no choice but to ask for some explanation for the money being spent and some reckoning of the benefits being realized. EDP managers began to find their budget requests closely scrutinized. Finally, senior management was paying attention and quickly learned that it was possible to manage an EDP department in much the same way as they managed the engineering department. During this stage the EDP manager was asked to assign priorities to existing and proposed applications. Doing so required the implementation of some system of measurement and control. The EDP manager had to begin to think in terms of the business and EDP's contribution to the bottom line. A new way of doing business was being forced upon the EDP manager. At the same time, users were being asked to justify their systems development requests. Chargebacks to the user for computing resource use became popular. The free ride was over.

We can trace the birth of IEMgrs to this point in time—although they were certainly not recognized as such. The need to conduct cost/benefit analyses forced EDP managers to begin to learn about the business they were supporting. At the same time, users needed to understand the relation between the technology and the value it delivered to their business unit. Although we didn't realize it at the time, we were seeing the birth of a partnership between EDP and users that would not be recognized for several years to come. This partnership was forced into existence by senior management. They wanted cost/benefit analyses that the IS manager was not prepared to conduct. The IS manager had to turn to the business unit manager to complete the analysis. As part of the analysis effort, the business manager had to learn more about information technology and its effect on the business functions and proposed projects.

Senior managers seeking to make informed decisions in the computer and systems area just as in other areas of the enterprise were now gaining control of the EDP function. They dictated to EDP managers what was to be done and by when. The EDP managers' role was beginning to evolve. At first it was strongly proactive as evidenced by the fact that they had to take the initiative in the early efforts at computerization. It was now showing signs of also being reactive as evidenced by the emerging role of senior management and a user community requesting, proposing, and justifying applications.

As the enterprise moved through the 1970s, computing became increasingly more sophisticated. New tools—some for the user community (fourth-generation languages)—were now available. The user community was growing comfortable with the technology and consequently was requesting more sophisticated applications. The term *management information systems* (MIS) replaced EDP. The term arose because applications were moving from the operational to the tactical level. The new MIS field and the MIS manager were maturing. This stage was marked by repeated promises that everything could be computerized.

Many MIS managers tried hard to regain the proactive position that had been lost a decade earlier. In too many cases they were trying to become empire builders. However, the seeds of a problem that would flourish into the early 1980s—autonomous actions on the part of the user community—were being planted.

Stage 4: Integration

During the 1970s, the computer industry expanded rapidly as technology raced ahead. Some have said that if no new technology was introduced at that time, it would have taken ten years for the business community to effectively utilize what was already available. Data and systems integration evolved as a direct result of centralization of the MIS function under a single management structure. New software technologies in the form of databases, database management systems, and fourth-generation languages made this integration possible. The microcomputer and the first commercially successful spreadsheet package ushered in a new era in computing for the user as the enterprise entered the 1980s. The broken promises and crippling applications development backlog of MIS departments could now be circumvented. Users now had tools that would allow them to do much of their own development work. They no longer had to line up at the door of the systems and programming offices to request high-priority action on their proposals; they could do their own thing, often without having to request additional monies. The cost of microcomputer hardware and software was falling within easy reach of many user budgets.

Thus, along with revolutionary changes in technology came equally significant changes in the role of both the user and the IS department (the M was dropped from MIS at about this time). During the integration stage there was clear movement toward an IS department that was in effect a utility and service organization for the user, who in turn had access to various tools for systems development. The IS department was evolving from a tightly controlled, centralized structure into a decentralized one. With this evolution, the strong corporate power base that the IS manager had developed became further weakened. End-user and departmental computing were replacing the more traditional systems and programming groups. Both user and IS department were initiating new systems for the benefit of the enterprise.

Many traditional IS managers had a difficult time dealing with this evolution. This stage was one of unrest for both the user and the IS department as each tried to determine its respective role in the enterprise. We see the beginnings of the manager with low skills in technology and business process, or IEMgr(tp), and the manager with more business process knowledge, or IEMgr(tP). At the same time, the IEMgr(TP) was gaining new and improved skills in both technology and business.

Stage 5: Data administration

In the current stage of evolution for most IS organizations, the IS department has recognized that information is a corporate resource that must be made available to all users. For this to happen, information must be managed appropriately. Data must be stored and maintained so that all users have access to them as a shared resource. In order to share resources, a corporate data model must be built and be application independent. This concept would allow users to develop their own applications to utilize that data. This stage is characterized by the ascendancy of the user, who now has chief responsibility for the integrity and proper use of organizational information resources. Few organizations have moved beyond the data administration stage. More recently the data administration phase is evidenced by the emergence of the client/server environment. The server holds the data while the client interrogates the server for information and reports.

Stage 6: Maturity

This stage might be called the frontier. If the organization has reached this stage, it has completely woven its information resources into the overall strategic fabric of the organization. The IS manager—or chief information officer (CIO), as he or she is known in some organizations—is a member of the senior management team and a significant contributor to decisions regarding the core business and the exploitation of information technology for competitive advantage. This person has a strong influence over how the organization does its business and even, in fact, what business it does. It is easy to see why few organizations have reached this stage; most are at some point between stages four and five.

The maturity stage will come to be characterized by the growth and maturation of the IEMgmt team. We have discussed the trend toward divesting the manager of several roles and responsibilities with the advent of IEMgrs. As that trend continues for managers with high business process skills, the IEMgr(tP) and IEMgr(TP), will play more important roles in technology decisions at the strategic level. The logical conclusion is that more companies will move into the maturity stage under the guidance and leadership of a fully involved IEMgmt team.

The stages hypothesis has often been applied to a single organization to determine the development of IS within the existing corporate structure and to indicate appropriate IS strategy. However, because the model is historical, some of the early stages are no longer relevant to organizations just getting involved with computerization. For example, the ready availability of user-friendly software allows the first-time user to begin working productively with sophisticated database applications. It would be incorrect to assume that every organization (or any organization for that matter) must pass (or even could pass) through every stage of the model. It is common for companies to skip stages or for different parts of a company to be in different stages simultaneously.

The Nolan and Gibson model is dated, but it is nonetheless of important strategic value to the IEMgmt team. Knowing the current stage of an organization, division, department, or user group can help the IEMgmt team formulate policy and strategy regarding further computer utilization. Some questions that the model addresses are:

- Are management practices consistent with the current stage of the company?
- Is the organization ready to take advantage of a particular technology?
- Is the systems and programming group technically prepared to support the new strategic directions?
- How is the organization positioned with respect to its use of technology as compared with others in its industry?

The Strategic Grid

The strategic grid (Exhibit 3-3), developed by F.W. McFarlan and McKenney [1983], is a tool for connecting the strategic position of the entire enterprise, its

Exhibit 3-3

Strategic Impact of Application Systems

	Strategic impact of existing application systems	
	Low	High
High (Strategic impact of application systems under development)	Turnaround	Strategic
Low	Support	Factory

planning commitment, and the appropriate management of information technology (IT). (As used here, the term *information technology* refers only to hardware and software systems.) The grid contains four main categories into which enterprises can be placed.

Support Category

The support role played by IS has its roots in the beginnings of commercial data processing, when transaction-based processes were automated (Initiation and early Contagion Stages). For organizations in this category, the objective of the IS department is cost reduction and the IS manager's success hinges on the achievement of this objective. Organizations in this category are usually well-established manufacturing or manufacturing-related firms. In such organizations, the IEMgmt team tends to be weak or nonexistent. It is unlikely to have an IEMgr(TP) but there might be a few IEMgrs(tP) in those business units that are more dependent on computing and information.

Turnaround Category

Organizations tend to move from the support category to the turnaround category as a result of external and internal factors and pressures. Newer and more cost-effective computer products and services as well as industry dynamics are the two major external factors. Through enlightened management as well as growing pressures from its end-user groups, the organization may move into the turnaround category. This category represents, however, only a temporary strategic position. If the organization does not follow up with additional development of strategic systems, it will move into the factory category. However, should such follow-up activity occur, the organization may eventually move into the strategic category. The turnaround category is a transitional category. The appropriate action for the IS manager in a turnaround-category organization will be to continue encouraging changes that have strategic value. The IEMgr(TP) is a critical component of that strategy. In many cases, the organization may have a number of power users who have initiated strategic applications. The IS manager would do well to partner with these users. The users are the group from which such future IEMgrs(TP) will come.

Factory Category

Organizations in the factory category have implemented systems with a definite strategic impact, although no new systems in the development portfolio are so labeled. Activities of the IS department in organizations in the factory category are more sophisticated than in the support category, but the IS department's role is still limited to current operational activities. The challenges are to improve existing strategic systems and sustain the strategic thrust of the organization through education programs and additional efficiency/effectiveness initiatives. Some of these efforts may require a technology push rather than a business pull. Again, the IEMgr(TP) is responsible for maintaining the strategic value of the application. If they are not already in place, the IS manager should identify future IEMgrs(TP) and encourage their development—first as members of the IS department and later as members of business units.

Strategic Category

For organizations in the strategic category, the IS department acts in true partnership with senior, process, and functional managers in strategy set formation. An effective IEMgmt team is in place. The IEMgr(TP) and IEMgr(Tp) are the information technology experts on the management team and are expected to identify, recommend, and implement changes that will affect the strategic direction, and ultimately the success, of the organization. Continual effort will also be required to protect the organization's position. The framework for accomplishing this must be collaborative. The entire IEMgr team also works to help IEMgrs(tP) maintain and improve products and services in the strategic portfolio.

Uses of the Strategic Grid

The strategic grid is a much more powerful tool for the IEMgr team than might be obvious at first glance. To exploit it fully, the team must first determine in which category the organization finds itself and in which category it would like to be, and then take appropriate action. For example, if the organization is in the factory category and the IS manager is trying to allocate the departmental budget across various competing projects, he or she should favor allocations to projects that maintain and improve existing systems rather than investing in new technologies and new applications. It is possible, however, that new technologies should be acquired if they contribute directly to the efficiency and effectiveness of existing systems. On the same theme, an appropriate planning system would be one that reacts to the existing business plan rather than one that blazes new trails. We return to this topic in Chapter 4.

The strategic grid has other applications for the IEMgmt team. The support and factory categories are static, whereas the turnaround and strategic categories are dynamic. Similarly, the support and factory categories are concerned with present operations, whereas the turnaround and strategic categories are concerned with future operations. Budget decisions should roughly favor operations in the case of support- and factory-category organizations and development in the case of turnaround- and strategic-category organizations. The choice of an appropriate planning system will follow a similar pattern. In general, IS planning will be reactive for organizations in the support and factory categories and proactive for those in the turnaround or strategic categories.

The first attempt at developing a strategic system may represent a major challenge to the organization, the IEMgmt team, and the IS manager. If IS managers wish to take a proactive role in the use of IT for strategic benefit, they will want to promote an application that is as near to a guaranteed success as possible. Having the appropriate IEMgr(tP) and IEMgr(TP) as project champions is an excellent approach. In those cases where such IEMgrs are not in place, the IS manager must take the lead. In any case, the process/function manager must be a partner. Their commitment will assure success.

Benefit/Beneficiary Matrix

It was through the efforts of Cyrus Gibson and Michael Hammer that the stages hypothesis and the strategic grid were synthesized into the benefit/beneficiary matrix (Exhibit 3-4). Their creation is in essence an operational tool. It makes use of a "domain" scheme to categorize an organization's use or need for information technology.

Domain 1

For organizations in the initiation and contagion stages of the Nolan and Gibson model, the primary purpose of computing is to improve the efficiency of functional departments. Most systems are initially developed to reduce the labor cost associated with highly repetitive activities (primarily those in accounting functions). As organizations advance in subsequent stages, they use automation to increase effectiveness in other functional areas. Domain 1 of the matrix contains functional units as the beneficiaries, and efficiency and effectiveness as the benefits.

Domain 2

As the Nolan and Gibson model shows, the introduction of the microcomputer and other end-user tools gave rise to a new beneficiary, the individual user.

Exhibit 3-4

Benefit/Beneficiary Matrix

Information Technology as a Strategic Weapon

BENEFIT	BENEFICIARY		
	INDIVIDUALS	FUNCTIONAL UNITS	ENTERPRISE
Efficiency	Domain 2	Domain 1	Domain 3
Effectiveness			
Transformation			

SOURCE: Cyrus F. Gibson and Michael Hammer, "Now That the Dust Has Settled, A Clear View of the Terrain," *Indications*, 2(5), July 1985, Index Group Inc., Cambridge, Mass.

Spreadsheets offer managers a means of improving the quality and timeliness of their decisions. Managers can define their own information needs and thereby improve their effectiveness. Clerical workers can use word processing to improve both the speed and accuracy of their work. Domain 2 therefore contains individuals as beneficiaries, and efficiency and effectiveness as benefits.

Domain 3

Michael Porter [1980] developed a value system model as an extension of value chain analysis. The model examines the relationships among an organization and its suppliers and customers. One of the outcomes from this examination is the identification of information technology applications that have the potential of strengthening these relationships. Information could be used to develop systems that expand and redefine responsibilities of individuals and functional units. Information could also create linkages to external forces in the value system. In summary, the strategic use of information can transform the organization both internally and externally. Organizations will realize some competitive advantages as a result. As an example, consider making a customer's order status available to them electronically. This creates linkages for the customer with sales, production, and shipping and strengthens ties to that customer as a result. Each of these functions is changed in order to accommodate the new system and realize the competitive advantages that result.

Use of the Benefit/Beneficiary Matrix

As we have seen, the matrix synthesizes the evolutionary development of IS in the organization. It is an excellent conceptual foundation for strategy set (mission, goals, objectives) development based on existing and new information technolo-

Exhibit 3-5

Type of Application by Matrix Cell

Information Technology as a Strategic Weapon

	BENEFICIARY		
BENEFIT	INDIVIDUALS	FUNCTIONAL UNITS	ENTERPRISE
Efficiency	Task Mechanization	Process Automation	Boundry Extension
Effectiveness	Work Improvement	Functional Enhancement	Service Enhancement
Transformation	Role Expansion	Functional Redefinition	Product Innovation

Source: Cyrus F. Gibson and Michael Hammer, "Now That the Dust Has Settled, A Clear View of the Terrain," *Indications,* 2(5), July 1985, Index Group Inc., Cambridge, Mass.

gies. It can also be used as an operational tool for exploiting IT by redefining it in terms of the nine cells shown in Exhibit 3-5. To use the matrix, an IEMgr(tP) will first determine what problem he or she wishes to solve and whether the beneficiary of the solution is an individual, a functional unit, or the organization. By determining the benefits, the IEMgr(tP) can position the problem in one of the nine cells in the matrix and through the IEMgr(TP) focus on the appropriate technology to solve the problem.

◆ ENTERPRISEWIDE RESPONSIBILITIES OF THE IEMgmt TEAM

With respect to their responsibilities at the enterprise, process, or functional levels, the IEMgmt team confronts many large and small challenges each day, and a good many of these challenges are unique—other managers do not have to deal with them. We are in the middle of a period that will be remembered as among the most revolutionary and dynamic in the history of the industrialized world; a period during which information has become of primary importance. The challenges we face demand special and different behavior on the part of IEMgmt. The IEMgr(Tp) of the early 1980s could be characterized as a reactive manager—one who responded to the plans and requests from all levels of management. But things have changed so dramatically in recent years that this characterization is no longer accurate. Information-intensive organizations have come to depend on the IEMgmt team. This shift has entailed a radical reshaping of the IS function, especially its interactions with middle and senior management. A new business partnership has been established between the IEMgr(Tp) and the rest of the IEMgmt team.

This section looks at the metamorphosis of the IS department's role in the "information organization." We begin by looking at three broad areas of corporate responsibility for IS. From there we move to a discussion of the proactive IEMgr(Tp); here we draw once again on the strategic grid introduced in this chapter. Next, we turn to the issue of high-level resistance to the redefined role for IS, touching on reasons for this resistance and suggesting several strategies for involving senior managers in the necessary process of transformation. This discussion leads to exploration of relations between the IEMgmt team and other business unit managers. A brief look at challenges that IS managers must confront follows with a look at the emerging CIO.

Stuart Sinclair [1986] defines three "domains" that help organize our discussion of the corporate-level responsibilities of the IEMgmt team: efficiency, effectiveness, and competitiveness. The main question pertaining to the first domain is "Are we doing things right?"—that is, is the organization minimizing its unit costs for each product mix? With regard to the second domain, the important question is "Are we doing the right thing?"—that is, is the mix of products and services optimal? And the key question relevant to competitiveness, the third domain, is "Are we headed in a direction consistent with our understanding of our environment?"—that is, does the organization have an overall strategy and is it sure that this strategy is the right one?

Exhibit 3-6 coordinates these three domains with IS functions at three major organizational levels: operational, tactical, and strategic. At the operational level, the IEMgrs(tp), because of their intimate knowledge of process and process activities, are in the best position to impact efficiency and effectiveness. Their process and technology expertise allows them to communicate recommendations for improvement to both the IEMgr(tP) and IEMgr(TP). At the tactical level, the IEMgrs(TP) are the key to further process-level improvements. Their high level of expertise with the systems that support the process empowers them to propose process improvement projects to the IEMgr(Tp) and IEMgr(tP) in the language of the respective IEMgr. They will typically manage the improvement projects. Their impact is more at the competitive level but does have residual benefits at efficiency and effectiveness levels. The most challenging domain is competitiveness. Here, the IEMgmt team must draw on all of their creative energies and insights to monitor trends and market conditions in order to identify new opportunities for the organization to pursue. This "gatekeeper" function is critical to the future survival of many organizations, especially those in information-intensive businesses.

Until recently, the IEMgr(Tp) seldom functioned in a truly proactive role at the enterprise level. Rather than participating in the creation of the corporate strategic plan, the IEMgr(Tp) received the corporate plan along with the charge to develop an information systems plan that would help the organization, its divisions, and

Exhibit 3-6

Domains of Information Systems at Three Levels

Organizational Level

DOMAIN	OPERATIONAL	TACTICAL	STRATEGIC
Efficiency	Reduce unit production and sales cost as much as possible Maximize turnaround times	Improve capacity planning Improve scheduling Improve inventory control and manufacturing resource planning	Optimize distribution systems
Effectiveness	Respond to all relevant inquiries	Ensure that all tasks are accomplished thoroughly	Maximize coverage of markets for sales and service
Competitiveness			Scan environment outside firm Identify and track threats and opportunities for different approaches Select different activities and assess impact for change

its departments meet their objectives. In this role, the IEMgr(Tp) responded to initiatives taken by senior managers and was expected to do the following:

- Establish policies and procedures to facilitate planning objectives.
- Acquire and allocate hardware, software, services, and staff resources.
- Ensure timely delivery of systems and services to meet corporate goals.

Although these responsibilities are integral to the IS function, they no longer accurately define the IEMgr(Tp) position in the organization. To remain competitive, many organizations have discovered that they must encourage new operational relationships between IS and other units—relationships that become part of the very fabric of the organization and that may change the way it conducts its business. It is our belief that these relationships will result in the emergence of the IEMgmt team and will usher in a new way of looking at the enterprise—through the eyes of the information technologist.

Carol Saunders [1986] was somewhat prophetic regarding the need for the IEMgmt team as she called for a radical restructuring of the IS manager's position:

> It then becomes necessary for the Information Systems Department not only to respond to technological changes and end-user needs, but to suggest ways in which IT can be used to continue and further the organization's competitive edge. Fundamental changes are required to move the Information Systems Department from IT distributors to corporate strategists. The most striking change is that the Information Systems manager no longer merely works within the framework of the organizational strategy set (i.e., mission, objective, strategy). Instead he [or she] helps develop that framework.

She did not anticipate that this restructuring might be accomplished through a team rather than through a single individual, the IS manager. On the same theme, John Rockart and Adam Crescenzi [1984] have identified a new role for senior management:

> Clearly it is time for top management to get off the sidelines. Recognizing that information is a strategic resource implies a clear need to link information systems to business strategy, and, especially, to ensure that business strategy is developed in the context of the new IT environment.

Although they did not realize it at the time, Saunders, Rockart, and Crescenzi had issued the clarion call for the IEMgr. They clearly see a critically important role for those with business and technology skills.

We see, then, that this strategic collaboration between business managers and information technology managers is achievable through the IEMgmt team. Such changes are evolutionary but we see signs that they are happening.

To better understand the evolution that must occur, we might recall McFarlan's strategic grid, which draws together the IS department's support and development roles (see Exhibit 3.3). Using the grid, we can get a picture of where an organization is positioned strategically and can determine whether its strategic position can or should change as a result of its current and planned use of information systems. We now return to the four categories of organizations defined by the grid, highlighting the proactive IEMgmt team's role in each context.

The Support Category

Organizations in this category use information systems for operational impact (i.e., cost reduction). They have not identified strategic applications, nor is it imperative that they do so. If the organization is appropriately positioned in this category, the IEMgr(TP) will concentrate on maintaining a steady level of support at minimal cost. If the organization is incorrectly positioned and is missing opportunities to implement systems with high strategic value, the IEMgr(Tp) and IEMgr(TP) will need to develop initiatives to move the organization toward the turnaround category. Depending on the organization's readiness, this approach may require a deliberate, well-executed IS education program starting at the executive level.

Turnaround Category

Organizations in this category have evolved from the support category as a result of proactive initiatives, first on the initiative of the IEMgr(Tp) and followed by support from the IEMgr(TP). In some cases, initiatives from the IEMgr(tP), from the IEMgr(TP), industry pressures, or some combination thereof may have been the catalyst. Regardless of the strategic application, the IEMgmt team, through the continuing support of the IEMgr(TP), will want to sustain the initiative by maintaining a flexible and receptive posture in seeking out additional opportunities. Joint efforts with users through R&D projects, demonstrations, dissemination of information on emerging technologies, and similar activities are appropriate.

The Factory Category

Organizations evolve into this category from the turnaround category. If it is appropriate positioning, the IEMgr(TP) should seek additional opportunities to enhance the efficiency and effectiveness of existing strategic systems. Additional IS activities should be similar to those for organizations in the support category. For organizations that should continue with the development of strategic systems but have not, the IEMgmt team should proceed much as in the case of moving an organization out of the support category. The difference is that the organization already has an understanding of how IT can be used to its full strategic benefit.

The Strategic Category

Once both the existing systems portfolio and the under-development systems portfolio have high strategic value, the IEMgmt team will have moved into a leadership role regarding corporate strategy set formation. Organizations in this category have established clear competitive strategies and a strategic planning process; they treat the IEMgmt team as a member of the executive team.

As an organization evolves from the support to the strategic category, the role of the IEMgr(Tp) necessarily changes from that of caretaker to that of change agent and, finally, to that of leader. Once this evolution has taken place, the following responsibilities will have been added to the role of the IEMgr(Tp):

- Participation in the development of the organizational strategy set
- Support of the business plan at corporate and departmental levels by bringing appropriate technology to the management team
- Management of integration of appropriate technologies into the way the organization functions and even into the determination of its business activity portfolio

It would be a mistake to assume that all organizations should or can evolve into the strategic category. Each category is characteristic of certain types of businesses. For example, well-established manufacturing-based organizations are typically found in the support category. The factory category, in contrast, typically includes service-based companies whose success in the market hinges on a few information-intensive applications but for whom the IS environment is otherwise relatively stable. The airline industry is a good example. But do not be led to think that their IS activity does not continue to be a challenging task. They must maintain their strategic edge by constantly investing in their existing strategic system(s). The turnaround category normally contains organizations in transition that are developing one or more strategic systems to gain competitive advantage. Many will be organizations that are more information-based than those in the factory category. In the strategic category are found the most information-dependent organizations. Financial services industries (banking, insurance, stock brokerage are a few examples) dominate this category.

For the proactive IEMgr(Tp), knowing where an organization is positioned—and where it should be positioned—is crucial. Armed with this knowledge, the IEMgr(Tp) can make informed decisions that are both realistic and likely to bring about genuine enhancements in the way information technologies contribute to the organization. The IEMgr has a key role in this scenario.

Evolution of the IEMgmt Team

We should comment on the evolution of the IEMgmt team as the enterprise moves through the four categories. In the Support Category, the IEMgmt team might consist of only the IS manager as the organization has not yet realized much strategic value from the IS function. To move the organization into the Turnaround Category the IS manager may have created an IEMgr(TP) position and attached it to the business unit in which the first strategic application was to be developed. That IEMgr(TP) may in fact report directly to the business unit manager. Such action is a strong statement of support and commitment from the IS manager. As the organization moves into the Factory Category, the business unit manager will begin to recognize that further enhancements of the application are needed to sustain the strategic advantage created by the application and will begin to evolve into the IEMgr(tP) member of the IEMgmt team. This will give rise to the IEMgr(tp) position as further enhancements will require implementing a continuous quality improvement program for the business unit.

◆ EMERGING PARTNERSHIP: USER MANAGER AND INFORMATION SYSTEMS MANAGER

While the IEMgr embodies the goal, or should embody the goal, of those organizations that wish to stay in business, we have to be realistic. Many organizations are not positioned for that model. Rather they are at some stage of transitioning to that model. In this section we discuss how that transition might take place. McFarlan's Strategic Grid is a good starting point for our discussion.

The Support Category

There are two cases to consider. Depending upon whether the organization is correctly positioned, the information systems manager will have different strategies.

Organization Is Correctly Positioned

For organizations in this category, the information systems manager collaborates with the user manager through the budget planning process to assure that the support required to continue with the existing applications is included in the budget. Changes in transactions volume or the adoption of more cost-effective technologies are two examples requiring attention. It would be a mistake to think that the support category reflects a stagnant situation. Rather, it reflects a situation in which the information systems manager must be aware of possible improvements that emerging technologies can offer. This requires knowing the problem areas, bottlenecks, and other issues that the process owners and functional managers consider important and responding to them. This means that the IS manager must become an IEMgr(Tp). The approach builds a good working relationship and prepares a foundation should it later become necessary to consider strategic applications.

Organization Is Incorrectly Positioned

Whereas the previous case depicts an information systems manager who is more reactive than proactive, this case is certainly the reverse, even if the process owner or functional manager realizes that their unit is missing strategic opportunities.

Turnaround Category

You will recall that this is a temporary situation. Organizations that are making the transition from the Support to the Factory Category must pass through the Turnaround Category. The process owners and functional managers may not be convinced of the wisdom in some of these new systems, especially if they are the output of a reengineering effort. This means that the information systems manager will have to take a considered approach. A relationship wherein each partner has an equal role in the change process is critical to success. The timeline for change must be driven by the readiness of the organization to assimilate the change. Most concerns center around skills training, job security, and anxieties that are attendant to most technology changes. The more radical the change, the more care that must be given to the readiness issue.

Remember that the partnership is embryonic at this stage. The information systems manager must adapt to the needs and concerns of the process owner and functional manager. At best, one would expect their knowledge of the technology to be minimal but they are open to technology change. Otherwise, the information systems manager would not have the forum needed to develop the first strategic application. It would be a good idea to involve the business unit manager and staff in an education and training program. Recommended readings, demonstrations, benchmarking, best-of-breed examples, and other delivery systems might work well here. The IEMgr(Tp) is responsible for developing the IEMgr(tP).

Factory Category

Getting the first strategic system in place is less than half the problem. Sustaining the strategic advantage that the system created is the more significant part of the problem. To be effective the process owners and functional managers must be learning about the technology so that they can initiate change and growth in the strategic portfolio. The astute IS manager should create an IEMgr(TP) position and assign it to the strategic system. Having this position report to the IEMgr(tP) will help build needed skills and the business partnership. The IS manager also must increase his or her understanding of the processes and functions to further enhancements of the strategic portfolio. A good sign that the partnership is growing is that when one of the partners is pursuing a new idea, the other is actively involved in the same idea. There is a definite synergy when both parties contribute their expertise together.

Strategic Category

By this time, there will be several strategic applications in place and several under development. Each partner will be knowledgeable of the other's disciplines. The IEMgmt team is well along in their development and team functioning. An open and continual communications link will be essential to maintain the company's strategic position.

◆ CHANGING NATURE OF THE CHIEF INFORMATION OFFICER (CIO)

The original task of the IS manager was to oversee the replacement of manual systems with computer-based systems to provide information faster and more efficiently. But that task is increasingly seen as fundamentally distinct from the task of the chief information officer (CIO), who focuses primarily on creative and innovative uses of IT. Indeed, in some organizations, the IS manager and the CIO are viewed as having two separate sets of responsibilities in two separate positions. In such cases, the CIO usually reports to the CEO in a staff position, although a line position (with perhaps the IS manager as a subordinate) is an alternative. In any case, the CIO is the "change agent" for new IT products, services, and processes. In those organizations that have an established IEMgmt team, the CIO can use the team to further develop the strategic use of information technology.

Perhaps the major responsibility of the CIO is to disseminate to other managers any relevant information on the latest technology developments and to help assimilate these new technologies into the organization where appropriate. Because this responsibility ultimately affects the development of strategy, the CIO does not typically have day-to-day operational responsibilities; he or she must be free to concentrate on the broader issues affecting the organization and its definition of its business. Successful CIOs need to be a combination of facilitator, promoter, agitator, businessperson, innovator, and communicator—not an easy blend to find in one person. At this stage in the history of IS, they are arguably a rare breed.

IEMgmt-Shared Responsibility with the CIO

By now you are beginning to appreciate the significance of the changing boundaries of the information systems function. Those boundaries were impacted at the operational level, then the tactical level, and finally, are now having their impact felt at the strategic level. This tendency raises several interesting considerations across the organization. We will discuss these at several points throughout the text.

What impact does shared responsibility have at the IEMgr level? Understand that the role is pervasive across all IEMgrs. We are not talking about a position or a single person. We are talking about an organizational culture in which all who would profess to be IEMgrs share roles and responsibilities. They can be thought of as a "virtual team." While they may never formally meet, they do share a common goal, that of exploiting information technology for the benefit of the organization and its people. They readily share information and ideas across the team. They draw on an enterprisewide information infrastructure. They are customer driven.

Strategic Direction Setting

As the information infrastructure aligns with the enterprise and processes become more formally part of the business fabric, the IEmgr will discover opportunities for further strategic benefit.

Information Technology Exploitation

The information systems department will have established an Advanced Technology Group. As they become aware of new and emerging technologies they will share that intelligence with the IEMgmt team. Through their professional associations, the IEMgrs in the business units will have discovered new benchmarks and best-of-breed examples. All of this information is input to the planning process, which leads to the next role for the IEMgr.

Business Systems Planning

We cover details of the systems planning process in Chapter 12. It is noted that all IEMgrs have both reactive and proactive roles to play in the organization's planning process. The cross-fertilization of ideas is the foundation for exploiting the potential locked up in the IEMgmt team.

Systems Development and Maintenance

As organizations evolve into the IEMgmt structure, systems development responsibility becomes pervasive. While not all IEMgrs will develop application systems, all IEMgrs are capable of developing application systems.

Along with systems development roles comes systems maintenance responsibilities. For this to work there must be an end-user systems development methodology in place across the organization. Information must flow easily across the organization and that cannot happen unless there is standardization at the systems development level. While the information systems department takes a leadership role here, the business units must participate in the design and implementation of that standard. This is a critical component of a successful IEMgmt effort and we return to the topic in Chapter 14.

◆ LEGACY SYSTEMS, INTEGRATION, CHANGE MANAGEMENT

Perhaps the most significant change in the last five years in hardware architecture is the movement toward a client/server architecture, and in data architecture, the movement toward an enterprise data model. Both have had, and are still having, a dramatic impact on existing application systems. We will have more to say on these changes later in the text. For now it is sufficient for us to discuss their impact on the applications portfolio. This is the topic of this section.

Many companies are trapped, in one way or another, in a hardware/software/data architecture of the past. They have a number of systems that were developed during a centralized, mainframe, CICS, COBOL era when applications were independent of one another, contained some of their own data, and communicated with one another through an intermediary database. Many of these systems still enjoy a useful life even though they are not designed for the contemporary information processing world of networks and client/server environments. As a result these systems (called *legacy systems* because they were developed in the past and still have business value) are somewhat inefficient by today's standards because they are not under the control of the end user, are function-oriented and not process-oriented, and are inaccessible to customers.

One might be tempted to say: "Let's redesign the applications for a client/server world." Senior management is hesitant to approve such drastic measures because they haven't yet realized the return on investment promised of the existing applications portfolio. The solution is to develop bridge software and graphical user interfaces (GUIs) that allow these systems to communicate with one another, to pass data back and forth, and to create access points for users and customers. Software tools such as dynamic data exchange (DDE) and object linking and embedding (OLE) have made such temporary measures possible.

In the long run, however, the enterprise will have to adopt a more permanent solution. Applications systems and databases of the future must have the following characteristics in order to create opportunities to establish competitive advantage for the enterprise:

1. There must be a single enterprise data model.
2. Data must be fully accessible to every knowledge worker.
3. Applications must be independent of the data.
4. Users and customers must be able to develop their own applications.

To create this environment will require significant change for many. For many it will also be difficult to fashion a realistic plan to migrate from where they are to where they need to be (as defined by these four criteria). Among the many problems we might list the following:

1. The current staff's technology skills are not client/server based.
2. With downsizing, everyone is working under stress and short deadlines.
3. A phased conversion plan is extremely difficult to develop and execute.
4. The transition from function to process is difficult.
5. The organizational culture and power base is changing.
6. Customer expectations seem out of reach.
7. Technology is driving our market position.
8. We do not have clear focus on the relative priorities of the above problems.

Let us look at four areas affected by these problems.

Developing a Partnership and a Leadership Role

First and foremost are the relationships among the four IEMgr types. We have already examined their responsibilities and have seen that they enter into a number of collaborative relationships depending on the task at hand. It is important that they recognize their changing roles—in some cases they take a leadership role, in others a partnership role, and in others a followership role. Along another dimension they fluctuate between proactive and reactive roles. In every sense, they are a team and they function as equals on that team.

Establishing a Collaborative Planning Environment

Planning is often a difficult task to do effectively. With so much work to do and deadlines to meet there is a constant temptation to short-change planning and get on with real work. We will see in Chapter 4 that there is a dual role for all IEMgrs. One role focuses on the corporate level and demands initiating actions on the part of each IEMgr to suggest ways of exploiting the technologies. The other involves supportive actions to help others implement their plans by providing support through the technologies. Taken one process or function at a time, this is a rather straightforward task, but in the aggregate it becomes difficult. The problem is balancing information technology expenditure across a number of processes and functions that vie for support as well as development resources. We examine the applications portfolio as an investment portfolio in Chapter 4.

Systems Integration

In many organizations, creating communications interfaces between existing applications is a temporary measure at best. Granted the solution may be in place for some time and may be transparent to the user, it is nevertheless a temporary fix. Consider, for example, an organization that has developed a number of function-based applications and is now reorganizing along business process lines. Whereas a single customer support system met the needs of a single product line, it may now have to interface with several product lines because the enterprise is now organized around customer-order-entry-to-order-fulfillment services. One would expect there to be a number of retrofittings and fixes to get the application operational across the process. It may be expedient to do this but it will not be in the best long-term interest of the enterprise. Eventually the systems will have to be designed to meet the needs of the process rather than the function.

Change Management: The Risk-Averse Culture

Systems professionals live in a world of constant change. Witness the advances in technology that require them to continually learn new application systems, new languages, and new hardware platforms. If they are to serve the enterprise, they must remain current lest the competition leapfrog them and capture market share. We all understand the tradeoff between change and risk. Traditionally they are inversely related to one another. Yet there is another perspective to consider. To *not* change exposes the enterprise to risk due to technical obsolescence and the loss of market share. *Too much* change exposes the enterprise to risk of inefficiency due to unfamiliarity with the technology. The times that we live in add another dimension to the tradeoff. In general, the enterprise must move toward a more risk-acceptance posture versus a risk-averse posture. To attain and sustain market share requires staying ahead of the competition, hitting narrowing windows of opportunity, improving cost/performance, quality, and time to market, and second-guessing the competition. That means taking chances and being willing to live with the consequences. That means taking some risks that might not have been taken a few years ago.

Reflections

GENERAL CONCEPTS

1. What organizational structure, if any, should exist between each member of the IEMgmt team and the CIO?
   How can this arrangement be implemented in the enterprise?
   What type of IEMgr should be the CIO?
   What type of IEMgr is the IS Manager?

2. Support the argument that the CIO need not be an IEMgr (none of the four types).
   In what kind of organization would such an arrangement be appropriate?

3. Which of the IEMgr(Tp), IEMgr(TP), or IEMgr(tP) are most important in the evolution of an organization to the Strategic Category?

4. How should the IEMgt team function?
   Do they really form a team, or does each individual act independently?
   Are there any circumstances under which they must function as a team? Describe.

5. Is the six-stage theory still relevant in establishing a starting point for the enterprise in any major information technology upgrading activity? Why or why not?

6. This chapter implies that CIOs and CEOs must collaborate so that an information-enabled enterprise can position itself for the global competitive market. Interview some CEOs and CIOs and get their opinions on what major issues arise regarding information technology and how they are resolved (satisfactorily or unsatisfactorily).

7. Although the concept of risk management is only introduced in the last section of this chapter, it has been suggested that the gap must be closed between old management rules and the new realities for competing in the next century. Traditionally, managers are supposed to be risk averse. Taking risks is dangerous for the enterprise and dangerous to one's career. It has not been viewed as a legitimate activity.
   Do you think this approach still holds? How much risk do you take in your job?
   Would you take more risk if the organization had a philosophy (backed by action) for taking more risk in grasping new opportunities without penalty?
   Is "trust" an important element of this issue?

As a preliminary study of the TQM movement (discussed in Part II), it is reported that 5 to 10 percent of American businesses will risk developing and sustaining the discipline, commitment, and involvement that TQM demands from every employee, and especially managers.

Verify that statement with some limited investigation of enterprises that have experienced TQM activity. Does TQM increase profits, eliminate waste and rework, and provide higher customer satisfaction and retention? Save your notes for Part II.

Reflections

STEP MODEL

1. What specific role can the Chief Information Officer (CIO) play in moving the enterprise toward maximum use of process, people, and technology?
    a. Is he or she confined to IS people? to the information technology infrastructure only?
    b. If the processes transcend departmental functions, and each department manager is responsible only for his or her own departmental functions (traditional view), how can the CIO and/or the IEMgmt team resolve the problem?
2. In a recent book by Charles Wang (Technovision, McGraw-Hill, 1994), he describes the relationship between the CEO and CIO as a "disconnect." He describes the business/IT relationship also as a disconnect. Read the book (it is a quick read) and report on his perspectives to the class.
    a. Interview a local business and compare the situation to the ones noted by Wang.
    b. If communication between the two parties (business/IT) is such a problem, how can it be addressed and resolved? Relate it to the STEP Model.
    c. Wang notes that IT vendors help to widen the gap. Do you agree? Relate it to the STEP Model.
    d. He also says that consultants widen the gap. Do you agree? Relate it to the STEP Model.
3. Traditionally, managers have been conditioned to be risk averse. Why take unnecessary risks? It is dangerous, leaves you vulnerable, and with the rapidly changing and uncertain marketplace, it appears that less risk is indicated. Do you agree with this statement? How does the concept to risk apply to the STEP Model?

Chapter 4

Assessing Strategic Opportunities

◆ ◆ ◆

Planning is the key to any organization's effective use of information resources. Downsizing has left most organizations with a much leaner staff, no corresponding reduction in the amount of work to be done, and the need to use limited resources to maximum benefit. This will not happen by accident.

At the same time, we must be sensitive to the overhead that planning requires. We simply don't want to waste people's time. That means that the planning process must be efficient, effective, and dynamic.

In this chapter we examine some of the basic tenets of an information-based planning process. The relationship between information technology and the business units is especially important. In that context we discuss several planning methods and close with a discussion of an integrated strategic information systems planning methodology.

◆ INFORMATION TECHNOLOGY AS A COMPONENT OF COMPETITIVE STRATEGY

A good manager must have vision and the capability to implement it. Vision and implementation might be group efforts with leadership provided by one or more individuals. The new breed of IEMgr is well prepared to be one of these leaders. Developing "strategies" is no longer just a long-range planning function by top executives within the enterprise as it has been perceived in the past. It is not a support activity infrequently performed over a period of years, documented, and mostly unread by a majority of the workforce. Instead, planning is a dynamic process that continues throughout the year.

Developing strategic initiatives and planning for their implementation are core management functions. The scope of the activity extends beyond the enterprise, participation encompasses all stakeholders, and any resulting master strategic

Exhibit 4-1

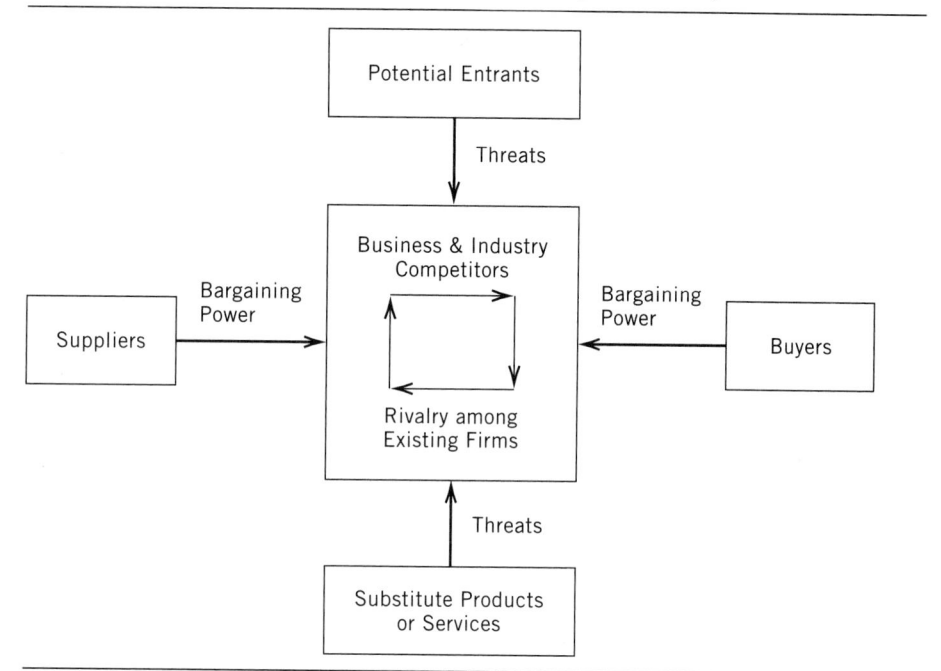

Competitive Forces Model
Value Chain Analysis and the Five Forces Driving Industrial Competition

```
                        ┌──────────────────┐
                        │ Potential Entrants│
                        └────────┬─────────┘
                                 │ Threats
                                 ▼
                        ┌──────────────────┐
     Bargaining         │ Business & Industry│       Bargaining
     Power              │    Competitors    │       Power
  ┌─────────┐           │                   │           ┌─────────┐
  │Suppliers│──────────▶│                   │◀──────────│ Buyers  │
  └─────────┘           │  Rivalry among    │           └─────────┘
                        │  Existing Firms   │
                        └────────▲─────────┘
                                 │ Threats
                        ┌──────────────────┐
                        │Substitute Products│
                        │   or Services    │
                        └──────────────────┘
```

SOURCE: Michael E. Porter's *Competitive Strategy; Techniques for Analyzing Industries and Competition,* Free Press, 1980.

---

plan contains a practical schedule of action items and responsibilities. The process is to create a vision of where the enterprise needs to go (with a rationale for attaining such a vision), convert general mission statements into operational objectives, develop strategies to get there, and finally, evaluate performance and adjust strategies to grasp new opportunities.

Porter [1980] suggests generic strategies to establish competitive advantage that are still applicable today. For each strategy, information technology has a substantial impact. His model is depicted in Exhibit 4-1.

In order to be a low-cost provider of products and services, costs are reduced by personnel reduction, more effective manufacturing and inventory control, and better use of materials. Here, information technology can help match enterprise requirements against available resources (human resources and production scheduling systems). A second strategy is aimed at offering unique and differentiated products and services. Computer modeling can assist in forecasts related to decision making about product/service gaps in the market and can help design new products and services to fill those gaps. A final strategy is to identify and meet specialized markets by using information technology to analyze historical data derived from internal and external databases.

In terms of Exhibit 4-1, these three strategies apply to each competitive force coming from potential entrants, suppliers, buyers, or substitute products and services. Porter's *value chain theory* provides a framework for segregating business into technologically and economically discrete activities related to productivity. In this way, advantages can be identified with information technology included as an integral part of the analysis. The importance of information technology is an assumption. The real question is whether or not technology will have any impact on the competitive position of the enterprise, especially in light of the recent merge of computers and telecommunications, which tends to immediately bring more competitors into the global marketplace.

In the early years of business computing, the quest for a high return on investment (ROI) emphasized cost reduction (more return) and inventory control (less investment) as the primary strategy to provide better information for decision making. Most of the targeted decisions in this effort were the province of low- to midlevel managers of operational and tactical level units. In recent years, there has been a major shift to strategic decision making in the form of new questions regarding the introduction of information technology:

Can it help sustain or improve market share?
Does the technology strengthen customer relationships through new value-added features?
Can the smaller organization benefit without destroying individuality?
Will expanded automation extend the life of products and/or services and suggest new markets?
Will suppliers or buyers exert more bargaining power through access to more immediate, complete, and relevant information?
Are threats from potential newcomers and substitute products minimized by enterprise knowledge on market shifts, new demands, and new opportunities?
Does the acquisition of the newest information technology eliminate potential customers who do not have the technology (such as developing nations) or promote relationships only with a new computer-fluent customer base?
Is too much dependency placed on information technology that reduces the human element (voice mail, electronic data interchange, automatic ordering and billing) in normal business operations? Is human intervention compromised by the system?
Does technology drive the business process or just support it? How flexible and user friendly are automated systems? What is the backlog and turnaround time for systems changes?

Who controls the process, humans or machines? Who controls strategic decision making?

What level of confidentiality and security is afforded by new and expanded use of information technology in global competition? Are contingency plans in place?

◆ PLANNING IS DYNAMIC NOT STATIC

There was a time when planning was an annual event, filled with a lot of fanfare, generating reams of data and analyses, reports that were read once and filed, and, in the end, signifying nothing. That has changed. Planning is no longer confined to a single month or quarter of the year. Planning is *continuous*. Effective strategic planning is a critical success factor. Planning is continually on the mind of every IEMgr. To think of it otherwise is to court disaster.

To see why this is so we need only look at one example. While the company is real, we have disguised it for obvious reasons. CommuWare develops a variety of shrinkwrapped communications software which they sell in the commercial market. Their customers cross all industries and are of all sizes. CommuWare is successful and is generally regarded as one of the leaders in their industry. They are a customer-driven organization and are ranked first in customer support.

Designing software for the commercial market is very complex and time sensitive. CommuWare is typical of companies in the software business in that each release of their software requires about 18 months to design, build, test, and implement. To that, add the fact that new releases must be introduced at intervals no longer than 6 months. Obviously they sell software in a highly competitive market.

What does planning look like at CommuWare? Obviously time to market is *the* critical success factor for CommuWare. Since it takes 18 months to roll out the next release and releases are introduced every 6 months, CommuWare must have at least three releases under development at all times and a fourth in the early definition phases. While timing is critical, so is the features and functions list in each release. Since CommuWare has a number of competitors, it must constantly watch the market for competitor releases and adjust its plans accordingly. CommuWare reviews the business justification for each release at each of the major development stages (design, build, test, implement) and has been known to cancel a release as late as the completion of testing. Why, you ask, would this happen? Simple. The competition introduced a new or revised product that rendered the next CommuWare release a wasted effort. Time to cut losses and abandon the not-yet-released next release. It seems radical, but it was the only business decision that made any sense. CommuWare depends heavily on its ability to continually analyze and forecast the market for communications software. Having to abandon a product at the eleventh hour doesn't make for a successful business. Our example is from a highly competitive industry, but aren't all industries becoming highly competitive?

◆ THINKING OUTSIDE THE BOX

Organizations are restructuring so they can compete successfully. It is a matter of survival. Business processes and the management of those processes need refinement and, in some cases, complete overhaul. Creative approaches are needed to meet these new and formidable challenges. Quick-fix solutions will not suffice; long-term solutions derived from thorough analysis are necessary to gain a competitive edge. Thorough analysis means strategic thinking, visionary and creative thinking, higher-order thinking. No longer is this type of thinking within the domain of only the higher levels of management; it must permeate all levels of the enterprise, especially members of the IEMgmt team and general operating business managers [Dala, 1994]. Nuances and intuition are an integral part of judgment and analysis of complex situations, especially where multiple criteria enter into the decision-making process.

Everything is in question and an inquiring mind is needed to examine all the options, terms and conditions, assumptions, and constraints. Again, the learning corporation needs learning workers; workers who can look ahead, see the problems and the opportunities, and take action accordingly. The drive for profit did not leave much time for reflective thought, preventative action planning, or contingency planning. The focus has been on production—not on people, nor on how they think. Plans were made, organizational structures were designed to accommodate workers' roles and positions, and people dutifully carried out their tasks. What has changed to welcome creative thinking as a respectable activity of the workplace?

Four events have led to a demand for creative approaches:

1. The TQM process requires all levels of management to design and implement systems, which requires creative thinking to be effective.
2. Information technology has become a change agent in the workplace; it is needed for workflow analysis (databases, information flow, administrative procedures, personal productivity) and for assessing new opportunities.
3. More enterprises are in financial difficulty and even though information technology is available it may not be used effectively.
4. The enterprise needs help in creating and implementing self-directed work teams; striving for diversity requires awareness not only of new cultures, academic background, and work experience, but also of new ways of thinking.

A framework for developing this new awareness is given by Exhibit 4-2. If one considers moving from the current state to a future one, there are three paths to

Exhibit 4-2

Creative Thinking and Innovative Acting

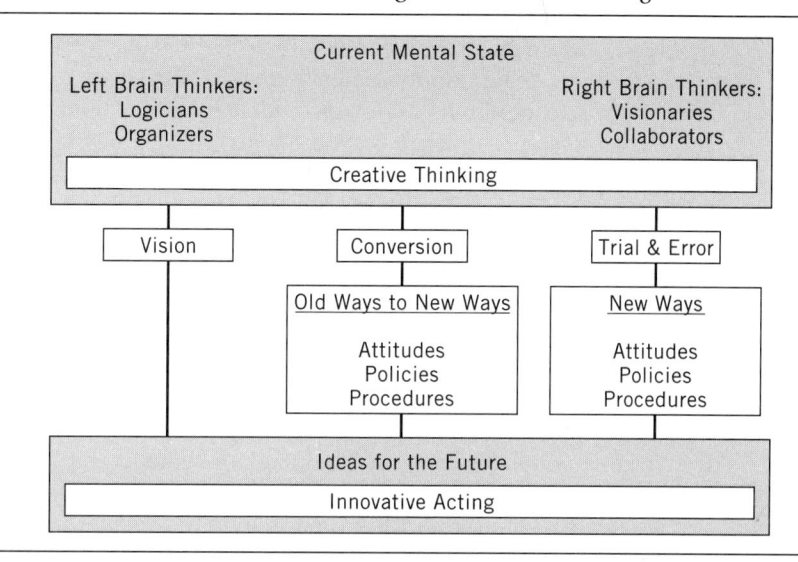

Current Mental State

Left Brain Thinkers:
Logicians
Organizers

Right Brain Thinkers:
Visionaries
Collaborators

Creative Thinking

Vision | Conversion | Trial & Error

Old Ways to New Ways
Attitudes
Policies
Procedures

New Ways
Attitudes
Policies
Procedures

Ideas for the Future
Innovative Acting

SOURCES: Some concepts for diagram derived from Cognitive Preferences Model (Logicians, Organizers, Visionaries, Collaborators, "Thinking Styles and Organizational Effectiveness," by Susan Straus, *European Business Report,* October/November 1992. Concept of creativity styles of vision, conversion, and trial and error from "What's Your Creativity Style?", *Information Week,* November 21, 1994.

---

follow. You can have a vision resulting from introspection, dreaming, or brainstorming sessions and jump right into an innovation or an implementation of the idea. The other two paths use past experience as a basis for future success. What worked before may work now and tomorrow. However, the old adage, "If it works, don't fix it," is no longer valid. Our experience from visiting numerous organizations in the corporate, government, and educational sectors shows that this type of organizational attitude is detrimental to growth and success. It is the wrong issue. It doesn't make any difference whether or not it works; everything is under scrutiny. What appears to be relevant today may not be relevant tomorrow and vice versa. The mindset of the workforce needs to be changed and it is the major responsibility of top-level managers to set this change in motion, not by words and mission statement, but with action. In the words of von Oech, "when you are searching for new information, be an explorer; when you are turning resources into ideas, be an artist; when you're evaluating, be a judge; and when you act, be a warrior" [von Oech, 1986].

In Exhibit 4-2, the creative-thinking block needs further discussion. What is creative thinking? Simply put, it means that you develop an *attitude* that enables you to search for ideas and to manipulate your knowledge and experience [von Oech, 1990]. According to von Oech, you constantly change perspective, play with your knowledge, and make the ordinary extraordinary. Rekindle the imaginary powers. Research indicates that different parts of the brain control different functions [Straus, 1992]. Left-brainers are sequential, linear thinkers with a penchant for detail. Right-brainers are conceptual, like to deal in relationships and pattern recognition, and welcome ambiguity. Also, Straus describes the cognitive preferences model of Ned Hermann in overlaying the left–right orientation with upper–lower traits, resulting in the four quadrants shown in the block "current mental state." The upper-left quadrant is logician; the other three traits are organizer, visionary, and collaborator.

The importance of "thinking style" recognition is not that organizations will change people's behavior to include all traits depending on the situation. The idea is that by recognizing the way others think, as a member of a team you can approach a problem with respect for others' opinions and with more patience. Diversity of opinion is valued and is beneficial in the long run. Further, it may be helpful to assign people with a good mix of quadrant traits to project teams so that a variety of alternatives are identified and considered. The process sacrifices some time in team deliberations (less efficient process) but is more productive (more effective solution) for the organization.

Right-brain thinking (vision and collaboration with others) is very important for creative problem identification and problem solving. Essentially, all three pathways to the future focus on new ways to conduct business and grasp opportunities. Innovation means taking those discoveries in the form of new ideas and acting on them. Arno Penzias states that people don't normally use logic to solve problems [Penzias, 1989]. Society and organizations reward successful problem solving and it behooves us to use the best methods possible. Information technology has limited usefulness in charting these creative paths. Pagels' text on complexity, computers, and mastering reality differentiates the brain from the computer [Pagels, 1989]. He describes the brain as self-assembled, understanding (what things mean as opposed to what is said), and visually perceptual with regard to pattern recognition. Computers have a difficult if not impossible time accomplishing these complex feats.

Complexity has been defined as a midpoint between order and chaos [Pagels, 1989]. If conquering complexity means finding the right problems and offering feasible, quality, and responsive customer-driven solutions and this is the major objective of the enterprise, then the people-machine mix must be maximized. Machines cannot make the leap from the creative-thinking block to the innovative-acting block of Exhibit 4-2. People are the prime movers of this transition. What we want is knowledge, not just information. Machines are information enablers that allow people to acquire that knowledge, make judgments, and be responsible and accountable for their actions.

Thinking about thinking is similar to learning about learning. The educational needs of the IEMgr include lifelong learning and the development of creative and critical thinking skills (see Exhibit 1-1). How does one hone such skills in exploring and processing information (higher-order thinking), as opposed to simply recalling and repeating information or (lower-order thinking)? Better yet, since both types of thinking are necessary for designing (higher order) and implementing (lower order), how can an integrated approach be presented by educators to facilitate this learning activity? A zig-zag pattern of formal lectures interrupted with creative and critical sidebars can force students to experience discovery and practice recall.

Higher-order skills can be defined in terms of thinking operations: comparing, interpreting, observing, summarizing, classifying, decision making, imagining, criticizing and evaluating, designing projects, identifying assumptions, and coding (programming) for discernible patterns of organizing data [Wassermann, 1987]. Once the characteristics are determined, Steinberg illustrates several myths about teaching/learning critical thinking and how to avoid them [Steinberg, 1987]. In summary, these fallacies can be replaced by observing these educational delivery requirements:

- Faculty need development in order to create an atmosphere conducive to critical thinking.
- Students should share the burden of critical thinking.
- Establish realistic goals for a thinking-skills academic program.
- Recognize that there are no completely right answers.
- Class discussion is an essential part of the approach.
- Everyone should be exposed to critical thinking programs.
- Critical thinking is a student-driven activity.
- Recognize the need for a combination of holistic and separate instructional approaches.

Brain-computer comparisons will be covered in Chapter 11 within the context of artificial intelligence (AI) and application-modeling tools for decision-support systems. At this point in the text it is important to raise the issue: Can machines be programmed to think and therefore traverse the pathway from creativity to innovation? Penzias is quite emphatic in his declaration that machines are fundamentally different from brains [Penzias, 1989]. Machines offer little competition to the human brain when it comes to creativity, integration of disparate information, and adaptation to unforeseen circumstances. Other authors, such as Levin, give more latitude to the term "artificial intelligence" and state that such programs do enable a computer to think [Levin, 1990]. They say that AI imitates the human learning process by which new information is absorbed and made available for the future. However, since AI depends on knowing the thinking process, which is uncertain, can it really copy intelligence? Also, because AI and its rule-based formal structure has not delivered on many promises, and because of the increased need to deal with images, analogies, and pattern recognition without application-specific software, there is much interest in neural networks.

By now the student should begin to appreciate the complex behavioral changes that information-enabled professionals must undergo if the organization is to fully exploit information technology. Our model suggests that creativity leads to innovation and innovation leads to increased value as perceived by the customer. For the IEMgmt team, especially the IEMgr(Tp) and IEMgr(TP), this may be a very difficult transition. Those whose roots lie in the technologies rely heavily on process, templates, logic, structure, and order. These are not the attributes that one would ascribe to creative and innovative professionals.

In order for the IEMgr to participate in continuous enterprise reinvention, his or her thinking styles must be tuned in to these needs of the future. The attributes, noted in Chapter 1 (Exhibit 1-2) are reexamined for comments pertaining to higher-order skill development. Leadership, the first listed attribute, is a most important and elusive trait. One cannot lead without vision and personal initiative to convert that creative vision into innovation. If complexity is present, the pathway becomes a maze. As noted earlier in this section, the people-machine mix depends more on people than machines to make the leap to innovation for complex situations. Knowledge, not data and information, can help to make the transition. The IEMgr cannot just learn about leadership principles, add some information enablement, and get effective results. The path of data to knowledge and wisdom (and its application to new situations) is noted by Talbott [1995]. In the transition, he states that data is organized for information, made meaningful to provide knowledge, linked to other knowledge to provide intelligence, and finally, with experience, becomes wisdom. The IEMgr must be able to get to wisdom through communication with others (good interpersonal skills, cooperative and collaborative attributes) and your inner self. Once this comfortable position is achieved using higher-order thinking skills, leadership is possible. Information technology can help to make the transformation of data into information. The rest of the sequence has to be driven by the individual (self-directed in work and life).

Other attributes on the list, such as enterprise systems knowledge, adaptability to the environment, and lifelong learning, are necessary to ensure that information technology is applied appropriately to the enterprise, that it is flexible to changing conditions, and that lifelong learning is a prerequisite condition for maintaining continuous improvement.

◆ NEED FOR PLANNING

Meaningful information technology planning is one of the most difficult managerial functions. Everyone is an active stakeholder in all aspects of acquiring, allocating, and using computer resources to gather, manipulate, and disseminate information. It may be argued that comprehensive and total planning for today's and tomorrow's uncertain and unstable marketplace is a waste of time. Why plan at all when dynamic forces interact immediately to cause accelerated change? The competitive environment seems to change without rhyme or reason; technology development races ahead of application in many chartered and unchartered directions; the vendor landscape changes daily; the global economy shifts dramatically in response to unstable balance of payments, fluctuating change rates, and the vagaries of international stock markets. Some master plans are obsolete before they appear in print. Certainly, it takes much time by many people to develop a strategic planning document.

The alternative, not to plan, is an option exercised by those enterprises that don't have or can't find the time to do so, or that believe that it is a futile endeavor. The dynamics of marketplace demand coupled with operational and immediate crises within the enterprise tend to make planning a supportive and secondary activity. Such a posture results in organizational chaos. The enterprise is adrift. Its people, anxious about their employability and promotability, respond conservatively (take no risks) to the work environment, and act independently to preserve the status quo.

For such organizations, cost containment becomes a major preoccupation and short-term solutions abound; systematic and integrated planning are not of paramount importance. Everyone enters the technology race and orders hardware, software, and services in an effort to meet those operational demands for fast response and customer service. The enterprise has no composite knowledge of its capability to respond since it has no information on who has what information technology for conducting effective company business. People are reactive, not proactive. The enterprise suffocates in the absence of a futuristic (planning) perspective.

Another approach is to adopt a *flexible* planning process which enables the enterprise to change direction rapidly. Harry Dent visualizes such organizations as a huge school of minnows—able to change direction instantly as if wired together into a central nerve network triggered by its leader [Dent, 1995]. Information technology can provide fast turnaround speeds if used properly. Some of the limitations of unresponsiveness to customer demand can be attributed to process. The process may be faulty in that any planning that does occur is sporadic, infrequent, and incomplete.

Yet one can encounter successful organizations that view planning as ever more important as the pace of change accelerates. The more complex and dynamic the environment, the more planning takes center stage and becomes an active, mainstream (not supportive) activity. This text takes the view that organizations should implement a flexible, all-hands, formal planning process that incorporates information technology and business planning. In some organizations, the role of the IS department is entirely reactive; in others, it plays both an active and reactive role in corporatewide issues such as telecommunications-computer connectivity, contractual terms and conditions with multivendor activity, outsourcing arrangements, and training and educational programs. IEMgrs have an active role in all phases of planning for information technology.

◆ THE PLANNING CHALLENGE

The challenge for integrating information technology into general business plans is not justification of process or identification of planners (IEMgrs and general operating managers at all levels), but rather identification of how it will be accomplished. Two historical and still essential issues in addressing this complex problem are whether (1) the process is business driven or technology driven, and (2) the process is controlled by top managers (top-down) or supervisory managers (bottom-up). In light of all the material presented thus far in this text, it is clear that the authors recommend that the process be business driven and undertaken by a representative group of all managers acting in collaboration.

If the process is business driven, the enterprise can respond to market demands more quickly and accurately. If managers are information enabled, it can do so more efficiently. If there is in place a flexible master plan updated on a continuous basis by all levels of management as an integral and important part of routine management tasks, the response is effective and efficient. Previous concerns of computer-illiterate senior managers are beginning to disappear; executives want portable, voice-input, software maneuverability, easy macroprogramming, information holograms (information literally floating around the desk), and an electronic consultant (intelligent electronic companion). These futuristic wishes demonstrate the imagination and vision of perhaps a new executive elite who want to be information enabled but don't have the time to devote to becoming a professional IEMgr.

The second issue of control by *all* managers may cause some advocates of action-oriented management practices to disagree. A typical hierarchy of all managerial levels is not efficient, may blur accountability, and may not be responsive to immediate operational needs. But the method is more effective (the right strategies by the right people for the right objectives). Teams can be action-oriented if they are empowered to make decisions and take action in addition to discussion and analysis. They may take more time to reach decisions but can make better and more objective decisions. IEMgrs are positioned to lead the process, create imaginative and empowered teams, and improve information flow throughout the enterprise. Planning horizons for developing business strategies, identifying needed applications, and prioritizing development should not be fixed. Planning should consider department, process/worker expertise and experience, organizational risk, operational disruptiveness, strengths and weaknesses, opportunities and threats, and timing.

◆ LINKING INFORMATION TECHNOLOGY TO BUSINESS PLANNING

Close observation of several enterprises reveals obsolete management structures. Governance is autocratic, departments are monolithic, and work is chaotic. They are trying to cope with mergers, downsizing, more demanding customers for quality and service, and longer hours. Information technology has made all this happen faster. More technology is not the answer. Different foci for management are the answer. A more holistic, human-centered, and process-oriented management style is needed. When this new management philosophy is adopted and accepted by the workforce, business planning can proceed concurrently with complementary information technology planning.

Specifically, how can the enterprise ensure that business and information technology be linked, strategically in design and operationally in implementation? Dimancescu has a four-fields mapping model for adding horizontal relationships (cross-functional information flows) to the toolbox of traditional time-driven schedules (milestone charts and other project management techniques) and work breakdown structures (WBS) [Dimancescu, 1991]. Any new management style must incorporate cross-functional relationships in its design so that total quality management (TQM) principles can survive. Once a total picture of information flow emerges and creates a "seamless" enterprise, the role of information technology will be clear, its impact on business activity assessed, and planning undertaken. Any information technology planning conducted prior to business planning runs the risk of unnecessary and/or inappropriate hardware and software purchases, data incompatibility, network connectivity problems, acquisition of inappropriate tools, poor hiring decisions, sustaining aging and costly legacy systems, and too much emphasis on technology at the expense of people and process.

Personal experiences with the TQM process in a variety of enterprise environments show that the link between information technology and business planning is ensured when the following four major commitments are made:

1. Promulgate long-range thinking over short-term results; pressure is then relieved from managers to meet quotas for the quarterly financial report; top-level managers obtain an understanding from governing boards and stockholders that immediate gratification in the form of tangible benefits will be secondary to the more intangible benefits of sustaining growth and existence in the next decade; this approach is demonstrated by thought and deed.
2. Establish some type of single body of managers or task force (across all functions and processes) whose mission is to create an inquiring atmosphere, to set the program in motion, and to monitor its progress.
3. Ensure that workers are trained, retrained, and educated (business, liberal arts, communications, problem-solving skills, and information-enablement) in lifelong learning.
4. Empower the task force with the authority to design and implement strategies, prepare budgets and spend funds, question all policies and procedures, reward productive teams and individuals, enter into negotiations with other enterprises, look for business value in all ventures, provide new performance criteria consistent with the new management style, engage all levels of management in higher-order thinking as well as lower-order thinking, encourage creative approaches to new opportunities, identify processes which can act as prototypes with high probability of success, and allow the pursuit of activities not relevant today but perhaps relevant tomorrow.

In addition, the new process should recognize the expertise of IEMgrs that is needed to integrate information technology components and lead the user community in developing applications and implementing systems. Managers with limited information enablement are needed to participate in strategic assessment, quality assurance, customer interaction, production, and staff work.

◆ THREE LEVELS OF PLANNING

Planning for information technology takes place at three distinct levels in the organization: strategic, tactical, and operational. The traditional triangle showing these three levels from top to bottom no longer applies in many of today's enterprises. In that context, one could impose the word "manager" in each segment and infer that top managers in the smallest upper-third of the information triangle were the smallest group and made policies, set the course, and were accountable for success or failure; middle managers developed procedures for tactical decision making; and supervisory managers (the largest group at the bottom) carried out the procedures.

Today, the shape of the geometry is unclear; what is clear is that middle managers are decreasing and although all three types of planning (strategic, tactical, and operational) remain in importance, they are conducted by teams of managers with diverse and cross-functional backgrounds. Management level is no longer relevant in these organizations. Old hierarchial organizational charts disappear; new structures are beginning to look like fishnets with raised "nodes" indicating a process is under investigation by a team [Johansen & Swigart, 1994]. Underneath there may be a formal functional alignment of people, but they are woven together in the net with a cord of information. In the newly emerging world economic order, which is transnational, regionally integrated, and information intensive, the network structure allows planning to occur across business units of varying types.

In addition to these new organizational issues, Exhibit 4-3 shows the complexity of the situation introduced by process teams cutting across planning levels, business functions, and organizational structure. Individuals can be caught in this fishnet of interrelationships. For whom does one really work in this matrixlike structure? Where is allegiance given (e.g., corporate division, reporting department, or project team)? If the lines of demarcation are not clearly drawn, which probably is the case in the real working environment, one's job and position in the enterprise changes frequently. In terms of information planning, it remains useful to describe the three planning levels of Exhibit 4-3.

Strategic information planning increasingly entails the participation of the IEMgr in general business-planning exercise. That is, the IEMgr is not only asked to develop specific systems to implement corporate strategy, but also is expected to participate in the actual development of that strategy. Strategic planning has two principal dimensions:

1. Strategy development, in which the external environment is monitored and strategic information is gathered

Exhibit 4-3

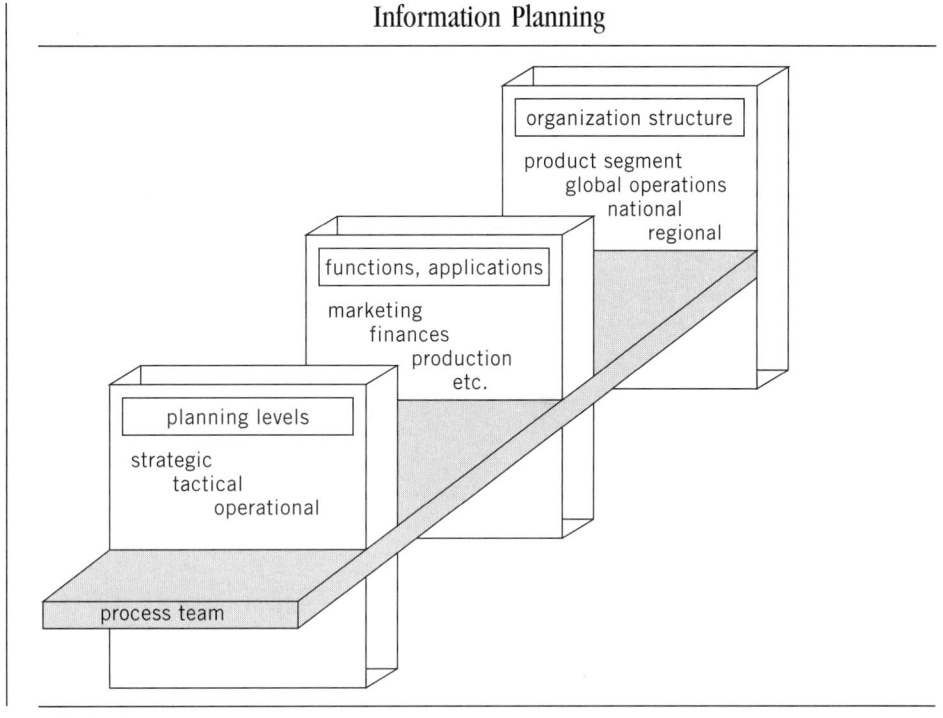

Information Planning

- organization structure
  - product segment
  - global operations
  - national
  - regional
- functions, applications
  - marketing
  - finances
  - production
  - etc.
- planning levels
  - strategic
  - tactical
  - operational
- process team

2. Strategy implementation, in which appropriate systems are designed and implemented to generate the information and computer support needed to accomplish strategic initiatives

Once informational goals and objectives are identified and prioritized (by organizational unit, task force, or process team), it becomes the responsibility of management to decide how to accomplish them. A number of projects to accomplish these goals and objectives illustrate how tactical and operational information planning is vital to the enterprise. The first type will address problem areas where performance is below normal. Shipping, scheduling, billing errors, delay in order fulfillment, production errors, increases in refunds and returned products from customers, system failures, delays in project completion, and larger-than-normal budget variances are typical problems to be addressed. The second type of project involves maintenance of the information system. Increases or changes in enterprise activity often will necessitate design and implementation changes in information system applications. These changes may be very minor considerations (increase database capacity of current computer system to accommodate increased size of customer base) or a major effort (computer system integration resulting from a buyout or merger). The third type of project relates to information systems development. Different information requirements arise in response to opportunities for new products or services and to technological advances more amenable to marketing, producing, and distributing those new products and services. Managers throughout the enterprise have to consider all three types of projects concurrently as they plan with the IEMgr to control information resources.

In addition to new applications development there is a major data planning component to address. The data model has been affected by three phenomena interacting almost simultaneously. The first is the delayering of the management hierarchy. Data must now be made available at lower levels (the individual worker) and at higher levels (senior managers). The midlevel managers who once interpreted or reinterpreted data and passed it up or down in the organization are gone (probably never to return). Those who receive the information must now "do it themselves." The second is the movement to a client/server architecture. The presumption is that data is now available to anyone, anywhere, at any time. The third is the evolution of the organization to a process rather than function structure. All three of these phenomena require that an enterprisewide data model be in place and accessible to all knowledge workers.

◆ INFORMATION SYSTEMS PLANNING METHODS

Having identified the three levels at which IS planning occurs, we now examine various strategic IS planning methods. In this discussion we assume that a no-planning option is not viable. Exhibit 4-4 does include this option, but only for the sake of completeness.

Standalone Planning

Organizations practicing standalone planning may generate a business plan and a systems plan but make no attempt to coordinate the two. Such organizations are usually found in the support category. Senior management is engaged in business planning but may be unaware of any uses of computing and/or information with potential strategic benefits.

The IS department in such organizations is in reactive mode, and its planning activity is limited almost exclusively to budget planning. If the organization is missing strategic opportunities to use IT, it will be largely the responsibility of the IEMgr team (which may be embryonic) to bring this situation to the attention of senior management (on the assumption, of course, that they perceive the problem). Education and demonstration programs for senior managers may be helpful in moving the organization from standalone planning to other options.

Reactive Planning

Reactive planning is the type most often used in modern organizations. A business plan is generated (without direct input of the IEMgr team) and passed

Exhibit 4-4

The Planning Spectrum

TYPE	DESCRIPTION	DEGREE OF INTEGRATION
No planning	No formal planning takes place, either business or information systems	No plan
Standalone	The company may have a business plan or an information systems plan, but not both plans	Business or IS plan
Reactive	A business plan is prepared and the information function reacts to it; traditional passive mode	Business plan drives IS plan
Linked	Business planning is "interfaced" with IS plan; systems resources are matched against business requirements	Business and IS plans overlap
Integrated	Business and IS planning occurs simultaneously and interactively; indistinguishable	System plan including elements of business and IS planning

down to the IS department. The IS department is then responsible for generating a systems plan to support the business plan. In this process the IS department assumes a completely passive role.

Linked Planning

Organizations in the turnaround and strategic categories often use planning systems that take into account information technology and how it can help meet certain business needs. In many cases, the IEMgr(TP) and IEMgr(tP) may have initiated the information technology idea. Such organizations are in a *change mode* regarding strategic systems. As we will shortly see, critical success factors (CSFs) may be used effectively by such organizations' IEMgmt team to help define information needs and to match systems resources against overall business needs.

Integrated Planning

Having business planning and systems planning occur simultaneously requires that the IEMgr team participate actively in the formation of the corporate business plan. In addition, other business unit managers must participate actively in IS strategic plan formation, especially with regard to assigning priorities, allocating resources, and making technology investment decisions. Fully integrated planning requires an IEMgr(Tp) who understands business processes and functions, and business unit managers who understand the value and role of IS. In other words, the organization must have at least an IEMgr(Tp) and several IEMgrs(tP). The number of organizations with such management resources is certainly on the increase.

Critical Success Factors

The Nolan and Gibson hypothesis gives us a good evolutionary view of IEMgmt teams, especially as this view relates to the process units of the organization. As we have seen, the emergence of the microcomputer in the late 1970s, coupled with the introduction of spreadsheet software, ushered in the era of the end user. It was not possible for the individual manager to access information and begin using it productively and efficiently.

The work of John Rockart and his colleagues [1979] at the Center for Information Systems Research at the Sloan School of Management at the Massachusetts Institute of Technology gave managers a major tool, called *critical success factors* (CSFs), to help them define their information needs and to link these with general business needs. CSFs, also called *strategic success factors* by Paul Tom [1987], are defined as those few areas of business activity that are measurable, have business value, are easily understood, and must go well in order for the organization to succeed. CSFs differ from industry to industry, from organization to organization (even within the same industry), and from one time period to another (even within the same organization). Five prime sources of CSFs have been identified [Bullen and Rockart, 1981]:

1. *The industry*
   There are usually a few CSFs common to every organization in a particular industry.
2. *Competitive strategy and industry position*
   Numerous factors distinguish one organization from another in a given industry. Size, location, and market niche are some of the possible differentiating factors. It is through such differences that CSFs unique to a particular business arise.
3. *Environmental factors*
   A number of exogenous factors can often give rise to CSFs. Recent changes in the balance of trade or exchange rates are examples. These factors are outside organizational control.
4. *Temporal factors*
   As a result of some extraordinary event, a particular CSF may be important, or even primary, but usually only for a short period of time.
5. *Managerial position*
   CSFs can also be defined for the functional units of an organization. These may be generic to that organizational level, as well as specific to that functional area.

Exhibit 4-5

Examples of Critical Success Factors

Medical Group Practices

CLINIC 1	CLINIC 2	CLINIC 3
Government Regulations	Quality and Comprehensive Care	Efficiency of Operation
Efficiency of Operations	Federal Funding	Staffing Mix
Patient's View of Practice	Government Regulations	Government Regulations
Relation to Hospital	Efficiency of Operations	Patient's View of Practice
Malpractice Insurance Effects	Patient's View of Practice	Relation to Community
Relation to Community	Satellite vs. Patient Service Other Providers in Community Relation to Hospital	Relation to Hospital

SOURCE: Rockart, John (1979), "Chief Executives Define Their Own Data Needs," *Harvard Business Review* (March-April).

Some examples of CSFs given in the work of Rockart and his colleagues follow.

Automobile industry

Image
High-quality dealer system
Cost control
Compliance with energy standards

Computer industry

Choice of market niche
Technological leadership
Orderly product development
Service and stability
Attraction and retention of high-quality personnel

Organizations in the same industry may have differing sets of CSFs. Exhibit 4-5 lists, in decreasing order of importance, the CSFs from three different medical group practices. Bullen and Rockart [1981] provide details on the interview process used to define the CSF set for a particular organization or department.

Even if the organization does not use CSFs in its planning process, individual departments can still use them for their own planning activities. And individual managers can use CSFs to develop departmental strategic plans and identify their own information needs.

◆ ENTERPRISE DATA MODELING

The movement from a function to a process structure must be accompanied by the development of an enterprise data model if the change is to have any chance of meeting business requirements. The vast majority of organizations grew their databases one at a time and in response to the needs of the business units. The enlightened few may have built a corporate model at one time but the onset of end-user applications development rendered much of that hard work obsolete. We have encountered a number of cases where end-users developed their own databases in order to feed the applications they were developing. In many of these cases, the data already existed at the corporate level but they were unaware of it and had no process to discover the existence of that data. The result is a collection of disjoint, unmaintainable, poorly defined, and redundant databases. Furthermore, there is no corporate dictionary, no standard definitions except by accident, no common database architecture, and several different shrinkwrapped packages being used to define, build, maintain, and report business-unit-level information.

We are reminded of a recent consulting engagement with a consumer products manufacturer in which several departments took issue with reports generated by the CFO claiming that their financial data was in error. After some painstaking investigation, it was discovered that the cause of the disagreement was a lack of data definition. Terms like "monthly sales" had different definitions across departments. The problem was solved with the design and implementation of an enterprisewide data model.

There is a good supply of productivity software tools to help construct the database and dictionary. The problem is organizational and behavioral for the following reasons:

1. An enterprise data model describes how the business wishes to function. That means policy and procedure will be affected by the data modeling effort.
2. Standard definitions must be agreed to for every data element. In most cases there will be as many definitions for an element as there are occurrences of that element in the business unit databases.
3. Who will claim ownership of each data element for the purposes of creation and maintenance? What about access privileges?
4. How will end-user developed systems be converted?
5. Will some data remain at the business unit level and not be part of the enterprise data model?
6. How will the enterprise convert from the current to the enterprise data model?

We will return to these issues in more detail in Chapter 12.

◆ MANAGING THE INFORMATION SYSTEMS PORTFOLIO

An organization's investments in technology are necessarily complex and diverse. Companies are being challenged to identify investments at progressively more strategic (and more highly leveraged) levels of corporate activity. However, this does not relieve the IS manager of the obligation to "invest," if only as a caretaker, in lower levels of the organization. The fact that a company might decide, as a point of strategy, to make aggressive investments in one functional area in no way means investments will not be made in other less strategic areas. In fact, there may be alternative investment strategies in different areas and/or at different levels.

Richard Nolan [1981] has recognized that the IS manager actually presides over a portfolio of investments made across many levels and functions, all requiring different strategies. Exhibit 4-6 illustrates the evolution of an investment portfolio. The first drawing indicates that investment can be made in systems at three different levels. The assortment of functions available for investment (e.g., marketing, manufacturing), each potentially with system investment opportunities in all three levels, is shown in the second diagram. Each segment in the now-divided pyramid represents the potential for investment consistent with the organization's strategic plan. The disproportionate size of the various wedges is indicative of the disproportionate opportunities that confront each organization. The last diagram shades a portion of each wedge to represent actual levels of investment. This portrayal allows the IS manager to visualize where investment penetration is being made compared to the opportunities for investment. Like any portfolio, a balanced approach to investing will minimize risks and harvest the relatively easy benefits of building tools in previously unimproved areas. However, this analysis will quickly indicate at a glance if a company is investing their IS resources in an unbalanced and pedestrian way, as the sample company in the third diagram seems to be doing by investing only at the operational levels across functions.

Although functional department investment is of initial importance to organizations, David P. Norton [1984] has pointed out that the nature of the investment may transcend functional alignments and may be a more important dimension along which to measure investment. Exhibit 4-7 shows that within any IS departmental functions or levels, IS products can be classified according to the following five application segments:

1. *Institutional Functions*
   Transactions or procedural systems that reflect an organization's business processes
2. *Professional Support*
   Computing support for groups of professionals (e.g., administrative assistants, engineers, programmers)
3. *Physical Automation*
   Automation of physical flows and processes

Exhibit 4-6

The Evolution of an Investment Portfolio

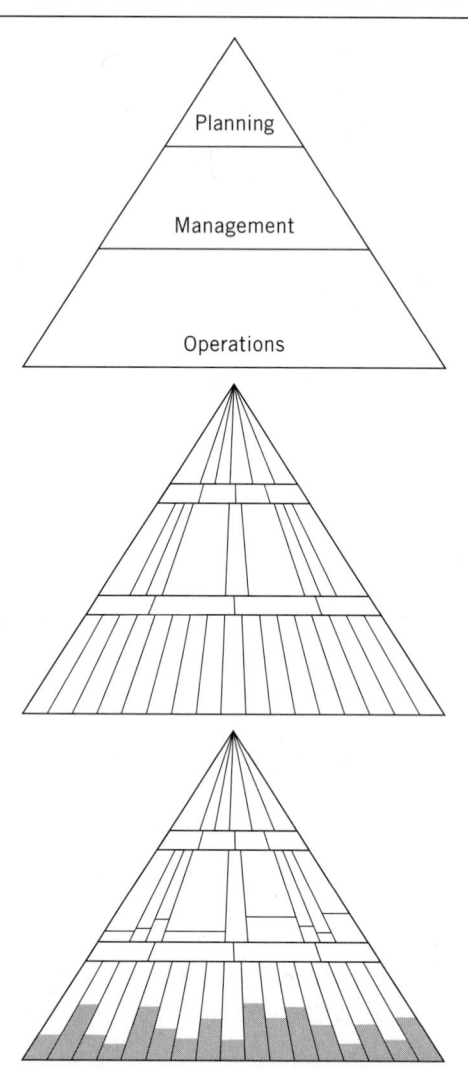

SOURCE: Richard L. Nolan, "Principal DP Asset: The Applications Portfolio," *Stage by Stage,* vol. 1, no. 2. p. 4. Copyright © 1982. Nolan, Norton & Co., Lexington, MA. All rights reserved. Reprinted with permission.

4. *External Products*
   Systems and information that serve as value-added products or services to customers
5. *Infrastructure*
   Investments made in foundation technology such as data architecture and network architecture

Exhibit 4-7

Product Segmentation's Impact on the Applications Portfolio

PORTFOLIOS	INSTITUTIONAL FUNCTIONS	PROFESSIONAL SUPPORT	PHYSICAL PROCESS	EXTERNAL PRODUCT	INFRASTRUCTURE
Input (spending) measure	VS spending as percent of sales	VS spending per person	VS spending per unit of output	VS spending as percent of product sales	Spending on infrastructure as percent of VS spending
User segmentation scheme	Functional department (e.g., accounting)	Job family (e.g., brokers)	Physical process (e.g., letters mailed)	Product line (e.g., commercial paper)	X
Output (return) measure	Output per support staff (e.g., transactions per employee)	Output per professional (e.g., revenue per employee)	Output per direct employee letters (e.g., processed per employee)	X	X

SOURCE: David P. Norton, "The Economics of Computing in Advanced Stages." *Stage by Stage,* vol. 4, no. 4. Winter 1985, p. 6. Copyright Nolan, Norton & Co., Lexington, MA. All rights reserved. Reprinted with permission.

The junction of functional user and application segments indicates to the IS manager the appropriate level of investment, as shown in Exhibit 4-8. This analysis allows comparison with general industry levels or specific competitors and permits historical comparison and management discussion. The process of categorizing spending by application segment encourages the IS manager to recognize important differences in various investments, differences that might otherwise remain hidden. This in turn helps the IS manager find the most appropriate means of organizing, measuring, and controlling each segment. Exhibit 4-9 shows some measurement alternatives in the area of spending, user segmentation, and output for various application segments.

For the IS manager increasingly called on to allocate scarce resources across a broad area so as to meet the demands of a multifaceted business strategy, minimize risk, and maximize returns, tools such as the Nolan and Norton application portfolio model are valuable techniques for staying in charge of the control and communications process.

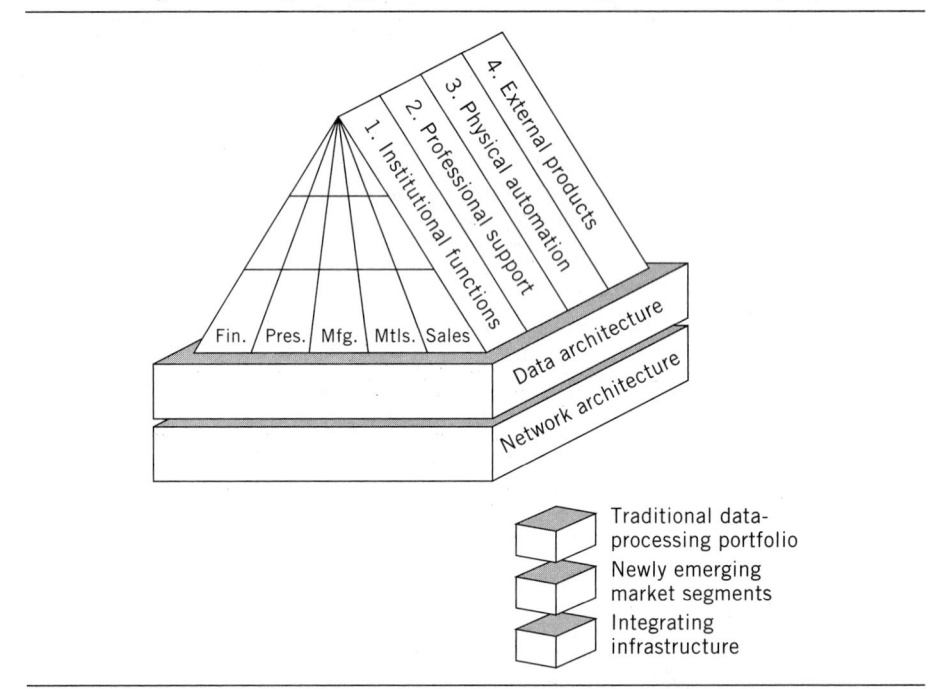

Exhibit 4-8 | Alignment of Spending and Business Strategy for One Company

SOURCE: David P. Norton, "The Economics of Computing in Advanced Stages: Part II—A New Framework for Management." *Stage by Stage,* vol. 4, no. 3. Fall 1984, p. 3. Copyright Nolan, Norton & Co., Lexington, MA. All rights reserved. Reprinted with permission.

◆ THE BUSINESS SYSTEMS PLANNING METHODOLOGY

Business systems planning (BSP) is a process for developing an IS strategy that is coordinated, at least partially, with the business strategy of an organization. The process is very structured and helps an organization establish a systems plan that satisfies its short-term and long-term information requirements. Developed by IBM in the late 1960s, this methodology was made available to IBM customers from 1970. It is still in common use as part of the data modeling procedures used today. The objectives of the process are to accomplish the following [IBM, 1984]:

1. Provide an information systems plan that supports the business's short- and long-term information needs and is integral with the business plan.
2. Provide a formal, objective method for management to establish information systems priorities without regard to provincial interests.
3. Provide for the development of systems that have a long life because these systems are based on the business processes that are generally unaffected by organizational changes.

Exhibit 4-9

Different Metrics Appropriate for Each Portfolio Segment

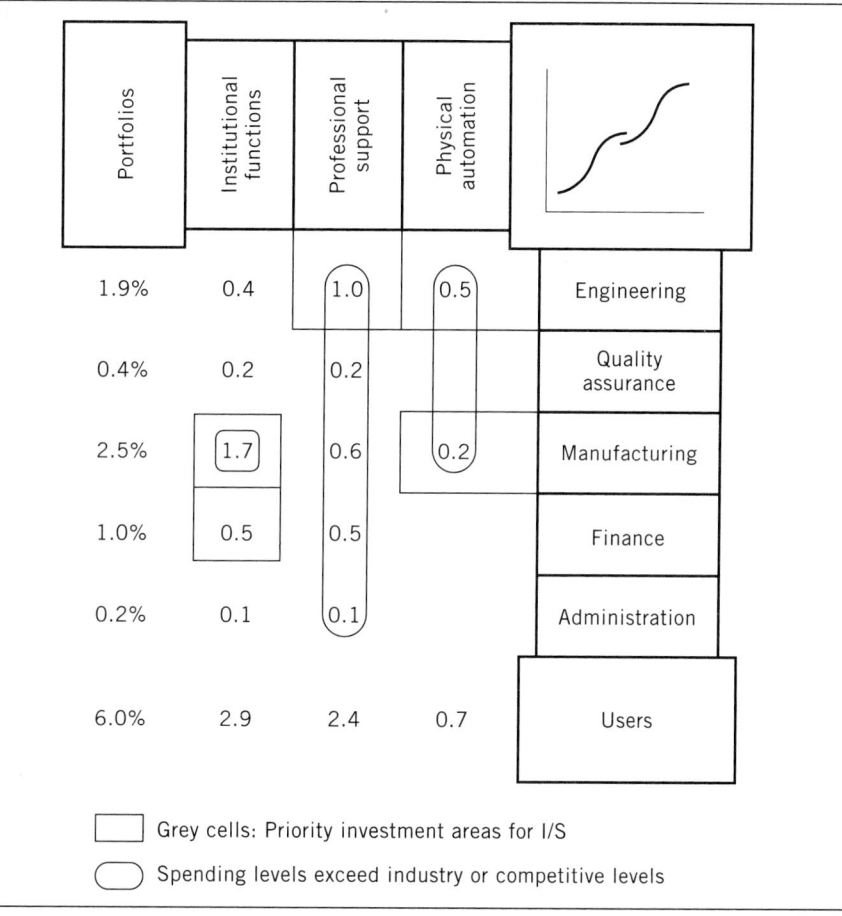

Portfolios	Institutional functions	Professional support	Physical automation	
1.9%	0.4	1.0	0.5	Engineering
0.4%	0.2	0.2		Quality assurance
2.5%	1.7	0.6	0.2	Manufacturing
1.0%	0.5	0.5		Finance
0.2%	0.1	0.1		Administration
6.0%	2.9	2.4	0.7	Users

☐ Grey cells: Priority investment areas for I/S

◯ Spending levels exceed industry or competitive levels

SOURCE: David P. Norton, "The Economics of Computing in Advanced Stages: Part IV—Focusing on the Investment." *Stage by Stage,* vol. 5, no. 1. Spring 1985, p. 6. Copyright Nolan, Norton & Co., Lexington, MA. All rights reserved. Reprinted with permission.

4. Provide that the data processing resources are managed for the most efficient and effective support of the business goals.
5. Increase executive confidence that high-return, major information systems will be produced.
6. Improve relationships between the information systems department and users by providing for systems that are responsive to user requirements and priorities.
7. Identify data as a corporate resource that should be planned, managed, and controlled in order to be used effectively by everyone.

Exhibit 4-10

Top-Down Analysis and Bottom-Up Implementation

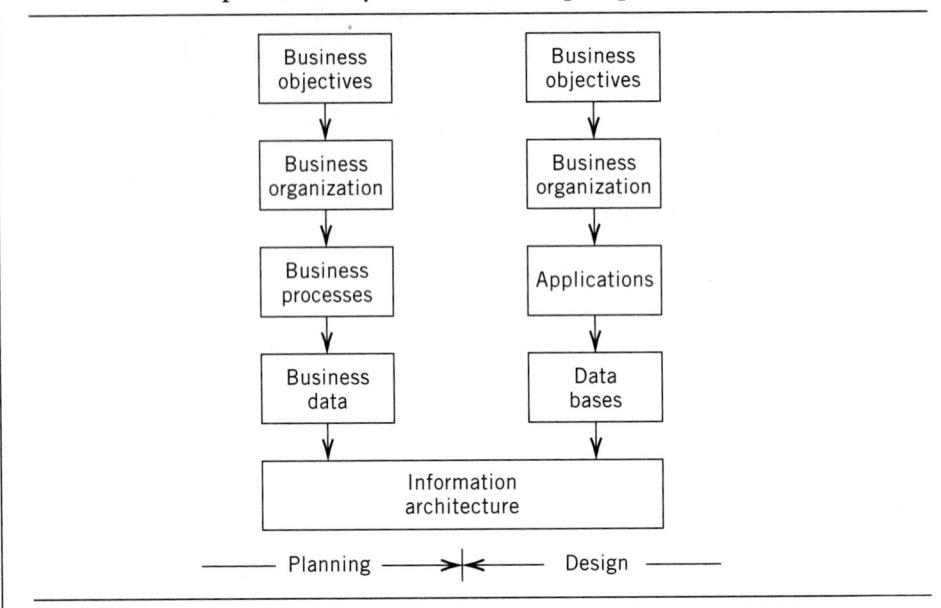

```
Business objectives          Business objectives
        ↓                            ↓
Business organization        Business organization
        ↓                            ↓
Business processes           Applications
        ↓                            ↓
Business data                Data bases
        ↓                            ↓
        Information architecture

——— Planning ———>|<——— Design ———
```

SOURCE: Reprinted by permission from *Information Systems Planning Guide,* © 1984 by International Business Machines Corporation.

BSP consists of both top-down planning and bottom-up design and implementation. In Exhibit 4-10, *business processes* consist of the activities that make up the value chain, and these in turn define the *business data* requirements of the organization. Both the business processes and the business data are identified through extensive interviews and discussion of the business plan. The planning phase is complete once the *information architecture* best suited to meet the needs of managers at all levels in the organization has been determined. The output of this step will be a definition of current system resources, the identification of additional resources that will be needed, and a prioritization scheme. The design and development phase begins with the information architecture phase and includes the development and modification of both new and existing databases. This analysis is needed so that new computer applications can be defined. The *applications* step consists of the definition of specific projects to be undertaken, development priorities, functional specifications, and finally, systems implementation. To complete the BSP methodology, the new applications support business processes, which in turn contribute to *business objectives*.

BSP is a planning approach that is more appropriate for organizations in the support or factory categories. Its strengths include the following:

- It involves senior management.
- It enhances communications among personnel at all levels of the organization.

- It sensitizes senior management to the costs, benefits, and capabilities of information systems.
- Being highly structured, it can be replicated and compared year to year.
- It is well-documented.
- It provides goals for the IS department around which an implementation plan can be structured.

Its weaknesses are that it is difficult to implement, is highly dependent on the interviewer's skills, and risks missing competitive opportunities. According to James Martin [1982], its major weakness is that its output is often not connected to existing databases and systems, thus increasing the communication problem with IS personnel and preventing the development of a specific IS plan.

◆ INTEGRATED STRATEGIC INFORMATION SYSTEMS PLANNING

Planning is a way of guaranteeing and maintaining a competitive advantage. Organizations that understand this statement also understand the importance of fully integrating IS planning at the senior management and departmental levels. The IS department plays a dual planning role, as the model we now present illustrates. One role is proactive and involves the IS department in strategy formation at the corporate level and application systems initiatives at the departmental level. The other role is reactive and involves the IS department as a support service to implement systems that help corporate officers and functional business units meet their planning objectives.

The model consists of five steps, each of which is discussed in detail in the following sections. Exhibit 4-11 illustrates the model.

Step 1: Environmental Analysis

Initiation of the environmental analysis is largely the responsibility of the IEMgr(TP) and IEMgr(Tp). In this step, both internal and external factors affecting the organization's use of IT are documented. Internal factors measure and define the organization's use of IT and potential changes or increases in that use. Documenting internal factors may entail locating the organization on the strategic grid in order to gain a better understanding of which planning methodology would be consistent with the organizational climate (i.e., the degree of formality or informality, level of detail, planning horizon, etc., that would be appropriate). The readiness of the IS staff to assimilate new technologies and trends also needs to be documented; it may be necessary for the IS manager to consider tradeoffs between long-range staff development and the timely hiring of professionals with the requisite skills.

Analysis of the external factors entails consideration of the organization's competitive position with respect to IT. This analysis includes an assessment of how IT has affected and can affect the industry as well as the organization itself.

Exhibit 4-11

An Integrated Strategic IS Planning Model

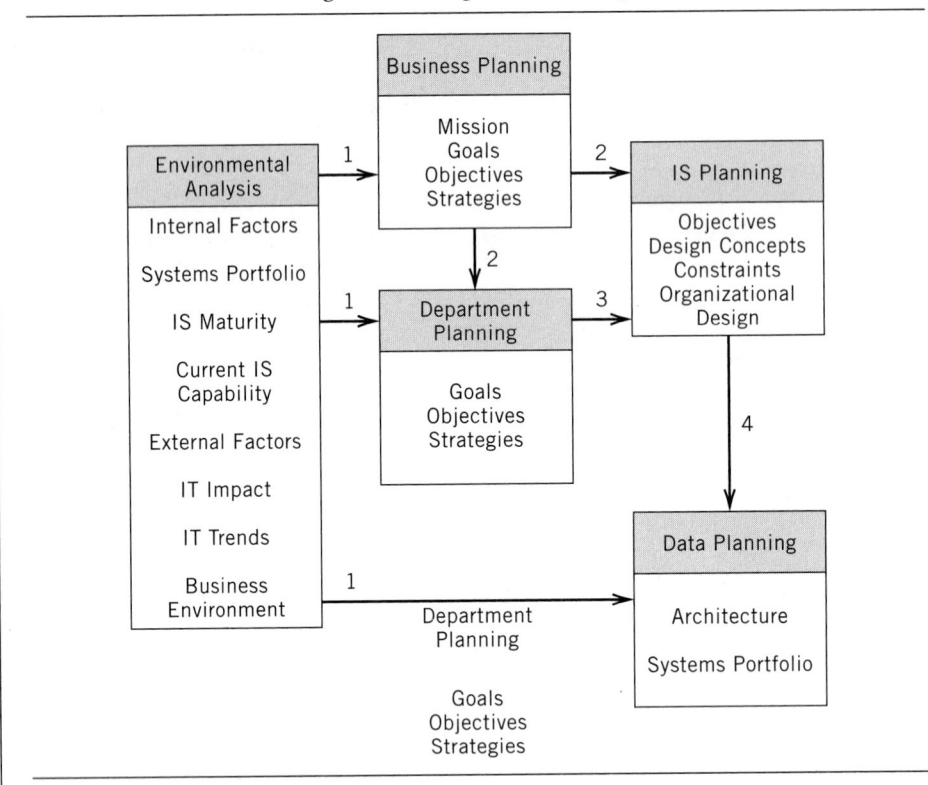

```
                    Business Planning
                    ┌─────────────┐
                    │   Mission   │
                    │    Goals    │         ┌─────────────────┐
   ┌──────────────┐ │ Objectives  │ ──2──▶  │   IS Planning   │
   │Environmental │1│ Strategies  │         ├─────────────────┤
   │   Analysis   │▶└─────────────┘         │   Objectives    │
   ├──────────────┤         │               │ Design Concepts │
   │Internal      │         2               │   Constraints   │
   │Factors       │         ▼               │ Organizational  │
   │              │  ┌─────────────┐  ──3─▶ │    Design       │
   │Systems       │1 │ Department  │        └─────────────────┘
   │Portfolio     │▶ │  Planning   │                 │
   │              │  ├─────────────┤                 4
   │IS Maturity   │  │   Goals     │                 │
   │              │  │ Objectives  │                 ▼
   │Current IS    │  │ Strategies  │        ┌─────────────────┐
   │Capability    │  └─────────────┘        │  Data Planning  │
   │              │                          ├─────────────────┤
   │External      │                          │  Architecture   │
   │Factors       │                          │                 │
   │              │1        Department       │Systems Portfolio│
   │IT Impact     │▶────────Planning────────▶└─────────────────┘
   │              │
   │IT Trends     │           Goals
   │              │        Objectives
   │Business      │        Strategies
   │Environment   │
   └──────────────┘
```

NOTE: Numbers indicate the time ordering of planned activities.

A traditional analysis of strengths, weaknesses, opportunities, and threats (SWOT analysis) common to strategic business planning will often be part of this exercise. Value-chain and value-systems analyses under the direction of the IEMgr(TP) are also useful. The IT trends that can be identified may suggest new strategic opportunities for the organization.

Environmental analysis is a proactive activity initiated and conducted on a continual basis by the IS department, although there is a growing trend among IEMgmt to do the same in their process or functional areas. Its resulting series of reports are input to planning meetings both at the corporate and business unit levels. The environmental analysis also provides information to help the IS department in its own planning activity. Trends and uses of IT may suggest to the IS department a number of changes that should be made in its network communications and database architectures to improve efficiency and/or effectiveness. As envisioned here, the environmental analysis is not a once-a-year exercise but rather a continual process that generates a steady stream of information on specific environmental issues. It is the responsibility of the IS manager to see that such information is appropriately directed throughout the enterprise.

Step 2: Business Planning

Using the information gleaned from the environmental analysis, the organization determines if it can use IT to make a significant change in the way it interacts with its markets. It might learn that it can gain competitive advantage by changing the markets in which it is doing business. A reevaluation of existing electronic data interchange (EDI) applications and trading relationships is part of this exercise. With the growth of public access networks (especially the Internet) and value-added networks (VANs), there will most certainly be new opportunities to consider. The output of this process will be a new or revised strategy set (mission, goals, objectives, and strategies) that will serve as input to all departments (including the IS department) for their planning. Each department translates this corporate strategy set into its own departmental strategy set.

Step 3: Business Unit and Department Planning

The environmental analysis might also suggest to the organization that it should look for internal applications of IT to improve the way that it currently conducts its business. Both this information and the corporate strategy set are the basic input data that business units and the functional-area departments will use to generate their strategic plans. At this level, IEMgrs(TP) will play a key role. They will have most likely participated in enterprisewide planning with IEMgrs(Tp) and will therefore have first-hand understanding of the planned technology direction and how process-level IT planning fits into technology infrastructure. In this planning model, the IEMgr(TP) is the linchpin between enterprise-level planning and process-level planning. As at the corporate level, three types of projects may result (problem resolution, systems maintenance, and new systems). Each can appear in unit and departmental plans and will become input to the IS strategic planning process. Value-chain analysis will often be used by the units and departments to identify areas of opportunity for competitive advantage.

Step 4: Development of the Strategic Information Systems Plan

The IS department, acting reactively, translates the corporate, business unit, and departmental strategies into a master strategic IS plan. Tools that might also be used to develop the strategic IS plan are the BSP framework, the strategy set transformation approach [King, 1978], and an ends/means analysis.

Step 5: Data Planning

Once the IS plan is in place, data-planning activity can begin. One approach is to define the information architecture (part of the BSP methodology discussed earlier) along with a portfolio of development projects (the application step of the BSP methodology). Data flow analysis and information flow techniques may also be used. The final step for the IS department is to prepare the necessary inputs to the budget planning process.

◆ CHANGING WINDOWS OF OPPORTUNITY

The only thing that is constant in today's business world is change. To be successful, organizations must be ready to exploit an opportunity when it arises. To wait and to think about it too long may mean to miss the opportunity. That is not to say that we proceed with reckless abandon. Rather, like all good athletes have been trained to do—anticipate and act. We already know what we will do when a particular situation arises. For example, the Advanced Technology Group will be watching certain technologies. When the price/performance of any one of them reaches a predefined level, we move immediately to implement it into our product/service portfolio. The analysis has already been done! All that was needed was to have the condition exist.

To build the infrastructure needed to make this happen is no small task. The methodologies for such things as project management, systems development, change management, problem resolution, and others must be well-defined and ingrained in every IEMgr and their staffs. Anything short of this will fail or at least expose the organization to needless consequences of high risk.

Reflections

GENERAL CONCEPTS

1. Given that planning is dynamic and not static, how should an organization keep its plan up to date?
    If it is so difficult to keep a rapidly changing plan current, why have a plan at all?
    How about changes to the plan?
    What process or structure would you recommend?

2. What criteria might you suggest for deciding which of several competing projects to undertake? You should be able to identify several.
    Can they be ranked according to importance? How might you do that?
    If you can identify criteria, how can you convert the project list to a prioritized one?

3. Describe an example of a product or service that you consider innovative and that brought new life into an existing product or service.
    Can you think of an example of a new product or service that creatively utilizes information technology and that does not presently exist?

How would you go about deciding whether or not to proceed with the venture?

4. Return on Investment (ROI) is an elusive quantity. Market share is quantifiable. Customer service is more intangible.

How can you demonstrate that information technology will improve customer service?

What is meant by customer service? What data about the customers are not known?

Can you devise a system for measuring (according to some criteria) improved customer service? Include new markets in a global environment and new product development.

5. Different parts of the brain control different functions (sequential vs. conceptual thinkers). Other research supports the notion that different people think differently. Select any topic and discuss it with several others. Use any methodology (such as Straus, 1992) for organizing the way each person approaches the issue or problem.

How does this exercise relate to the current movement toward self-directed work teams?

Can individuals change their behavior patterns to accommodate working on team projects?

Does the enterprise get an advantage from several opinions on major issues? Or, is it better and faster to limit input and take action?

How does "risk" enter into team projects, divergent thinking patterns, and innovation?

6. Managing the information systems portfolio has been the responsibility of the IS manager. Now with increased influence of end users in every aspect of the acquisition and use of information technology, it appears that the process is more difficult.

From the perspective of the CIO, how would you manage the applications portfolio of the enterprise?

Using the SWOT (Strengths, Weaknesses, Opportunities, and Threats) technique, analyze an enterprise, or organizational element of the enterprise, for developing a priority listing of its application portfolio.

7. Examine an enterprise using the competitive forces model of Porter (Exhibit 4-1).

Reflections

STEP MODEL

1. How can the STEP Model accommodate ideas for new and innovative products and services? In the last chapter, creative ideas can be risky.

2. In the people dimension of the STEP Model, in order to progress with self-directed work teams instead of separate and distinct individual initiatives, the model suggests that different motivations are needed to progress effectively. Individuals will focus more on process and less on the department, more on team

performance and less on personal performance, and more on interpersonal skill development and less on task completion. Are these new individual directions correct and consistent with total quality management concepts?

3. The applications portfolio becomes hotly debated when the question of priority arises. Progress on any STEP Model pathway is directly related to the implementation of the right applications at the right time by the right people (end users and/or IS staff).

   a. Examine one application area for information technology enablement (new application, major upgrade of an existing application, or a software conversion effort) and justify it for development and/or implementation. What criteria will you use?
   b. Should you compare it to other application proposals?
   c. How would you make sure that it is somewhere on a STEP Model path.

Chapter 5

Organizational Deployment of the Information Function

❖ ❖ ❖

*T*he organizational placement and structure of the information systems function has undergone numerous changes over the past several decades. Some of these changes were the result of historical accident, others were the result of deliberate planning, yet others were in response to market pressures and technological advances. In this chapter we trace that historical evolution and then consider some of the general approaches to structure as they have played themselves out in the information systems arena. As we consider the current situation we see yet another evolutionary phase unfolding. It appears as though the information systems function, as it continues to become pervasive throughout the enterprise, is, at the same time, disappearing into the organization much as the telephone disappeared into the organization several decades ago. We do not want the student to think that organizational problems of the information systems function are solved as a result. The evolution we are experiencing is carrying the information systems function to a new level—one that promises to bring it into a critical role in determining the future success of the enterprise. As we will see, that role involves everyone, in different capacities, in the successful assimilation of information technology into literally every aspect of corporate life.

◆ TRENDS IN INFORMATION SYSTEMS ORGANIZATION

As one might view the evolution of the information systems organization and its placement within the organization, it might seem to be one based more on impulse than on considered decision. Upon closer examination, it did follow upon a sequence of business needs and the resulting decisions that made sense at the time. The fact that structures oscillated back and forth between centralized and decentralized was the result of considered decisions. Let us begin our discussion by tracing that evolution.

The Initiation Stage

Because the first commercial computer applications were in the accounting area, the data processing staff normally reported to the head of the accounting department. As providers of a service, the data processing staff had to worry about ensuring the timely delivery of correct reports to the accounting department and responding to application development requests from them. Moreover, the data processing supervisor had to deal with only a single technology (batch processing on a single mainframe). From an organizational standpoint, life was fairly simple. The pressure to change came from a growing need to support other business functions.

The Contagion Stage

As other functional managers became aware of the potential benefits of IS applications in their areas, it became necessary for the data processing supervisor to establish relationships with other departments and implement procedures regarding the allocation of development support and production time. Policies had to be developed to accommodate the needs of these new users. At the same time, the accounting department saw its control of computing resources erode as others began to contend for computing time and programming resources. The data processing supervisor was often under great pressure from his or her old boss to play favorites and give the accounting department preferred treatment.

Many departments were able to convince senior management that their needs were very different from those of the accounting department and that it was in the organization's best interest to let them establish their own computing resources. This pressure was quite effective. The data processing supervisor, who reported directly to the head of the accounting department, did not fully understand the needs of the users in other departments and was not, in any case, in a position to meet them. Letting other units establish their own computing facilities was a means of avoiding a confrontation with the accounting department and letting everyone get on with their own business. This laissez-faire management approach was more expedient.

As the number of requests for applications continued to grow, it became necessary for data processing to form its own department to serve users who could not justify their own equipment and staff. This new department was typically located on the same organizational level as its user groups.

The Control Stage

The unbridled growth of computer use eventually caught the attention of senior managers, who temporarily brought a halt to rapidly increasing expenditures for computing resources by making the data processing manager (by now known in many organizations as the MIS manager) responsible for implementing controls and cost/benefit measures. This was unfamiliar territory for the MIS manager, who had never before needed to learn cost/benefit analysis techniques, to estimate systems development times, or to establish monitoring and control procedures. Senior management began looking at the MIS department as it would any other service department in the organization. In so doing, they evaluated the MIS department using tried and true cost-justification criteria. The MIS manager, who had previously been protected from such close scrutiny, was now competing on the same playing field as other middle managers. It was a strange field too—with new and strange rules governing how decisions were made! The power and politics of the management team had to become part of the MIS manager's tool kit.

The MIS manager had been promising systems for literally anything users requested. As monitoring and control systems went into place, it became evident how poorly managed the MIS department was. Excessively late, overbudget projects were the rule rather than the exception. As we have seen, the typically poor management skills of the MIS manager (remember they were "techies") and the department's failure to deliver on promised systems resulted in a serious loss of credibility and user confidence.

The Integration and Data Administration Stages

As computer applications became more sophisticated and MIS took on a more visible role in business affairs, many organizations recognized that they would have to use their computing resources more efficiently and effectively. This meant that the MIS manager needed a broader corporate perspective to actively assist functional managers in the search for ways to use information technology to good advantage. A new kind of relationship began to develop between the IS manager (another name change to herald the new partnership) and other functional managers. The immediate result was that the IS manager had an opportunity to regain user confidence and to be treated and received as an equal among functional managers. At the same time, however, pockets of computer applications began to spring up independently of the IS department. These "islands of technology" (CAD/CAM, desktop publishing, word-processing centers, robotics, etc.) presented (and still present) a difficult organizational structure issue for the IS manager, who had to define the department's position regarding their operation. In many cases, the professionals responsible for various islands of technology knew more than the IS staff did about the use of the technology, so centralizing such islands under the IS department might prove detrimental. From a senior management perspective, there was no clear-cut solution, so the IS manager was on his or her own to recommend and defend a particular organizational decision.

The Maturity Stage

At present, organizational use of information technology has moved beyond the organization itself and into the marketplace. Relationships with customers and suppliers are heavily affected. In fact, the IS manager is being called on to establish working relationships with customers and suppliers so that the organization may retain its competitive position. Few if any organizations have reached the maturity stage—a point at which information technology is fully integrated in the organization at every level and the IS manager is a full-fledged member of the senior management team.

What is happening suggests that this will come about—perhaps faster than we would think. The more recent trends toward downsizing, customer-driven organizations, process structures, and worker empowerment suggest a metamorphosis is occurring. Information technology is at the core of these trends. Organizations realize that the last opportunity for efficiency, effectiveness, and productivity enhancements can come only from exploitation of the technology. The IS department, through its manager, is being pulled into the battle by the business units. Rather than struggling for a more viable role they are now having to demonstrate that they can be both proactive and reactive members of the management team. It is truly a time of great challenge and high risk. Witness the two- to three-year tenure of the typical CIO.

◆ TRENDS IN DEPLOYING THE INFORMATION FUNCTION

Information systems departments have adopted diverse organizational structures and alignments as a result of historical evolution, accident, planned change, or the pressures of corporate culture—forms that may or may not be appropriate for a given organization. The rapid transition toward an end-user-oriented environment has rekindled the issue of whether the department should be centralized or decentralized—in short, it has begged the question of the IS department's position or alignment within the corporate structure. Moreover, the reporting responsibilities of the IS manager in a context in which autonomous uses of information technology are dispersed throughout the organization are not clearcut. This fact, too, raises the question of structure and alignment.

Form follows function. And nowhere is that more pertinent than in the information systems department. We have established that organizations need to be designed so that they are more responsive to the needs of the customer. Once those relationships are defined, it makes sense to talk about how the information systems department should be configured to support business activity. Few enterprises do this.

These and related issues are the focus of the remainder of this chapter. We begin by tracing the evolution of the IS department's location in the organizational structure; to do so, we revisit the stages hypothesis [Nolan and Gibson, 1974; Nolan 1979] discussed in Chapter 3. Next we look at typical organizational placements for the IS department. We then take up the question of which structural options make best use of the IS department—that is, which options best position the department to contribute significantly and consistently to the organization's competitive arsenal. We look at centralized and decentralized

Exhibit 5-1

Advantages of Centralization/Decentralization

CENTRALIZATION	DECENTRALIZATION
More specialized expertise develops	Service can be isolated, focused
Economies of scale are achievable	Greater assignment options
Skills more readily backed up	Specific accountability
More focus on long-range planning	Greater responsiveness
Easier standardization	More autonomy provided
More autonomy	Expertise dispersed
Central control and integration	Experimentation fostered
Fewer redundancies	

structures for the IS department. Finally, we explore reporting relationships, with special emphasis on CEO styles of work and their effect on the IS manager.

Centralized to Decentralized

A major factor in structuring the IS department is the issue of centralization. For example, Operations can either be grouped centrally (as is traditional) or be decentralized (i.e., with its people and equipment divided into groups that support functional or business process units). The choice of approach depends on the IS manager's perception of the relative advantages illustrated in Exhibit 5-1.

A Centralized Structure

A centralized IS department manages all corporate computing activities from a single office. This does not imply (as was once true) that all processing takes place at one location. It is entirely possible that under a centralized structure the IS department may have several remote computing facilities that depend on one or more processors for their computing power. Large networks of processors and terminals can be part of a centralized structure as can standalone processors.

A centralized organizational structure is therefore defined as one in which the following holds true:

- One line manager is directly responsible for all IS issues (standards, policy, procedure, communications, and security).
- There are defined corporatewide procedures and controls for systems analysis, design, and programming practices.
- Data administration is under the control of one office.

Centralized organizational structures do offer a number of advantages. Certain corporate-level reports serve consolidations of divisional—and even departmental—

level financial and operating activities and are therefore easier to generate in centralized as compared to decentralized organizations. Standardized data items and summary rules aid in report preparation and interpretation. Problems with incompatible hardware and software and communications tend to disappear under a centralized structure; having to write bridge software and conversion software is very costly and problematic and generally is not recognized in a centralized situation.

Centralization also provides more staffing options and opportunities for career advancement than do other types of organizations. It is easier to hire and keep talented people because there is greater specialization, career advancement, and project variety in a centralized as compared to a decentralized setting. Staff turnover and shortages are easier to absorb, too. Finally, better resource allocation and control systems are possible, and economies of scale as well as greater leverage with vendors result from a centralized organizational structure. More productive use of resources is a likely benefit of these economies of scale.

A Decentralized Structure

In a decentralized organizational structure, information processing occurs at several sites that are managed independently. Each of these sites functions in the same way as the centralized organization just described. A decentralized organizational structure is thus defined as one in which the following hold true:

- Several processors function independently of one another, perhaps under different sets of standards and operating procedures.
- Each unit may have its own analysis and design procedures and controls.
- Special-purpose databases, data administration, and applications are in place at each unit.

The decentralized organizational structure has a number of advantages. Having the development staff closer to users means that the staff has greater access to product-specific knowledge and can thus provide a higher level of expertise in application development (and probably a higher degree of user satisfaction as a result). The development staff tends to be more responsive to user needs and to avoid the conflict over resources that crop up in centralized organizations. Enhanced responsiveness means that production work can be scheduled for single user groups rather than across units with differing priorities. For cost control and cost-benefit purposes, a decentralized organization is typically better; users are more sensitive to cost considerations because they deal with these costs in their project proposals and feasibility studies. The likely result is a more productive use and allocation of resources as well as users who are more sensitive to these issues. (Users' profitability is at stake, and therefore they are more likely to pay attention to costs than they would in a centralized organization.)

A Hybrid Structure

What we are seeing in most organizations is the trend toward a hybrid of the centralized and decentralized structures. This has been brought about by the emergence of client/server architectures. The server is a centralized enterprise database with some supporting commercially available application packages. This resource is available, through a network, to the users (the clients). The enterprise database was designed to be applications independent. That allows applications development and maintenance and operations to be decentralized out to the client areas. There are obvious advantages to this over both the centralized and decentralized models. First, the client is in full control of their data resource. There are, of course, previously agreed-upon standards that the client unit adheres to. The client's primary responsibility is the creation and maintenance of certain data elements that are used across the organization. Apart from that, the client unit operates quite independently of the rest of the user community and the IS department. Applications development is prioritized within the client unit and the client computing resources are managed within the client unit. What we see in this hybrid is the separation of information systems functions into some that remain the province of the IS department (network management, data administration, and standards setting and enforcement) and some that are decentralized to the user groups (applications development and maintenance, some database maintenance, and some operations). This trend will continue and the IS department's centralized responsibilities will become transparent to the organization—somewhat like the telephone is today.

Which Structure Is Best?

According to John Rockart and colleagues [1978], there are three major dimensions to be considered in any discussion of centralization or decentralization; systems management, systems operations, and systems development. Each can be positioned with an independent degree of centralization or decentralization, as Exhibit 5-2 illustrates.

In general, organizations tend to have more centralized operations and less centralized development activities. In fact, the trend toward decentralized applications systems development is so strong and well-entrenched that one might well be resigned to the fact that it will become even more so in the years to come. It would seem to be a trend that will continue—and with good reason. Management and control activities are so varied that wide differences are seen in practice from company to company. Jack Buchanan and Richard Linowes [1980] have refined the three-dimensional view by specifying that development and operations have an execution component as well as a control (management) component that might separately be centralized or decentralized. Thus, a company might allow functional units to determine their own computer use or project activity (i.e., decentralized execution) but have highly uniform and structures

Exhibit 5-2

Dimensions of Centralization/Decentralization

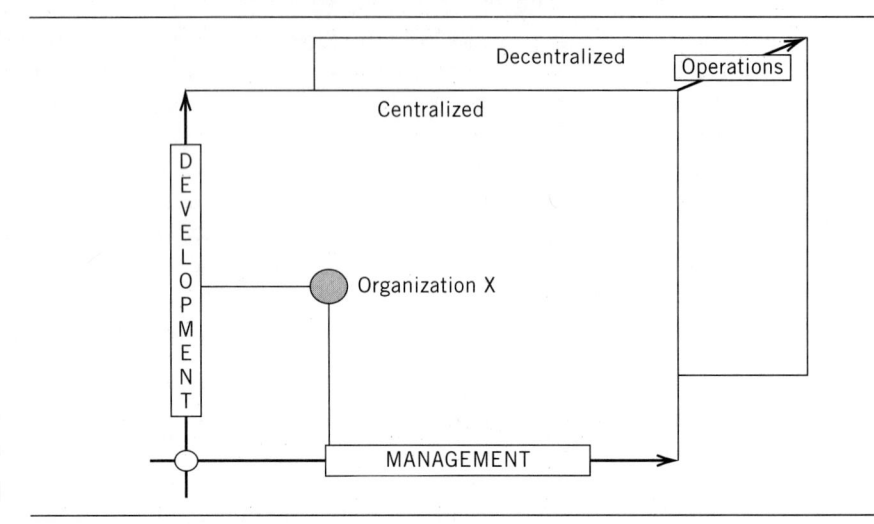

```
                    Decentralized     [Operations]
              Centralized
    D
    E
    V
    E
    L
    O      ● Organization X
    P
    M
    E
    N
    T
         ○────── MANAGEMENT ──────→
```

standards or budget restrictions (i.e., centralized control). This is the hybrid structure described above. Other permutations are also conceivable. Using Buchanan's schematic (altered for presentation), Thomas H. Johnson of Nolan, Norton & Company has revealed patterns that differ from industry to industry (Exhibit 5-3). Even though the breadth or height of each square illustrates the amount of variation that exists between companies in the same industry, it is the general contrast in patterns from industry to industry that stands out.

Centralization or Decentralization of Tasks to be Executed

Within areas as complex as management, development, and operations, individual elements may be treated differently. For instance, the use of an IS product might be decentralized whereas security authorization could remain centralized. Buchanan and Linowes illustrate the probable pattern of decentralized versus centralized tasks to be executed in the data-processing unit (Exhibit 5-4). This pattern varies from unit to unit. Manufacturing, for example, could have a system configuration that is more decentralized than that of accounting.

Function to Process

Yet another factor to consider is the extent to which companies are changing their organizational structure from one that, heretofore, has been organized along business functions to one that follows a process structure. Since companies are focusing more on a customer-driven mode of operation and since form follows

Exhibit 5-3

Decentralization Postures of Three Industry Groups

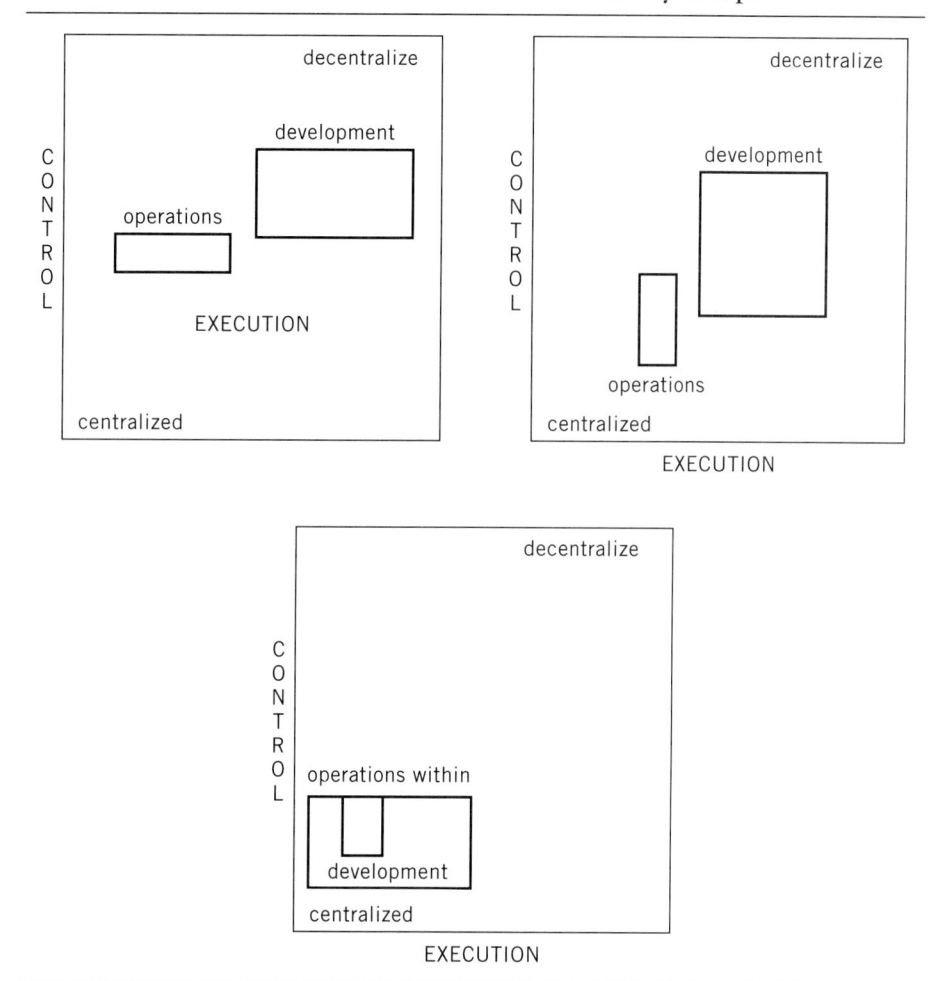

```
         decentralize                              decentralize
              development                              development
C                                    C
O     operations                     O
N                                    N
T                                    T
R                                    R
O                                    O    operations
L          EXECUTION                 L
    centralized                          centralized
                                                  EXECUTION
```

```
                    decentralize
      C
      O
      N
      T
      R
      O    operations within
      L
                development
           centralized
              EXECUTION
```

SOURCE: Thomas H. Johnson, presentation entitled "Characterization of Distributed Data Processing," Nolan, Norton & Co., Lexington, MA, 1982.

function, it follows naturally that they would adopt a process structure. For the IS department this presents some rather interesting problems as well as opportunities. Such an orientation requires that information systems professionals learn, not about a single business function, but rather about a process that contains most, if not all, of the business functions. Fortunately this problem is only temporal. On the opportunity side, the IS department can now focus support on the processes that can be measured and relate directly to value-added activities. That means that the IS department can measure its value to the company. It also means that

Exhibit 5-4

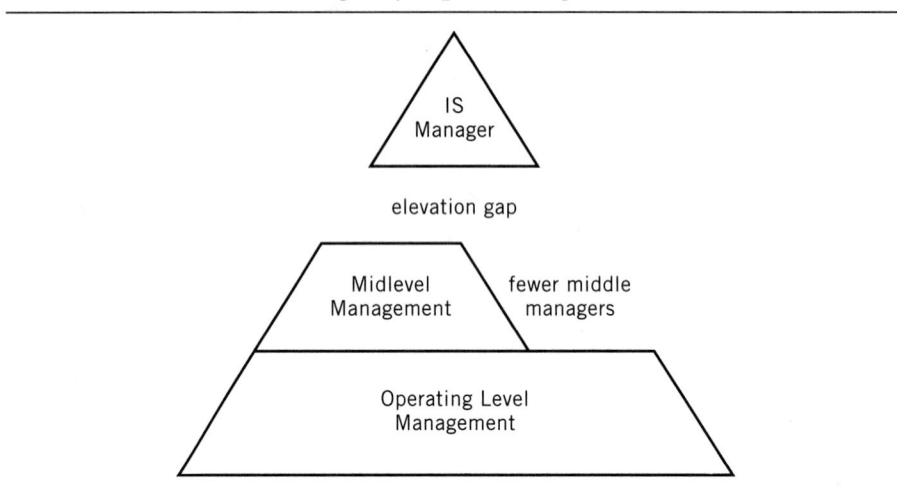

Technologically Expanded Organization

```
         /\
        /  \
       / IS \
      /Manager\
     /_____\
     
     elevation gap
     
      _____
     /        \    fewer middle
    / Midlevel \   managers
   / Management \
  /_____\
  /              \
 / Operating Level\
/   Management    \
/_____\
```

SOURCE: Derived from Darrell E. Owen, "Information Systems Organization—Keeping Pace with the Pressures," *Sloan Management Review,* 27(3), Spring 1986, p. 64. Reprinted by permission of the publisher. Copyright 1986 by the Sloan Management Review Association. All rights reserved.

the IS department can further decentralize its functions to these processes. And finally, it means that the IS department can build partnerships using the processes that define their company's business activities as the foundation.

Cross-Functional and Self-Managed Teams

A natural byproduct of the process orientation is the emergence of cross-functional and self-managed teams. To develop applications in a process structure it is necessary that teams representing a number of business functions be created. In many cases this expands the matrix concept across the entire organization. That raises the complexity of systems development project management to new heights. For instance, this escalates priority setting and resource allocation from within a single functional discipline to typically all functional disciplines.

Mainframe to Client/Server: The Current Situation

Having traced the historical evolution of the IS department in the organization, we see that both the breadth and depth of the IS manager's responsibilities have changed dramatically since the data processing days. The hardware environment has evolved from single-batch to remote-batch to terminals, to micros, to distributed and networked systems, to client/server architectures. Software applications have evolved from simple accounting to control systems to decision-making systems, and special-purpose uses (as reflected by the islands of technology) have also emerged. Software has become so sophisticated and affordable that the typical professional can become analyst and programmer to supply many of his or her own needs. Organizations no longer rely heavily on skilled programmers; users can and are doing their own applications development work independently of the IS programming staff. The natural cause of computer proliferation has created a cadre of IEMgrs (TP and tp) at the extremes of using technology and process effectively. Early IEMgrs tended to be self-motivated and self-directed. They had a need, envisioned the application of technology, and took the initiative to learn and implement it.

The organizational reach of the IS manager's job has also undergone major changes. Senior managers expect a greater corporate-level contribution from the IS manager and have raised the IS manager to a higher and more responsible position in the organization. This has created what at least one author, Darrell Owen [1986], has called an "elevation gap." As Owen explains, this gap gives rise to several concerns. The most immediate is that the expectations of senior management are raised, and the IS manager is not always prepared to meet those heightened expectations. Another concern is that because the IS manager is increasingly drawn into corporate issues, he or she has less time to spend actually managing the IS department's operations. In those IS departments that need a lot of attention from the IS manager, there will be problems. As new technologies and methodologies are added, the department ends up supporting them without the necessary degree of managerial control. Exhibit 5-4 graphically illustrates this elevation gap.

Also, we see the emergence of the IEMgr(Tp) about this time. This appearance was not the result of initiatives on the part of IS managers as much as it was forced upon them by senior management. The IS manager, because of circumstance, had to become an IEMgr(Tp). We turn now to consider the functional areas within the IS department and how they are being impacted.

Applications Development

Applications is moving into the hands of users. We are quickly reaching the point where applications development will become the responsibility of the user. This does not exclude information systems professionals from participating in applications development, it just changes their role and responsibility. For applications that are process- or function-based we recommend that the project manager be the IEMgr(TP) from the process or function. Among the team members will be specialists from the IS department. Their role is that of guiding and consulting. Their guiding role is to keep feasible alternatives in front of the team for their consideration. Their consulting role is to offer their subject matter expertise wherever and whenever it is requested.

Data Resources

The movement from function to process structures requires that an enterprise-wide data model be in place. Processes must draw information from across several functional areas in order to operate effectively; there must be a data model in place to serve the processes. Organizations that grew up without such a model in place have a major task at hand to build such a model. The data model reflects how the organization does business and that means the setting of policy and procedure.

Software Infrastructure

The megasystems that drive the business will continue to be the proper domain of the IS department. These systems provide support to those who support customers (both internal and external) and IS must assure that those who support customers are having their needs met. Everything must be measured in terms of customer satisfaction. This is a new way of valuing the software infrastructure but it is a necessary way if the organization expects to remain competitive.

Hardware Infrastructure

The effectiveness of software infrastructure is limited by the effectiveness of hardware infrastructure. Accessibility (both local and remote), ease of use, and responsiveness are critical to provide world-class support to those who serve customers.

Standards

With the continuing decentralization of information systems functions comes a need for standards across those functions. Consider, for example, applications development. Some of the areas that will be considered for standardization will be documentation, maintenance procedures, choice of development tools, testing, training, naming conventions, and others. The IS department is the only entity that should be considered as steward of those standards. They are therefore responsible for defining those standards (in collaboration with the user community). We will have more to say on this topic in Part III.

◆ PERVASIVENESS AND DECENTRALIZATION

As computing continues to become more pervasive throughout the enterprise there will be a strong push and pull toward decentralization. Perhaps a more accurate observation would be that the computer—much like the telephone—will disappear into the woodwork of the organization. It is there when we need it, wherever we need it, and we aren't too concerned about who manages it.

IEMgr and Power User Relationships

The push toward decentralization comes from the IS department. Those who initially carried the moniker "power user" were looked upon as loose cannons by the IS department. They were a never-ending stream of users who bothered the IS professional with inane and obscure questions that raised doubt as to whether they were doing real work for their department or whether they were just playing with the technology. From the perspective of the IS department, the power users seemed to be neglected by their managers. They were seemingly free to roam around in the technology at will. Their managers paid little attention probably because they did not understand what was being done even though the power users could offer a rationale for their activities when asked.

Despite the nuisance, the power user could be a valuable resource to the astute IS manager. Power users were the first professionals who understood both the business function and the technology. In a sense, they were the stone age IEMgr(TP). If channeled properly, they were a bridge into their department for the IS manager. If ignored, they could discredit any attempts by the IS manager. And so IEMgrs now represent the pull toward decentralization. It is in their best interest to make sure that the technology serves their area of responsibility.

Work Group Computing

Initially, departmental computing needs were confined to one business unit; soon, the pressure grew for even more sophisticated systems to place the organization in a more favorable strategic position. Departmental computing groups began to see that the strategic benefit of their systems could be enhanced by integrating them with one or more systems that have logical or physical linkages in the value chain. This necessitated the development of systems that transcended departmental boundaries and dealt more with a defined business activity rather than a function-specific activity. Indeed, in those organizations that are reconfiguring themselves around business processes, that requirement naturally emerges. Early in this evolution we saw the emergence of work group computing.

Work groups initially arose out of a need to access data that resided in separate departmental databases or resided in a corporate database but to which one department did not have access. Once the security issues were resolved and read-only access privileges established, obstacles were neutralized and applications enhancements were possible. More recently, as processes became the focal point, business function experts began to investigate process improvement and reengineering possibilities. Success required collaboration between functional areas. The work group took on a new mission, that of business redesign as a pathway to establishing competitive advantage.

With work group computing, the IS department must establish standards, documentation, security, and controls. Because systems development and processing activities occur beyond the purview of the IS department, it is more difficult for the department to know how things are being done and whether they are being done according to standards. The IS manager, the process owner, and the business unit manager have a joint responsibility in this regard. We return to this discussion in Chapters 13 and 14.

◆ ORGANIZATIONAL STRUCTURES: SOME BASIC CHOICES

So far we have discussed the IS department as an organizational entity. In this section we look inside the IS department and discuss a variety of organizational structures. Specific attention is paid to how these structures fit into the context of the contemporary enterprise.

Apart from reacting to the influence of corporate organizational strategy, IS managers can select organizational options that facilitate distinctive strategies appropriate to the IS department. These options may derive from the IS strategic plan, the skills and experience of IS personnel, the professional preferences of those personnel, and other sources. What follows is a discussion of some common organizational schemes along with their advantages and disadvantages.

Functional Structure

This is perhaps the oldest form of IS department. With this alignment, personnel are grouped by what they know. For example, programmers are separated from analysts, systems programmer duties are grouped by software product, or systems and programming staff are grouped by the technologies they work with. Exhibit 5-5 is an example of one functional alignment. This describes a small department. As the department grows, new specialization areas will appear on the organizational chart. These specializations might form around hardware platforms (minis, client/server, PC, etc.), software platforms, or within application areas such as marketing, finance, manufacturing, distribution, and so on. Exhibit 5-6 lists the advantages and disadvantages of the functional structure.

Project Structure

IS personnel can also be grouped by the tasks they perform, regardless of the skills required. For example, operators can have broad responsibilities for running several computers or pieces of equipment. The task of systems and programming professionals might be divided between maintenance or large projects. Task alignment can either broaden or restrict the variety of work in comparison to skill alignment. Exhibit 5-7 illustrates one popular way in which IS professionals' work responsibilities are compartmentalized.

This approach is more typically found in large organizations where a method helps keep attention focused on many important activities. Some of the pros and cons of the project structure are listed in Exhibit 5-8.

A variation on this alignment is the service alignment. Jobs can be organized by the group to which a service is being provided. Systems and programming is

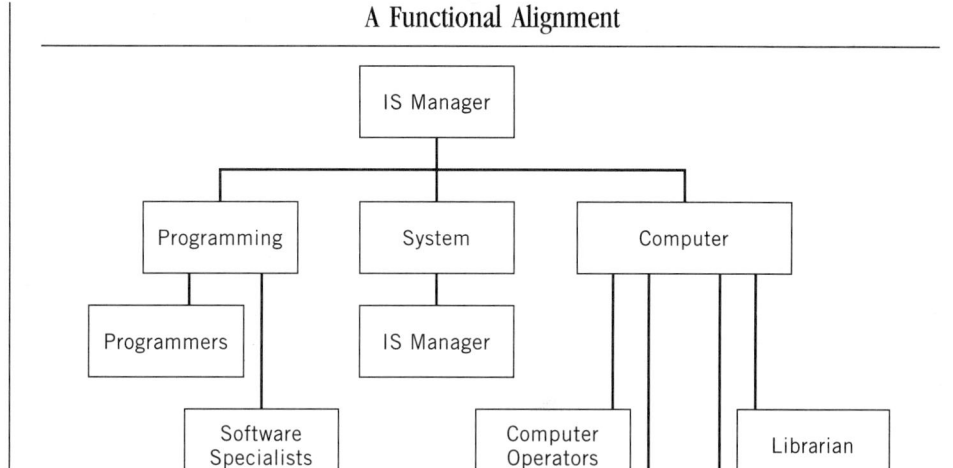

Exhibit 5-5

A Functional Alignment

```
                        IS Manager
        ┌───────────────────┼───────────────────┐
   Programming           System              Computer
        │                   │           ┌───────┴───────┐
   Programmers          IS Manager   Computer        Librarian
        │                            Operators           │
   Software                              │            Scheduler
   Specialists                       Data Entry
```

often segregated into groups conforming to user departments (manufacturing, marketing, etc.). In certain large companies the entire IS department (including operations and technical support) is aligned in such a manner; only IS service and support groups such as training administration or quality assurance might remain centrally grouped, and these units provide services to functional support groups while the IS manager coordinates as the common boss.

As a result of delayering, process structures, cross-functional systems development, and interorganizational partnerships, we are seeing a growth in the

Exhibit 5-6

Advantages and Disadvantages of a Functional Alignment

ADVANTAGES	DISADVANTAGES
Everybody understands his or her tasks	The IS manager spends too much time on problems arising among organizational elements
The structure confers stability	Training and development opportunities are poor
Greater opportunity for the development of specialized skills	Higher risk of project failure
Provides a system of checks and balances	Communication within the department is more difficult
Standardization with a functional area is easily possible	

Exhibit 5-7: A Project Alignment

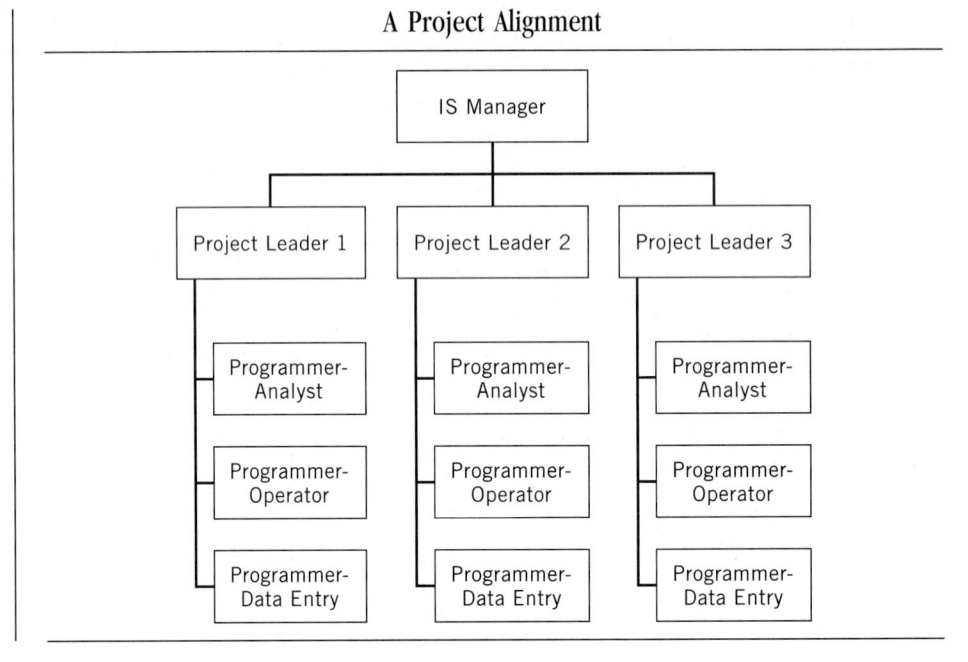

```
                        IS Manager
                            |
        ┌───────────────────┼───────────────────┐
   Project Leader 1   Project Leader 2   Project Leader 3
        |                   |                   |
   Programmer-        Programmer-         Programmer-
   Analyst            Analyst             Analyst
        |                   |                   |
   Programmer-        Programmer-         Programmer-
   Operator           Operator            Operator
        |                   |                   |
   Programmer-        Programmer-         Programmer-
   Data Entry         Data Entry          Data Entry
```

frequency of project structures among organizations. Some of the project teams are permanent (self-directed work teams, and process structures); others are temporary (task forces, applications development). There is every reason to believe that this trend will continue.

Matrix Structure

This structure is a hybrid that simultaneously accommodates functional and project approaches. According to this structure, units maintain a dual allegiance: one to a functional group and the other to a project group (see Exhibit 5-9). As

Exhibit 5-8: Advantages and Disadvantages of Project Organization

ADVANTAGES	DISADVANTAGES
Everyone understands departmental work	Structure is not highly stable
Structure is highly receptive to new ideas	Structure demands continuous management attention
Structure offers greater adaptability	Few opportunities to develop special skills
Shorter chain of command, which makes each person more visible	No clear career path

Exhibit 5-9

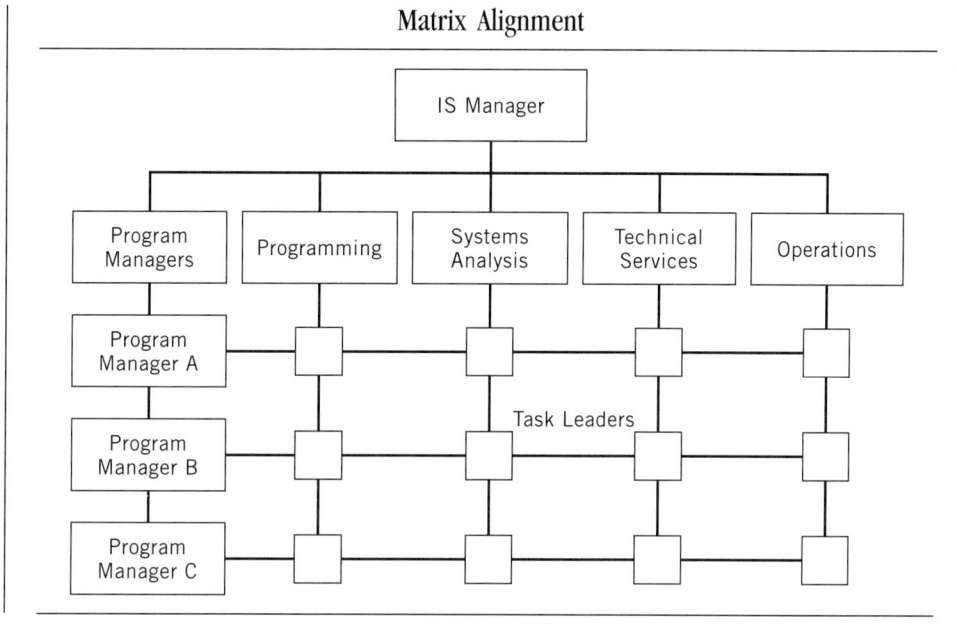

Matrix Alignment

```
                        IS Manager
                            |
    ┌───────────┬───────────┼───────────┬───────────┐
 Program    Programming  Systems    Technical   Operations
 Managers               Analysis    Services
    │           │           │           │           │
 Program ──────□───────────□───────────□───────────□
 Manager A
    │           │           │           │           │
 Program ──────□───────────□──Task Leaders─────────□
 Manager B
    │           │           │           │           │
 Program ──────□───────────□───────────□───────────□
 Manager C
```

one might suspect from an environment with parallel lines of authority, managing can be complex and fraught with bureaucracy.

A large, dynamic organization that prides itself on flexibility would be likely to use a matrix structure. This approach has the advantages and disadvantages listed in Exhibit 5-10. The matrix structure can be a supportive environment for the development of information-enabled professionals. To see why this is so, consider the responsibilities of the project managers vis-a-vis the function managers. Project managers are responsible for getting projects done on time, within budget, and according to customer specifications. The function managers are responsible

Exhibit 5-10

Advantages and Disadvantages of a Matrix Organization

ADVANTAGES	DISADVANTAGES
Better assessment of individual skills and professional development	Success is highly dependent on interaction between functional manager and project manager
Better utilization of specialization skills	Project management more difficult; project manager does not have line authority
Highly flexible and adaptable to changing environments	Greater potential for political difficulties
	Problems in communication because of dual reporting

for staff development and deployment. If we view the development responsibility as one that includes multiskilling the worker, we have an ideal environment for developing IEMgrs.

Task Force and Self-Directed Work Team Structures

With the trend toward enterprise structures becoming more business process aligned, the IS department has adapted its structure accordingly. Task forces, some of which become self-directed entities, are becoming commonplace. For example, an IS department might separate its business analysts, applications programmers, and technical support staff by business processes and assign them to the process owners. IEMgrs(TP) can be developed in this manner. While decentralized for work assignment, they remain centralized for skills development. This matrix-type structure assures meeting user needs as it retains the advantages of centralizing those functions for which there are economies of scale. This is a good example of form following function.

In this structure the task forces and self-directed work teams are often self-sufficient. They turn to the IS department for technical support, training, and consulting. Observe that the IS department becomes reactive in this structure and the task forces and self-directed work teams become the proactive element, an interesting twist and one that shows considerable promise in customer-driven enterprises.

◆ EVOLUTION TO A SUPPORT ORGANIZATION

By now we have suggested that the IS department is evolving to a higher form both in terms of how it functions internally and how it relates to its external user community. In this section we discuss these notions further. We see additional examples of "form follows function."

Internal Considerations

The degree to which support services are emphasized relative to the major functions to which they provide assistance is an organizational question with implications for how power is distributed to line managers, staff managers, and ultimately the IS manager. The training function can serve as an example. When the duties and attendant resources of training belong to line managers of systems and programming operations, and so on, there is a greater latitude and autonomy for each group than if training were provided by a separate group under a training manager. If training support comes from a separate organizational unit it could mean less control for each line manager but with possible service benefits that come from economies of scale. If the training manager of this separate unit reports directly to the IS manager, not only are this manager and other line managers nominal peers, but the IS manager is in a position to become more involved in deciding on training resource deployment and thus to exercise more detailed control. The same analogy can be extended to quality assurance and other internal support areas.

This method of gaining (or, conversely, distributing) control might be consistently applied to all internal support functions. Or it might be used selectively to emphasize or deemphasize a selected function. For instance, IS managers might have database administrators report directly to them as a way of devoting attention to and exercising control over data administration services.

External Considerations

Understand that this interaction is a collaborative of the IS manager and IEMgmt. Furthermore, the customer-driven philosophy of organizational structure carries into the IS department just as it does other units of the enterprise. The IS manager has been and will continue to play a more senior, executive role within the organization. Essentially, the perspective of the IS manager must become executive in nature, so that the manager's methods of directing the IS department can stay in tune with overall business and organizational goals and needs. To this end, the IS leader must develop an acute ability to separate the critical from the important, the vital from the meaningful, and the essential from the popular. In any case, IS managers and IEMgrs are now major players in the success of the organization as it attempts to exploit information technology.

Although personal involvement and "managing by walking around" will still be necessary, the future IS manager must more directly influence the organization's use of information technology by establishing specific policies and procedures. As the territory for which the IS manager's department is responsible increases and as more actual developmental undertakings fall to user departments, the IS manager, in collaboration with IEMgrs, will increasingly rely on setting rules and guidelines, however liberal, to exert influence. Tailoring appropriate policies requires a strategic vision, political sensitivity, and a keen awareness of behavioral issues.

Then there is the unrelenting pressure to make increasingly productive use of information technology. IEMgmt must take a leadership role here and set an organizational strategy that is characterized by the right blend of aggressiveness and caution. On the one hand, experimentation, although encouraging new uses, also has the potential of wasting or misdirecting effort and diffusing a rigorous pursuit of benefits. Too much control, on the other hand, can stifle the kind of creativity that uncovers obscure but revolutionary applications of technology. Moreover, overly heavy control may discourage even clear-cut and obviously beneficial applications. As illustrated in Exhibit 5-11, if one accepts that too little technology will decrease technical benefits because fruitful opportunities for automation will be neglected, but too much technology will decrease benefits by encouraging wasteful and inappropriate usage, then it follows that some hypo-

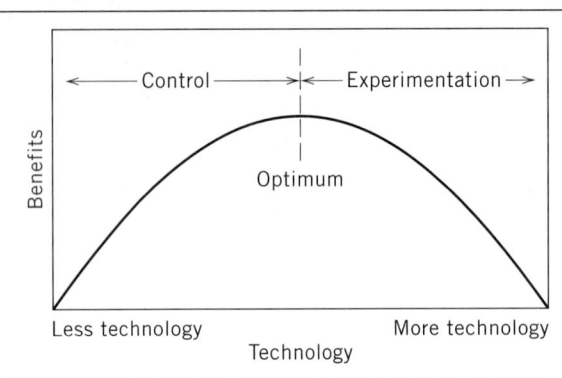

Exhibit 5-11 | **Control and Experimentation in the Introduction of New Technology**

[Graph showing Benefits vs. Technology as an inverted parabola, with "Control" on the left side and "Experimentation" on the right side, meeting at "Optimum" at the peak. X-axis ranges from "Less technology" to "More technology".]

thetical middle ground—the "optimum" in the exhibit—will maximize the benefits of technology. The goal of the IS manager and IEMgmt is to find that optimum point.

All of this translates into a major challenge for all information technology stakeholders in the organization. The organization's investments in technology are necessarily complex and diverse. There are no silver bullets, no all-seeing sages. We are in a new world and are learning how best to deploy our information resource through on-the-job experiences. Companies are placed in difficult situations where windows of opportunity open and close overnight and narrow as the competition joins the battle. The need to invest is clear. How to invest is not so clear.

◆ STEERING COMMITTEES

Some would argue that the IS manager should not report to a senior executive but rather to a steering committee [Richard Nolan in Lasden, 1980]. The argument is that the senior manager does not have enough time to devote to the IS manager. In organizations undergoing significant restructuring and maturation with respect to its use of technology, this argument may be valid. However, there will be value in having the CEO participate in the steering committee in order to bring the IS manager into the corporate strategic planning process. In those organizations that do have a steering committee in place, they generally act as a board of directors. Their basic responsibilities will be to establish priorities, control expenses, and make policy decisions. To be more specific, they are the direction-setting body when it comes to the integration of corporate strategy and IS strategy. This happens through the planning process (see Chapter 4). Implementation of the strategic plan involves resource allocation, determining the level of resources to be made available, and their deployment. The organizational placement and deployment of staff is part of their responsibility too. Finally, some method of evaluation must rest with the steering committee. After all, they are charged with the best use of technology and therefore must also be responsible for its contribution to the goals of the organization.

◆ REPORTING TO THE CEO

A situation in which the IS manager reports directly to the CEO of an organization may come about as the result of careful and deliberate planning or it may simply be an accident. It may also be the result of a decision that was correct at some point in the organization's history but is no longer appropriate. In any case, although reporting to the CEO carries a certain status, it also entails meeting certain implicit expectations, handling certain kinds of corporate political issues, and understanding certain behavioral dimensions. The risks are high; job security is low. For the successful IS manager, the rewards to both the organization and the individual are great.

John Rockart offers the following thoughts on when it makes sense to have the IS manager report to the CEO [Lasden, 1980]:

- When the CEO is analytically minded and wants to use this approach to manage the organization
- When the IS manager is managerially as well as technically skilled
- When the IS department has developed to the point where it is considered a true management resource

In this reporting relationship, the IS manager must realize that the CEO will be evaluating him or her with the same yardstick used for other senior managers reporting at this level. If the IS manager is continually sensitive to the bottom-line impact of decisions, has good business sense, can communicate effectively, and—most importantly—can self-govern, he or she will survive. Herbert Halbrecht contends that most IS managers cannot survive in this type of environment [Lasden, 1980]. Being a technician is fundamentally irrelevant; what is needed is a business leader who happens to have, as the tools of his or her trade, information technology. In other words, he or she must be an IEMgr(Tp).

For organizations that do elevate IS to the top, there are several noteworthy hazards and "disconnects" [Wang, 1994]. When the CEO gets involved in IS development details, he or she may impose a perspective that will subvert the primary purpose of a system, rendering it less effective for the actual user. In addition, IS managers who enjoy easy access to the CEO may be less inclined to build real consensus among users and the result may be a dangerous buildup of resentment. Furthermore, a busy CEO who is given a direct role in making decisions about IS may be distracted often enough to keep the IS department perpetually in limbo.

For any manager who has access to the top, effective communication with subordinates becomes more difficult; people invariably do not speak to such a manager as freely as to those with less elevated connections. Nonetheless, some CEOs, such as Terrance Hanold (president of Pillsbury in the late 1960s and early 1970s), have IS managers report directly to them, on the reasoning that other managers will grasp the importance of IS and be more likely to use it [Lasden, 1980].

◆ OUTSOURCING: AN INTRODUCTION

Our discussion of the placement of the IS department and its organizational structure would not be complete without some mention of outsourcing. More details of the topic are in the next chapter.

We have lost count of the number of times we have read about organizations downsizing by adopting an outsourcing strategy only to find that they gave away their ability to quickly respond to strategic opportunity when it arose. The net result is capsizing, not downsizing. Every organization has a number of core competencies that are critical to their success and competitiveness. The internal services that support these core business activities are also a critical part of their food chain. Someone once said, "Either support a customer or support someone who supports a customer." To do otherwise is to be a candidate for outsourcing. Such services as payroll, food service, grounds maintenance, and security are obvious candidates for outsourcing.

What about information systems? Are there any opportunities for outsourcing here? The answer to this question begs another question. What parts of the information systems function are strategic and which aren't? In that answer lie the opportunities for outsourcing the information systems function. Some obvious possibilities are operations, help desk, training, and network management. A bad choice is applications development. While we choose not to name them, we are aware of organizations that have outsourced applications development only to realize that they no longer had control over a strategic resource. We became aware of some of these situations through being asked to help such organizations get out of their outsourcing arrangement.

Let us turn to a discussion of several areas that might be appropriate for outsourcing—keeping in mind the trap of giving away our strategic coins for the sake of lowering the cost of doing information processing business.

Operations

First on the list would be operations. This would be a limited form of facilities management and might prove cost effective if for no other reason than keeping the technology up to date and keeping a trained technical support unit in place. For some organizations this area has been particularly troublesome.

Network Support

The larger the organization the less likely it would be to outsource this support function. There will be economies of scale here and the IS manager should work the numbers.

Hot Line

This is an interesting consideration which we are seeing being outsourced more frequently in recent months. The issue is one of keeping a staff up to date on the latest revisions and new applications. As end-user software becomes more sophisticated and varied, it becomes more difficult for an organization to provide quality and timely support. Outsourcing this function is no more difficult than changing the phone number of the help desk. It is an area worthy of consideration.

Applications Development

Except for very complex and time sensitive situations, this function should rarely be outsourced. Contracts may be let on occasion but to completely outsource this function would be to put a company's competitive position at risk. For one, the company would give up some of the flexibility that is needed as applications are developed and business conditions change during the process. Also, what the company may place at the top of the priority list, the vendor may not. If your vendor typically has large companies as clients and your company is small, you may not get the preferential treatment you would like.

Reflections

GENERAL CONCEPTS

1. As applications development continues to pass into the hands of the end user, what major problems would you foresee?
   How might they be mitigated?
   How is this transition related to Nolan's stages model?

2. Information systems departments have continually oscillated between centralized and decentralized structures. Eventually a hybrid of the two will evolve and stabilize.
   Which functions should be centralized and which should be decentralized? Why? What is the effect of moving from mainframe computer systems to client/server networks in the design of different centralized/decentralized structures?

3. As organizations move from a function to a process structure, what would you perceive as the major problems to be resolved?
   How would you recommend they be resolved?

4. Experts tend to agree that the project form of organizational structure is returning.

Assuming this return to project orientation is the case, what major problems do you foresee in such a transition? How would you recommend they be avoided?

5. IS managers and other IEMgmt team members have within their groups supercomputer-fluent "power users" for selected systems and applications hardware and software.

   How can this power be harnessed to the advantage of the enterprise?
   Does the enterprise have reward systems in place to address the unique contributions of each of these groups?
   How can work group computing be integrated into any scheme to harness this power?

6. Self-directed work teams can get out of control. Sometimes they address issues well beyond their scope or do not include problems within their scope. The project is too political, or too complex to solve during the next few months. Each team member may have a different set of criteria for evaluating work selection and priority.

   What conditions must be established with teams so that they work in harmony and address real concerns of the enterprise?
   Examine the various types of control and how they can be effectively managed.
   Examine a self-directed work team in an industry for issues, problems, and solutions. Are the solutions unique to that enterprise or can they be used for others?

7. A recent text by Wang [1994] suggests several ways for CEOs and CIOs to come to grips with information technology as an "enabler." He uses the term "disconnect" regarding business managers and IS professionals.

   Are IS professionals disconnected from the enterprise? If so, why and how?
   How can business strategic planning be conducted to ensure that information technology is included in all phases of activity?
   Why is outsourcing such an important concept in strategic planning for the enterprise?

Chapter 6

Acquiring and Managing Computer Resources

◆ ◆ ◆

◆ GROWING IMPORTANCE OF USER/VENDOR RELATIONSHIPS

Computing is everyone's concern. Planning for computing is everyone's business. An important trend of the past decade is that managing these resources has become ubiquitous. Now and in the future, all levels of functional and work group managers will participate actively in planning and implementing information technology for personal and organizational productivity. The current procurement and allocation scene is somewhat chaotic in that all workers buy and use computers collectively for some major and enterprisewide applications but act independently for most localized applications. Outside of work, individuals enjoy the benefits of rapidly decreasing microcomputer prices with increased throughput and capacity using very user-friendly software.

Once computing becomes a full enterprisewide activity where strategies and operations depend significantly on the information-enabled organization and its workforce, the process-people relationship becomes more complex and difficult to manage in a coordinated, collaborative, and synergistic way. Social, political, legal, psychological, ethical, and practical issues emerge and complement economics factors in decision making for information technology. In addition, computers no longer are divorced from information communications (networking) technology. Madron's [1991] text demonstrates that the size of the installation and micro-mini-mainframe classification schemes alone have little value in understanding human-computer interaction. Thinking in terms of client-server systems, multitasking, and multiuser functions is more helpful in designing an information-enabling environment.

In order to manage information, both people and technology are needed. The situation has changed dramatically from the past four decades when decisions were identified and made by a handful of operating executives and/or information systems professionals. Now, management functions are scattered throughout the firm. Individuals, departments, and divisions buy products and services from a more diverse, aggressive, and sometimes shortlived vendor establishment armed with an arsenal of product options.

Numerous and frequent contract negotiations replace a few major procurements over a five-year time frame. Long-range master plans are needed to provide some framework for addressing the rapidly changing global business landscape; short-term solutions must be consistent with a flexible master plan, which is updated on an annual basis. Managers should be information enabled themselves so that they can be effective in computer resource acquisition and allocation. IEMgrs have to be "renaissance" persons [Mensching, 1991] and fit technology to the organization in a human-centered and business-savvy manner.

Case study research by the authors on quick-fix solutions (short-term answers not related to long-range planning) indicates these conclusions for computer systems development:

1. End-users may have ready knowledge on the technical aspects of computing (machine capability, memory, speed, and commercial software), but flounder when files are incompatible with other systems, when vendors are not available for operational deadlines, or when maintenance problems exist beyond the warranty.
2. Funding for system enhancements and training for use of software is more difficult to justify than the original purchase.
3. Purchases on sales and special promotions are not preceded by analysis and feasibility studies.
4. Overeager and seductive vendors make promises to get the sale and because of personnel displacement or replacement do not follow up on after-sale services.
5. IS professionals may very well have not been involved in the procurement and therefore have no obligation to help in addressing problems or renegotiating contracts.
6. Contractual terms and conditions are specified by the vendor and not the user.
7. Access authority to the new system is undefined.
8. Expectations among IS professionals, users, and vendors are not delineated, causing confusion, finger-pointing, frustration, and anxiety for all.

A better approach aimed at preventing these shortfalls is for the organization to create a process which requires a long-range *and flexible* master plan for information technology. Such a plan would be consistent with enterprise goals and objectives and developed following TQM methods (especially team empowerment, collaborative concepts, and "process" orientation). It is necessary for users and IS professionals to collaborate on policies and procedures. Vendor relationships should be developed for the long term with renegotiations based on predetermined issues.

◆ OUTSOURCING ISSUES: PART I REVISITED

In order to relate planning for procurement of information technology and resulting vendor relationships to the topics discussed in Part I of this text, an appropriate starting point is the STEP Model introduced in Chapter 1 and reproduced here with the staff-technology plane (enterprises having achieved high quality, improved customer service, and fast response through the proper mix of people and information technology) given more focus on information infrastructure and the types of IEMgrs needed to plan and act for computer resources (Exhibit 6-1).

All four types of IEMgrs are needed to either sustain the position of the enterprise or move the enterprise to the vortex (T,P,S) by overcoming deficiencies in technology capability and/or in user application of technology. The IEMgr(TP) is capable of designing and implementing technology applications for their function or process. Other IEMgrs with varying degrees of technology and process (tP, tp, and Tp) are in either the IS department or business function area and serve in more passive and supportive roles. For IEMgrs(Tp) with more expertise in technical matters, their primary responsibility is to ensure that IT is linked to business functions and processes and that the infrastructure is planned and implemented for flexibility and nonobsolescence.

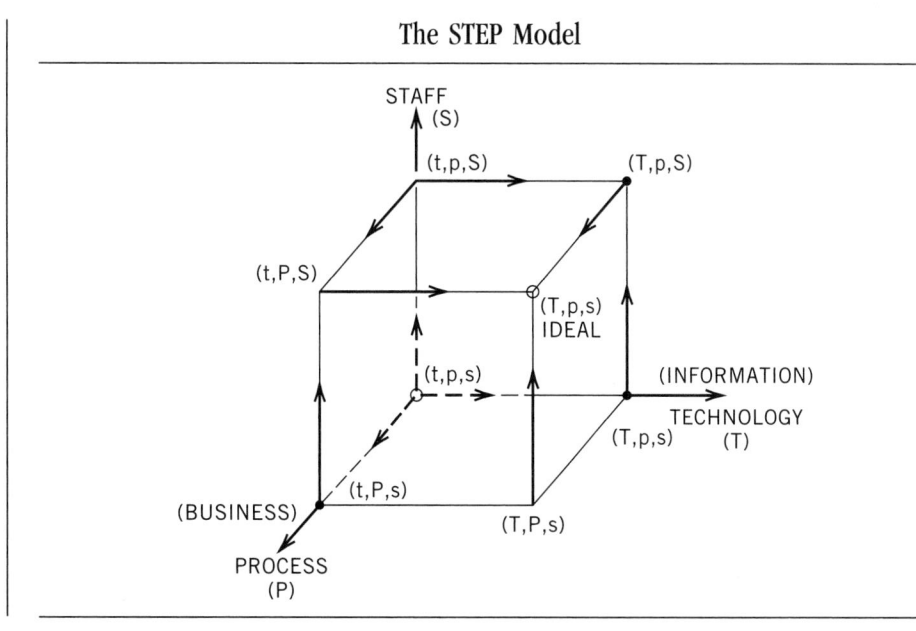

Exhibit 6-1 | The STEP Model

Before we can discuss why, when, and how outsourcing can be incorporated into this model by the various types of IEMgrs and their business colleagues, it is instructive to review some topics of Part I and relate them to the general procurement process and raise the major outsourcing issues. Later in this chapter, we will address these issues with more detail and suggest guidelines to assist the IEMgr in determining whether to outsource, and if so, for what types of activity. Here, outsourcing is used in the most general way and means using personnel other than in-house staff for computer-related activity. It does not include vendor-supplied assistance for normal maintenance of hardware and software. It does include myriad consulting services associated with computer systems definition, negotiation, installation, and other management and training functions.

In Chapter 1, the changing nature of the workplace and the concept of strategic opportunity is introduced. It may seem obvious that the first outsourcing issue is strategic advantage. Does the operation provide strategic advantage and differentiate the enterprise from competitors [Lacity and Hirschheim, 1995]? Does it maximize flexibility and control? Clearly, from the research of Lacity and Hirschheim and from experience of the authors in both soliciting and providing outsourcing activity, the decision is based on numerous variables, is not a yes/no response, and has little commonality with other organizations. Their research of 40 companies and 61 outsourcing decisions shows that approximately half of those decisions involving "selective outsourcing" met objectives and satisfied users. The other extremes (20% or 80% outsourced) have met with some degree of failure because of management failures: less-than-expected cost savings, inflexible contracts, lack of response to current business demands, and poorer customer service.

Outsourcing can be viewed as a continuum from 0 percent to 100 percent. The process may very well include more than one vendor. Cross describes a scenario for the BP Exploration Operating Company, which used a team of three major contractors to work together to deliver a single seamless service to 42 businesses around the globe. They relinquished operations to focus on IT doing business, not running the business. Cost reduction was set as the most important target; after a poor-performing year, the targets were reset to service responsiveness, quality, and customer satisfaction. Selective outsourcing is approximately near the middle and appears to be the best approach. The adjective "selective" means that some analysis must be performed to determine at the outset what activities are appropriate for outsourcing. It is not good enough to list a few questions about strategic nature, elusive requirements, disruptiveness to operations, and available expertise. Some framework is needed to direct the analysis in an informative and complete manner. After a few more comments on the remaining chapters of Part I, we will provide such a framework for analytical review.

Chapter 2 presents the learning organization and the four types of IEMgrs needed to direct the effort for information enablement of the enterprise. It emphasizes adapting to the environment and identifying the skills necessary for these managers to address the changing environment in an effective way. In terms of information technology procurement, it is difficult to gain the experience of the vendor community in a short time. Vendors conduct procurements on a continuous basis. The enterprise enters into major procurements randomly and infrequently. The enterprise has the advantage of knowing its business operations, which may be somewhat different from those examined by vendors in the past. Certainly, the managers and their decision-making styles may present new and different challenges to the vendor responding to a solicitation document for hardware, software, or services. Business outcomes can be an effective way to drive the procurement process. In-house personnel are in the best position to prepare those outcomes with or without the help of outsourcing.

In Chapter 3, we return to the concept of information technology as a strategic and competitive weapon by examining the "stage" of automation of the enterprise. Where is the enterprise in data processing growth? What condition does it want to achieve and in what time period? What organizational level (operational, tactical, and strategic) is to be addressed with information technology and in what precedence for what benefit? The information systems applications portfolio needs to be examined for criteria to be used in evaluating each application so that enterprise competitiveness can be determined. If the wrong information resources are procured at the wrong time and for non-mission-critical functions, the enterprise will not be enabled sufficiently to survive. Simply obtaining state-of-the-art hardware and software is not good enough. The theme of this text is based on the proper mix of people and technology for effectiveness. Unless the people are enabled with technology and are empowered to use it for personal and organizational effectiveness, funds will have been wasted.

In Chapter 4, Porter's [1980] competitive forces model serves to highlight decision making in the form of issues regarding the introduction of information technology, some of which are to improve market share, strengthen customer relationships, develop new markets, and promote new customers, as well as dependency on automation and control of the process. Planning is portrayed as a dynamic and continuous activity involving managers from throughout the organization. Procurement of information technology requires the same planning approach and should focus on major business initiatives. In order to conduct the procurement process, workers need to be creative and exercise higher-order thinking skills. Everything is under scrutiny; everything is examined for effectiveness and efficiency. Total quality management (TQM) procedures force these issues not only for business operations but also for the quest of procurement solutions to business problems and opportunities. Creative ideas must lead the way for innovative actions. Focus on business processes helps to uncover problem areas and new opportunities.

In Chapter 5, radical changes in traditional information systems organizational structures and positions within those structures are presented. High-level IS managers find themselves drawn more into strategic business decision making and having less control with operations. End-users are exercising more control in almost every aspect of computing from data entry and query to local data processing and report generation to application development. Centralization versus decentralized control of computing throughout the enterprise is a hot issue. In general, organizations tend to have a mix of centralized operations and less centralized development activities. The trend will continue. Decentralization is exacerbated by business process teams armed with empowerment for fast response; these teams will not want to wait for a detailed systems analysis of all enterprise requirements before they act. Systems development methods will have to be more flexible and responsive to end-user needs in order to meet market demands. Procurement methods will have to account for this changing and much more collaborative information systems scenario. How, when, and by whom information technology is acquired and allocated will directly affect the ability of the enterprise to respond to strategic opportunities.

◆ SELECTIVE OUTSOURCING: A FRAMEWORK

Now that procurement of information technology has been shown to relate to a number of variables and to be a complex process, it is important to return to a major point of the previous section. What framework can we use to analyze the enterprise so that all of these important issues are addressed in search of a flexible and continuous process of acquiring and managing information across the enterprise? Managing computer resources from organizational assessment to acquisition to allocation is delineated in Exhibit 6-2 as a computer resource management model (CRMM).

In order to make any decision concerning outsourcing, one must first know what is involved in the complete process at the outset. Exhibit 6-2 provides a detailed chronicle of events in the procurement process and was derived from data on 20 organizations over a period of 10 years and additional experience by both authors over two decades of soliciting and providing outsourcing services. The case study profile is included in Appendix A.2.

At this point, it is instructive to peruse the list, item by item, and ask: Is it feasible for this activity to be conducted by outsourcing? What portion, if any, of this activity should and can be relegated to an outside agency? In fact, this self-assessment (collection of data from the CRMM list and subsequent analysis) could be conducted by an outside agency. Such a procedure would constitute a "selective outsourcing" mode which then could be evaluated to determine which of the feasible options are slated to become a reality. A feasible option is one that has technical, operational, economic, political, and practical soundness. After listing the feasible options, additional information for each option is needed, such as: strategic importance to the enterprise; change over the next five years; integration with other current systems; and in-house knowledge about linking IT to business plans.

As we have said, outsourcing is an activity on a scale from 0 percent to 100 percent. The emerging trend is to be selective at approximately the 50 percent mark. Different companies may want to be slightly higher or lower depending on

Exhibit 6-2 — Computer Resource Management Model (CRMM)

Stage I: Assessment

Management of the Organization
- Structure and Modification Mechanisms for Change
- Philosophy, Goals, Decision-making and Managerial Styles
- Operating Procedures and Work Flow (Formal and Informal)
  - Organization Charts: Hierarchy, Project, or Matrix
- Levels of Authority: Responsiveness and Control

Perception of Automation
- Strategic and Operational Feasibility: Definition of Feasibility
- Business Function Operations
- End-User Information Systems Literacy, Fluency, Power Users
- IS Professionals: Education, Expertise, Interests
- Current and Future Requirements; Untapped Opportunities
- Planning
- Organizing for Automation or Automation Changes
- Master Computer Resource Plan
  - Control Issues: IS and End-User Application Development
  - *Task Forces: TQM System and Authority
  - Impact on Organization (Local, National, International)
- Request for Proposal Guidelines
  - Development, Production, and Implementation
  - Technical, Economic, Legal, Contractual, Administrative Issues
  - Level of Specificity, Scope, Constraints

Stage II: Acquisition

Contents of Selection Plan
- Authority, Review, and Control of Process
- Organization, Scope, Timing, Constraints
- Communication and Ethical Issues (Internal and External Reporting)
- Validation and Confidentiality
- Continuity and Continuance of Selection Committee

Implementation of Selection Plan
- Master Plan Conformance: Business Plan and Information Systems Plan
  - Application Priorities and Schedule, Organizational Impact
  - Computer System Redesign, Resource Changes and Constraints

Make or Buy Decisions
- Computer System Hardware, Peripherals, Data Communications, Software
- Support Services (Consultants On-Site, Off-site), Modification, Maintenance

Contract Negotiation
- Solicitation of Bids
- Terms and Conditions of Contract: Mandatory and Desirable Requirements
- Data Collection, Evaluation System, and Analysis
- Clarification of Bids, Contract Award, Installation, and Acceptance

Stage III: Allocation

Master Plan Conformance and Continuous Evaluation System Renegotiation
- Organizational Assessment, Annual RFP Modification
- The Three Stages Revisited: Assessment, Acquisition, and Allocation

---

*The underlying concept for the total quality management (TQM) approach is to have cross-functional task forces with authority.

computer intensity of business operations. Data suggest, that it is not a good idea to approach either extreme position. Also, this list is only a starting point for the process. It is expected that some of the items will increase or decrease in importance and others will be added or deleted as the procurement process proceeds. It is almost impossible to estimate accurately future business conditions, new technology, and adaptation of workers to new environments, positions, and team projects. The staff-technology plane of our cubic STEP model appears to be a simple concept but is quite elusive.

◆ OUTSOURCING PROCESS

Now that you are armed with feasible outsourcing options derived from a list of activities defining the procurement process, what other information impacts decision making, allowing us to arrive at the *most* feasible options? In Exhibit 6-3, other factors in the outsourcing process are identified.

We have discussed in depth the top block (CRMM) and top-left block (Outsourcing Options) in the previous section. Advantages and disadvantages are provided by Exhibit 6-4 and need no further explanation.

External factors, such as new markets and products, and opportunities and threats from internal and external agencies, require some type of SWOT (strengths, weaknesses, opportunities, and threats) analysis. Without an analysis of this type, any procurement of information technology is destined to fail to enable the enterprise. Once all of this information is collected, the enterprise can evaluate its information technology infrastructure and its governance arrangements between end users and centralized IS departments. Now, the feasible options list can be reduced to the *most* feasible options list and the enterprise can return to implementing the computer resource management model (CRMM). The CRMM can be annotated for outsourcing feasibility and the process converted to an enterprise project, perhaps documented with a project management software tool. Such a procedure has the advantage of acting as a communications device for various managers, ensuring that some activities must be completed before others begin, and providing a timeline with task accountability for each activity.

◆ IMPLEMENTING THE COMPUTER RESOURCE MANAGEMENT MODEL

Today, educators and practitioners perceive that immediate and complete hardware and software solutions are commercially available. The existence of on-the-shelf solutions usually prompts two questions from the end-user community:

Why should there be such a long wait for quality results in the organization's applications development cycle and/or procurement process? If there is a formal applications priority list, why can it not be easily modified and then expedited

Implementing the Computer Resource Management Model

Exhibit 6-3

Outsourcing Process

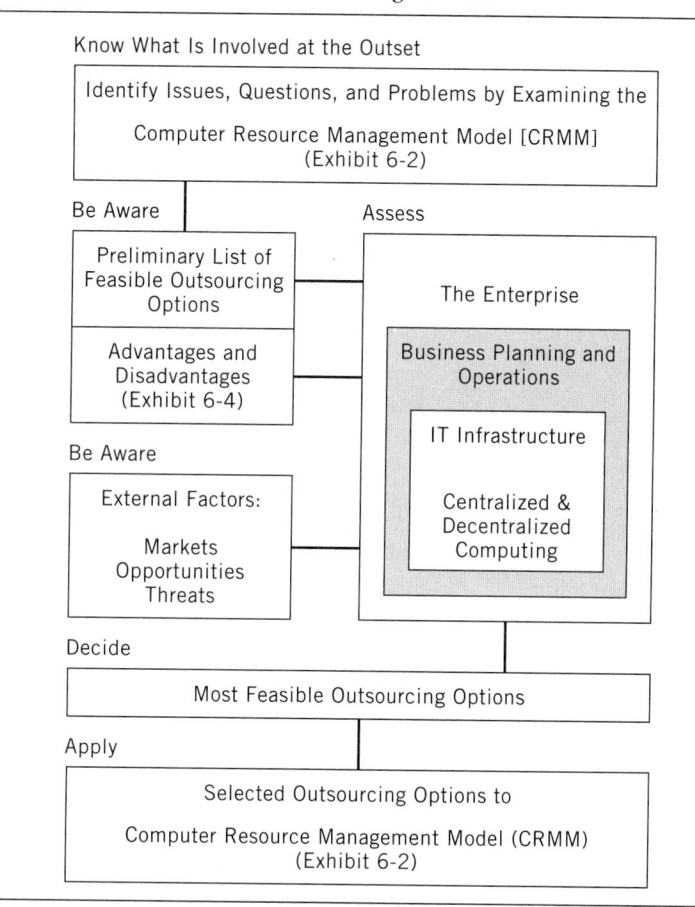

Know What Is Involved at the Outset

```
Identify Issues, Questions, and Problems by Examining the
Computer Resource Management Model [CRMM]
(Exhibit 6-2)
```

Be Aware / Assess

- Preliminary List of Feasible Outsourcing Options
- Advantages and Disadvantages (Exhibit 6-4)

The Enterprise
- Business Planning and Operations
  - IT Infrastructure
  - Centralized & Decentralized Computing

Be Aware

- External Factors:
  - Markets
  - Opportunities
  - Threats

Decide

Most Feasible Outsourcing Options

Apply

Selected Outsourcing Options to Computer Resource Management Model (CRMM) (Exhibit 6-2)

---

with judicious use of commercially available software and turnkey solutions, perhaps even with end-user involvement?

During the past decade, case study data were collected from a wide variety of educational, governmental, and business environments to uncover a model to help organizations assess and implement appropriate computer resource acquisitions addressing these two questions. Thirty-eight case studies were examined for common and unique attributes relating to managerial issues of information systems planning and implementation. General conclusions were converted into operational action items in the form of collaborative strategies for IEMgrs(Tp) and other business managers to define requirements and manage contract negotiations. Later sections of this text discuss and delineate conclusions in that order. (Case study data are presented in Appendix A.2.)

When IEMgrs(Tp) are relegated to monitoring routine data processing operations, information processing capability becomes stagnant. Their managerial

Exhibit 6-4: Outsourcing Advantages and Disadvantages

EXPECTATIONS	COMMENTS/TRADEOFFS
IS expenditure reduction up to 50%	Forecasting inaccurate, unreliable
More computer power, lower cost	May not need it
Fewer salaried personnel, fewer benefits	Severance packages, lost best employees
No capital expense	No depreciation
Less chance for obsolescence	Reliance on vendor to be state-of-the-art
Good for small firms	Dependence on vendor & expensive
Less in-house training for IS staff	More training for end-user community
New vendor approaches & experience	In best interest of vendor or client?
Opens new opportunities for business	Some disruption in conducting business

ploys are either to avoid the problem completely (no support for user-developed and immediately responsive systems), or to assist end users in the process (through long-term user-IS agreements). The search for a more comprehensive solution is encumbered by the demand for immediate and global response, quality enhancement, cost containment, increased productivity, cash liquidity, just-in-time manufacturing and inventory, outplacement alternatives, and organizational downsizing moves. An overview of the procurement process is shown in Exhibit 6-5.

For more user-controlled and independent operations, daily operations have been shown to contain conflicting procedures. Departmental data sets are separate entities and, because the data elements themselves may not have unique definitions, data integrity is at risk. In addition, some reports for top-level management for assessment of organizational fiscal status require segments of information from several operating functions. Unless the distributed databases are integrated to a master system with true connectivity to central computing resources, the process requires manipulation of end-user data files. Case study data suggest that quick-fix solutions by consultants and/or in-house staff have not been satisfactory. Some examples are noted, as follows:

- Funding for extended in-house services or for outside consultants is not available.
- IEMgr(Tp) or end user has neither time nor expertise to assess requests.
- Assessments involve the wrong personnel with competing motivations and objectives.
- End users do not provide accurate information concerning application requirements.
- Overeager vendors provide solutions without an implementation plan.
- Insufficient attention is given to contract terms and conditions and systems deliverables.

Implementing the Computer Resource Management Model

Exhibit 6-5

Vendor Relationships and Contracting: The Process

Computer Resource Management for the Enterprise

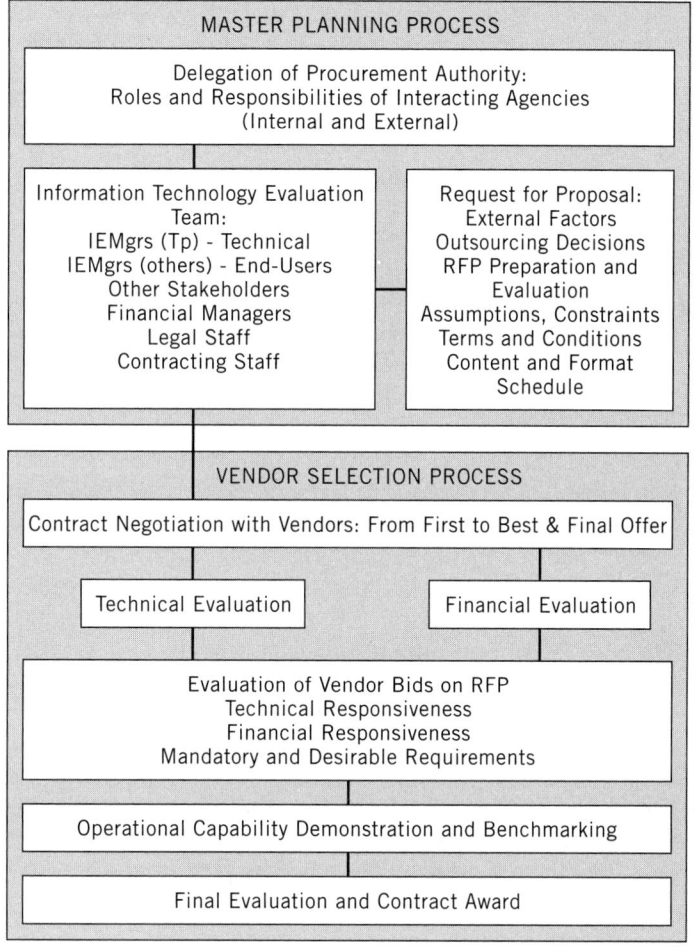

MASTER PLANNING PROCESS

Delegation of Procurement Authority:
Roles and Responsibilities of Interacting Agencies
(Internal and External)

Information Technology Evaluation Team:	Request for Proposal:
IEMgrs (Tp) - Technical	External Factors
IEMgrs (others) - End-Users	Outsourcing Decisions
Other Stakeholders	RFP Preparation and Evaluation
Financial Managers	Assumptions, Constraints
Legal Staff	Terms and Conditions
Contracting Staff	Content and Format
	Schedule

VENDOR SELECTION PROCESS

Contract Negotiation with Vendors: From First to Best & Final Offer

Technical Evaluation | Financial Evaluation

Evaluation of Vendor Bids on RFP
Technical Responsiveness
Financial Responsiveness
Mandatory and Desirable Requirements

Operational Capability Demonstration and Benchmarking

Final Evaluation and Contract Award

- Documentation is either too technical or too simple and user literacy is not considered.
- Contingency measures for delayed installation or maintenance are not identified.
- The postimplementation roles of IEMgr(Tp) and end users are unclear.
- Access to the computer system by other departments or enterprises is undefined.
- Expectations among end users, IEMgrs, consultants, and vendors are unclear.

The need is for the establishment of a long-range master plan with complementary short-term solutions producing a responsive, manageable environment under control. Traditional organizational models, although applicable for many segments of computer-related management issues, do not address all of these issues. Case data support a CRMM as described in Exhibit 6-2. The CRMM design encompasses the three managerial stages of assessment, acquisition, and allocation of information technology.

Today, instant communication and seductive advertising reduce the computer resource management process to one-page solutions. The solutions appear to be user friendly, inexpensive, properly designed by experts, and cost conscious. Computer-fluent staff can scan the computer supermarket shelves and find a combination of hardware and software to meet vaguely identified needs.

This scenario is supported by case data in almost every situation. More interested and informed end users rush to bypass the perceived lengthy process of dealing with complex and interrelated issues. Small pockets of funds in departmental budgets are available for such independent solutions and the vendor community is quick to respond with immediate delivery of hardware and software. A more comprehensive study reveals that total investment by these independent groups over a longer time period is costly and financially unsound.

What is really expected from the end-user community, and does IEMgmt(Tp) staff establish organizational philosophy for them?

Research shows that this major issue is not generally addressed. If the organization does examine the desired level of literacy, the review occurs *after* acquisition of computer resources. User activity is a function of computer literacy and, in tomorrow's world, computer fluency. Computer fluency expectation levels affect management procedures, responsibilities and accountabilities, resource constraints, priority of application development, and overall risk-return analyses. Organizational problems of uncontrolled computer system procurements force research efforts toward management of information technology and away from pure technical aspects.

Prioritization of resources, computer literacy expectation levels of all personnel, and end-user computing philosophy are an integral part of the planning and control imperative. For many organizations experiencing frequent change of computer capabilities in hardware, software enhancements, and distribution of computing, a formal declaration of authority for computer system procurement does not exist. There is a difference between organizational policy for centralized control and the reality of the situation when users acquire and implement standalone, low-cost, microcomputer systems. Strategies are needed to develop a master plan.

◆ COLLABORATION STRATEGIES

Several design and acquisition issues have been discussed and demonstrate the large scope and complexity of the process. The fact that some organizations do not enter into the formal computer resource management process (selection plan, RFP, negotiation) is understandable. The planning effort is a tremendous undertaking and together with the continuous and frequent changing of key personnel certainly discourages such systematic approaches. If selective outsourcing activity has been utilized as suggested by this text, some of these time and personnel problems are reduced. If the organization is willing to commit time to the project at the outset and focus on an adaptable long-term solution, then the proposed approach is beneficial to the organization. The financial portion of the contract focuses on cash flow and tax breaks. A phased-in approach with documented milestones and prioritized applications can be implemented. In this way, some results can be realized while the process unfolds.

Vendor relationships should be developed for the long-term with renegotiations based on predetermined issues. Procedures establish not only the impact of business/educational programmatic changes, but also opportunities afforded by technology updates on computing resources. As hardware and software products proliferate and costs continue to decrease, other extensive systems studies and procurement groups do not have to be reestablished. The mechanisms should be in place for addressing the issues with the benefit of historical records to prevent duplication of effort. Microcomputing, including local and wide area networks, need not be a threat since it can be centrally controlled, even though the processing power is locally realized.

The proposed CRMM approach with its committees and task forces is focused on design of the best system for the total organization. Such activity does not result from technology available at the time; impact assessments of technology are made on all aspects of the organization before any procurement action is taken. All facets of end-user computing become planned activity. Any software development by users becomes part of the total effort and does not produce clusters of independent databases and file incompatibilities. Additional overall benefits of this proposed approach are to reduce costs, minimize risks, properly utilize available resources, and improve management. The key concept is to quickly develop the master plan, appoint the right people to a loosely coupled network structure of task forces, and produce results on some predetermined and timely schedule.

Such an approach requires that top-level managers, including corporate information officers, provide forums where ideas can be introduced openly and where a full discussion of emerging strategies can be converted into action. Since information technology must be mobilized to support these strategies, the specific roles, responsibilities, and accountabilities of the action teams, or task forces, must be identified at the outset. This activity will require that line managers and IS professionals enter into more detailed formal agreements addressing the rationale for and implementation of information technology for gains in personal productivity, business value to the organization, image of the firm, and/or quality of products or services. The forums should not be complaint centers for current operating problems; these comments could be handled by a separate action team concentrating on those issues, perhaps conducting workflow analyses in much the same manner as total quality teams explore current operations for streamlining productivity.

Most of the forum activity should be visionary in nature. They should assess corporate strengths and use them effectively to grasp opportunities both in the near term and in the long-range picture. A summary of these and other collaborative strategies among end users (line managers), IS professionals, and vendors is provided in Exhibit 6-6.

◆ DEVELOPING THE REQUEST FOR PROPOSAL (RFP)

The Request for Proposal (RFP) document provides specific deliverables for the process. The level of effort to develop a solicitation document should be consistent with the expected return from the resultant information processing capability. Guidelines for major managerial aspects of the RFP process (Exhibit 6-7) are provided for acquisition of computer resources as an integral part of managing information technology for effective organizational competitiveness and productivity. Strategies incorporated in this document should emerge from task force discussions, findings, conclusions, and recommendations. The selection team for information technology is concentrated on procurement but will have the benefit of the wisdom, experience, and cross-functionality of task force activity to justify its request for proposal. Exhibit 6-8 identifies action items for developing an RFP.

◆ NEGOTIATING THE CONTRACT

It is important to promote an atmosphere where philosophy, discussion, and action are synergized to produce the best solution for each unique enterprise. Contract negotiation suggests a rather lengthy process. Since arbitration and debate are encouraged by these guidelines, terms and conditions are extensively examined. Conclusions resulting from a discussion of issues form the basis of a written document, which then is enforceable. If areas of dispute do arise, there exists a reference document upon which to base the arguments. A self-assessment guide for managing contract negotiations is presented (Exhibit 6-9) for assisting organizations in reviewing their environment for management issues.

The overall purpose of a written agreement is to ensure that both parties understand the terms and conditions of the requested service. In an effort to prevent timely and costly litigation, not only should the client take the time to prepare some type of document for computing capability acquisition, but also the document should be reviewed by legal staff.

◆ CONCLUDING COMMENTS

Can this computer resource management model and guidelines be used by the average nontechnical administrator and/or the computer systems professional?

Exhibit 6-6: Recommendations for General Procurement

1. **Secure top-level support for managing information technology**
    a. Authorities to control on-going process
    b. Dissemination of information formally to all organizational elements
    c. Implementation plan with flexibility for new users and applications

2. **Develop specific set of objectives for management program**
    a. Scope, constraints, milestones, membership roles and responsibilities
    b. Critical success factors and actions needed to exploit them

3. **Create a forum for ideas**
    a. Discussion of process and criteria for justification of resources
    b. End-user involvement, including applications development
    c. Impact of process on organizational philosophy and business practices

4. **Resolve the issues**
    a. Most effective and practicable solution for the business
    b. Technical, economic, operational, political, and human factors
    c. Focus on productivity and total quality management issues

5. **Assess solutions**
    a. Programmatic or staffing changes for alternative solutions
    b. Internal and external impact on organizational structure and workforce
    c. Technology and management advances and impact on alternative solutions

6. **Plan the selection process**
    a. Schedule for procurement process and evaluation
    b. Immediate, short-term, and long-range acquisitions
    c. Procedures for all phases and all participant roles and responsibilities

7. **Establish RFP process and working RFP**
    a. Comprehensive framework as continuous reference document
    b. Flexibility on scope and constraints for normal and fast track processing

8. **Address design issues**
    a. Total systems solution with integrated segments, or phases
    b. Inclusion of all computer-related operations in systems design
    c. Exploration of standalones, networks, and connectivity concerns
    d. Outsourcing possibilities as integral part of solution

9. **Execute selection plan**
    a. Fixed timeframe for developing evaluated costs
    b. Formal procedures for solicitation, contract negotiation, and bids
    c. Definitions of terms used in contract to resolve semantic differences
    d. Clarification of mandatory and desirable requirements
    e. User-driven standards and specifications

10. **Negotiate and annually renegotiate the contract**
    a. Acceptance of systems and/or services by all key participants
    b. Evaluation standards, procedures, and timing

Exhibit 6-7   **Collaborative Strategies for IEMgrs**

1. Securing top-level support for managing information technology in these key areas:
    Authorities to control ongoing process by collaborative task forces
    Task Force makeup: cross-functional teams of IEMgrs and business unit managers
    Formal dissemination of information to all organizational elements
    Implementation plan with flexibility for new users and applications
    Strategies with vision and integration for IT into business plan
    Decision-making criteria and impact on IT procurement
    Requirement for planned implementation for migration to new technologies
    Creation of new reward systems commensurate with project-oriented work
    Support of educational program for new organizational structures
    Encouragement to design and implement self-directed work teams
    Discouragement of independent IT activity
    Integration of IT in financial planning process
    Requirement that IEMgrs and vendors communicate for effectiveness
    Emphasis on strategies with action plans and not reactive crisis management

2. Developing a specific set of objectives for management, including:
    Scope, constraints, milestones, membership roles, and responsibilities of task forces
    Critical success factors and actions needed to exploit them
    Identification of corporate strengths and application opportunities
    Identification of corporate weaknesses and their conversion into strengths
    View of future technological advances (5 to 10 years) in hardware, software, and services

3. Creating a forum for ideas, including:
    Discussion of process and criteria for justification of resources
    End-user involvement, including applications development
    Impact of process on organizational philosophy and business practices
    Establishment of a communications system using groupware and other mechanisms
    Several task forces loosely structured to address issues, problems, and opportunities
    Allowance for immediate and long-term solutions
    Authority clearly established for planning, control, and implementation

4. Resolving the issue through:
    Emergence of the most effective and practicable solution for the business
    Consideration of technical, economic, operational, political, and human factors
    Focus on productivity and total quality managements issues
    Schedule of activity consistent with task force recommendations
    Resolution of application portfolio problems, priorities, and conflicts
    Resolution of charging scheme; budget planning and expenditures

5. Assessing solutions in terms of:
    Programmatic or staffing changes for alternative solutions
    Internal and external impact on organizational structure and workforce
    Technology and management advances and their impact on alternative solutions
    Focus more on business value and less on information technology development

Exhibit 6-7

Collaborative Strategies for IEMgrs *(continued)*

6. **Planning the information technology selection process, including:**
   Schedule for procurement process and evaluation
   Immediate, short-term, and long-range acquisitions
   Procedures for all phases and all participant roles and responsibilities
   Full consideration of, and accountability to, task force recommendations

7. **Establishing RFP process and working RFP, including:**
   Comprehensive framework used as continuous reference document
   Flexibility on scope and constraints for standard and fast-track processing
   Historical record for justified changes to RFP as new information emerges
   Continuous dialogue back to task forces for additional information
   Focus on the need for long-term relationships with vendors

8. **Addressing design issues, such as:**
   Total integrated systems solution with phases of migration to new information technology
   Inclusion of all computer-related operations in systems design plan
   Exploration of standalones, networks, and connectivity concerns
   Outsourcing possibilities as integral part of solution
   Specific criteria for vendor evaluation and establishment of evaluation system
   Provision for a secure, easily accessible, and comprehensive database
   Requirements-driven architecture, not just current computer system adaptation
   System for creating and implementing system standards for hardware and software
   Provision for physical standards (e.g., optic fibers, equipment, services)
   Pathways for expansion of internal computing to external electronic highways
   Database entry, access, and change authorities: who, why, what conditions, how

9. **Executing the selection plan by establishing:**
   Time frame for developing evaluated costs for vendor comparisons
   Formal procedures for solicitation, contract negotiations, and bids
   Definitions of terms used in contract to resolve semantic differences
   Clarification of mandatory and desirable requirements
   User-driven, business-oriented standards and specifications
   Product modules, phased-in approaches, application priorities, and schedule
   Nontechnical evaluation: training, openness for future change, flexibility
   Vendor procedures, constraints, responsiveness consistent with client objectives
   Confirmation of vendor, line managers, and IS working relationships afterward

10. **Negotiating and annually renegotiating the contract, according to these criteria:**
    Acceptance of systems or services by all key participants
    Evaluation standards, procedures, and timing
    Insurance that vendors communicate only with authorized team
    Product criteria: quality, performance, reliability
    Vendor criteria: trustworthiness, long-term relationship, financial stability
    Feedback to appropriate task forces on status of process and any new developments
    Development modification procedures, conditions, limitations, and costs
    Continuance of this concept of shared participation and ownership of automation
    Communications of the process to senior-level management: costs, benefits, trade-offs
    Consistency with corporate philosophy for integration of information technology
    Commitment to service line management: immediate and long-term plans

Exhibit 6-8   **Actions Items for Developing a Request for Proposal (RFP)**

1. **The race for installation.** Analysis and design activities are costly and do not show immediate return for the expenditure. Frequently, these phases are accelerated for purchase of hardware and software.
   a. Conduct an assessment to make a conscious decision of the level of detail to be undertaken for analysis and design. Somewhere between the extreme positions of very general specifications to very specific terms and conditions lies a balanced portrayal of information for the RFP.
   b. Ensure that this effort is commensurate with return/investment and risk/return ratios. Identify intangible benefits, hidden costs, and expected productivity gains for new opportunities.
   c. Be consistent between the desired level of detail required of vendors and the RFP.

2. **Authority and control of selection procedures.** Procedures may be documented but not implemented. IEMgrs may not be situated high enough in the organization to provide objective leadership and together with representation from the end-user community, control computer resources.
   a. Place IEMgrs at a level high enough to form an action team with authority and responsiveness.
   b. Establish formal authorities for computer resource allocation with input from end users.

3. **Advisory planning groups.** The process of managing information technology does not end with advisory group recommendations; it must be a continuous process in order to have serious impact on the organization.
   a. Create advisory groups and/or teams to design, implement, and oversee all aspects of the process.
   b. Develop operational mechanisms to maintain progress and to allow for new users, new applications, and new priorities consistent with changing business requirements and opportunities.

4. **Information technology evaluation team.** Since the evaluation process is multidisciplinary (end users, technical experts, contracting and purchasing personnel, legal, and finance) the makeup and size of the group will depend on the current and intended scope of computing in the organization.
   a. Select a team with expertise for proper evaluation of the product and/or services sought.
   b. Assign as chairperson an experienced business operating manager with leadership abilities.

5. **End-user computing.** Since end-users must be an integral part of the procurement process to achieve success in using that information technology effectively, issues of applications development and other related user activity must be addressed at the outset.
   a. Formalize end-user and ISM relationships (among different types of IEMgrs) for each aspect or procurement.
   b. Document specific objectives which exploit strengths and reduce weaknesses.
   c. Capitalize on new business opportunities made possible by technology and people.
   d. Ensure that managing information technology is consistent with business planning.
   e. Provide for mainframe/network connectivity and hardware/software compatibility.

Concluding Comments

> **Exhibit 6-8**
>
> **Actions Items for Developing a Request for Proposal (RFP)** *(continued)*
>
> 6. **Administrative versus other types of computing.** This issue is philosophical, power-based, and political. Since computing resources are an expensive budget item, overall policy guidance should be substantiated with justified arguments. Examples: administrative vs. instructional use of computers in higher education; administrative vs. research and development for business.
>   a. Utilize computer selection evaluation group to examine and suggest solutions for priority conflicts (total fund allocations and schedule for implementation).
>   b. Create a system for measurement of computer literacy and fluency levels for all administrators, staff, and computer professionals.
>   c. Establish organizational standards, and incorporate these capabilities in RFP requirements.
>
> 8. **Impact of new technology on organization.** Although it is not always possible to anticipate all aspects of impact of computer system upgrades on an organization, it is necessary to realize impact assessment as a goal at the outset of the process. The RFP represents not only technical and financial specifications for computing, but also indicates future thrusts to be supported by information technology.

Yes. This case data collected over a decade from a variety of environments suggest universal concepts that apply to information technology assessment, acquisition, and allocation.

Does each organization have to apply the entire process (selection plan, RFP, negotiation) in order to realize the benefit of automation?

No. The CRMM approach applies to any type of organization at any staff level (division, department, individual end-user). The guidelines are arranged according to the stage of automation for ease of reference.

Is a formal RFP really necessary, and is it practical in terms of the effort needed to draft it?

Yes. In order to be competitive today, response is important. In addition, accurate, complete, and reliable information is critical to success. It is clear from this study that organizations with operational objectives, creative use of the right information to the right people at the right time, and structured, documented approaches to computer resource management are competitive. Some form of RFP, even if it addresses only a few carefully selected and important issues, is necessary. The questions it asks of users and information systems professionals in justifying the purchase and relating it to business operations are invaluable and highly practical.

Is a process really needed in view of the advent of new decision-systems support tools, prototyping methods, and user-development activity?

Yes. It is most important that organizations adopt some form of master plan for computer resources during a time when solutions proliferate and more informed

Exhibit 6-9: Self-Assessment Guide for Managing Contract Negotiations

1. Hardware, Software, and Services
   a. Strategic and operational cost/performance data, support services, training
   b. Requirement for vendors to respond to predetermined format
   c. Individual component costs, depreciation factor, discounts
   d. Data communications issues: definitions of system responsibilities
   e. Phase-in methods: annual modifications and business disruptiveness
   f. Purchase, lease, or other payment plans: proper comparison of bids
   g. Maintenance specifications: end-user standards and requirements
   h. Operational capability demonstration and references
   i. User-friendly systems and applications software
   j. Concurrent usage of system: response, peakloading, priorities
   k. Processing throughput measurement
   l. System expandability: memory, communication channels, user stations
   m. Connectivity and compatibility issues: internal and external systems

2. Additional Software Issues
   a. Ownership, site licensing, maintenance: intellectual property issues
   b. Ethical and legal issues with all aspects of use of software
   c. Conversion terms and conditions: data entry, programming, testing
   d. Memory requirements and compatibility with system upgrades
   e. Levels of priority: utilization, recovery, debugging, file management
   f. File protect options for updating and enhancements
   g. Customizing features: buyer allowances and prohibitions
   h. Control of processing schedule: end-user options
   i. Acceptance criteria and timeframe for trial period
   j. Termination clauses

3. Other Contracting Terms and Conditions
   a. Backup system: procedures, costs, and responsibilities
   b. Training requirements: computer literacy assessment, nature and location
   c. Documentation of all phases of management of information technology
   d. Implementation planning: schedule, actions, action addressees
   e. Technical assistance from vendor: constraints, costs, accessibility
   f. Multivendor systems: authorities and responsibility tree
   g. Cost guarantees and time period for which applicable
   h. Replacement of hardware, software, peripherals: Cost for upgrades
   i. Confidentiality issues of contract negotiation, implementation
   j. Formal renegotiation procedures: timeframe and conditions
   k. Account management: personal contacts after award and for implementation
   l. Cancellation provisions and payment schedule for changed arrangements
   m. Protection against natural disasters
   n. Provision for major organizational changes (including mergers, acquisitions)
   o. End-user involvement through all phases of contracting
   p. Noncompliance penalties: timeliness, completeness, opportunities lost
   q. Site preparation: physical conditions, remote sites, cable installations

users engage directly in information technology. The new tools must be used for the right applications. Prototyping methods can be very successful if the organization fully supports the technique. End-user computing and user development of applications requires formal agreements with information systems staff. The RFP, or some similar solicitation document, together with the selection plan and contractual theory, can serve to avoid costly mistakes and serve as the basis for the solution.

Are there some intangible and serendipitous benefits from this more comprehensive approach?

Yes. If master planning and control mechanisms are implemented, personal motivations and employee professional growth and computer fluency become more of the fabric of the organization and provide an integrated and synergistic total solution. The path through the maze of new and numerous options is unique to each institution. As each organization plans for automation, the questions uncovered by case-study data together with practical recommendations should be helpful in planning a strategy for success and implementing an effective program.

Reflections

GENERAL CONCEPTS

1. The large number of options for the enterprise to evaluate can be very confusing. Applications software updates emerge every month, computer companies are partnering to meet the competition, personnel turnover has increased due to downsizing measures, and the enterprise still has the responsibility to provide immediate services. Without information technology, it cannot be competitive.

    How do these new user-vendor relationships make it even more difficult for the enterprise to be effective in acquiring and allocating computer resources? Are all the right people at the right time brought into the acquisition process?

    In an effort to address these very important questions, inquire about the procurement process in some actual enterprise.

2. Outsourcing for hardware, software, and/or services must be addressed by the enterprise for survival. A conscious decision must be made to use or not use information technology (equipment and services) in each major aspect of operations.

    Why should the enterprise consider outsourcing? What methodology would you propose to evaluate outsourcing as a viable option? Is it a yes/no decision?

    How is the text's STEP Model related to this activity?

    What are the specific roles of IEMgrs in this process of outsourcing?

3. How can the CRMM model be used to identify options in outsourcing activity? Examine outsourcing activity in a particular enterprise.

    What is their process? Is it formal?

Is the process followed? How flexible is it? How political is it?

4. If most organizations do not intend to develop a formal RFP for procuring hardware, software, or services, of what use is the CRMM and detailed information on developing RFPs?

   What are the dangers of allowing departments independently to acquire applications software, even if the costs are minimal?

   What are the advantages and disadvantages of using many computer vendors (especially software vendors) for your enterprise activities?

5. Examine some local computer vendors for their opinions on issues and problems in providing equipment and services.

   What are their major complaints? What do they have to do to get the business?

6. Contract negotiations require technical, operational, financial, legal, and contractual skills. Vendors hone these skills every day. Unless a major procurement is underway, typically the enterprise does not assemble a team of people covering this array of needed expertise.

   Are vendors at a decided advantage in negotiating contracts?

   What can the enterprise do to prepare for dealing with multivendor operations?

   What can the enterprise do to sustain state-of-the-art information technology and at the same time conduct business without disruption?

   Is it worth the money to use consultants to help in developing strategies for information technology planning? How can you determine a cost/benefit ratio for such services?

Reflections

ISI CASE STUDY

Industrial Supplies, Inc. (ISI) - Roles and Responsibilities

Objective:

To configure an upgraded computer system for an industrial supplier of products (grinders, tools, etc.) from some automation with standalone microcomputers and outsourced services to a fully automated system needed to compete today and tomorrow.

Client: End-User Community

Prepare the outline of an RFP, explain it to the vendors, negotiate with each vendor, and award the contract (with justification).

President
Vice President for Business Operations
    Information Systems Department
    Marketing and Sales
    Human Resources Management

Corporate Office, Bridgeport
    Managers, Branch Offices

Chief Financial Officer
    Accounting (A/R, A/P, Ledger, Pay)
    Planning, Budgeting
    Purchasing

Manager of Operations
    Customer Accounts, Inventory

Vendor A and Vendor B

Propose bids independently. Meet technical requirements of RFP, present bids, and compete for the contract.

    Account Manager
        Financial Data for Bid
        Chief Negotiator for Contract

    Technical Support
        Hardware/Software Specialists
            Configuration Design
            Operations and Maintenance
        Applications Software Specialist
            Capabilities of System
            Training and Education

Client: Computer System Selection Team

    Chief Negotiator
    End-User Representation (Applications)
    IS Representation
    Legal and Contracting Representation

Instructor Comments

Before conceptual material on the design and acquisition of computer systems from the perspective of the end user is presented, each participant is to assume a "role" for the positions listed. It is not necessary that you have experience in these positions, only that you think of applications in those areas. In fact, you might find that wearing a new hat is an interesting approach and provides you with the intellectual freedom (creativity) needed for objective analysis.

Reflections

ISI CASE STUDY

Industrial Systems, Inc. Case Study: Business Functions and the Process

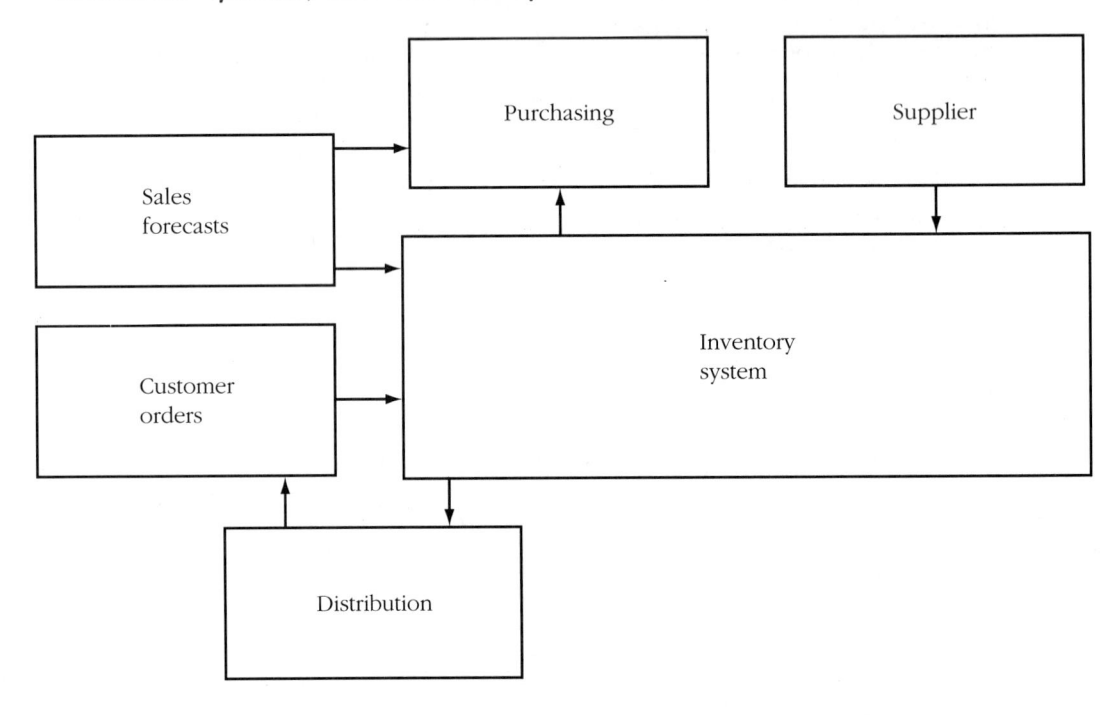

```
                    ┌──────────────┐        ┌──────────────┐
                    │  Purchasing  │        │   Supplier   │
                    └──────────────┘        └──────────────┘
┌──────────────┐           ▲                       │
│    Sales     │           │                       │
│  forecasts   │───────┐   │                       │
└──────────────┘       │   │                       ▼
                       ▼   │
                   ┌────────────────────────────────────┐
┌──────────────┐   │                                    │
│   Customer   │──▶│          Inventory system          │
│    orders    │   │                                    │
└──────────────┘   └────────────────────────────────────┘
       ▲                       │
       │                       ▼
              ┌──────────────┐
              │ Distribution │
              └──────────────┘
```

Business Functions

Corporate Planning, Information Systems
Marketing, Physical Distribution

Finance and Accounting
Human Resources

Reflections

ISI CASE STUDY

Background

ISI is an old Yankee wholesale supply house which has been in business for three decades. It is managed by a family (president and other officers) and has prospered very well without extensive automation. The corporate headquarters is in Bridgeport and uses approximately 100 applications programs (customized dBase3+ programs) at independent offices in Bridgeport, New Haven, and Waterbury. Software is written in BASIC and C.

Applications are menu driven. Other relevant information is:

- $20M/yr gross revenues with 10%/yr increase
- 500,000 data elements in inventory
- 50 quarterly catalogs for special clients (1000 elements with special pricing)
- 6 on-line clients (EDI) with growth rate of 2/yr for 5 yrs.
- 10,000 active clients, 100,000 passive clients (retain records for 10 yrs)
- 500 active suppliers, 100 passive suppliers
- A/R, payroll, ledger outsourced to DP processor
- A/P standalone, in-house
- manual inventory system (card file) with batch updating daily
- regular work days
- one person IS staff with minimum expertise
- IS consulting firm on retainer
- some funds set aside to upgrade
- 100 employees
- 10,000 transactions/month

It is unreasonable for you to take this scenario, expand (make up) more information on it, prepare specifications for vendors to bid on the IS upgrade, negotiate the contract (evaluate a competitive bid process), award the contract, make sure that there is an implementation plan, and finally complete the process in only a few sessions. We have included some background information in this chapter; however, subsequent chapters will use this information to explore concepts presented later.

The important concept is not accuracy of content but rather the process. The medium (process) is the message!

It *is* reasonable for you to comprehensively examine the process which acts as the framework for issues, problems, and suggested actions. One of your tasks (individual or group) is to read all material, select what information is relevant for this particular case, and within your "role" apply it accordingly. Not all aspects of the process apply to all work situations; however, the case contains all the issues involved in computer resource (information technology) management.

End-users:

- Feel free to change the scenario proposed as a starting point
- Communicate the changes, additions, deletions to the vendors
- Keep track of the negotiations, direct the activity
- Keep each vendor team's specific bids in confidence
- Manage information; think about managing information across the enterprise

Case Study Deliverables

(Regardless of whether role-playing/teams are used as a methodology)

1. Although this chapter addresses all aspects of the computer resource objectives, make ISI competitive in the marketplace with faster customer response, on-line product availability and pricing, improved purchasing procedures, just-in-time inventory system, streamlining of sales order and distribution systems, and other strategic and operational enhancements.
    a. End-User Community—Develop system specifications (RFP) in the form of a detailed outline of components suggested in the text.
    b. Vendors—Commence preparing a bid on the RFP by designing a total systems configuration including technical and economic factors.
    c. Computer System Selection Team—Outline strategy for conducting contract negotiations for end users; ensure that systems specifications are detailed enough for the competitive bid process.
2. Use the exhibits of the chapter to guide you through an exploration of ideas for solving the problems associated with current strategies and operations and for arriving at alternative solutions.
3. For this segment of the integrated case, more emphasis is placed on a strategic master plan for ISI. A thorough analysis of requirements should evolve from a corporate vision and policies commensurate with that vision. It is recommended that vendors just listen to a series of sessions where end users describe the current and future requirements. The questions from the vendor community are intended to clarify the RFP and form a vendor strategy for submitting a bid (in a later chapter).
4. Documents Produced (Outlines Only)
    a. Request for Proposal—outline prepared jointly by end user and selection team
    b. Vendor Preliminary Notes—needed for preparation of bid at later time
    c. Selection Process—prepared by selection team
    d. Diary of Activities—team and individual, oral and written reports
5. Schedule—This segment of the case study will require several sessions in order for students to grasp the concepts, analyze the data, discuss the limitations and assumptions, and produce outlines for later use in more formal documentation. As subsequent chapters are covered and more clarification sessions are conducted among the groups, the outline will become more detailed and vendor bids will become more competitive.

PART II

♦♦♦

Redesigning Business Processes

As organizations reconfigure themselves to improve their customer service focus, their structure almost always changes to one that is process oriented rather than function oriented. This change is usually done in parallel with a business process reengineering effort and brings with it a total cultural revolution across the organization. Not since the Industrial Revolution have our businesses undergone such radical change. Among the many issues that surface and that must be dealt with in order for this change to be successful, we list the following:

1. How does one adopt a process view of the organization when all of our education and training is grounded in the business functions and command and control structures?
2. What does business process redesign entail and what tools are available to help us?
3. What about the human resource changes that we will have to undergo as part of the redesign effort?
4. What role will the IS department and the IEMgt team play in our business redesign efforts?

In Part II these four areas of concern are discussed in each of the four chapters. Chapter 7 introduces the process view of the organization by defining business processes, categorizing processes, and then discussing the role of each member of the IEMgt team. This is a new concept in information technology management and one that will continue to change as organizations become accustomed to working in the new process environment. All we can hope to record is the situation as it is today; tomorrow, it will surely be different.

In Chapter 8 we introduce the idea of business process redesign and explore the various levels of redesign. We will see that business process reengineering, process quality management, and continuous quality improvement are different stages of redesign. The role of the IEMgt team is discussed for each category of business process redesign. Also, in Chapter 7 we turn to the tools of analysis and the preparation of the workforce for business process redesign. Workforce preparedness is an area of particular interest to senior management because it has accounted for many of the problems in moving the organization from a function to a process structure. We discuss this situation in detail in Chapter 8. Part II closes with a look at the changing role of information technology as a service organization to the business processes.

Chapter 7

Emerging Process View of Organizations

❖ ❖ ❖

*O*rganizations are not what you thought they were. They have changed in rather remarkable ways in the last few years. The changes are so fundamental that they challenge the basic premises on which the role and responsibility of the IS department have been established. Both the IS manager and the IEMgmt team need a new set of operating rules. In this chapter we begin our study of the business, not as a set of stovepipes (one for each business function) but rather as a collection of businesses within businesses and business partnerships within the larger framework of the enterprise. Critical to our study will be to consider the role of the IS department, the IS manager, and IEMgmt team.

❖ WHAT IS A BUSINESS PROCESS?

Information technology has figuratively turned the organization on its side. The Industrial Revolution introduced the command and control structure and business functions as an organizational structure that would last until only a few years ago. For a variety of reasons to which we have already alluded, this structure no longer meets the needs of the information-age enterprise. The need to focus all of our efforts on satisfying customer needs rendered the hierarchical structure not only obsolete but in fact a barrier to world-class customer service. A new way of looking at the organization was needed. The early works of Michael Porter [1980, 1985] set us to thinking about the food chain—that sequence of activities that create product and service as inputs move through a sequence of operations that add value to our company's product or service. For example, the simple analysis of the sequence from order entry to order delivery forced us to consider the entire process and how it might be improved, or reengineered, to meet quick-response goals and other quality measures that impact customer satisfaction.

By redefining the enterprise along the lines of processes, appointing a process owner, and assigning teams to processes, new life and a renewed sense of direction has been infused back into organizations. It has given senior management an opportunity to put the worker closer to the customer, and empowered decision making at the lowest level capable of making the decision, and given workers a stake in the success of their organization. By defining processes down to a microlevel, workers can see the results of their efforts whether their customers are internal or external. It becomes very clear whether a given task adds value or not and it gives workers a basis on which to make improvements that directly impact the goals of the enterprise.

Definitions: Bounding the Process

Briefly, a business process is any sequence of activities that consumes resources and adds value to a product or service. We see immediately, then, that we can define the business in terms of its processes and we can do so at increasing levels of detail. For example, we might define an organization in terms of its core business processes such as new product development, order generation, order fulfillment, and customer service. Each of these core business processes can be further defined in terms of the support processes that make them up. A business can therefore be represented as a hierarchy of processes rather than as a set of business functions. Harrington [1991] defines a typical manufacturing business with the 11 processes listed in Exhibit 7-1.

We visualize the enterprise graphically in Exhibit 7-2. With this perspective let us not forget that underlying these processes are business functions which we learned from our formal education. (The education community has some catching up to do!) In fact one might think of the business as a matrix whose rows are business processes and whose columns are the business functions. Wherever a business function is part of a business process place an "X" at the intersection of that row and column. An example is shown in Exhibit 7-3.

Exhibit 7-1 | **The Definition of a Business as a Set of Business Processes**

- New product development
- Product design release
- Production planning
- Materials management
- Hiring
- Billing and collections
- After-sales support
- Human resource training
- Customer needs analysis
- Order entry
- Order fulfillment

Exhibit 7-2: Visualization of Core Process and Support Processes

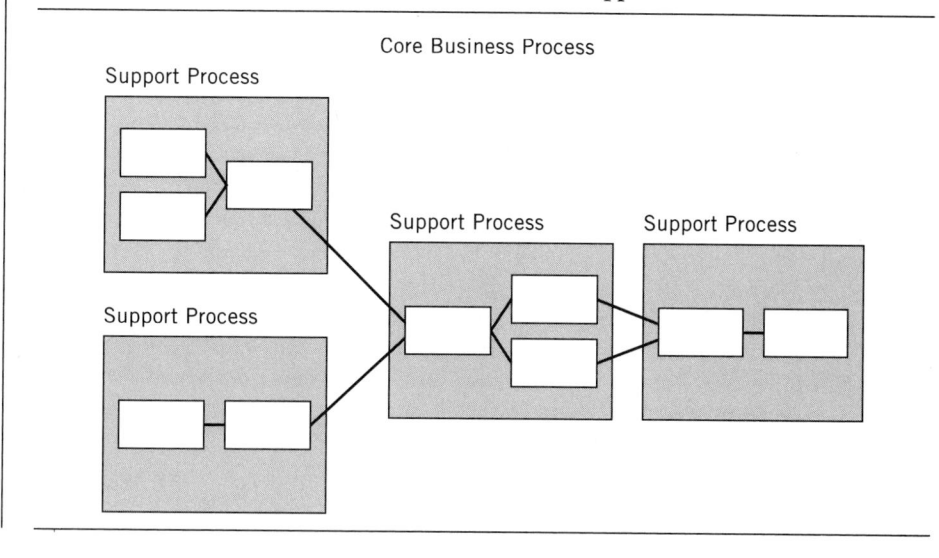

When an organization begins to define itself in terms of business processes the question of boundaries between processes immediately comes up. How should these boundaries be established? What about processes and subprocesses? If a task force is to be commissioned to reengineer a process, how are the boundaries of the study to be determined? These and several related questions must be answered before proceeding with any definition or study. Harrington [1991] offers us some help in this regard. There are two dimensions to consider. The first is the

Exhibit 7-3: Matrix View of Business

	\multicolumn{5}{c}{*Business Functions*}
PROCESSES	R/D	MFG	MKT	FIN	HR
New product development	X	X	X		
Product design release	X	X	X		
Production planning		X		X	X
Materials management		X			
Hiring		X	X	X	X
Billing and collections			X	X	
After-sales support			X		
Human resource training		X	X	X	X
Customer needs analysis	X		X		
Order entry		X	X	X	
Order fulfillment		X	X		

Exhibit 7-4

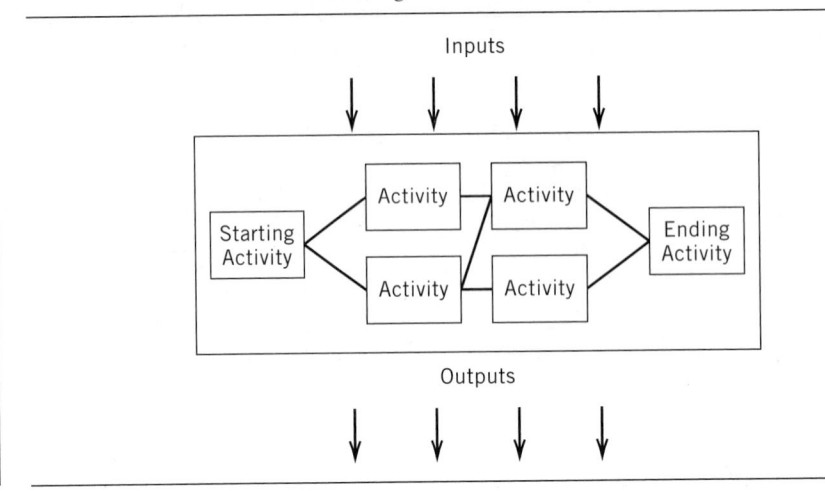

Bounding the Business Process

Inputs ↓ ↓ ↓ ↓

Starting Activity → Activity → Activity → Ending Activity
           → Activity → Activity →

Outputs ↓ ↓ ↓ ↓

chronological beginning and ending activities that define the process. In other words, what event signals the beginning of the process and what event signals the end of the process? The second dimension defines the inputs and outputs to the process. Here the decision is what will be considered an input (output) and what will be considered part of the process. Exhibit 7-4 depicts the boundary considerations.

Taking the business process view of the organization offers several benefits over the more traditional functional view. First and foremost is that it offers a customer orientation that cannot happen in the functional view. Every process either supports the customer directly or supports someone who supports the customer. Process changes can be directly related to customer benefits. Second, strategic plans can be directly linked to operations. This follows from working backwards from customer needs to the business processes and the discovery of better ways of meeting customer needs. The third benefit is strategic in that it helps in cycle time reduction. Cycle time reduction has become the critical success factor in the delivery of product and service. Like it or not, we live in a hedonistic society where instant gratification is the norm, not the exception. Customers expect to have their needs instantaneously met. Backordering or delays for any reason are the kiss of death. Finally, efficiency is the last of the four major benefits. Apart from improving quality or timeliness, we look at the other side of the ledger and look for ways to improve efficiency without sacrificing effectiveness.

Components: Personnel, Technology, Process

For many organizations the process level is where their current emphasis is placed—witness the rush to business reengineering. Despite all of the hype and hoopla, the failure rate of reengineering efforts is very high. The reasons are many: incompetent reengineering experts, lack of organizational readiness, lack of understanding of senior managers and the required commitment, and poor understanding of what a reengineering effort involves. Our belief is that many of the failures can be avoided. To see why this is so, let us examine each of the component parts of the STEP Model.

Staff

Underlying the change from function to process structures there has been an equally dramatic change in the technology infrastructure. This has given rise to a need for an equally dramatic requirement for retooling the skill sets of the workers. Many workers are concerned for their future job security, and rightly so. Reengineering is talked about in the same breath as downsizing the workforce. For many, the two are synonymous and have resulted in less-than-enthusiastic support of reengineering efforts. The paradigm is shifting: The "gold watch at 30 years" is gone. Longevity is no longer the reward for good and faithful service. Rather, continued service is contingent on workers' ability to add value. To workers this means that they must look for opportunities to contribute, even more so in the face of reengineering efforts. (For more on this topic see any one of the following books: Araoz & Sutton, 1994; Bridges, 1994; Dent, 1995; and Marshall, 1995).

Technology

About 15 years ago someone said, "If we stopped developing new technology today, it would take us at least ten years to fully utilize what already exists." This statement was made before the personal computer was a commercially viable product, before the Internet was any more than a research conduit for colleges and universities, before networks, and before multimedia. The point is that technology is racing ahead and no one individual or company can keep up with and assimilate the power that is available today. But to remain competitive, companies must keep up. The dilemma is even more pronounced when one considers keeping workers up to date in the use of the new technologies. In too many cases companies have been quick to jump into a new technology without really giving it closer scrutiny. We pose a discussion question that asks whether the high failure rate of reengineering efforts might be attributable to a gap between the appropriate technology and the adopted technology.

Process

The current crop of managers did not have the opportunity to study business processes while they were in school. The paradigm under which they were educated and are operating is the command and control structure and business functions model. We have already shown that this is obsolete and a new model is required. The transition is difficult for a number of reasons that include the shift of power from manager to worker, the change in role of manager from boss to coach and facilitator, and the focus on customer-driven processes. To realize the benefits that accrue to process-oriented enterprises requires training and preparation in change management, organizational readiness, project management, total quality management, worker empowerment, self-managed teams, and several other disciplines that have yet to find their way into the mainstream of university curriculum.

◆ BUSINESS PROCESS CATEGORIES

In this section we further examine business processes by following an example of new product development given by Thomas Davenport [1993]. New product development is one of the core processes found in most companies. It is composed of a number of support processes that define, at a more granular level, the new product development core process. Exhibit 7-5 is a matrix view of new product development.

The support processes are those identified by Davenport [1993] and are listed in the sequence in which they are performed. By viewing new product development in this manner, those responsible for each support process understand their role in the core process. When we relate this core process to serving customers, we automatically are led to consider ways to reduce the cycle time for new product development. Even at the support process level the same observations hold true. In the old functional organization there is a saying that merits repeating here. It goes something like this: *You people in marketing are selling products that don't exist and expect the engineers to perform miracles and the engineers, in*

Exhibit 7-5

New Product Development Process and Support Processes

	MKTG	R&D/ENGR	MFG
Needs Analysis	X		
Research	X	X	
Market Test	X		
Component Design		X	
Product Test		X	
Product Release		X	
Process Design		X	X
Equipment Design		X	X
Production Start			X

Exhibit 7-6: Cycle Time Reduction through Concurrent Engineering

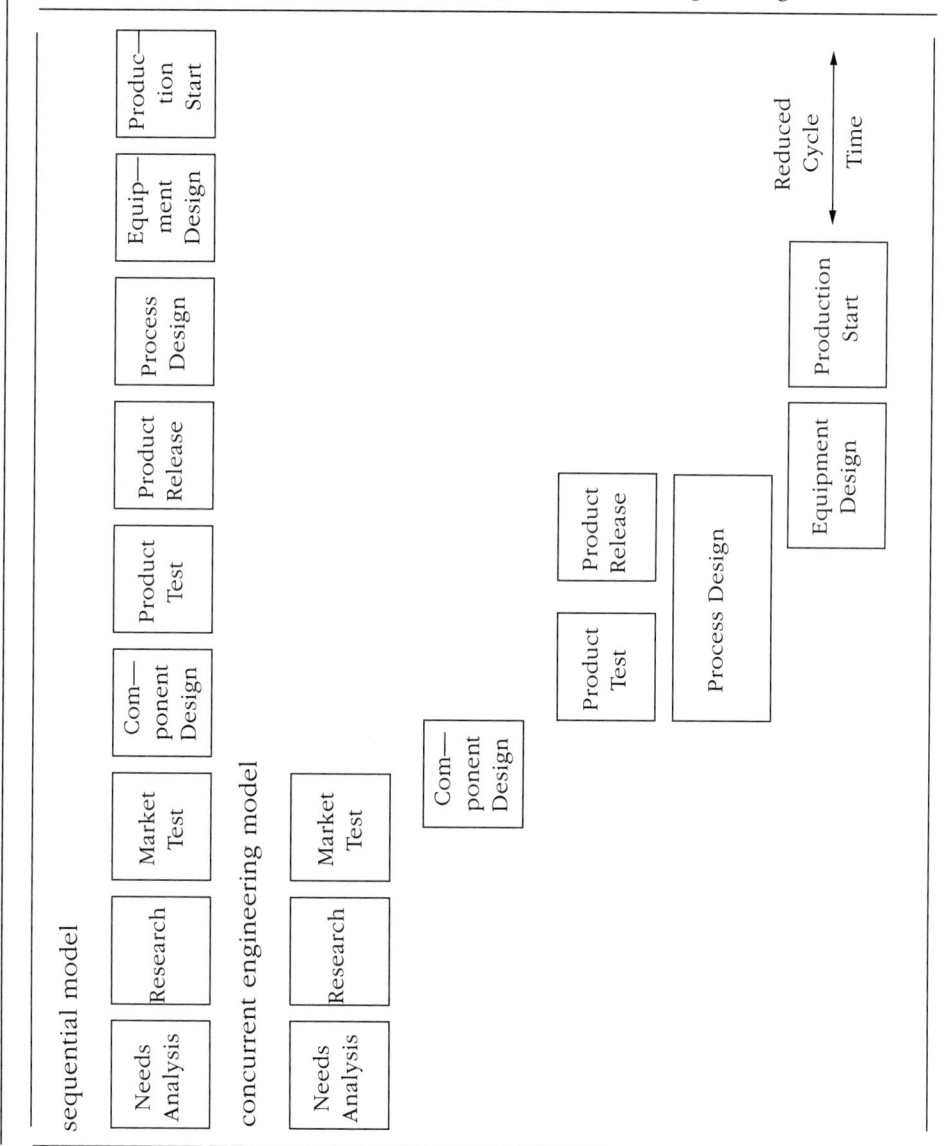

sequential model: Needs Analysis → Research → Market Test → Component Design → Product Test → Product Release → Process Design → Equipment Design → Production Start

concurrent engineering model: Needs Analysis → Research → Market Test → Component Design → Product Test → Product Release → Process Design → Equipment Design → Production Start (with parallel overlap producing Reduced Cycle Time)

turn, are designing products that can't be built. Moving to a process structure eliminates the barriers between functions and allows for such breakthroughs as concurrent engineering. Concurrent engineering simply introduces some parallelism into the sequential process as shown in Exhibit 7-6. This not only reduces cycle time but also creates a communications link across the support processes.

The result is a more effective and efficient new product development process that raises the probability of meeting customer expectations.

Note what has been accomplished and how it has been accomplished using concurrent engineering. It is reasonable to assume that activities such as Market Test and Component Design can be somewhat overlapped. At some point during Market Test we would have enough information to at least begin Component Design. However, Component Design could not be finished until some time after Market Test was completed. There obviously is some risk in this approach. For example, Market Test might finally conclude that a radical redesign was needed. That might render much of the earlier Component Design inappropriate. The same arguments hold true for overlapping Process Design with Product Test and Product Release and Equipment Design with Process Design. The question for IEMgrs, especially the IEMgr(TP), is how much concurrence can be scheduled into the process while recognizing the increased risk that must be incurred.

◆ ROLE PERSPECTIVES

Across the spectrum of IEMgr types there are a variety of roles that impact the process structure. In this section we discuss each and see how the enterprise benefits from the partnerships that evolve among the IEMgrs.

External and Internal Views

Consider the deployment of the IEMgrs as shown in Exhibit 7-7. The IEMgr(Tp) serves at the enterprise level. He or she maintains an enterprisewide perspective on the adoption and use of technology. To the extent that a technology may be beneficial to one or a few processes it must be assessed at the enterprise level

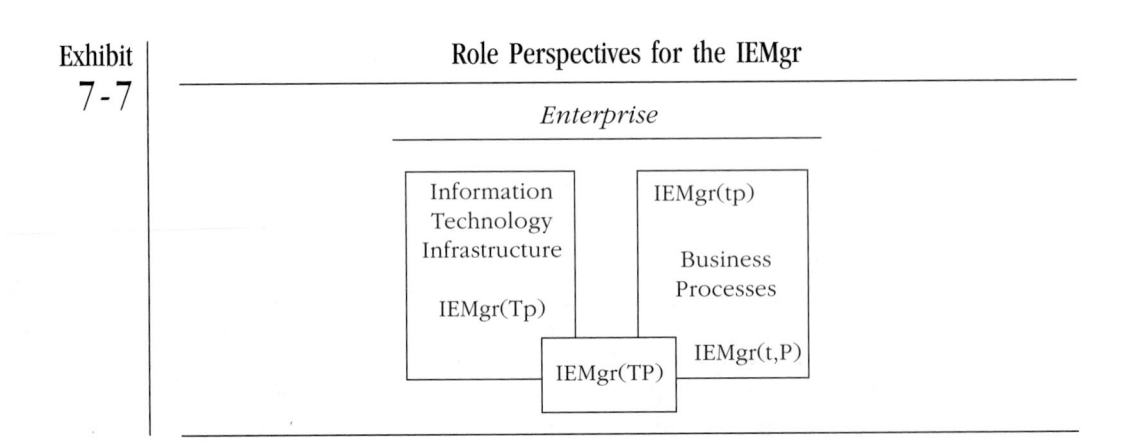

Exhibit 7-7 Role Perspectives for the IEMgr

Enterprise

- Information Technology Infrastructure
  - IEMgr(Tp)
- IEMgr(tp)
  - Business Processes
  - IEMgr(t,P)
- IEMgr(TP)

before any decision to acquire can be made. While it may be true that a single process can fully cost justify the acquisition of a new technology, it is more often true that the technology may have to fit elsewhere as a condition of acquisition.

At the process level the dynamic is somewhat different. The IEMgr(TP) is the bridge between the enterprise and the process when it comes to technology. Remember that the IEMgr(TP) may report into the IS department or the business unit responsible for the process he or she supports. That means that the IEMgr(tP) has a voice, through the IEMgr(TP), in matters related to technology acquisition. The role here is quite influential because the IEMgr(TP) has both technology expertise and process expertise. IEMgrs(tP) are ultimately responsible for the success of the process they manage and must maintain a business perspective first and a technology perspective second. Through their IEMgrs(tp) they are aware of problem areas and opportunities for improving the process at the operational level.

What we have described here is an IEMgmt team with responsibility across the continuum from technology and strategy to process and operations. The fact that all four members of this team have at least a conversational-level understanding of both the technology and the process gives them a common language. This is very different than the traditional subject matter experts trying to understand one another when they have little common ground from which to start their discussions. The number of projects that have failed simply because there was no mutual understanding is staggering. We see, then, how critically important it is to raise the minimum level of understanding of technology and process among all members of the IEMgr team in order for them to be effective.

Process Owners and Scope of Authority

The IEMgr(tP) is responsible for the process that he or she manages. As such all other members of the IEMgr team assume a support role to the IEMgr(tP). Remember, either support the customer or support someone who supports the customer. That is at the very heart of how a process structure is to operate. The process must serve the customer whether the customer is external or internal. The IEMgr(tP) is charged with meeting the performance measures that define success for the process. The IEMgr(Tp), and IEMgr(TP) are support to the IEMgr(tP) in assuring that success.

◆ THE QUALITY IMPERATIVE

Now that some preliminary comments have established that the process view has emerged, that this view requires specific boundaries for the process, and that people, technology, and process must be integrated into strategic and operational working relationships, a more detailed look at the quest for quality is in order. In this section, we discuss the major issues involved in achieving quality (strategy and vision, team leadership, customer expectations, and built-in quality design) and identify some measurement tools for analyzing customer requirements, business process, and value-added factors. Finally, implementation issues are examined through three recent activities conducted by the authors. In Chapter 8, we return to the IEMgr and to the direct relationship between information enablement and business process.

It is clear that the emphasis on quality and process has permeated all enterprises (business, government, and education). It is also clear that the movement is in its infancy. Therefore, some failure is to be expected. If an enterprise enters into the competitive race with quality, customer service, and responsiveness as target activities, the concept goes well beyond streamlining administration, cost reduction through downsizing and lower inventories, and repositioning of workers; it encompasses every fiber of the organization. There are three factors critical to success: (1) definition and measurement; (2) shared responsibilities between IS staff and end users; and (3) effective quality assurance (QA) teams. Good intentions do not guarantee success.

The major difficulty in applying these factors and numerous others identified throughout current literature (and through personal experience of the authors) is that terms such as *definition, measurement, shared responsibility,* and *effective teams* have different meanings for different organizations. Measurement can be self-defeating if the parameters are restrictive, the evaluation is too subjective, and the expectation for achievement is set too low. Shared responsibility may be just a convenient mechanism to apply blame for failure. Teams can be effective if they accomplish their objectives, regardless of appropriateness of those objectives; further, the team could finish ahead of schedule and therefore be efficient.

There is no single recipe which can be used across all enterprises. Before we examine quality assurance, functional deployment, and/or TQM in the form of a comprehensive model, other terms, phrases, and questions emerge and increase the complexity of such model-building. Hammer and Stanton's excellent text [1995] on the reengineering revolution is a compendium of information on the elements of success, making it work, and case studies and anecdotes on results of various levels of reengineering by different businesses. In addition, they list some lessons learned from the failures and some characteristics of the type of "reeengineer" needed to convert those lessons into a working formula. Because of the importance of his research, we list their conclusions in the following two sections (lesson learned and characteristics of a new type of reengineer) and have added our comments on each issue.

Lessons Learned

1. *Reengineering is a very difficult and ambitious undertaking regardless of the size of the enterprise, and there is no single formula to guarantee success.*

Why refer to historical data if it cannot be applied to one's organization today? This is a common question that can be answered by suggesting that if lessons learned from previous ventures are not examined for relevance to your organization, then failure is almost assured. Relevance is a changing term. What is relevant today may not be relevant tomorrow and vice versa. All factors may not apply, but certainly some are worthy of consideration. It is better to have some data than to operate in a vacuum. What is required of each organization conducting or considering a quality management program is creative thinking, or higher-order skill application as described in Chapter 2.

The restructuring process is total and irreversible. Before such a commitment can be demanded of the enterprise, full analysis of the implications for people and processes is necessary. The STEP Model requires that we first establish an empowered workforce before charging ahead into a reengineering effort. Only then are we assured that the risk exposure due to a noncommitted workforce will have been neutralized. The very difficult questions of impact on workers and on the way they conduct business cannot be "handled" by neglect, dodging, or refusal to confront them. Some type of diagnostic self-assessment system is needed to uncover these issues at the outset. Later in this section of the text, we propose a model for raising the important issues to be addressed.

One of the first obstacles to overcome is employee resistance to change. Hammer suggests five key mechanisms: incentives, information, intervention, indoctrination, and involvement. All of these mechanisms are important to reshaping every aspect of a business, government agency, or institution of higher education.

2. *The primary ingredient is leadership. Without it, the venture will fail.*
The definition of leadership is hotly debated even today: Is it art or science? Can it be taught or is it inherited? What is the difference between leadership and management? Whatever the definition, everyone recognizes it as soon as someone rises above the crowd and "leads" others with zeal and personal magnetism to fulfill a mission. Our experience in leadership roles in business, government, and education validates the notion that authority alone cannot make it happen. The leader of tomorrow must be earnest in his or her convictions, be patient with others (delegation and empowerment to self-directed work teams), and be action-oriented (with a proper amount of reflection and discussion to uncover the problems and issues). Adair and Murray [1994] describe leadership in terms of pulling others toward a vision or goal; management provides the policies and procedures to get there.

For the quality-driven organization, both leadership and management are necessary. A combination of management and leadership skills may very well be embodied in a single individual; however, in order for the venture to succeed, there must be many such individuals working within self-directed project teams. The team should display leadership with strategic initiatives and management through the effective implementation of those initiatives. In addition, information technology enablement of these managers can significantly increase the probability of success.

Again, staff, technology, and process are the key points in the STEP Model. Success depends on the ability of the enterprise to recognize relative worth and add value. These attributes are consistent with our information-enabled manager.

3. *The other major ingredient is a team dedicated to the process, to customer needs, and to itself.*

   The most difficult aspect of this concept of team priority is the reality of the workplace in that workers may not be allowed such team loyalty over their own business unit. In addition to the items listed by Hammer & Stanton [1995], our experience with many different types of workgroups, committees, and task forces with varying periods of activity (short and long-term objectives), validates his comments and further demonstrates that teams:

   a. Are difficult to create properly; much of the time, workers are added to teams because of availability and not expertise, personality, and commitment to team objectives.
   b. Take a lot of time to coalesce into a working, trusting, and cohesive unit.
   c. Must share information accurately, completely, and quickly in order to be effective, especially in this scenario of quality assurance; information-enablement is mandatory.
   d. Must brainstorm continuously if continuous improvement is a goal; rules must be established to allow everyone to contribute to the discussion while staying on mainstream topics.
   e. Must have reward systems to recognize team accomplishments.
   f. Use project management and other tools and techniques as appropriate to tasks.
   g. Document progress with milestones so that current members can keep on track and new members do not lose time coming up to speed.

"Progress" and Enhancement of the Quality of Life and Work

People, technology, and process have been around a long time and have not always interacted in the most effective and efficient fashion; everyone wants better quality, but not everyone wants to pay the price for it; lifelong learning is a fact of life for today and tomorrow, and the separation of work from leisure time is beginning to be fuzzier (flexible schedules, virtual environments). Rapidly changing world conditions increase complexity. Complexity increases confusion, chaos, and the search for new competitive advantage. Quality is an important ingredient and it should not be sacrificed for quantity, profit margin, or market share. In tomorrow's environment, this will not be possible.

What Is Meant by Quality?

Guinta and Praizler [1993] suggest that quality fulfills requirements, is on time, and is within costs. If we assume that quality, time, and cost are competitive variables, then tradeoffs become the center of the problem-solving process with less-than-favorable results. Instead of reacting to this tradeoff analysis, why not work on all three variables concurrently? Build in the quality up front, not after the product or service has been delivered and its failings have been discovered; examine workflow and cycle times for increased response and less variation. Optimize productivity with better design-production linkages. Zahedi [1995] presents a detailed account of almost every aspect of quality information systems which have been derived from total quality management concepts. This orientation has proven to be useful in developing our quality deployment model in the next section.

What Is Meant by "Value-Added" and Can it Be Measured?

Most reengineering efforts are internally-oriented when it comes to process improvements [Roth, et al., 1995]. They suggest that in order to profit under new conditions (globalization, information technology proliferation, and fragmented customer markets), it is necessary to integrate the needs and desires of customers into the culture and processes of the provider. Their "customer value integration" model makes sense and is consistent with the definition of quality—it fulfills requirements of the customer. Usually, measurement of efficiency (doing things right) is easy, especially if the activity is transaction oriented (time based, event driven, and/or task specific). Measuring effectiveness (doing the right thing) is more difficult.

In terms of business process improvement, Harrington [1991] offers several mechanisms for measuring not only efficiency and effectiveness, but also adaptability (flexibility of the process to handle future changing customer requirements). In addition, he addresses value-added assessment in the streamlining process. His assessment procedure sorts out those activities needed to produce output and contribute to customer requirements with real value added and those which add business value. If you can't measure it, you can't control it, and therefore, you can't manage it.

Strategy and Vision: Are They Different?

Davenport's [1993] text quickly focuses on the difference as it applies to process innovation. Strategy is defined as a long-term statement of the firm or business unit; vision is more tactical and describes how well a process should work in the future. They support the notion that customer input is vital to process innovation and that the corporate mindset must be directed outward to the customer base.

Productivity: What Is It?

Productivity is an elusive quantity. Certainly it is no longer measured as a ratio of output to input. Neither of these terms can be completely quantifiable. New technologies and economies of scale, diverse workforces, decentralized decision making, and renewed focus on tangible and intangible value-added concepts have moved the analysis from efficiency to effectiveness. Most attempts to increase white-collar productivity with technology have failed because of the thrust on more *efficient* systems [Larson and Zimney, 1990]. Since information flow (and information technology enablement) is necessary for organizations to survive, the concept of productivity must change from efficiency to effectiveness orientation. In terms of white-collar workers, this transition means new structures under which to work, new skill requirements, and new management techniques incorporating teams and collaborative arrangements among workers from different functional business units.

Organizational Integrity

Creating a working environment responsive to these new and complex interrelationships also is difficult to manage. Even if the starting and ending points of the trip from traditional organizational structure to a completely new process-oriented, team-driven, and project-directed environment are known, the transition is apt to be strategically and operationally disruptive, be complaint-driven on the part of workers and perhaps customers (in the short-term), have less ROI in the short run, incur resistance from some staff, cost more to train and retrain, and require a rethinking of rewards and incentives.

Before the organization can incorporate a total quality movement, all aspects of this transition must be examined at the outset with full commitment by key managers at every level of the organization. This comprehensive examination of the enterprise will provide "integrity." A new value system is being placed on everyone's shoulders; workers must believe that the organization is fully behind the effort if any chance of success is to be obtained. During the past decade, organizations undertaking TQM that did not have consistent strategies and implementation (everyone on board and supporting the movement) had severe difficulties along the way [Hammer, HBR, 1990]. One way to audit organizational integrity is proposed by Marshall [1995] in his "disconnect" scheme. He suggests that disconnects occur when there is a gap between what the company says it will do versus what it does.

The disconnects of leadership, business and customers, workforce relationships and processes, and organizational systems require intervention so that they can be "connected." Much of the time, these disconnects are evaluated in terms of ongoing work processes. Some departments are outside the process loop when they should be directly involved in reengineering design. Other key individuals are unaware of events simply through self-selection of information (they may not

> **Exhibit 7-8**
>
> ## Opportunity Assessment Matrix
>
> Opportunities are assessed in the form of a checklist for which data is collected on the following items:
> - sample period dates
> - number of items processed
> - processing cost
> - batch processing operations
> - processing efficiency
> - processing complaints
> - cycle time (time to move product or service)
> - calendar time to move product or service
> - lead times
> - cost of work in progress
> - cost of raw materials
> - rejected parts, services
> - rework, rechecked work
> - number of handoffs of work
> - queues (wait times)
> - travel distances of work operations
> - number of people involved
> - major process problems

want to know what is happening, or they discover their unawareness at the most inopportune time). There also exist disconnects between the enterprise and potential customers. Opportunities should be addressed much the same way that work processes occupy our attention [Adair & Murray, 1994]. Adair and Murray offer a data collection device for assessment of opportunities for redesign (Exhibit 7-8).

Now that some major concepts and terms have been introduced, it is time to place them in some framework for further discussion and, in some cases, for providing practical guidelines to apply the concepts to your enterprise. The last section of this chapter will present specific examples of application of our model to business and education environments.

◆ QUALITY FUNCTION DEPLOYMENT MODEL

Quality function deployment is a framework, or methodology, designed to prepare and implement total quality management (TQM) principles in any enterprise. It is an attempt to integrate people, technology, and process in a synergistic way for efficiency, effectiveness, and adaptability using a workforce of IEMgrs for personal and organizational productivity. Exhibit 7-9 depicts a 12-stage model for discussion of all issues; it has been developed following traditional systems development methodology (analysis-design-implementation

Exhibit 7-9

Stage Quality Function Deployment (QFD) Model

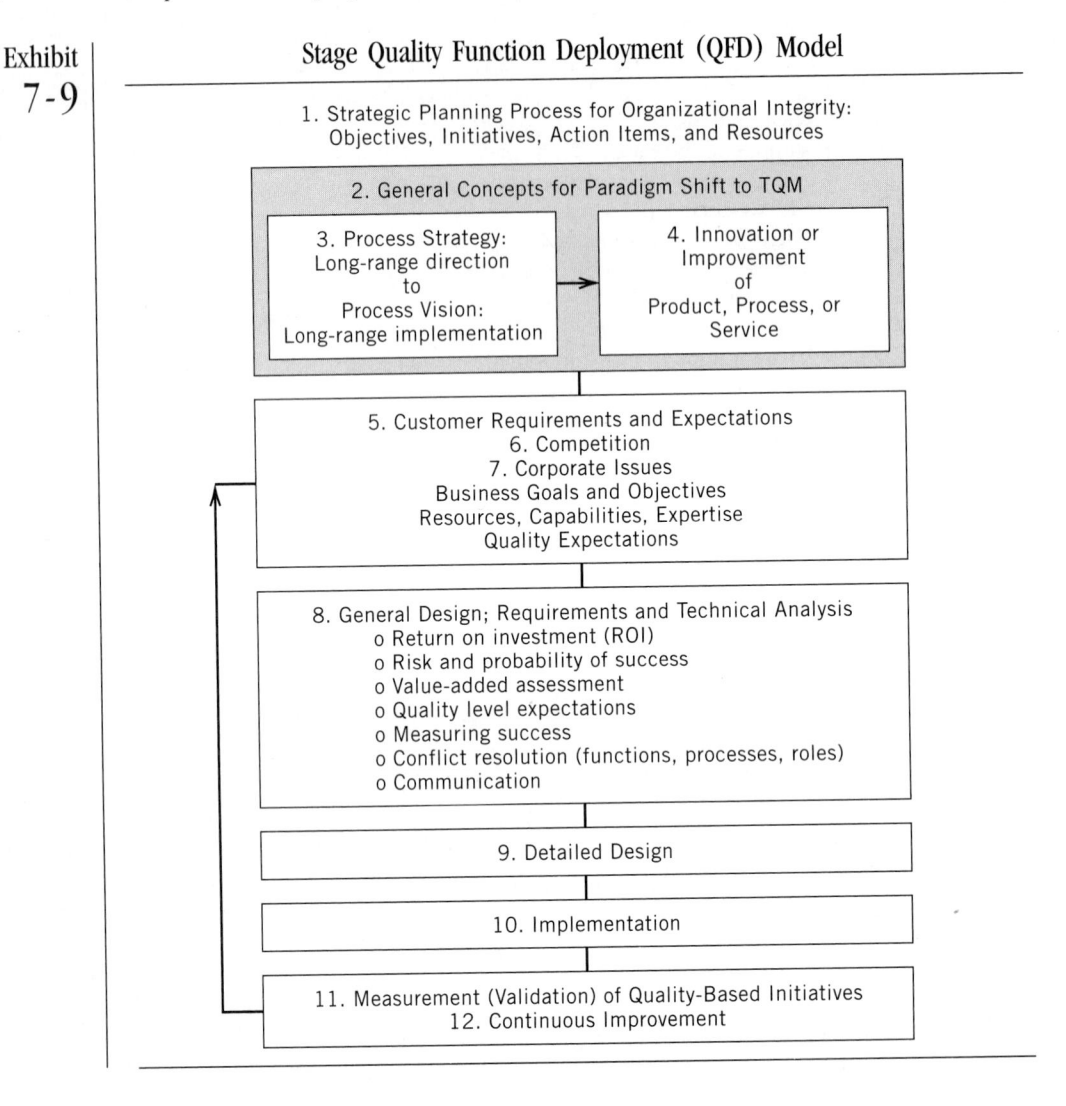

1. Strategic Planning Process for Organizational Integrity:
   Objectives, Initiatives, Action Items, and Resources

   2. General Concepts for Paradigm Shift to TQM

   | 3. Process Strategy: Long-range direction to Process Vision: Long-range implementation | → | 4. Innovation or Improvement of Product, Process, or Service |

5. Customer Requirements and Expectations
6. Competition
7. Corporate Issues
   Business Goals and Objectives
   Resources, Capabilities, Expertise
   Quality Expectations

8. General Design; Requirements and Technical Analysis
   o Return on investment (ROI)
   o Risk and probability of success
   o Value-added assessment
   o Quality level expectations
   o Measuring success
   o Conflict resolution (functions, processes, roles)
   o Communication

9. Detailed Design

10. Implementation

11. Measurement (Validation) of Quality-Based Initiatives
12. Continuous Improvement

sequence) with quality attainment as the main objective instead of developing an information system for a business function (sales order processing, marketing research, production scheduling, accounts payable).

Stage 1: Organizational Integrity

For organizations serious about doing the right things and doing them right, some formal mechanism must be in place before any action takes place. In their zeal for embodying the TQM concept, some organizations embark on this journey without careful analysis of all tradeoffs. Often, TQM is precipitated by a crisis (dramatic drop in sales over the past quarter; too many customer complaints and/or losses; lost opportunities because of inability to respond fast enough; stockholders want more profit next quarter; competition too keen; administrative bungling; bureaucratic red tape). Examples and case studies abound in texts, periodicals, and current magazines.

The trick is to prevent crises from happening. Obviously, this is not possible in all cases; however, it can be a serious strategic initiative. Preventive stances are always more difficult to enact than simply reacting when the need arises. If no formal mechanism is in place to establish, document, implement, and validate the process of quality attainment, it is destined to fail. A common argument against the enterprise undertaking a proactive and preventative mode is that everyone is too busy fighting the alligators on a day-to-day basis to engage in prolonged discussions leading to a solution for next year. Jobs and performance are on the line today. Careers and performance measures in the future may change dramatically, but who knows when (or if) that will really happen? The status quo, if the corporation is solvent and prospects are bright, is appealing. On the other hand, we know that the status quo will not suffice anymore. So, a mechanism can be created for the long term with implications for the short term. One master plan for business with information enablement is indicated.

Documentation is an important part of Stage 1. Without it, the enterprise cannot keep on track, especially if the track changes course to meet business conditions and/or opportunities. A historical memory is necessary. Every minute of every meeting need not be transcribed. At a minimum, several issues must be integrated into the documentation package: major strategic initiatives focused on business goals and objectives, actions to implement those initiatives, resources available and needed to conduct those actions, and some accountability for the actions. As decision making moves even closer to the client (more direct interaction, feedback, and responsibility to customers), it is more important to share information among individuals, departmental groups, and project teams. A formal communication system is necessary as workers move within and to/from the enterprise (turnover). With fewer middle managers to act as the glue to the communication network for conducting business, the corporation without organizational memory (documentation, communication) cannot survive.

Stages 2, 3, & 4: Paradigm Shift from Function to Process

During this process of developing strategic initiatives, it is important to conduct a major sort: separation of innovative development from merely improving the product, process, or service. Once the sort is made, then the enterprise should address both directions concurrently. Once these directions are documented, long-range and short-term initiatives can be assessed for importance, relative priority, and other factors identified later in Stage 8. The paradigm shift is from function to process with special attention on initiatives (strategic direction of the enterprise) and process vision (strategic actions for processes needed to get there).

Stages 5, 6, & 7: Customer Requirements, Competition, and Corporate Issues

The customer may not always be right, but any feedback from current customers and prospective customers is important. They constitute a part of the stakeholder community along with stockholders and employees, and in recent years are much more demanding of quality, service, and price. The patience level of customers is low; this attribute is consistent with society in general. The norm is immediate response and gratification. The enterprise cannot afford to maintain status-quo relationships with the customer base; customers are a moving target and they are moving fast.

Although there are success stories with reengineering ventures, Hammer concedes that about 70 percent fail to accomplish their goals [Moad, 1993]. With this statistic in mind, it is in the interest of the competing organization to move toward the next generation of customer value added, namely customer value integration [Roth et al., 1995], where more intimacy over a longer time period is encouraged. In order to engage in this concept, customer value parameters are needed together with a listing of value creation issues (Exhibit 7-10). Roth and coauthors suggest using structured interviews to fully understand customer needs and beliefs. Next, questionnaires are derived from initial interviews followed by additional interviews on questionnaire data analysis. Finally, steps for improvement are determined.

The competition wants those same customers. Whatever the method used (direct observation, focus groups, face-to-face interviews, telephone surveys, written surveys, and/or user groups), the objective is to distill the data into a customer value profile [Adair & Murray, 1994]. Once a customer profile of requirements is obtained, it can be compared to what the organization can provide. This gap is refined further by analyzing one's organizational "perception" of customer needs and comparing them to actual customer data. This procedure is very similar to the benchmarking procedure employed in computer systems contracting. Several negotiation sessions between vendor and client are needed to ensure that both parties understand each other's position, requirements, and provision.

Many corporate issues have been addressed with regard to total quality management. It bears repeating that many spectacularly unsuccessful efforts of TQM are attributable to lack of planning. Planning is time intensive. In the upcoming decades of global competition and instant communication, it is conceivable that an organization would say that it is a waste of time. By the time the plan is ready for implementation, the customer market has changed and the corporation is retooling for the next wave—so, why plan? This fallacious thinking was discussed extensively in Chapter 4, the conclusion reached being that some plan is better than none. A flexible plan (continuously updated) is better than a plan created in four-year intervals. A formal plan can be used in benchmarking results against listed variables, even if those variables change frequently.

Quality Function Deployment Model 167

Exhibit 7-10

Information Economics Scorecard

Evaluator	Business Domain					Technology Domain				Weighted Score
(factor →)	roi • +	sm • +	ca • +	mi • +	cr • +	or • -	sa • +	du • -	tu • -	ir • -
Business Domain										
Technology Domain										
Weighted value										

- Where:
  - ROI Measurement
    - ROI = Enhanced simple return on investment score
  - Business Domain Assessment
    - SM = Strategic match
    - CA = Competitive information
    - MI = Management information
    - CR = Competitive response
    - OR = Project or organizational risk
  - Technology Domain Assessment
    - SA - Strategic IS architecture
    - DU - Definitional uncertainty
    - IR - IS infrastucture risk

SOURCE: Reprinted from Parker, Benson with Trainor text, Fig. 13.1, p. 145, *Information Economics: Linking Business Performance to Information Technology,* Prentice Hall, 1988.

Once goals and objectives have been established and are consistent with documented and formal strategic initiatives demonstrating those directions, more information on available resources is needed. This information is not limited to head count and financial statement data. Often, resources within a corporation are not really known. The human resource database may not contain information on all employee skills; it may contain summary data on where the individual is working and on his or her current position description.

Full impact analyses are needed to fit current employees into new careers of the newly reengineered corporation. New processes need different skill sets. New innovative opportunities may very well need a different type of manager (i.e., IEMgr). Resources take on a more encompassing meaning as the environment becomes more complex. In any event, it is worth the time to thoroughly identify corporate strengths, mainly in the area of people, and make an effort to retain and retrain rather than lose the most important resource through downsizing. Attempts to recapture the resource later may come too late.

Alternatively, the organization could conduct an internal human resource survey to identify current and future aspirations of employees given that they have some idea of corporate direction and personnel requirements. This vision is very important. We return to it in greater detail in Chapter 9. If the process is a formal information systems project and is an integral part of the "organizational integrity" concept discussed at the beginning of this segment, in the long run the enterprise would benefit. In the short-term, the quarterly report would show an investment, thereby raising the ROI. Business process reengineering concepts indicate that the commitment is 100 percent and that organizations should settle only for ten times improvement within a year or two. Practically, this goal may be unrealistic in light of the turmoil caused by such abrupt and disruptive change. The point is that focusing only on quantitative measures for ROI may be a disservice to the organization. Other intangible factors with long-term consequences should be considered.

Stage 8: General Design—Requirements and Technical Analysis

Return on Investment (ROI)

If you have lost staff through downsizing, your financial investment has decreased, making the return/investment ratio larger. If you make the remaining people do their work and the work of those who left, return is higher and the ratio increases. If this scenario continues too long, good people burn out and retire early, and others move to better environments, or deliver less quality and response, or just ignore workplace demands and wait for retirement. This scenario is not unlike the situation today. Again, using quantitative data exclusively for ROI does not provide a complete picture, especially when elusive terms like *quality* and *customer service* enter into the calculation. A very definitive treatment of decision-making tools and concepts, applied specifically to information technology projects and their linkage to business processes, is provided by Parker and Benson [1988]. Their text goes beyond traditional cost/benefit analyses to include value based on business performance and strategic impact. These principles are applicable to any type of project, namely, quality management efforts led by information-enabled managers.

Risk and Probability of Success

The Parker and Benson text [1988] incorporates several chapters on business and technology domain values, corporate values, risks, and corporate decision-making. It is not the intent of our text to digress into these areas with specificity; however, the general concepts highlight our thrust for comprehensive coverage of business performance. In this section, we defer to the statisticians and their models of domains and information economics. In an effort to provide the reader with some notion of their direction, we show you Exhibit 7-10, which identifies the features of the process without undue detail. The text applies the model to the business environment incorporating risk in ROI determination. Using the concept as a framework, the application can be extended to TQM projects.

The factors examined are indicated on the scorecard which attempts to measure by subjective scoring (scale of 0–5, a range from no relationship to corporate goals to 100 percent related to corporate goals) the desirability of the project. Risk factors are negative. The two domains are business and technology. The result is a ranking of projects by score, thereby giving a relative economic value of each project to the enterprise. Clearly, their four chapters on this topic [Parker & Benson, 1988] suggest more detail on the procedure. "Weighted values" in the scorecard means that some subjective judgment must be made on the importance of that factor, or value, to the enterprise. It can be argued that one can make the analysis move toward preconceived results as a trial-and-error procedure is enacted. Change the weights, change the results to agree with your desires. This procedure is not very different from evaluating vendor bids on some point basis just to arrive at a relative ranking for a starting point in the negotiations. In the federal government, the concept has been used to evaluate resource change proposals for the zero-base budgeting process. The government's focus is the best way to spend resources for mission-critical operations.

Value-Added Assessment

The general concept is to evaluate before and after processing. In reengineering, it means collecting data on current procedures, tracking value accrued during a transformation process, and then calculating the increase in value over and above the original condition. Value added is the difference between the before and after processing cycle. If the important parameter is time, the transformation is a decrease in value, such as noted earlier by Exhibit 7-6. In accounting, the difference would appear as accumulated costs during the life of the change.

Harrington [1991] submits that real value-added (RVA) activities are those activities viewed by the customer to meet expectations. A value-added assessment analysis (VAA) is needed to increase business value and reduce or eliminate no-value activity. MacDonald's value process model [Morton, 1991] marries a value chain and an organization flow diagram to produce a picture of the organization at any one time.

Quality-Level Expectations

What are the minimum quality levels acceptable to the customer? Note that a customer-driven orientation is indicated in this question. The corporate quality imposition should be set against the customer standard; if the customer standard is unknown or unclear, some type of assessment (previously discussed in this chapter) is in order. Quality-level expectation is like computer literacy. It depends on the enterprise. What are the standards, if any? Do different people have different standards for different positions? How do career aspirations (moving from an IS department into a business unit) enter into corporate expectations?

Similar questions can be noted for quality of information technology and quality of business processes. Software quality is an important topic. Information systems managers have wrestled for years with design and development of quality applications. The quality of code is uneven, compliance to standards is less than perfect, and reliability of the product is wanting, according to Hanna [1993]. She proposes process management systems as a way to ensure reliability and consistency in software development. The methodology includes task structures, planning techniques, project management techniques (individual and team projects), and development of skills needed to build the product. Users are involved in the standardization process, automated tools are employed (such as Ernst & Young's Navigator System, Application Development Workbench from KnowledgeWare, Inc., and Information Engineering Facility from TI). Hanna's article identifies several other quality assurance tools dedicated to the premise that quality is crucial to success.

If errors are not detected in the design/testing phase (built-in quality), they will occur during implementation when more is at stake. For example, Microsoft delayed introducing Windows95 several times. There is too much at stake with error-ridden software; it could ruin the company's reputation. Compared to other business functions, information systems projects seem to have a higher failure rate. It is understandable since funding is based on the success or failure of each project, sometimes without sufficient funds to track the interrelationships among business units (integrating effect). Accurate estimates are very difficult to obtain; turnover is higher than other manager levels; and response is perceived to be job critical. No one is impressed with the milliseconds saved by incorporating C++ and object-oriented elegant analyses. Timely results have been the reward system; now, they have to be timely for the enterprise to survive and to have the quality to remain competitive.

Poor project estimating can be corrected. Try to reduce changes as much as possible, unless the methodology incorporates prototyping, which presupposes that many changes will occur. The prototype is placed online as soon as possible (weeks) with some features needed for the application; other features are added according to current and new requirements. For this method, users are active participants in every phase of the project. Object orientation, a process which separates phases of a project into "activity objects" and tasks, moves our thinking from unique tasks to tasks common to several processes [Lederer and Phasad, 1992]. At the task level, all the data and processing power is self-contained to execute the application segment. Segments are clustered for larger applications. In a project-planning sense, cost, schedule, and status differentiate tasks from one another. The approach negates the concept of overrun tolerance; object orientation provides the basis for a more systematic approach to using historical data and experience to best advantage.

Measuring Success

Most measures of success have been based on dollars. They are quantifiable and can be derived from transactions, events, and other quantifiable measures. Often, success or failure is noted after the fact; measures are created to get a handle on results to see where we have been and, hopefully, to use that data to help predict future prospects. Very little measurement activity helps us to manage. Much of the time, there is too much information, especially in this world of connectivity. Also, there are too many reports left over from legacy computer systems. Users are immersed in the cybernetic culture whether by choice or not. They are information enabled to varying degrees and use the technology for personal productivity, sharing it on teams. Measures of performance are becoming tied more to results and less to aptitude for the next promotion. At a major industrial firm's computing center, the CIO had an entire wall dressed with numerous page-size charts, all in different colors to indicate project status. The charts were changed weekly; none of them were available to others in the organization. They were impressive but did not measure customer satisfaction; they only indicated whether or not the project was on, behind, or ahead of schedule. A successful week was one where there were no "red" charts (behind schedule).

Measurement systems must give feedback to be beneficial to the performers and to the organization. For example, this text has been reviewed by at least five professionals in this field; they will follow the text to its completion. Without their serious input to the process, we could publish a text that few academicians would buy. Athletic endeavors have measurable standards (win or lose) and feedback from fans, coaches, and other players. Scientists have measures and feedback systems. Why not business managers? With the current emergence of reengineering management in addition to business processes [Champy, 1995], jobs and careers are becoming even more elusive. If "jobs" disappear, what takes their place? Are we headed for another identity crisis in the workforce?

Our experience indicates that organizations are becoming aware of the need for feedback on performance. Higher-level managers in business and education are receiving peer review. The problem still exists that usually ratings are based on past performance. Why not review strategic initiatives and follow them to completion with performance review milestones? Furthermore, the measurement parameters should be identified at the outset, not when the work is done. Individuals would welcome knowledge of performance criteria when they are hired and before any work is done. Time should be allocated for performance review. Perhaps outside services could be used in developing the criteria, conducting the interviews, analyzing results, and reporting (tactfully) findings. With the advent of teams, special criteria may apply and may be different from those used for individuals in the past.

Conflict Resolution

It is inevitable that more conflicts will emerge from any quality movement. Drastic changes in business strategies and operations, streamlining administrative workflow, project teams, and new cost containment policies mean more conflict. If systems, processes, and procedures have been benchmarked, that is, the organization has fully uncovered its operation (internally), has defined the competition, and sorted out the best solutions for today and tomorrow, then it has considerably reduced conflict and increased the chance of success. The benchmarking process has been around for a long time but has not been actively implemented in the business arena. Harrington [1991] provides an extensive account of methods, guidelines, and actions for a comprehensive audit of all internal business process activities (functions, processes, and roles).

Communication

Good communication is implied throughout each issue covered in this chapter. Communication is essential in the form of feedback loops, documentation packages, team and individual reporting, measurement of performance review, involvement of the user in each stage of the quality development process, leadership, information sharing and groupware, assessments for opportunity and risk, and resolving conflict. Information enablement can help to make human communication more effective through personal and organizational productivity tools.

Stages 9, 10, 11, and 12: Detailed Design and Implementation

These stages have been discussed in the immediately previous sections of this chapter. Once the first seven stages are firmly and completely in place, the remainder of the process takes care of itself. The process is continuous; milestones are generated on a continuous basis. The key idea is to build an adaptable and responsive system.

◆ APPLICATION OF THE QFD MODEL

Business Example

The twelve-stage Quality Function Deployment (QFD) Model was applied to a major industrial firm incorporating total quality methods in numerous major projects throughout the enterprise. Although corporate staff had been indoctrinated in TQM methodology over the past few years and several projects were completed, it was decided to implement the proposed model in a new corporate-driven venture with a team of self-directed and cross-functional managers during a three-month time period. This very recent project was designed to bring academe and business together in addressing the theory and practice of assuring quality in an ongoing operation. The team consisted of two faculty from Fairfield University (R. DeMichiell and J. Keenan) and thirteen managers from nearby Sikorsky Aircraft in Stratford, Connecticut. Both academic and business objectives were identified for a project selected by the enterprise after evaluation by the team and high-level Sikorsky management (Stages 1–4). During these stages (strategic planning for innovation and improvement of service), all problem areas (e.g., incompatible schedules, different motivations, and the cross-functional nature of the project) were examined for consensus, which was quickly obtained.

The next three stages (expectations, competition, and corporate issues) consumed a major part of the effort because of the academe-business relationship, diversity of the team in expertise, and delineation of project deliverables. Such discussion is understandable for projects involving new concepts (TQM) applied to existing processes across departments (manufacturing, production control, quality assurance, information systems). The specific project involved the final machine shop inspection (FMSI) process for parts and assemblies destined for helicopter manufacture. Top management support was provided at the outset and throughout the project for staff empowerment.

Three subgroups of team members were self-selected for specialized project work on analysis of cycle process times for work orders, on physical logistics of each activity in the FMSI process, and on analysis of the inspection process. These subgroups were defined by the team after numerous plenary sessions with all members discussing and resolving the issues. As the project proceeded from Stage 8 (general design) to Stage 9 (detailed design), communication among the teams, university faculty, and corporate management was assured by weekly meetings and documentation of analyses, findings, and recommendations. It was necessary for all parties to review progress, make sure that the next steps were still appropriate, and modify the schedule. In this way, the return on investment parameters dominated discussion and expectations were fulfilled or adjusted for more complex operations.

Near the conclusion of the QFD procedure and just prior to the implementation phase, a forum was held to bring together academe and business to formally report on findings and recommendations for implementation. The audience was asked to comment on the implementation plan (responsibility and accountability for action, schedule, benchmark measures, and continuous improvement methods).

For Stages 9-12 (implementation through continuous improvement), systems techniques were employed in the production, analysis, design, and interpretation of process and workflow diagrams. This methodology included distance measurements, critical path time, wait time, cycle time, and value-added time. Data was collected on the shop floor by team members with assistance from process quality inspectors. Project management methods were employed in scheduling and reporting of results at appropriate milestones. Integration of the process with the extensive materials resource planning (MRP) software system was investigated for accuracy, completeness, and data integrity; in addition, usage of programmable laser measurement devices was examined for effective utilization. Administrative operations were streamlined and other opportunities were uncovered for further improvements.

Follow-up on the implementation occurred within a few months of completion of the project. All recommendations were enacted with favorable results. Although the project did provoke many arguments among the cross-functional teams, the net result was a more effective procedure with tangible value-added components. As expected, team members spent much more time on the project than anticipated; the frequent communication among members tended to be somewhat inefficient due to prolonged discussion of some key issues, but did result in effective solutions. In addition, each team member was required to keep a journal separate from team reports. This approach helped members to stay abreast of all activity and at the same time build confidence in their individual contributions to the venture. For some members who never had been directly involved in such a project, it helped in organization and reporting findings. When it came time to deliver the oral reports at the "forum," the historical information proved invaluable.

Higher Education Example

The same QFD Model is being used in the quest for business school accreditation at Fairfield University by the Chair of the Task Force, R. DeMichiell. During the past few years, the model has been used for developing a strategic plan for quality education development. At this time, the program is in the implementation stage with measurement (validation) of quality-based initiatives through a self-study report and visitation of the accrediting body imminent. The most difficult aspect of this example was the starting point (Stages 1 and 2—strategic planning process and the paradigm shift to TQM). Faculty tend to resist new approaches, especially if they are nontraditional and are business driven. For the business enterprise, many TQM ventures have occurred during the past decade.

For higher education, there have been innovations precipitated by information technology (more and better microcomputers, user-friendly software, connectivity enhancements through networks, and integration of computing into discipline-specific curricula; however, the more bureaucratic institutions have not absorbed the technology as fast as it has emerged. Although the University is relatively young (approximately 50 years old), its business school has been in existence for almost two decades, and has grown from a handful of department faculty to a school of 30 faculty during that time period. Until recently, faculty have been very comfortable with the curriculum developed slowly over the years. Each year, new curriculum changes arise and are addressed by a general meeting of faculty. Usually, sweeping changes in content or methodology do not characterize the process.

With the advent of the TQM movement in industry, the declining student body (in general and in schools of business), infringement of corporate education and training programs, new business demands for more communicative, business-savvy, and information-enabled graduates, and more selective students (and parents), complacency cannot be tolerated if the institution is to survive. For private colleges and universities (such as Fairfield, a Jesuit university), the need to use limited resources prudently is highlighted by the situation. The business school had to react to the new and rapidly changing environment. Only a full sweep of activity with fully empowered faculty could make such a transition. The first step, to gain acceptance of a zero-based approach to the curriculum and of the dissolution of discipline-driven procedures for creating new and innovative courses, is more than a paradigm shift; it is a major paradigm shift from everything in place to development from nothing.

The transition was made with considerable discussion, argument, and finally consensus. An elaborate information system was designed to record progress and keep faculty productive and on schedule. A documentation system for identifying strategic initiatives from the action teams, committees, and task forces and converting them into action statements was created at the outset. Anyone, at any time, could suggest an initiative. All documented initiatives were placed on the agenda, discussed, and resolved by faculty at several plenary and small group sessions throughout the year. Each initiative followed the QFD Model in principle and did not need to be repeated stage by stage.

In addition to the difficulty of startup activity, another problem area was value-added assessment. Learning activity consists of transactions; however, they are much more intangible than business statements. How does one evaluate a learning method, such as the use of case studies in the classroom? The more experienced and professional faculty have to step forward and provide insights to content and methodology changes, especially if the changes are dramatic. Often, older faculty have not experienced the use of information technology in the classroom and may be hesitant to try it now. Younger faculty may have the technical base, but do not have classroom experience and may not have had the opportunity to demonstrate leadership in classroom teaching. The educational reward system (rank and tenure) has not caught up with the need for new curricula, teaching expertise, and research in the use of instructional technology in the classroom. Old reward systems are not conducive to risky new approaches in educational reform. Reinvention of the curriculum and its delivery system is risky.

However, reasoned judgment prevailed and a new process of business school reinvention occurred. The result over the past three years is the production of over 25 initiatives encompassing 100 action items. At this point, approximately 90 percent of the action items have been completed with the addition of 25 more action items. At the beginning, perhaps a quarter of the faculty were resistive, half were complacent, and another quarter proactive. Three years later, most are proactive and some are complacent and supportive. When it became clear that administration supported the process with thought and action, it did not take long for resistive faculty to join the program. In addition, when the accrediting agency was complimentary to the strategic plan and associated early actions, a boost in morale was experienced and helped to launch even more dramatic initiatives.

Some programs met with resource difficulties at first, but later receipt of grants afforded some relief. The Dean's Office became more of a resource provider for traditional and visionary ventures; the faculty took control of the reins and in an orderly way with the office of the dean, orchestrated the process. A single task force (faculty and Dean's Office) directed the effort, held the meetings, reported progress to the faculty and the accreditation agency, and provided general leadership to the movement.

Reflections

GENERAL CONCEPTS

1. How does one adopt a process view of the organization when all of our education and training is grounded in the business functions and command and control structures? (This question and the following related subquestions were presented at the beginning of this part.)
   a. What does business process redesign entail and what tools are available to help us in the conversion process?
   b. What about the human resources changes that we will have to undergo as part of the redesign effort (downsizing, rightsizing, upsizing, reshaping, reinventing)?
   c. What role will the IS Department and the IEMgmt team play in our business redesign efforts?
2. Why is the concept of a "process owner" particularly difficult to understand?
   a. Expand on the brief discussion of this topic in the chapter by examining one or more businesses, government, or education institutions for clarification of this issue.
   b. Does organizational structure have an important impact on process ownership?
3. A Quality Function Deployment (QFD) model suggests a framework to integrate

people, technology, and process in a synergistic way for effective enterprise competitiveness. Select an enterprise which has recently undergone some total quality management (TQM) effort and using the model respond to the following questions:
 a. Which of the twelve stages was handled particularly well and why?
 b. Was the model, or some other form of detailed model, used in the process? Comment.
 c. Attempt to evaluate the amount of time (person-days) spent on each stage of the model. A person-day is one person spending one day, or two persons spending 1/2 day each, and so on.
 d. Since no guidelines are provided in the text on these stages, is it reasonable to assume that the application of QFD to an enterprise is a unique experience? Could you devise a scheme for evaluating (with parameters and/or criteria) such a deployment plan before deployment occurs?
 e. Why all the fuss about organizational integrity? About measurement of success?

Reflections

STEP MODEL

1. How can the enterprise stay on a STEP Model path with the massive turnovers in personnel? It would appear that once momentum is gained along a path, disruptions in conducting business (caused by personnel turnover and the decrease of middle management positions) and perhaps in new strategic initiatives (new top-level executives), would tend to derail any planned effort to move forward on that path.
 a. How would you keep everyone on the path?
 b. Does the QFD Model suggest any directions you might recommend?

Reflections

ISI CASE STUDY

Introduction

Now that some basic facts of ISI have unfolded and instructor and students may have modified the case according to their interests and experience, it is time to begin the iterative process of redefining both the RFP and vendor bid preparation. Ultimately, a sufficient degree of convergence will take place to provide the enterprise with a best solution and the vendors with a reasonable profit.

In this chapter, a more in-depth look at the nature of ISI is needed. What is the management philosophy? Can the current business functions be changed to reflect a "business process" perspective? ISI does not produce anything; it buys and sells products that other companies produce. It is clear that ISI has no IEMgrs; in fact, there is only one person responsible for automation. Most of the expertise is obtained from consultants who plan for applications development and implement standalone solutions on microcomputers in piecemeal fashion. Their focus is on internal operations and not corporate growth. There is little external data available and the marketing effort relies on old connections.

The Quality Imperative

In order to move to the "quality imperative," ISI needs a formal vision statement other than the current objective of maximizing short-term profit. Top-level management probably should start over and develop a strategy for master plan development which includes information technology as an integral part of the process. A "process" orientation must replace current operations. Self-directed work teams are needed to improve quality of customer service. A total systems view is needed to incorporate a new electronic database with business operations (see the business functions flowchart of Reflections-ISI for Chapter 6).

Deliverables

Since there is no recipe for this massive transformation of a corporation stuck in a time warp with a command and control, authoritarian, task-oriented methodology, the challenge for students undertaking this case is to develop a framework to accomplish the change. In this respect, the following comments may be helpful:

1. End users and selection team—Much thinking is needed by these two groups because without the vision, policies, and philosophy for change, ISI will not survive.
b. Vendors—Commence drafting a configuration (physical and logical diagram of the hardware and software) of ISI current situation with an eye for improving it with information technology.

In examining the business applications portfolio, all groups should focus on the "value-added" concept, productivity measurement, and organizational integrity. Once the vision is stated and ISI says it will proceed to implement the master plan, will actions support the idea? The quality function deployment model (Figure 7-9) is useful in approaching this problem.

Chapter 8

Business Process Redesign

◆ ◆ ◆

In this chapter we consider various levels of change that an organization might entertain as it looks to improve the efficiency and effectiveness of its business processes. Having just begun to view the enterprise from the perspective of process rather than function, it might well be expected that there are numerous opportunities for improvement. These enhancements will range from the simple to the sublime. We need a strategy for approaching change. The objective of this chapter is to give you a model for change. In the next chapter we present several tools you will need in order to analyze business processes.

◆ DOWNSIZING AND RIGHTSIZING: REPOSITIONING WORKERS

One of the major obstacles to any business process redesign is the anxiety that workers feel when they know that their job may be on the line. Under such stressful conditions it would not be unusual for there to be little interest in participating in the redesign project on the part of those who feel that their jobs are at risk. The realities of the situation are such that some will lose their jobs and only some of those that are displaced will be able to find comparable work elsewhere in the company. Others will be dismissed and will have to fend for themselves outside the company. For this reason it is paramount that the individual develop a strategy for the future. That strategy must place the individual in charge of his or her own career. The responsibility cannot be delegated as might have been the case in the past. Those days are gone. They will not return.

For the individual worker there are some options. You need to answer a few basic questions. Where are you in your career? Where do you want to be? How do you get there from here? These questions are easily formed but difficult to answer in many cases. The realities of job loss due to downsizing are so prominent in the minds of IEMgrs that we spend some time discussing strategies and action plans. This topic is covered in Chapter 9.

◆ BUSINESS PROCESS REDESIGN HIERARCHY

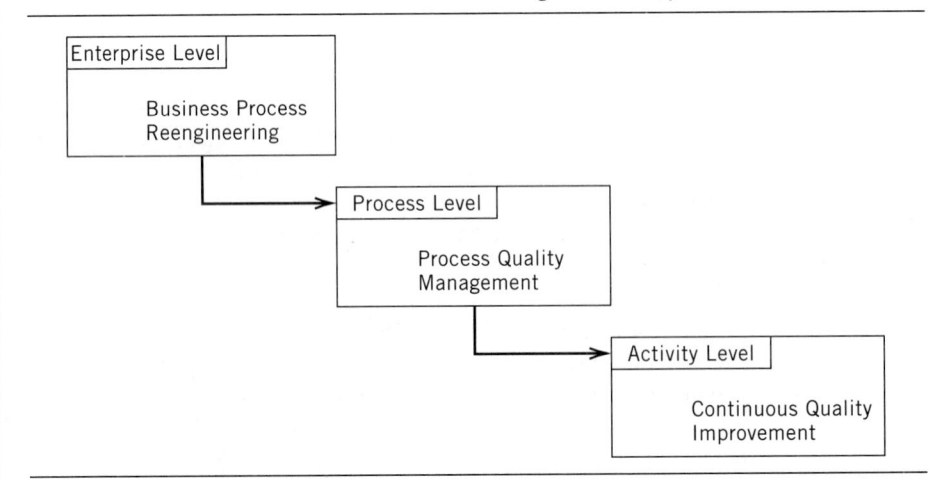

With respect to business process redesign there is a hierarchy of change that we need to understand. Exhibit 8-1 is a graphical representation of this hierarchy. IEMgmt can enter the hierarchy at any level. Obviously, the more serious the problem the more likely it is that the entry point will be at the enterprise level, for at this level the enterprise is looking for quantum improvements. Oftentimes the need for reengineering is triggered by a major threat to market position. Efforts at reengineering are undertaken by the IEMgr(Tp) and IEMgr(TP). For processes that are well-designed or have been reengineered, the IEMgr(TP) and IEMgr(tP) will take more of an improvement role and focus on a particular process looking for ways to make further improvements in the reengineered process. Finally, within a particular process at the activity level, the IEMgr(tp) will look for minor adjustments to the process. To be most effective we recommend that IEMgmt begin as near the top of this hierarchy as the organizational climate will permit.

In this chapter we will look at each part of this hierarchy. Of particular importance will be the role of the IEMgr at each level of the hierarchy. We will see that their roles are quite different and will retain their customer service focus at all times. In fact, we will see that the IEMgmt team is the most effective way to fully utilize information technology at all levels of business improvement efforts.

Enterprise Level—Business Reengineering

Michael Hammer and James Champy [1994] are credited with introducing the discipline of reengineering and offer the following informal definition:

Exhibit 8-1

Business Process Redesign Hierarchy

Enterprise Level

Business Process Reengineering

Process Level

Process Quality Management

Activity Level

Continuous Quality Improvement

When someone asks us for a quick definition of business reengineering, we say that it means "starting over." It *doesn't* mean tinkering with what already exists or making incremental changes that leave basic structures intact. It isn't about making patchwork fixes—jury-rigging existing systems so that they work better. It does mean abandoning long-established procedures and looking afresh at the work required to create a company's product or service and deliver value to the customer. It means asking this question: "If I were re-creating this company today, given what I know and given current technology, what would it look like?" Reengineering a company means tossing aside old systems and starting over. It involves going back to the beginning and inventing a better way of doing work.

The formal definition that they offer is that reengineering is "the fundamental rethinking and radical redesign of business processes to achieve dramatic improvements in critical, contemporary measures of performance, such as cost, quality, service, and speed." In other words, we don't ask how can we do this better; rather we ask, why are we doing this at all? This, then, is the starting point for any organization that is intent on quantum improvements in the performance of their business activities. Later in this chapter we will discuss the "how to's" of reengineering by offering a business reengineering methodology.

The Role of the IEMgmt Team in Business Process Reengineering

With few exceptions, business process reengineering efforts will require information technology and the creative efforts of those who have a fundamental and detailed knowledge of the current business process. Certainly the IEMgr(TP) would be expected to have this broad expertise. Unfortunately, not many enterprises have the luxury of employing such talented professionals. Until the colleges and universities are able to supply graduates with the required conceptual understanding, enterprises will depend on partnerships between information technology professionals and business process experts.

In any case, senior management expects business value from the IEMgmt team, especially from the CIO and the IS manager. In those cases where the IS manager does not have a fundamental grasp of business functions and processes, this will be very difficult. In fact, many of the reengineering failures can be attributed to this knowledge gap. That is not to say that all would be well if the information technology expert had business function knowledge or, conversely, the business unit managers had information technology expertise, for that is not the case at all. Even under the best of circumstances business process reengineering is very high risk. Failure rates as high as 70 percent and even higher are commonly reported.

The entire IEMgmt team should participate in the reengineering effort. The key player will be the IEMgr(TP). For those organizations that do not have such professionals on staff, the reengineering effort will depend on a strategic partnership between the IEMgr(Tp) and IEMgr(tP). This partnership will most often be best served by having the IEMgr(tP) direct the project. This assures a business-driven solution, as it should be. A technology-driven solution under the leadership of the IEMgr(Tp) is generally less desirable.

Process Level—Process Quality Management

Having completed the reengineering of one or more business processes, we next turn to further improvements in the reengineered processes. While the best efforts of the enterprise may have been brought to bear on a business process, it is unlikely that the process will be perfect as initially reengineered. After some experience with the newly reengineered process, there will be further discoveries as to how the process might be marginally improved. The method we present is one developed by Maurice Hardaker and Bryan K. Ward [1987] in a *Harvard Business Review* article. It is a method for comparing the effectiveness of existing processes, targeting those for which further improvement is possible, and launching the appropriate improvement projects. The details of their method are discussed below.

The Role of the IEMgmt Team in Process Quality Management

Under the leadership of the IEMgr(TP), process quality management projects will be undertaken. Such efforts will usually be undertaken as a follow up to a business process reengineering effort. However, in this case, the reengineered process will be further modified based on experience and input from the IEMgrs(tp) that work with the process. The IEMgr(TP) will review a number of proposals and commission those that show high promise.

Activity Level—Continuous Quality Improvement

Continuous quality improvement is based on a philosophy that we can always do better. It means continuously observing a process at the activity level and asking how it can be done better. It is the tinkering that Hammer and Champy refer to, but tinkering with a process that has undergone the reengineering and process improvement efforts. The IEMgr(tp), working at the activity level, will often be the first to spot opportunities for adjustments to a process step that will improve effectiveness, efficiency, or productivity. Even the most minor improvements, continuously discovered and implemented, will have a measurable cumulative effect. Attention at this level will produce world-class results.

◆ BUSINESS REENGINEERING METHODOLOGIES

A number of methodologies have been put forth for business process reengineering (BPR) [Adair & Murray, 1994; Andrews & Stalick, 1994; Davenport, 1993; Harrington, 1991; Johansson et al., 1993; Morris & Brandon, 1993; and Roberts, 1994]. There are books on reengineering management [Champy, 1995] and reengineering yourself [Araoz & Sutton, 1994]. We have tried to compare these methodologies as shown in Exhibit 8-2.

Exhibit 8-2 — Comparison of Selected Reengineering Methodologies

ADAIR & MURRAY	ANDREWS & STALICK	DAVENPORT	HARRINGTON	JOHANSSON ET AL.	MORRIS & BRANDON	ROBERTS
Understand the Customer and the Market	Frame the Project	Identify Processes for Innovation	Define and organize for Improvement	Identify Candidate Core Processes	Identify Possible Projects	Opportunity Assessment
Develop a Process Vision	Develop a Process Vision	Identify Change Levers	Analyze the Business Process	Assess Processes	Conduct Initial Impact Analysis	Conduct Current Capability Analysis
Determine Business Imperatives	Redesign the Business Process	Develop Process Vision	Redesign the Business Process	Choose Process	Select Level of Effort and Define Scope	Redesign the Business Process
Develop Strategy	Conduct Proof of Concept	Analyze Business Processes	Implement	Develop Process Vision and Redesign	Analyze the Business Process	Do Risk and Impact Assessment
Choose the Right Process	Plan the Implementation	Redesign and Prototype the New Business Process	Monitor & Adjust	Communicate and Validate New Process Design	Define Alternatives & Simulate	Develop Transition Plan
Survey and Benchmark to Set Process Goals	Get Implementation Approval	Implement		Implement	Perform Cost/Benefit Analysis	Run Pilot Test
Perform Baseline Analysis Implement	Implement	Communicate Results		Compare Results Against Plan	Select Best Alternative Implement	Modify Infrastructure Implement
Monitor and Adjust	Monitor & Adjust	Monitor & Adjust		Monitor and Adjust	Monitor & Adjust	Monitor & Adjust

Given these variations we will offer yet another methodology. The approach suggested here is more a concatenation of the best of breed of those described in Exhibit 8-2 than it is any original contribution by the authors to the growing body of literature in BPR.

Identify Process

Determine Organizational Readiness

This is a critical step. Usually, business reengineering is equated to reducing staff and layoffs. To ask people to fully participate in and commit to a project that they feel may result in their job disappearing, is asking a lot. In more serious cases, where the very survival of the enterprise depends on a successful reengineering effort, some of these doomsday perceptions may take a back seat to organizational survival. Survival somehow transcends individual priorities.

Identify and Bound the Business Processes

We suggest that temptations for the killer reengineering project be resisted. While certainly dramatic and filled with opportunities to be the hero, the risk is not worth it. We prefer an approach that considers a number of alternative projects and clearly draws the boundary between what is in scope and what is out of scope. This is very important because there will always be a strong temptation is to include more than can be reasonably accomplished. On the other hand, do not define the process so narrowly that quantum improvements are not possible. Good judgment is called for! Once a number of alternatives are identified, a risk versus reward analysis can be conducted. This approach, or some other comparable analysis, will provide a ranking of reengineering efforts and a method of choosing which one(s) will be commissioned.

Evaluate Performance

This action, and the next step, will complete the analysis phase and provide senior management with the data they will need to make an informed decision. Performance metrics that focus on what is important to the customer (and what is measurable) must be established. Some determination will be made as to the performance goals that are desired.

Perform Gap Analysis

Comparing the desired performance goals to the current performance goals will establish a gap. For each alternative, compute the gap, and translate the gaps into business value. This should provide ample information for decision making and for which process should be chosen. There will be a temptation to select more than one process for reengineering. Consideration of information technology resources must be imposed on the evaluation of each process.

Select Process

While this may seem ceremonial, it is not. We have already identified some of the issues that must be considered. They include organizational readiness, risk, and business value. To that list add cost/benefit analysis for other nonreengineering projects contending for resources, and breakeven analysis. If this is the organization's first reengineering effort, perhaps a low-risk project should be chosen even if others have greater business value. An early success may encourage the organization to try again, whereas a failure may risk losing support for any plans for a second effort.

Plan the Reengineering Project

Planning may seem like nonproductive work to many, but the price that must be paid for no planning or for poor planning is too great. Reengineering projects are already exposed to enough risks from organizational resistance, the rapid pace of technological change, narrowing windows of opportunity, market instability, competitive forces, and so on, and to add to the list something that the organization can mitigate is foolish. Spend the time on solid planning.

Identify Alternative Process Designs

This is the most creative part of the effort. Simply put, start with a blank piece of paper. What would the process look like if you were designing it for the first time? Forget about the fact that Harold and Mary are the best IEMgrs(tp) and whatever solution is adopted must utilize Harold and Mary. If Harold and Mary are that valuable to the enterprise, there will be several alternatives for using them productively. The message is clear—don't constrain your thinking by what is now being done and by certain people occupying certain slots on the organization chart. In the spirit of Hammer and Champy—start from scratch!

Conduct Risk Analysis

For each of the identified solutions, conduct a risk analysis. This approach identifies the probable risk-versus-gain outcomes and hence provides a metric for ranking the alternatives.

Choose Alternative Process Design

Given output from the risk analysis, this should be relatively straightforward.

Implement the New Process

Pilot Test New Process

If possible, pilot test the solution. In the majority of cases this may not be possible and management will have to trust their instincts, the soundness of the procedure they followed, and the results it provided.

Cut-over to New Process

Cut-overs can be parallel, phased, or direct cut-over. Parallel cut-over has both the old and the new process working in parallel so that the results from the old process can be compared with the new as a check on the validity of the new. This is the most expensive option but the least risky of the three. Phased cut-over allows a new process to be introduced to different parts of the organization. It has the longest implementation time of the three and is often used when staffing is the constraint. Direct cut-over simply turns off the old process and turns on the new. It is the least costly but riskiest of the three. The situation will often dictate which one should be used. Cost, space, time, and labor required are some of the criteria that have to be taken into account when choosing the cut-over approach.

Monitor Performance

The monitoring activity is prerequisite to process quality management initiatives as well as continuous quality improvement programs, in that order as Exhibit 8-1 shows. Generally an organization will follow a reengineering effort with a number of process quality management projects. Once the process is stabilized, the switch is made to a maintenance mode characterized by a continuous quality improvement program.

The Role of IEMgmt in Business Process Reengineering

One is tempted to relegate business process reengineering efforts to the IEMgr(Tp), but that would be a mistake. In fact, business process reengineering is one area in which the IEMgr(TP) and IEMgr(tP) are best prepared to deliver results. While there are numerous reasons why business process reengineering efforts fail, one that stands out is to depend on the IEMgr(Tp) and the IEMgr(tP) to make it happen. While each certainly has either technology or process as their area of expertise, neither can marry technology and process at the level of creativity required to effect quantum improvements in the process success criteria. The IEMgr(TP) is the linchpin to every successful effort.

◆ PROCESS QUALITY MANAGEMENT

Process quality management (PQM) can be a follow-up to further improvement of reengineered processes or as the starting point for those organizations that are not ready for BPR. Exhibit 8-3 is the schematic of how we recommend PQM be used for process improvement. PQM is a series of steps that begin with the organization's mission statement and end with a monitoring activity to assure the

Exhibit 8-3

Business Process Redesign Process Flow Model

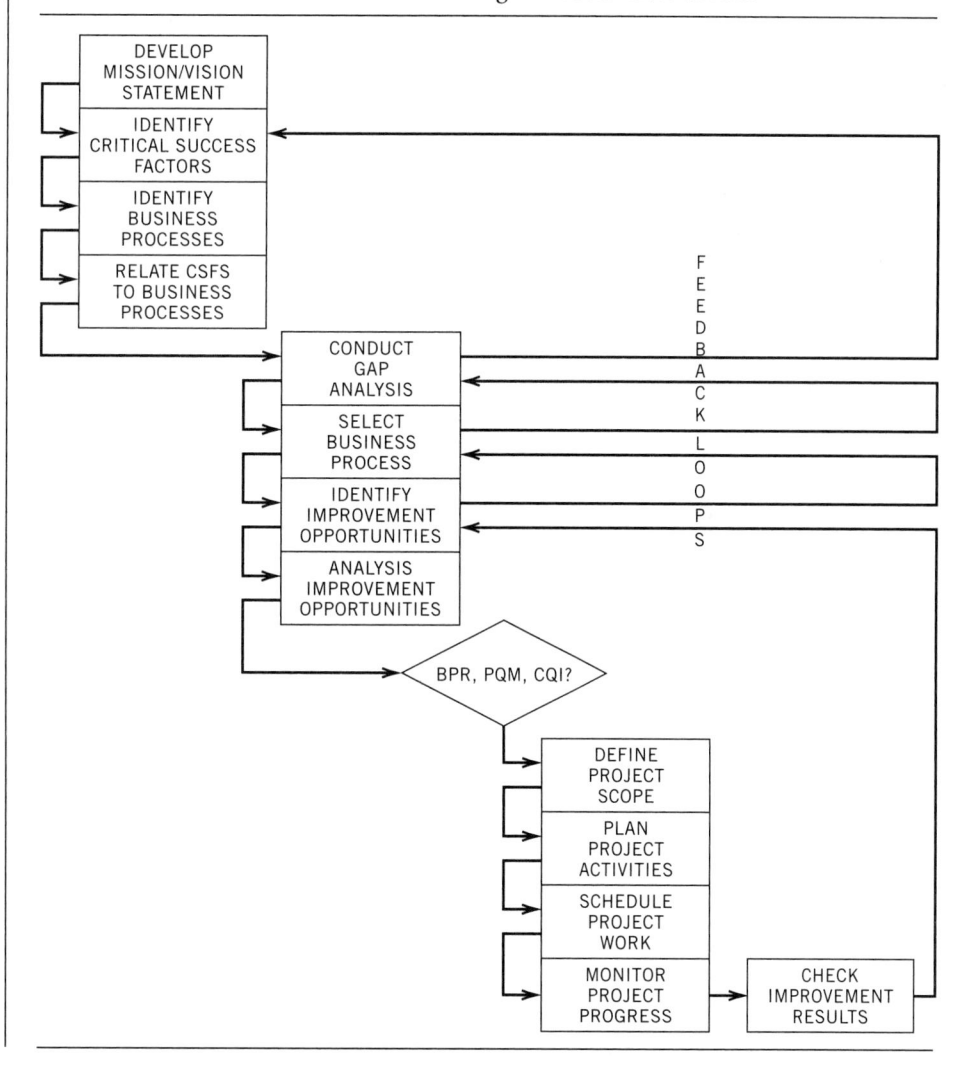

```
DEVELOP MISSION/VISION STATEMENT
    ↓
IDENTIFY CRITICAL SUCCESS FACTORS
    ↓
IDENTIFY BUSINESS PROCESSES
    ↓
RELATE CSFS TO BUSINESS PROCESSES
    ↓
CONDUCT GAP ANALYSIS
    ↓
SELECT BUSINESS PROCESS
    ↓
IDENTIFY IMPROVEMENT OPPORTUNITIES
    ↓
ANALYSIS IMPROVEMENT OPPORTUNITIES
    ↓
<BPR, PQM, CQI?>
    ↓
DEFINE PROJECT SCOPE
    ↓
PLAN PROJECT ACTIVITIES
    ↓
SCHEDULE PROJECT WORK
    ↓
MONITOR PROJECT PROGRESS → CHECK IMPROVEMENT RESULTS
```

FEEDBACK LOOPS

desired process performance improvement has been realized. While not as dramatic in results as a BPR project, it does offer significant performance improvement with less risk. It is therefore a reasonable alternative in organizations that are not ready to support a full reengineering effort.

For the purpose of illustration we have created a case study. The company is hypothetical. The case study was originally developed for use in a project management seminar and later incorporated in a book on the topic [Wysocki et al., 1995].

Case Study—O'Neill & Preigh Church Equipment Manufacturers

The numeric data in this case study is adapted from Hardaker & Ward, "How to Make a Team Work," *Harvard Business Review*, Nov.-Dec., 1987, pp. 112–117.

O'Neill & Preigh is the largest manufacturer of church furnishings and equipment. They sell both stock and custom-designed furnishings for churches in North America and are listed among the Fortune 500 companies. Their products are among the highest quality in the industry and O'Neill & Preigh are recognized as the industry leaders.

All is not well however. For the past six quarters business and profitability have dropped off dramatically. It is generally agreed that part of the problem was the result of the aggressive pricing strategies of a Southeast Asian conglomerate that recently introduced their products into the American market. As a result, O'Neill & Preigh has lost market share.

Ben E. Dictus, the president, has just concluded an executive committee meeting at which it was decided that radical measures were needed. Ben was aware of business process reengineering but felt that the senior managers were so steeped in tradition that such a radical approach would meet with great resistance and anxiety. He did have some confidence that PQM was a good starting point. At some later time he hoped that the culture would support a more thorough effort, however. A complete study of the existing enterprise would therefore be undertaken. There would be no sacred cows. To launch this project Ben started with the mission statement.

Write Mission Statement

One of the interesting features of PQM is that it starts at the most basic and fundamental level of an enterprise—its mission statement. It only makes sense that one understands how the enterprise views itself with respect to what it wants to be before it launches a program to improve itself. Knowing where it is and where it wants to go is prerequisite to setting its direction.

After considerable discussion at the annual Executive Committee Retreat, the senior management team revised the O&P mission statement. It now reads:

> Restore market share and profitability within two years, and prepare the company and the marketplace for further profitability and growth.

Exhibit 8-4	O'Neill & Preigh Critical Success Factors
	1. Best-of-breed product quality 2. New products that satisfy market needs 3. Excellent suppliers 4. Motivated, skilled workers 5. Excellent customer satisfaction 6. New business opportunities 7. Lowest delivered cost

Identify Critical Success Factors

The next question to answer is: What measurable activities or events relate to the mission? That is, what has to go right in order for the mission to be attained and the enterprise to reach its goals? Usually 6 to 8 critical success factors are sufficient to describe an enterprise.

The senior management team conducted a series of three half-day sessions to revise the company's critical success factors in light of their current market situation. Exhibit 8-4 shows the revised O&P critical success factors.

Define Business Processes

In Chapter 7 we discussed identifying and bounding the business processes that describe the enterprise. This exercise should decompose the enterprise to the support level. To conduct a reengineering effort at the core business process level is not appropriate. For large organizations it would not be unusual to have as many as 200 processes identified at the support level. There is no magic number and each organization will be unique.

Rather than risk missing creative opportunities for improvement, they decided to bring in an outside consultant. Sal Vation was hired to lead them through the project. He was an expert in business reengineering and process improvement. After the appropriate briefing sessions, Sal had mapped out an approach and started by having the senior managers help him identify the business processes. In less than one day of meetings they had identified and agreed upon the business processes shown in Exhibit 8-5.

Relate Critical Success Factors and Business Processes

One measure of the importance of a specific support process is the number of critical success factors (CSFs) that are affected by the process. For this exercise construct a matrix whose columns are the critical success factors and whose rows are the support processes. For each support process place an "X" in the column of every critical success factor affected by that process (Exhibit 8-6).

Exhibit 8-5	O'Neill & Preigh Business Processes
P1.	Research the marketplace
P2.	Measure customer satisfaction
P3.	Advertise products
P4.	Monitor competition
P5.	Measure product quality
P6.	Educate vendors
P7.	Train employees
P8.	Define new product requirements
P9.	Process customer needs
P10.	Develop new products
P11.	Monitor customer complaints
P12.	Negotiate manufacturing designs
P13.	Define future skill needs
P14.	Select and certify vendors
P15.	Promote the company
P16.	Support installed products
P17.	Monitor customer and prospects business
P18.	Announce new products

Measure Process Effectiveness

With the business processes identified, Sal asked the senior managers to evaluate how well each process was being performed. They rated them on a scale of A to F with A being exceptional and F embryonic. Sal incorporated this information in the "Quality" column of Exhibit 8-6. The "Count" column of Exhibit 8-6 is simply a count of the number of CSFs each process impacts. It answers the question: Which business processes influence which critical success factors and how does management view the effectiveness of each process?

Identify Candidate Process

As an indicator of which processes require attention we use a combination of the number of CSFs affected by each process and the quality of that process. Processes of low quality that impact higher numbers of CSFs will require attention. That information is summarized with the Zone Chart inset in Exhibit 8-6. It shows, for example, that the six processes in Zone #1 are the most problematic, the nine in Zone #2 have less need of improvement, and those in Zone #3 have lower priority still. Regarding those in Zone #1, Ben might consider creating six teams, one for each process. Or alternatively, using some other criteria, he could prioritize the six processes in Zone #1 and work on them according to their priority. Another approach might be to address those processes that directly impact customers, in which case teams would be formed to study P2, P7, and P16.

Process Quality Management

Exhibit 8-6

O'Neill & Preigh Quality Impact Matrix

critical success factors:
- Best-of-breed product quality
- New products that satisfy market needs
- Excellent suppliers
- Motivated, skilled workers
- Excellent customer satisfaction
- New business opportunities
- Lowest delivered cost
- Count
- Quality

business processes:

Process	BoB	New mkt	Suppl	Workers	Cust Sat	New biz	Cost	Count	Quality
P1 Research the marketplace		X			X	X		3	C
P2 Measure customer satisfaction	X	X			X	X		4	D
P3 Advertise products					X	X		3	B
P4 Monitor competition	X	X	X	X	X	X	X	6	D
P5 Measure product quality	X	X	X		X		X	5	C
P6 Educate vendors	X	X	X			X		4	E
P7 Train employees	X	X			X	X	X	6	C
P8 Define new product requirements		X	X	X	X	X		4	C
P9 Process customer orders					X		X	2	B
P10 Develop new products	X	X	X		X	X	X	6	B
P11 Monitor customer complaints	X	X			X			3	D
P12 Negotiate manufacturing design	X	X	X		X	X		5	D
P13 Define future skills needs		X		X		X		3	C
P14 Select and certify vendors	X	X	X			X	X	5	C
P15 Promote the company				X	X	X		3	C
P16 Support installed products	X				X		X	3	E
P17 Monitor customer and prospects business		X			X	X		3	B
P18 Announce new products					X	X	X	3	C

Distribution matrix:

	E	D	C	B	A	#
						7
		1	1	1		6
			1	2		5
zone 1	1	1	1			4
		1	1	4	2	3
zone 2				1		2
						1
zone 3						0

zone 1	zone 2	zone 3
P4	P10	P3
P7	P5	P17
P12	P14	P9
P6	P8	
P2	P11	
P16	P1	
	P13	
	P15	
	P18	

Identify Improvement Opportunities

For each process identified above for further study, the teams conduct a detailed analysis using the tools presented in the first four sections of Chapter 9. Their objective is to identify specific areas or activities within a process for improvement. There may in fact be many areas that can be identified. They may be addressed separately and their cumulative improvement impact monitored. In some cases, a target level of performance (perhaps a best-of-breed analysis of similar situations at other companies) can be defined and improvements cumulated until that target is achieved.

Prioritize Improvement Opportunities

In cases where one improvement at a time will be undertaken, some strategy is needed to rank order the improvement projects. This rank ordering might be based on such factors as potential improvement level, risk, cost, time to implement, level of difficulty, how well bounded the improvement area is, extent of managerial control over the improvement area, and other criteria.

Manage Process Improvement Project

At this point the standard project management process is invoked. A detailed specification is written; time, cost, and people resources are estimated; and a detailed work plan is put in place. As work commences on the improvement project, it is very likely that other opportunities may suggest themselves. Rather than revise the current plan to incorporate these, they should be added to the set of opportunities, prioritized, and undertaken as appropriate.

Monitor Process Performance

With the improvement project completed and the improvement implemented, it is time to monitor the improvement results that are obtained. Further work may be needed to reach target improvement goals in which case additional opportunities within the same process will be undertaken.

The Role of IEMgmt in Process Quality Management

The initiative for a PQM effort can arise from either the IEMgr(TP), the IEMgr(tP), or a joint initiative of both. If there is a quality standard against which process performance is measured, it may provide a tripwire that initiates an investigation. These quality standards will relate to efficiency and effectiveness measures, timeliness, complaints, returned products, cycle time, and other quantitative measures of the process. The IEMgr(TP) should have implemented systems that track the process's impact on related CSFs.

◆ CONTINUOUS QUALITY IMPROVEMENT

We are now at the activity level within a process. Here we tweak steps or tasks within an activity. These are minor adjustments that are made at the operational level. The recommended adjustments come from IEMgrs(tp).

Identify Quality Improvement Areas

The process team has expectations for the quality and performance level of every activity in the process. At all times they are looking for ways to meet or exceed those levels. They are not looking for quantum leaps in improvement;

those improvements have already happened through previous reengineering and process improvement efforts. Rather, they are looking for those many little changes that improve only some aspect of the process. Maybe it's just one way to react in a certain situation so that the customer is just a little more satisfied with the level of service received. In any case a number of possibilities will be identified.

Perform Gap Analysis

The IEMgrs(tp) will suggest several areas where improvements are possible. The current performance level will be compared with the expected performance level. The difference, the performance gap, will be determined for every activity under consideration.

Prioritize Quality Gaps

The activities can be rank ordered by some criteria. This activity could occur from the largest gap to the smallest gap. It might be by *likely impact,* with the highest potential impact ranked first. In any event, some procedure will be used to identify the activity that will be considered for improvement. We suggest using the problem-solving methodology, cause-and-effect diagrams, and forcefield analysis tools to assist in this analysis.

Manage the Activity Improvement Project and Monitor Performance

The improvement project must be planned. We suggest following the methodology outlined earlier. That method as well as several others are well-documented in the literature. This is important because we have found that quality improvement projects tend to spawn other quality improvement projects. That is, you will "discover" from one project ways to make further improvements with other projects. Good management control is a plus.

The Role of IEMgmt in Continuous Quality Improvement

IEMgrs(tp) are the driving force in continuous quality improvement efforts. They will often manage these projects or at least be principal members of project teams. Because technology plays such an important part in many activity improvements, their technology fluency and their ability to communicate with IEMgrs(TP) will be valuable.

◆ PROJECT MANAGEMENT

Introduction

Everyone manages projects in work and life. Daily activities at work are planned, conflicting schedules at home are resolved, committee work is delegated to individuals for task completion, and children conduct science projects for the annual fair. All of these activities are time based and most of them have milestones for a progress check. Many of these activities are process based and involve decision making and sequential completion of tasks. The process can be rather simplistic (a few interrelated activities) or complex (multiple priorities, interrelated deadlines, adherence to limited resources, and numerous people involved in one or more major activities).

All of these activities need attention in the form of project management. The format can be a manual list of activities for simple and straightforward projects, but an electronic (software) format is necessary for multiple activities encompassing multiple departments and staff members. The array of commercially available software and the increasing demand for project management seminars attest to the fact that the topic is important, perhaps even vital to survival. Clearly, some enterprises continue to exist without the benefit of either manual lists or elaborate online project management; in the near future, they will not be able to cope with the accelerated change over the long term. Short-term fixes are common and respond to crises; funds are shifted to make the payroll, quarterly reports favor the stockholder, resources are not utilized to maximum capacity; and lost time in executing various stages of the master plan contributes to cost overruns. Some of the more important aspects of project management (structure, software, cycle time, rightsizing, and middle management) are mentioned briefly before a summary of the principles, tools, and techniques of this methodology.

Organizational Structures

The familiar command and control structures introduced at the turn of the century are rapidly disappearing. In their place we have task forces and self-directed work teams. Empowerment of the worker lies at the foundation of these new structures. With that empowerment comes the need for solid project management skills.

Software Applications

Many of our readers remember the days when a computer application had only to meet the needs of a single department. If there was a corporate database, we accessed it to retrieve the required data and passed the data through an applications program to produce the requested report. If there was no data or we simply did not know of its existence, we created our own database or file and proceeded accordingly. In retrospect, our professional life as systems developers was relatively simple. Not so any more. We are now developing applications that cross departmental lines; applications that span organizations; applications that are not clearly defined; applications that will change because the business climate changed. All of this means that we will have to *anticipate* change in our projects and be skilled at the management of that change.

Cycle Time

The window of opportunity is narrowing and constantly shifting. Organizations that can take advantage of these opportunities are the ones that have addressed the problem of reducing cycle time. Taking too long to roll out a new or revamped product may mean missing a business opportunity. Project managers must know how and when to introduce multiple-release strategies and project schedule compression strategies to help meet these requirements which happen at unexpected times even though we expected them.

Rightsizing

With the thinning of depth and breadth in many organizations there is a need for the continuing professional staff to find ways to work smarter, not harder. Project management includes a number of tools and techniques that help the project manager respond to the increased workloads.

Middle Management

Peter Drucker, in a landmark paper ["The Coming of the New Organization," *Harvard Business Review,* Jan.-Feb. 1988], depicts middle managers as those who either receive information from above, reinterpret it, and pass it down, or who receive information from below, reinterpret it, and pass it up the line. Given the politics and power struggles at play the quality of the information is suspect. One might question the need for such middle management activities when the computer is perfectly capable of delivering that information to the desk of any manager who has a need to know. As a result, we have seen the thinning of the organization's layers of middle management. Do not expect them to come back.

Job Functions and Tasks for Project Management

Project managers are called upon to perform a variety of functions and tasks. In order to set the stage for varying expectations of project participants, the following list provides some framework for allocating functions and tasks:

1. Project Planning (Strategic and Tactical)
    a. Develops preliminary study with project team and identifies business problem, requirements, project scope and benefits.
    b. Identifies key project results and milestones.
    c. Develops project plan and work-breakdown structure, and communicates to team and client.
    d. Determines needed resources, including client involvement.
    e. Estimates timelines and phases.
    f. Influences selection of project team members.

g. Assigns project responsibilities based on assessment of individual skills and development needs.
h. Defines clear individual roles and performance expectations.
i. Establishes acceptance criteria.
j. Determines appropriate technological approach, including use of prototyping CASE or other tools.

2. Managing the Project
    a. Continually reviews project status.
    b. Reviews work against key results criteria.
    c. Uses systematic method for logging project status—checks against schedule.
    d. Uses change management/request procedure.
    e. Uses project meetings to measure progress against plan; communicates changes and issues.
    f. Assesses skill needed; documentation of meetings, work, conversations, and decisions.
    g. Measures quality through testing against requirements.
    h. Conducts project reviews and walkthroughs (with appropriate client involvement).

3. Leading the Project Team
    a. Involves team in planning.
    b. Uses both formal and informal methods to track project status.
    c. Recognizes individual and team accomplishments or results.
    d. Manages performance issues in a timely manner.
    e. Effectively delegates tasks based on individual strengths and weaknesses.
    f. Maintains open-door policy for staff ideas and concerns.
    g. Sets performance and development objectives for staff.
    h. Schedules and holds regular team meetings.

4. Building Client Relationships
    a. Involves working jointly with client in defining project goals and key results.
    b. Works with client to assure alignment of project to overall business goals.
    c. Listens and responds actively, documents client needs, changes, and demands.
    d. Implements procedures for controlling and handling change.
    e. Develops client understanding of the system and trains for systems use.
    f. Reports (formally, orally, and in writing) periodically to client.
    g. Establishes lines of responsibility and accountability to client.

5. Targeting the Business
    a. Manages in accordance with IS visions and values.
    b. Links overall IS architecture principles to project management system.

c. Effectively interfaces with corporate database management.
   d. Plans for impacts on related systems/departments to achieve maximum efficiency.
   e. Understands business needs, time, and cost pressures.
   f. Keeps current with business and technology developments in competitors.
   g. Aligns project with corporate and business priorities and direction.

Definition of a Project

To put projects into perspective we need a definition—a common starting point. Often, people call any type of work a *project*. Projects actually have a very specific definition. If a set of tasks or work to be done does not meet the strict definition, then it cannot be called a project.

> A project is a *sequence* of *unique, complex,* and *connected activities* having *one goal* or purpose and which must be completed by a *specified time, within budget,* and *according to specification*.

Sequence of Activities

A project comprises a number of activities for a defined piece of work that must be completed in some specified order. The sequencing is based on technical or best-practices requirements and not on management prerogatives. It is often helpful to think in terms of inputs and outputs. The output of one activity or activities becomes the input to another activity or activities. Avoid the trap of specifying sequence based on resource constraints or statements such as "Pat will work on activity B as soon as she finishes working on activity A."

Unique Activities

The project has never happened before and will never happen again under the same conditions. Something will always be different each time the activities that comprise this project are repeated. Usually the variations from time to time will be random in nature—a part is delayed, someone is sick, a power failure occurs, and so on. These are random events that we know will happen—but when, how, and with what impact on the schedule we are not exactly sure. It is these random variations that give rise to the challenge for the project manager.

Complex Activities

The activities that comprise the project are not simple repetitive acts, such as mowing the lawn, running the weekly payroll, washing the car, or loading the delivery truck. Rather, they are new activities and require special skill levels, creative input, and judgment to be done effectively.

Connected Activities

There is some order to the sequence in which the activities that make up the project must be completed. Connectedness follows from the fact that the output from one activity is input to another. The alternative is a list of tasks that are unconnected but must all be complete in order for the project to be complete.

One Goal

Projects must have a single goal, as compared to a program, which can have many goals. Programs are, therefore, a collection of projects that may have to be completed in a specific order for the program to be completed. There will be situations where a project may be divided into several subprojects, which are each projects in their own right.

Specified Time

Projects have a specified completion date. This may be self-imposed by management or externally specified by a customer. Often, the deadline is beyond the control of anyone, such as firing a rocket at a distant comet as it swings near the earth's orbit or holding a trade conference. In both cases, the project is over whether or not project work has been completed.

Within Budget

Projects also have resource limits (people, money, machines). While these may be adjusted up or down by management, they are considered fixed resources by the project manager.

According to Specification

The customer or recipient of the deliverables from the project expects a certain level of functionality and quality from the project. These may be self-imposed or customer-specified but are fixed (temporarily) as far as the project manager is concerned. There are any number of factors that will cause project specifications to change. For example, the customer may not have defined their requirements completely, or the business situation may have changed (happens in long projects).

Project Parameters (Cost, Time, and Resources)

Scope, cost, time, and resources define a system of four constraints that operate on every project. They are an interdependent set in the sense that as one changes it may cause us to change the others so that we can restore equilibrium to the system. Because they are important to the success or failure of the project, we will discuss them briefly.

Throughout the project management life cycle, cost is a major consideration. The first consideration occurs at an early and informal stage in the life of a project. The requesting client may simply offer a cost figure about equal to what they had in mind for the project.

Depending on how well thought out it was, their number could be fairly close or wide of the mark. Consultants will often encounter situations where the client is only willing to spend a certain amount for the work. In more formal situations, the project manager prepares a proposal for the work to be done. That proposal will include a good estimate of the total cost of the project.

To a certain extent, cost and time are tradeoffs. Time can be reduced but cost will increase as a result. Time is an interesting resource. It can't be inventoried. It is consumed whether we use it or not. For the project manager, the objective is to use the time allotted to the project in the most effective and productive ways possible. Once a project has commenced, the prime resource available to the project manager to keep the project on schedule or get it back on schedule, is time.

While all resources can be discussed in terms of cost, we choose to identify resources (equipment, physical facilities, inventory, etc.) separately. These are capital assets that have limited availabilities, can be scheduled, or can be leased from an outside party. Some are fixed; others are variable only in the long term. In any case, they are central to the scheduling of project activities and the orderly completion of the project.

The parameters of cost, time, and resources must be kept in equilibrium, a condition which can be envisioned as a triangle with the parameters as sides of equal length. When changes occur to extend or shorten one leg, the impact is felt on the other parameters and the result is imbalance. This cause suggests solutions to return the triangle to a more balanced figure by compensating with more time, less resources, and/or additional costs. If a project management life cycle model is used (preferably, enhanced with software), several approaches can be applied to the model in search of the best solution to achieve a balanced project.

Project Management Life Cycle

Over years of consulting and training in project management we have observed a number of project management methodologies that differ from one another. On closer examination, we have uncovered a number of underlying principles present in the more successful methodologies. The result of this experience is the project management life cycle first published in Weiss and Wysocki [1991], later revised [Wysocki, Beck & Crane, 1996], and summarized here for review by future IEMgrs. Although we have discussed at length different aspects of the planning process, goal orientation, and teamwork requirements in Part I, these topics need to be readdressed with regard to project planning.

Planning, or rather, effective planning, is painful. Planning doesn't seem like real work. Projects are always behind schedule and so we are tempted to skip planning and get down to the real work of the project. Experience has shown that good planning can actually decrease the time required to complete a project, even taking the planning time into account. Planning reduces risk and increases productivity by 50 percent. We find it interesting that project teams do not have time to plan but they do have time to do the work over again.

Every project has one goal. It is the agreement between requestor and provider as to what is to be accomplished from this project, the *deliverable,* if you will. The goal tells us where we are going so that when we get there we will know it. In our project management life cycle the goal is bounded by a number of objective statements. These objective statements clarify the fuzzy boundary of the goal statement. Taken as a pair, the goal and objective statements scope the project. They become the framework within which the entire project planning process is conducted.

Finally, projects are done by teams. We have to escape the notion that an individual is singly responsible for the success (or failure) of the project. True, you can point to examples where the efforts of an individual brought the project to successful completion, but these are rare events. In contemporary organizations the project team is often cross-functional and spans organizational boundaries.

Scope the Project

This phase of the project management life cycle is the one most often given the least attention. In this phase an initial statement of the project is put forward. A document called the Project Overview Statement (POS) is prepared. The POS is a brief document (usually one page) that describes, in the language of the business, what problem or opportunity is being addressed by the project, the project goal and objectives, how success will be measured, and what risks, obstacles, and assumptions may affect the project outcome. The purpose of the POS is to gain the approval of management to proceed to the next phase, which is the generation of the detailed project plan.

The POS, or some form of it, is in wide use. It is also called a Document of Understanding, Scope Statement, Initial Project Definition, or Statement of Work. In some cases attachments may be required. We are aware of organizations that require cost/benefit analyses, return on investment analysis, internal rate of return estimates, and breakeven analysis as part of the input for deciding whether a project should proceed to the detailed planning phase.

Develop the Detailed Plan

In this phase details of the project plan are developed. While this may be an exercise for one or a few individuals, it is often a formal planning session attended by those who will impact or be impacted by the project. The deliverables from this planning session include the detailed description of each work activity, the resources required to complete the activity, the scheduled start and end date of each activity, and the estimated cost and completion date of the project. In some organizations there may be any number of attachments such as feasibility studies, environmental scans, or best-of-breed analyses. Once this document, called a *project proposal,* is approved, the project enters the next phase where the final details of the work schedule are completed and work commences.

Launch the Plan

In this phase the project team is specified. The actual people assigned to work on the project will be identified, exact work schedules will be determined, and detailed descriptions of tasks to be done will be developed. The completion of this final planning activity signals the beginning of the monitoring phase.

Monitor/Control Project Progress

As soon as project work commences, the project enters the monitoring phase. A number of project status reports will have been defined and used to monitor project progress. Change management is a big part of this phase and procedures will have been installed to process change requests. Here the feedback loop is activated as change requests will always cause some amount of project replanning to take place. Problems will also occur as work finishes ahead of or behind schedule. A problem escalation procedure will have been defined to handle these situations.

Close Out the Project

The final phase begins when the customer says the project is finished. In this phase a number of closing activities are undertaken. Deliverables are installed, final reports and documentation are filed, a postimplementation audit is done, and a postproject celebration is held.

IEMgr's Role in Managing Projects

The IEMgr can be a valuable asset to managing projects either in directing the effort (if applications include major components of hardware, software, services, and/or information analysis and design support services) or in participating in a team effort (if applications include some information technology with business functions or processes primarily occupying center stage). In terms of the project management life cycle some roles of the IEMgr are noted in each of the five phases:

Phase I: Scoping the Project

Experienced IEMgrs (knowledgeable about business processes and information technology) are in a unique position to identify problems in workflow information processing and relate them to business goals, objectives, and opportunities. The internal loop within the scoping procedure forces the enterprise to examine carefully time, cost, and resources and their interplay for ensuring the proper scope of the project. If the project is too large, it is apt to be very complex and perhaps unmanageable; it may be a "program" and require analysis and management of several projects. If the project is indeed a project, it may require further analysis for delineation of subprojects. If the project is too small, team members may overlap too much in task completion, resulting in inefficient use of personnel resources, loss of opportunity in exploring other projects, and limited return for the investment of time.

It is our experience that students and practitioners tend to be in either of these extreme (and undesirable) positions because they do not spend enough time on this phase. They are too ready and willing to proceed with action. More time planning here will uncover the proper and measurable success criteria, assumptions, obstacles, and risks.

Phase II: Developing the Detailed Plan

Once the project scope is determined, the IEMgr can assist in identifying activities and estimating their duration. Operating business managers will be instrumental in listing them; IEMgrs can portray them electronically to show which activity must be conducted before another starts. Activity interrelatedness is important so that the project proceeds at the fastest pace and so that integration of activities can take place. This project network diagram can lead to another helpful graphic, the milestone or Gantt chart, which depicts the clusters of activities according to start/stop times and perhaps the persons accountable for taking action and reporting progress.

Phase III: Launching the Plan

Now that the project objectives are planned, it is time to ensure that team makeup is appropriate in number and kind. Except for information-specific projects, the IEMgr's contribution is limited in the initial steps of this phase. Even after the team is organized and rules have been established to proceed with the project, the IEMgr's role is to participate mostly as a reactive member of the team. Resource loading and scheduling and documenting work packages are the shared responsibility of each team member.

Phase IV: Monitoring and Controlling Progress

If sufficient care has been taken to plan a flexible structure for project management (highlighted due to appropriate software), change of plans can be accommodated more easily. Problems can escalate; solutions may not be immediately forthcoming. The IEMgr can maintain and produce a database for portrayal of time-based performance measures so that graphical images summarize progress of the project.

Phase V: Closing the Project

Here the IEMgr functions only as a team member, and reacts to problems of client acceptance; delivery of the project on time, ahead of, or behind schedule; and quality of results.

Reflections

GENERAL CONCEPTS

1. One of the major obstacles to any business process redesign effort is worker anxiety. Top-level managers look for early retirement packages, middle managers scramble for repositioning in another firm, and supervisors retrain for different positions. IEMgrs (all types of information-enabled managers) are part of this workforce and are just as transitory. A recent book by William Bridges, *Managing Transitions* (Addison Wesley, 1991), addresses many of these issues and offers some advice to help managers help other staff and themselves make the transition.
   a. What aspects of the book are helpful to you and why?
   b. Is his approach realistic and/or applicable to the average worker?
   c. Are you in his "neutral zone" and if so, how do you propose to escape from it (reactive and resistant worker, passive resistant worker, or ideal proactive leader)?
   d. How good are you at absorbing new changes? Can you absorb them fast enough to complete old and new tasks together with planning for new positions/careers?

2. The comparisons of reengineering methodologies (Exhibit 8-2) has been compiled from a plethora of information from numerous sources.
   a. Select an enterprise (business, government, or educational institution) and compare its reengineering methodology to the one method that most closely resembles its application. Discuss.
   b. Has the enterprise followed the method faithfully? Where did it succeed and fail?

3. How does an organization determine readiness for business reengineering? Comment generally.
   a. Create a check list of items to be used in a management audit designed to evaluate whether an organization is ready for this process. This is a major undertaking and will require you to examine questionnaire creation, validation, and other measurement criteria.
   b. Invent some type of scoring system for responses to a questionnaire; this procedure should lead to a yes/no/maybe decision regarding reengineering.

4. Examine the O'Neill and Preigh Case Study in this chapter.
   a. What elements could be added to the case to make it more complex?
   b. What assurances are there that quality will be continued?
   c. What other opportunities can be explored?

5. Examine the job functions and tasks for project management in the text as applied (specifically) to any enterprise by interviewing one or more project planners.
   a. Document what was conducted and what was not done.
   b. Comment on each aspect of the listing in the text as it applies or does not apply to the enterprise.
   c. Select a few items from one of the five categories and comment in depth on those issues.
   d. How does one lead a project team? The key ingredients are listed in the text; how does one accomplish each of these? Use specific examples from your life or work to illustrate the concepts and actions.

6. The project management life cycle is discussed in this Chapter with added references to other texts. Our discussion suggests that much planning is necessary in order to be successful.
   a. Why is planning so painful for most people?
   b. Why is client acceptance located in the closing-out phase rather than at the beginning? or in each of the blocks?
   c. Can you think of ways (other than those enumerated in the text) in which the IEMgr can facilitate each of the phases?
7. What are the misunderstandings involved in "progress reports?"
   a. How can major changes in cost, time, and resources affect progress reports?
   b. What would be the best way to handle these major changes and retain some continuity of progress reports?

Reflections

STEP MODEL

1. The STEP Model shows that growth of the individual in meeting current work demands and in developing a career is paramount for the "earning organization." Continuous education and continuous improvement are precepts of the total quality movement.
   a. How can you enable yourself with information technology (people-technology plane of the model) so that the enterprise progresses toward the ideal?
   b. Are you ready for the behavioral changes needed to enter, or accelerate the use of, the world of information technology?
2. What does project management have to do with any one pathway on the STEP Model?
   a. If you have never managed projects, do not manage them now, and wouldn't like doing it, why take the time to learn the concepts and tools?

Reflections

ISI CASE STUDY

Introduction

It was necessary to use creative thinking skills to address ISI problems to move the corporation from a stagnant business operation to progress forward, become competitive, and grasp new opportunities. Business process redesign principles of this chapter should be helpful in addressing new concerns at the same time that current operations are rescued from further disaster.

a. Is the organization ready for change? If not, what approach is needed?
b. What are the factors critical to success?
c. Can you identify specific improvement opportunities and prioritize them?
d. How can you begin to develop an IEMgmt team when there are no IEMgrs?
e. What are the first steps in organizing a business reengineering effort?

Project Management

One way to commence any new major project is to use principles focused on the management of that project. We live in a world of projects and processes. Why is it that organizations hesitate to use these time-honored principles, and the software which supports them, in addressing complex situations like ISI? For such a massive change, it is not only necessary that the right events of the project are identified, but also their sequence and timeliness require documentation.

Deliverables

a. Using the project management life cycle and some project management software product (MS Project, MacProject, Timeline, etc.), construct milestone charts encompassing all the elements of the project.
b. Review the computer resource planning model (Exhibit 6-2), recommendations for general procurement of information technology (Exhibit 6-6), and action items for developing an RFP (Exhibit 6-8) in identifying the events, or activities, needed for the project charts.
c. Review the background information provided on ISI in Reflections for Chapters 6 and 7 for leads in defining the future direction of the company.
d. Once the project charts are constructed, ensure that the activities represent a realistic timeframe for development and implementation of the reengineering process and for negotiating and implementing a contract for hardware, software, and services to provide information enablement to the organization and its people.

Chapter 9

Human Resource Development

◆ ◆ ◆

*O*rganizations are undergoing a complete metamorphosis in their relationships with their workers. We are admonished to reengineer the corporation, to reengineer our business processes, to reengineer management, and even to reengineer ourselves. In the midst of all this reengineering, workers are told that the "gold watch at 30 years" is gone forever and, furthermore, their continued employment will no longer be the reward for good and faithful service. Continued employment is contingent on their ability to add value to the enterprise. Long-term employment is no longer part of the corporate model. "Take charge of your career" is the message from senior management. Easy to say, but how does the corporation facilitate it, how does the manager make it happen, and what can the worker do to cope with the growing pressures of job, career, and security? Practical solutions have not been forthcoming. Few prescriptive measures are available—no silver bullets are expected. Career planning is now based on a new set of rules—many of which are still being written.

Let us take a closer look at the problem. Organizations have short-term needs requiring development of the appropriate mix of skills among their workers and then deploying them in the best way possible. At the same time, workers have both short- and long-term goals for skills development and personal career growth. To the extent that workers can continue to progress toward career goals and are challenged in so doing, there is reason for them to remain with the employer. In order for this scenario to materialize, both employers and the workers must collaborate in providing a professional development environment that maximizes personal and organizational productivity. Many will find this to be an uncomfortable situation. They will be on unfamiliar ground—not quite sure what to do, what works, what doesn't, or where to go for help.

The crisis is further exacerbated by a number of trends and changes impacting business. As companies become more customer focused they have found that an organizational structure based on business processes is more effective than functional hierarchies based on command and control philosophies. Adopting a process structure results in jobs that require multidisciplined individuals working *on cross-functional teams. In many cases these teams become self-managed—requiring yet another set of skills that include problem-solving, creativity, negotiating, project management, consensus building, decision making, and a host of interpersonal skills.*

At the organizational level, traditional information systems staff are being dispersed into the business units; at the same time, business units are having to share their staff with the many cross-functional teams and task forces that are being commissioned. In the face of all this, professionals are left with a bewildering array of decisions regarding their future and how to secure it. The security of an organizational "home" is gone. They are adrift. The notion of job doesn't have the same meaning that it did a few years ago. One has to wonder whether career ladder is still a meaningful concept. Which way is up? Maybe "up" is obsolete or at least needs to be redefined.

Today, more and more managers come into the workforce computer fluent, but fall short when it comes to the effective use of technology. While they understand the need for retooling the technical skills of their staff, they are not as comfortable training their staff in the equally important business and interpersonal skills. Let's face it, managers are not human resource specialists, nor are they career counselors or training directors. Without help, confusion and lack of direction are the likely outcomes. It should come as no surprise, then, that managers will have difficulty working with their staff in career planning. Staff are told to take charge of their careers, yet have no support system in place to help them. In summary, neither group has the tools for effective skills training and professional development.

In this chapter we explore this changing world and offer a prescriptive model for the IEMgmt team to use in the development and deployment of information-enabled professionals. We have used this model in the past with good results.

◆ UNDERSTANDING INFORMATION-ENABLED PROFESSIONAL DEVELOPMENT

This topic may seem out of place in a book like this, but it has become a critical issue in virtually every organization, especially those that depend on information-enabled positions to remain competitive. Reengineering and rightsizing have resulted in thinner staffing levels and heavier workloads for the less-experienced survivors. Much of the downsizing has reduced the experience level among those who remained. Unexpected turnover further exacerbates the problems and the stress levels. Managers are fearful that if they spend too much effort on skills development their staff will have increased their market value and will leave for more lucrative positions. A seeming dilemma has been created and there doesn't seem to be any relief in sight.

Furthermore, the changes in the technology infrastructure have given rise to a new set of problems—maintaining a skilled workforce. The valued skills of the mainframe professional have limited value in a client/server and PC world. Not too many years ago it was sufficient to identify a needed skill, send the individual for the appropriate training, and then wait for the opportunity to apply the newly learned skill. That leisurely pace is not part of the current business landscape for three reasons. First, the typical worker does not have the time to spend a week in San Diego learning DB2. The effect of the downsizing effort has been to spread the same level of work across fewer workers. Since people are busier, they do not have time to attend seminars despite the importance of learning the new skill. Second, the need for the new skill is immediate. It arises literally overnight and there simply isn't the time to respond in a sensible fashion. Third, a number of managers have turned to just-in-time training. They reason that if they invest in skills development much before it is needed, the staff member will have an opportunity to ply his or her new skills with another employer. Rather than risk this, the manager tries to schedule training at exactly the time it is needed so that the individual will have an immediate application of the new skill when he or she returns to the work place.

While this dilemma is very difficult to resolve, that doesn't release either managers or workers from their obligations for skills training and career development. We cannot offer a silver bullet but we can, and do, describe an approach that works. As you will see, the responsibility is shared between the manager and the subordinate. Both will be asked to take on a role different from the one under which have been operating. They will be somewhat uncomfortable in that shared role because it breaks new ground for individuals and as partners.

We present this material not only for the benefit of the enterprise and its managers, but also for the benefit of the individual. As students of information technology, you will soon be looking for a position in industry. This section will give you a jump start by helping you understand your role as a lifelong learner and how to survive and grow in the information-enabled professions. Now is the perfect time to begin thinking about your future and this section gives you the foundation tools to do just that. Exhibit 9–1 is a schematic of the process we use.

Describing Tasks, People, and Skill Requirements

The first step for management is to describe the supply and demand for skills. To do this we recommend generating two databases. The first is called the information-enabled professions database (IEPD). It describes the roles performed by an information-enabled professional, the tasks that comprise each role, and the skills needed to perform each task. The second is a staff skills profile database (SSPD) that describes the skills present in the current workforce. By specifying the roles to be performed in a specific job and comparing them with the skills profile of the professional staff, the manager can determine the difference between the skills on hand and the skills needed—the so called "skills gap." The same calculation can be done for individuals. They can be compared

Exhibit 9-1

Process Flow Diagram for the Career Development Process

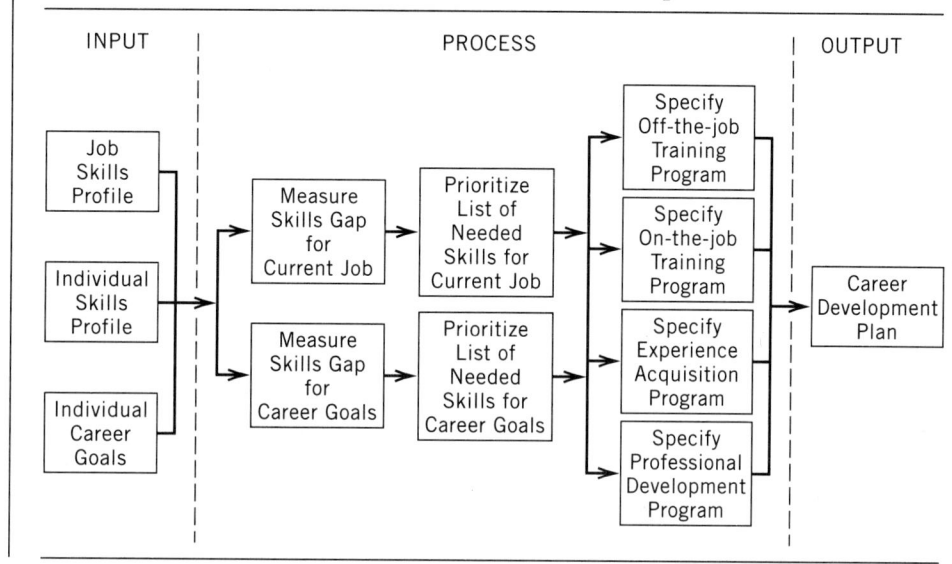

```
INPUT                    PROCESS                                          OUTPUT

Job Skills Profile  ──┐                                  ┌─▶ Specify Off-the-job Training Program ──┐
                      │   Measure         Prioritize     │                                           │
                      │   Skills Gap      List of        ├─▶ Specify On-the-job Training Program ───┤
Individual       ─────┼─▶ for         ─▶  Needed Skills ─┤                                           ├─▶ Career Development Plan
Skills Profile        │   Current Job     for Current Job│                                           │
                      │                                  ├─▶ Specify Experience Acquisition Program ─┤
                      │   Measure         Prioritize     │                                           │
Individual       ─────┘   Skills Gap  ─▶  List of        │                                           │
Career Goals              for              Needed Skills └─▶ Specify Professional Development ──────┘
                          Career Goals     for Career Goals   Program
```

against the job they are now doing or some future job they would like to do. The difference between their skills profile and the job skills profile is their skills gap.

Building the Information-Enabled Professions Database

To build the IEPD, list all of the information-related roles that a person in a particular position is required to perform. For each role list the tasks that comprise the role and finally the skills required to perform each task. One can envision the IEPD as a matrix whose rows are the tasks and whose columns are the skills. An entry in a cell of this matrix means that the skill represented by the cell column is required to perform the task identified by the cell row. Since most tasks will require multiple skills, there will be several entries in each row of the task/skills matrix. In this model a job can be defined by combining roles. Since roles are described in terms of the tasks that comprise them, and tasks in terms of the skills needed to perform them, a job can be described in terms of the skills needed to perform the job.

Staff Skills Profile Database

The (SSPD) comprises one record for each person. One can envision the SSPD as a matrix whose columns are the same as the columns of the IEPD and whose rows represent each of the staff members. For a given staff member there will be entries in several cells in their row. These entries will describe the skills profile of that individual. Looking ahead a bit, a person can assess her ability to perform a particular job by comparing her skills profile with the skills needed to perform the job. More on that later.

Bloom's Taxonomy

In order to build meaningful career development plans that are consistent and efficient, it is necessary that we have an orderly process of evaluating individual skill levels and define job skill requirements using the same scale of measurement. There are several tools that purport to do this. The one we have chosen is Bloom's Taxonomy. It is easy to learn and reasonably objective. This removes much of the subjectivity from an otherwise arbitrary means of determining the level of competency that an individual possesses. It also eliminates the need for competency testing. This approach will be met with some alarm by purists, but we contend that any method that is cumbersome and costly to implement and maintain will simply not be used. What we propose is practical and feasible.

Definition of the Taxonomy

Bloom's Taxonomy is a six-point scale that measures the level of competency that an individual possesses with regard to a specific skill. We will use it to measure both the individual's skill level and the skill level needed for each skill required to perform a particular task. The difference between the skill level required by a task and the skill level possessed by the individual is a measure of the training needed to perform that task. If this difference is zero or positive, the individual meets or exceeds the skill level requirement on that skill. If the difference is negative, the individual requires additional training. The more negative the difference, the more training is required. Listed below are the definitions of each of the six competency levels we will be using.

Knowledge

Knowledge, as defined here, involves *the remembering or recalling* of ideas, materials, or phenomena. For measurement purposes, the recall situation involves little more than bringing to mind the appropriate material. Although some alteration of the material may be required, this is a relatively minor part of the task. To use an analogy, if one thinks of the mind as a file, the problem in a knowledge test situation is that of finding in the problem or task the appropriate signals, cues, and clues which will most effectively bring out whatever knowledge is filed or stored. Knowledge does not mean that the student can actually perform or use the knowledge in a practical manner.

Comprehension

Comprehension means that objectives, behaviors, or responses represent an understanding of the literal message contained in a communication. In reaching such understanding, the individual may change the communication in his mind or in his overt responses to some parallel form more meaningful to him. There may also be responses which represent simple extensions beyond what is given in the communication itself. For example, carrying the relational database architecture to the next level would mean that the individual understands the concepts and principles underlying such databases. This level of understanding might also include being able to explain the logic behind such architectures.

Application

At this level the individual uses abstractions in particular and concrete situations. The abstractions may be in the form of general ideas, rules of procedures, or generalized methods. The abstractions may also be technical principles, ideas, and theories which must be remembered and applied. An example of application is that the individual will use an abstraction correctly, given an appropriate situation in which no mode of solution is specified. This level includes the ability to apply generalizations and conclusions to real-life problems, to apply scientific principles, postulates, theorems, or other abstractions to new situations. For example, having established the database problem, the individual would be able to discuss why and how a relational architecture could be used to meet the specified database requirements. This level of competency also includes the actual application of the concept to the real problem.

Analysis

This is the breakdown of a communication into its constituent elements or parts such that the relative hierarchy of ideas is made clear and/or the relations between the ideas expressed are made explicit. Such analyses are intended to clarify the communication, to indicate how the communication is organized, and the way in which it manages to convey its effects, as well as its basis and arrangement. Analysis deals with both the content and form of material. Continuing the example, the individual would be able to dissect the relational architecture and explain the application of the component parts in the context of the real problem. This presumes then that the individual would be able to adapt the real problem to the principles involved.

Synthesis

This is the putting together of elements and parts so as to form a whole. This involves the process of arranging and combining parts in such a way as to constitute a pattern or structure not clearly there before. At this level of competency the individual is able to adapt the architecture to the real problem.

Evaluation

This is the highest level of competency in the taxonomy. Judgments emerge on the value of material and methods for given purposes. Quantitative and qualitative judgments are made about the extent to which material and methods satisfy criteria. Use of a standard appraisal is commonplace. The criteria may be those

Exhibit 9–2

Descriptive Phrases for Each Competency Level

COMPETENCY	LEVEL	BRIEF DESCRIPTION
Knowledge	1	I can define it
Comprehension	2	I understand it
Application	3	I have used it
Analysis	4	I know how each part works
Synthesis	5	I can adapt it to other uses
Evaluation	6	I know when to use it

determined by the individual or those which are given to her. This level is distinguished from the others because the individual is able to make a determination as to when this architecture is the best choice and to defend that decision based on the evaluative criteria.

For ease in remembering the definition of each of these categories, we will use the shortened definitions given in Exhibit 9–2.

An example of the use of Bloom's Taxonomy is shown in Exhibit 9–3. The exhibit gives an example of the competency levels applied to the prototyping methodology.

Self-Assessments

There are three assessments that are needed in order to generate a career development plan: career interests profile, learning styles profile, and the skills profile.

Career Interests Profile

The career interests profile is a self-administered questionnaire that captures basic preferences of the individual for a hypothetical job (i.e., preference to work alone rather than on teams, or problem-solving situations rather than repetitive tasks). There are several commercial products available to collect this data.

Entries in the task/skills and people/skills matrix are described in this section. Basically, we need to determine the level of each skill needed to perform a specific task and the level of each skill that an individual possesses. To do this we need a metric that measures skill level from beginner through expert. Rather than devise one, we have found that Bloom's Taxonomy does quite well in practice.

Learning Styles Profile

The material in this section is adapted from the works of Donna M. Smith and David A. Kolb, *User's Guide for the Learning-Style Inventory* (McBer and Company, 1986). We are indebted to them for providing exactly the right tool for managers to collaborate with their subordinates to build effective training programs.

Exhibit 9–3

Example Application of Bloom's Taxonomy

TYPICAL COMMENTS ON PROTOTYPING COMPETENCY

I can define it

"I've heard that term before. Isn't that a method for developing an application in stages where at each state the user works with the application and then suggests additional functionality for the next stage?"

I understand it

"Prototyping addresses the situation where users aren't able to clearly specify what they want the system to do. You give them a simple version with only a few features, they learn more about what they want by using this simple version. This allows them to specify new features which you program in and they use the new system. This cycle of learning, modifying, and learning continues until either they are satisfied that the system performs as they wanted it to or the system just isn't meeting their needs. Sometimes the completed system is quite different than originally intended because of the learning that took place. There are also prototypes that are not real systems. Once the prototype is stable it is discarded and the system written in a more efficient language."

I have used it

"Last quarter I completed a system for wage and salary administration that followed a prototyping approach. It took 16 versions and the user was quite satisfied. The system went into production status two weeks ago."

I know how each part works

"The learn-by-using phase is really quite powerful. While it was originally intended to serve as a learning device for the user it also works as a learning device for the developer. You know we are always criticized because we don't understand the functional area in which we are developing systems. I have found that I learn as much about the functional area as the user learns about systems functionality. It's clearly a win-win approach."

I can adapt it to other uses

"I see a good application of prototyping in the design phase. By creating several system designs in phases much like in prototyping we can cut the design time, have a better chance of getting the correct design in place, and save on programming changes later in the development cycle."

I know when to use it

"I think we should measure the characteristics of the system to be developed and, based on those characteristics, decide which SDM to use. Prototyping is especially useful when we are under severe time constraints. Users are unclear about what they want, we are trying a new idea, or we are developing a DSS. On the other hand, prototyping is not appropriate when data resources are not available, when users cannot commit the required time, or when we don't have the appropriate software tools to support the prototyping methodology."

Exhibit 9-4

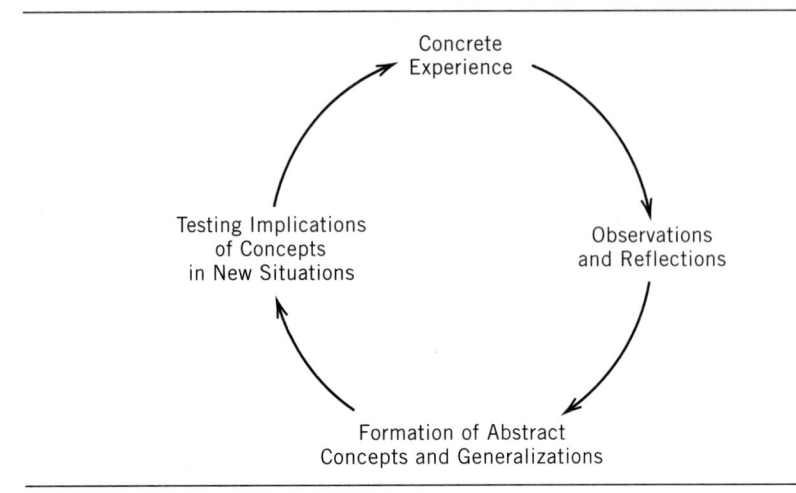

The Experiential Learning Model

```
           Concrete
          Experience
         ↗           ↘
Testing Implications    Observations
   of Concepts          and Reflections
in New Situations
         ↖           ↙
      Formation of Abstract
    Concepts and Generalizations
```

Definition of the Learning Styles Inventory (LSI)

People learn from concepts, books, and experience. Conventional adult learning theory suggests that adults learn by doing and by receiving input from a variety of sources encountered in their daily activity. Furthermore, individuals learn differently, according to their preferred learning styles. The theory is called *experiential learning* and was the original work of Kurt Lewin in the 1940s. We won't need to discuss the historical and theoretical foundations of the LSI. Rather, we will show how it can be indispensable for manager-subordinate collaboration and for development of good training programs.

The foundation of the Experiential Learning Model is the learning cycle. As shown in Exhibit 9–4 it explains how experience is translated into concepts, which in turn influence new experiences. There is an immediate and concrete experience, which is the basis for observations and reflections. These observations and reflections are assimilated and distilled into a theory or concept— however informal—from which new implications for action can be drawn. Finally, the cycle ends with testing the implications for their use as guides in creating new experiences.

The model suggests that effective learning requires four different abilities: Concrete Experience abilities (CE), Reflective Observation abilities (RO), Abstract Conceptualization abilities (AC), and Active Experimentation abilities (AE). The adult learner can call on any one or a combination of these abilities given the situation. Flexibility and adaptability are paramount for the effective learner. Unfortunately, the ideal situation is seldom reached. Rather, each of us has dominant abilities and suppressed abilities when it comes to learning styles. A simple analogy with learning to swim may help ground your understanding of the model.

Concrete Experience
> Throw me in the water and I will learn how to swim on the way down.

Testing Implications of Concepts in New Situations
> I want someone at my side coaching me and helping me so that if I start to drown, he can rescue me.

Observations and Reflections
> I would like to watch and analyze how someone else swims and then try it for myself.

Formation of Abstract Concepts and Generalizations
> Do you have a book I can study that will tell me how to swim?

Note that these styles progress from pure experiential to pure analytic. There is nothing wrong with any of these learning styles. The whole point is that we should discover an individual's style and then try to avail him or her of opportunities to learn according to preferences.

Learning Style Inventory Training Modes

Concrete Experience

Some people like to perceive the world through their senses and to immerse themselves in reality and rely heavily on their intuition, rather than step back and analytically think through the situation.

Abstract Conceptualization

Others like to grasp new information through symbolic representation—to think about, analyze, or systematically plan, rather than use their intuition or senses as a guide. Concrete Experience and Abstract Conceptualization can be thought of as two extremes on a continuum.

Reflective Observation

These individuals prefer to observe others involved in the experience rather than jump right in and try it out.

Active Experimentation

In contrast to the Reflective Observer, the Active Experimenter would rather just jump in and try it out. They process new experiences by doing rather than watching. Reflective Observation and Active Experimentation can be thought of as two extremes on a continuum.

If we put these four dimensions together we have one dimension that describes how we perceive new information (Concrete-Abstract axis) and one dimension that describes how we process what we perceive (Active-Reflective axis). Both dimensions can be represented as shown in Exhibit 9–5.

LSI Learning Styles

No single mode can entirely describe your learning style. In fact, each person's learning style is a combination of all four modes. As you go through the process

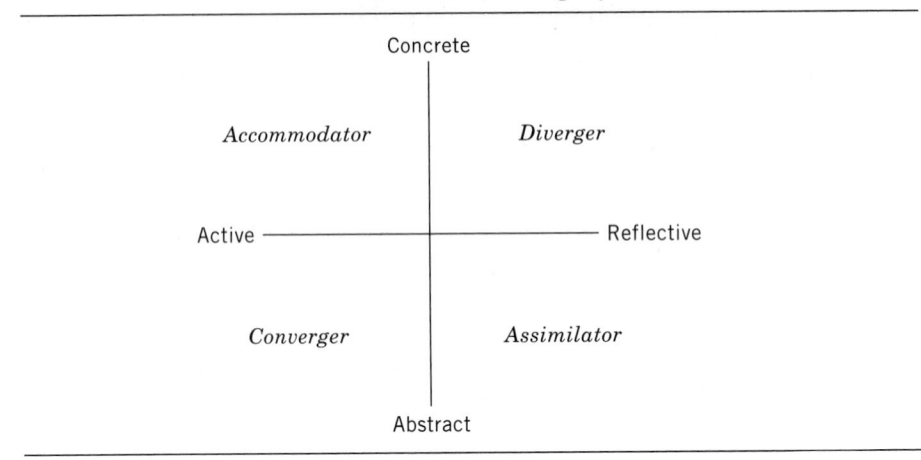

Exhibit 9–5 The Four Basic Learning Styles

```
                    Concrete
                       |
      Accommodator     |    Diverger
                       |
   Active  ————————————+———————————— Reflective
                       |
        Converger      |    Assimilator
                       |
                    Abstract
```

of learning you actually pass through all four modes beginning with the dominant mode. The four learning styles that result from combining the scores on the four modes are described in the following.

Accommodator

Accommodators are best at Concrete Experience and Active Experimentation. Their greatest interest lies in doing things—in carrying out plans and experiments and being involved in new experiences. Accommodators tend to be more risk-taking than people with other learning styles. They tend to excel in situations where one must adapt oneself to specific, immediate circumstances. In situations where a theory or plan does not fit the "facts," Accommodators will most likely discard the theory or plan. They tend to solve problems in an intuitive, trial-and-error manner, relying heavily on other people for information rather than on their own analytic ability. The Accommodator is at ease with people, but is sometimes seen as impatient and pushy.

Diverger

This person is best at Concrete Experience and Reflective Observation. This person performs better in situations that call for the generation of ideas, such as would occur in a "brainstorming" session. Divergers tend to be imaginative and emotional. They have broad cultural interests and tend to specialize in the arts.

Converger

This person's dominant learning abilities are Active Experimentation and Abstract Conceptualization. A person with this style does best in situations such as conventional intelligence tests, where there is a single, correct answer or solution to a question or problem. This person's knowledge is organized so that through hypothetical-deductive reasoning he or she can focus it on specific problems. Convergers are relatively unemotional, preferring things rather than people.

Assimilator

Assimilators excel in inductive reasoning and assimilating disparate observations into an integrated explanation. Their learning styles are strong in Reflective Observation and Abstract Conceptualization. Like Convergers, Assimilators are less interested in people and more concerned with abstract concepts, but less concerned with the practical use of theories. For Assimilators it is more important that the theory be logically sound and precise; in a situation where a theory or plan does not fit the "facts" they would be likely to disregard or reexamine the facts.

Exhibit 9–6, adapted from Smith and Kolb [1986], summarizes the learning strengths and preferred learning situations for each learning style.

Exhibit 9–6

Preferred Learning Situations and Styles

LEARNING STRENGTHS	PREFERRED LEARNING SITUATIONS
Concrete Experience • Learning by intuition • Learning from specific experiences • Relating to people • Sensitivity to people and feelings	• Learning from new experiences, games, role play, etc. • Peer feedback and discussion • Personalized counseling • Teacher as Coach/Helper
Reflective Observation • Learning by perception • Careful observation before making judgments • Viewing things from different perspectives • Introversion—looking inward for the meaning	• Lectures • Opportunities to take an observer role • Objectives tests of one's knowledge about an issue • Teacher as Guide/Task Master
Abstract Conceptualization • Learning by thinking • Logical analysis of idea • Systematic planning • Deductive thinking	**Theory Reading** • Study time alone • Clear, well-structured presentation of ideas • Teacher as Communicator of Information
Active Experimentation • Learning by doing • Ability to get things done • Risk taking • Extraversion—acting to influence people/events	• Opportunities to practice and receive feedback • Small group discussions • Projects and self-paced learning activities • Teacher as Role Model of how to do it

Individual LSI Data

Let us look at some actual LSI data. It will help firm up your understanding of the tool. First, the LSI data comes from your answers to 12 questions. A typical self-assessment is:

I learn best when:

    _____   I am receptive and openminded
    _____   I am careful
    _____   I analyze ideas
    _____   I am practical

To respond, you merely rank each of these alternatives with the numbers 1 through 4. A rank of 4 goes with the phrase that best describes how you learn. A rank of 1 goes with the phrase that seems least like the way you learn. The responses are then summarized and reported as scores on the four modes. The scores are graphed as shown in Exhibit 9–7.

The data describes an individual who scored high on Abstract Conceptualization and Reflective Observation. The data was obtained from an information systems professional whose career focuses on training, planning, and writing. It is fairly typical of professionals with such interests. Not everyone learns the same. There are, in fact, four styles that we identify here. The following statements should give you a good understanding of exactly how each style differs. None is more correct than any other. All are valid approaches to adult learning.

Exhibit 9–7

Graphical Representation of LSI Data

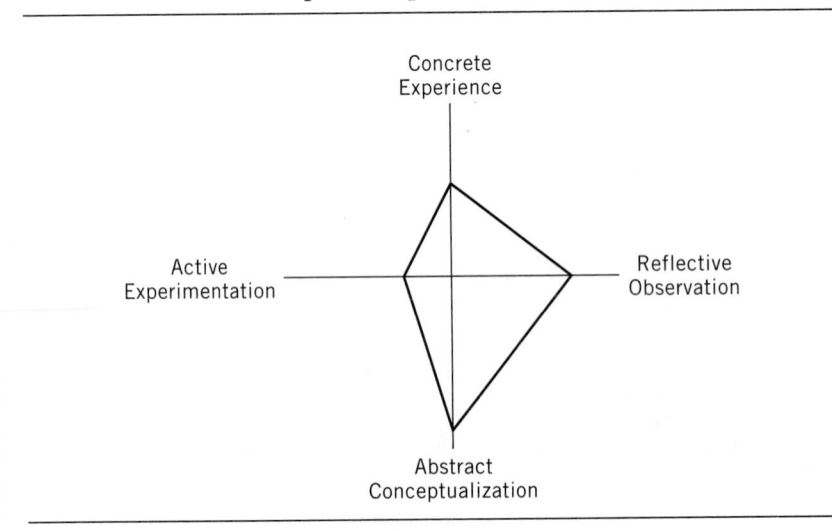

(A kite-shaped diagram with four axes labeled: Concrete Experience (top), Reflective Observation (right), Abstract Conceptualization (bottom), Active Experimentation (left).)

Job Analysis

A job analysis generates a matrix whose columns are the different jobs in a class of jobs (programmers, analysts, for example) or in some functional subunit and whose rows are the skills associated with the listed jobs. The matrix entries are the competency levels required for each skill in order to be fully functional in that job. A blank indicates that the skill is not required for that job. Exhibit 9–8 shows a typical job analysis for programmer positions within an applications development unit in the information systems department.

Skills Profile

The individual's skill profile consists of a competency level (1–6) for each skill that appears in any current job description. Of immediate interest to the individual's line manager is the skills profile for those skills required of the individual in order to be fully functional in his current job. Of longer-term interest to both are those skills which may not be required in the current job but which are relevant to the longer-term career goals of the individual.

Exhibit 9–9 shows the format of a skills profile for a hypothetical person. The row entries are the skill, the competency level, and the skills gap. A blank entry for a skill means that the individual has not achieved even the lowest-level competency. In effect this means that the individual is not aware of the term denoting the skill or maybe has heard the term but cannot define it. The individual's skill profile shows, for each skill required in her current job, the skills measured against the skills required in the job. Any gaps are readily observed. Exhibit 9–10 is a hypothetical profile for a programmer/analyst. As an alternative, the skills profile may show all skills, whether or not they are relevant to the current job.

The Skills Gap

The skills gap can be computed directly from the task/skills matrix and the people/skills matrix as illustrated in Exhibit 9–10. The individual's skill profile is continually updated as she completes off-the-job and on-the-job training, gains experience in using learned skills, and completes professional development activities. This is one of the inputs we will need to determine training requirements.

Definition of the Skills Gap

The skills gap is defined as the difference between an individual's competency level on a particular skill and the competency level required on that skill for a particular job. If we look at that difference over all skills required for a particular job, we have our first cut at the training required in order for the individual to become fully functional in his current job.

Exhibit 9–8

A Partial Job Analysis for Programmer Jobs

TECHNICAL SKILL	PGMR	PGR/ANALY C	PGR/ANALY B	PGR/ANALY A
Data Structures				
Data Query	3	3	4	5
Database				
Design Fundamentals	2	3	4	5
Client/Server	2	2	3	4
Programming				
Job Control Language	2	3	4	5
Programming Language	3	4	5	6
Structured Programming	3	4	5	6
Structured Testing Methods	3	3	4	5
Application Development Tools				
Debug	3	3	4	4
Editor	3	3	4	4
Code Generators	3	3	4	4
Screen Editor	3	3	4	4
Utilities	3	3	4	4
Operating Systems Fundamentals	2	3	4	5
Product Knowledge				
Interaction between Products	2	3	4	5
Software Promotion Principles	1	2	3	4
Assist Trng/Supv of Team Members	-	2	3	4
Technical Support				
Troubleshooting	-	2	3	4
Analysis & Programming Design				
Design Specifications	-	2	3	4
Screen Design	2	2	3	4
Dataflow Diagrams	2	2	3	4
Pseudocode	-	2	3	4
Technical Limitations				
Hardware	2	3	4	5
Software	2	3	4	5
Physical Design Specifications	-	2	3	4
Assist/Provide User Training	-	2	3	4
Test Planning	3	3	4	5

Exhibit 9-9

Individual Technical Skills Profile

NAME: Anna Lyst
CURRENT JOB CLASS: Programmer/Analyst A
APPROVED BY:

EMPLOYEE ID#: 46352
LENGTH IN POSITION: 2 yrs

_____ _____
Mgr/PDP Supervisor   date   Employee   date

CURRENT TECHNICAL SKILLS PROFILE

Skill	Level	Gap	Skill	Level	Gap	Skill	Level	Gap
Data Query	5	0	Op Sys Fund	5	0	User Trng	4	0
DB Design	4	-1	Prod Inter	6	1	Test Plan	4	-1
Client/Server	4	0	SW Promo	6	2			
JCL	5	0	Trnng/Supv Team	2	-2			
Pgmg Lang	6	0	Troubleshooting	6	2			
Struct Pgmg	4	-1	Design Specs	5	1			
Struct Testing	4	-1	Screen Design	5	1			
Debug	4	0	Dataflow Diag	5	1			
Editor	4	0	Pseudocode	4	0			
Code Gen.	5	1	HW Limitations	4	-1			
Screen Editor	5	1	SW Limitations	5	0			
Utilities	4	0	Phys Design Specs	4	0			

Measuring the Skills Gap

As an example, let us look at the skills profile of a typical programmer/analyst, C. The column headed "Person" is the skills profile for that programmer/analyst C. The columns headed P/A_C, P/A_B, and P/A_A are the competency levels required for each skill required in each of the three programmer/analyst jobs. The columns headed Δ_C, Δ_B, and Δ_A are the skills gaps for each of the skills required for those jobs. They were computed by taking the entry in the Person column and subtracting the corresponding entry in the P/A_C, P/A_B, and P/A_A columns. Positive numbers indicate a skill level that exceeds the required competency level for that skill. Negative numbers indicate a skills gap. It is those negative numbers that will be the focus of our training program.

The skills gap analysis can be extended to any number of future jobs. The individual could add additional columns that describe the skills requirements of a series of positions leading to his career goal. A comparison of skills requirements specified by his manager to meet current job requirements and skills requirements on his career path will help identify those that are in agreement with both the manager's needs and the individual's needs. This will be valuable input to the career development plan discussed later in this chapter.

Exhibit 9–10

A Typical Skills Gap Calculation

TECHNICAL SKILL	PERSON	P/A$_C$	Δ_C	P/A$_B$	Δ_B	P/A$_A$	Δ_A
Data Structures							
Data Query	2	3	-1	4	-2	5	-3
Database							
Design	2	3	-1	4	-2	5	-3
Client/Server	2	2	0	3	-1	4	-2
Programming							
JCL	3	3	0	4	-1	5	-2
Prgmg Lang	5	4	1	5	0	6	-1
Struct Prgmg	3	4	-1	5	-2	5	-2
Struct Test Meth	2	3	-1	4	-2	5	-3
Appl Dev Tools							
Debug	3	3	0	4	-1	4	-1
Editor	4	3	1	4	0	4	0
Code Gen	3	3	0	4	-1	4	-1
Screen Editor	3	3	0	4	-1	4	-1
Utilities	3	3	0	4	-1	4	-1
Operating Systems	3	3	0	4	-1	5	-2
Product Knowledge Interactions	2	3	-1	4	-2	5	-3
SW Promotion Prin	1	2	-1	3	-2	4	-3
Assist Trng/Supv	-	2	-2	3	-3	4	-4
Technical Support							
Troubleshooting	-	2	-2	3	-3	4	-4
Anal & Pgmg Design							
Design Specs	1	2	-1	3	-2	4	-3
Screen Design	2	2	0	3	-1	4	-2
Dataflow Diag	2	2	0	3	-1	4	-2
Pseudocode	2	2	0	3	-1	4	-2
Technical Limits							
Hardware	2	3	-1	4	-2	5	-3
Software	2	3	-1	4	-2	5	-3
Phy Design Specs	2	2	0	3	-1	4	-2
Assist/Provide User Trng	-	2	-2	3	-3	4	-4
Test Planning	1	3	-2	4	-3	5	-4

Prioritizing the Skills Gaps

There are two ways to prioritize skills gaps as described in the following.

By Importance to the Job

Those skills which align with the most important job tasks are skills that should be addressed before those that relate to tasks of lesser importance. While the initial implementation relates skills to job, the intent is to define jobs in terms of tasks, and tasks in terms of their required skills and competency levels. While managers certainly have an intuitive sense for those skills which are important to the job, there is a need for standardization across jobs. This standardization is more easily accomplished at the task level. Tasks are more easily prioritized than skills. Furthermore, tasks are performed while skills are not.

Another added benefit will be to aid in the planning of the professional development segment of the career development plan. As one looks to the future the individual will want to know how skills relate to tasks to prepare for increasing job responsibilities. This activity requires mastery of the skills needed to perform certain job-related tasks. This approach provides an opportunity to take on some new job responsibilities while preparing for the more difficult ones through further professional development and training.

By Degree of Difficulty in Learning the Skill

In those development situations where the individual is being groomed for a completely different job, for example, project management or people management, for the first time, it may make sense to rank the skills to be learned. The ranking would be from easiest to hardest to learn. As the easier skills are learned the individual can assume job tasks that require the learned skill. One advantage to this approach is that it gives the individual some early successes with the new job responsibilities. These are strong motivators.

◆ CAREER DEVELOPMENT PLANNING

Career development planning has arisen either by choice or by circumstance in most organizations. For some organizations this has been an easy change, as some version was already part of the corporate culture. For others, career planning has been quite difficult due to a variety of reasons discussed below. The mainstream thinking is that career development planning is a joint responsibility of manager and subordinate with the subordinate taking the lead role. We explore this topic in detail in this section.

Organizational Culture and Commitment

We work in organizations whose culture has undergone radical restructuring in the last few years. Corporate culture now asks: What have you done for us lately? The individual must be able to demonstrate value added—and not just once, but repeatedly. It is now incumbent on the worker to seek out opportunities to bring value to the enterprise or risk layoff. Organizations are looking for ways to reduce operating costs and think they have found it through reengineering and the consequent reduction of the workforce. Some have, but most have only further aggravated the problem—calling for more staffing reductions. The corporation might well ask: How are we to remain competitive in such turmoil and change?

The individual might well ask: What am I to do to secure my future? Both of these questions can be answered with the same answer: Design and implement a comprehensive career management system. That is the topic of the sections that follow. We advocate a joint career-planning approach where both manager and individual have essential roles to play.

Individual Responsibility

The individual is responsible for meeting the requirements of his assignment but moreover, is responsible for his own professional future. Focusing on his career development, the individual must ask and answer several questions such as:

1. What do I want to be (now, short term, long term)?
2. Where am I now?
3. How do I get there from here?

For many workers, the decision as to what they want to be in the future can be only vaguely determined. There are many self-help books available and having a mentor may also be helpful. There must be some sense of direction before it makes sense to take the next step. That sense of direction can be defined in terms of the skills needed to perform in that future role. Where you are now is easy to answer. It only requires a skills assessment be done. The difference between what is needed and what you have in the way of skills gives you a picture of the skills gap. That skills gap can be further analyzed to formulate a plan for removing it. That plan will include such items as further formal education, skills training, on-the-job experiences, mentoring, networking with other professionals, observing the practice of a skill you need, assisting an expert, reading, and self-study.

Manager's Responsibility

The manager is responsible for producing results within a specified timeframe that must be accomplished using available human and capital resources. Focusing on the human resources, the manager must ensure that the staff complement has the requisite skills to meet the unit's goals. In the absence of those skills it is the manager's responsibility to provide for the recruiting of new employees and the training (on the job and off) of existing staff to align the staff skill set with the needed skill set.

Joint Responsibility

In the short run it should be obvious that both the manager and the individual must collaborate in the planning and implementation of career development and skills training. For the manager, the bottom line is that the individual acquire the skills to meet defined needs of the unit. For the individual, the bottom line is that he is able to progress toward his career goal and skills requirements in the short term. If the long-term career goal of the individual can be met through the current employer, great. Realistically, that situation will not be the case and the individual will seek other employment at such time that the current employer can no longer meet short- and long-term skills development needs and career goals.

◆ CAREER DEVELOPMENT PLANS

The development of effective training plans is not an easy exercise, especially since neither the manager nor the individual can be expected to have expertise in the area. The tools that we present in this section take that shortcoming into account. The following process is somewhat intuitive and not too time consuming. As long as the commitment and shared responsibility are understood, there should be no problem implementing these procedures.

Components of a Career Development Plan

Once the individual has identified his career interests, it is time to begin developing a plan that will lead in that direction. We call this a *career development plan* (CDP) and it consists of skills training to meet current and short-term job requirements and skills acquisition for long-term professional growth. The CDP also includes experience acquisition and professional development activities. In other words, there are four parts to a CDP that follow the sequence shown in Exhibit 9-11.

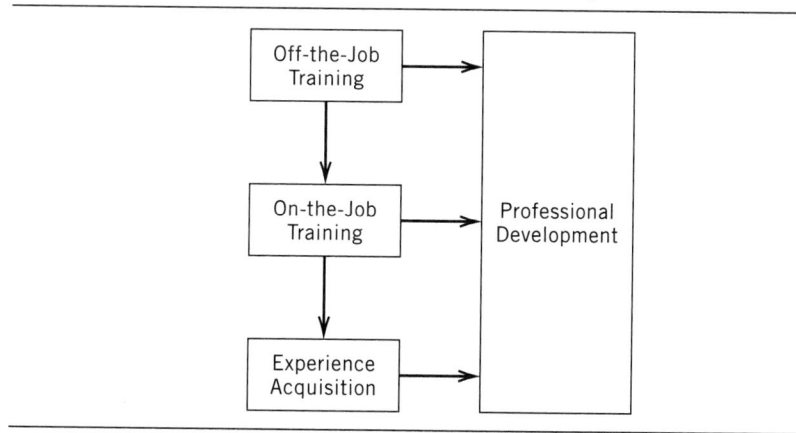

Exhibit 9-11

Components of the Career Development Plan

Off-the-Job Training → On-the-Job Training → Experience Acquisition → Professional Development

Off-the-Job Training

Off-the-job training offers the individual their first exposure to a new skill. The skill is not related to current job requirements but is either a skill to be used in a future job-related task or is exploratory in nature and related to longer-term interests. This type of training may include such activities as self-study, observation, seminars, short courses, readings about a methodology or tool, and so on. Note that off-the-job training does not imply off the premises. It simply means that the training activity is not associated with performance of a current job responsibility. This differentiates it from on-the-job training, which is associated with training in preparation for, or in parallel with, performance of a current job responsibility. Off-the-job training can be initial training in a new skill or advanced training to develop expertise at a high level in the skill. In either case it will eventually lead to on-the-job training.

On-the-Job Training

On-the-job training involves the practice of a skill that has been learned in an off-the-job training activity but has not been practiced. It is conducted on the job and under the watchful eye of a mentor, someone who possesses the skill being practiced. The mentor may be a co-worker who possesses the skill, or the individual's manager. The mentor watches the performance, corrects as required, and repeats the process until the individual has acquired enough competency in the skill to perform the tasks requiring the skill without direct observation by the mentor. Once this stage of skill development has been reached, the individual may begin acquiring experience to further hone this newly acquired skill.

Experience Acquisition

The newly acquired skill is practiced independently until the required competency level has been reached. At this point the individual is ready to move to another or higher level of performance in that or another skill area.

Professional Development

In this part of career development the individual looks outside their immediate job requirements for other professional development opportunities. This may include such activities as learning about another technology, learning a skill needed in a future job, expanding knowledge of the business of the enterprise, learning about a business function, reading, self-study, professional society involvement, short courses, seminars, information gathering from professionals, and so on.

The Career Development Planning Process

The actual process of developing a career plan is a collaborative effort of both the individual and his manager. Exhibit 9–12 is the schematic diagram of that

Career Development Plans

Exhibit 9-12 | Process Flow Diagram of the Career Development Planning Process

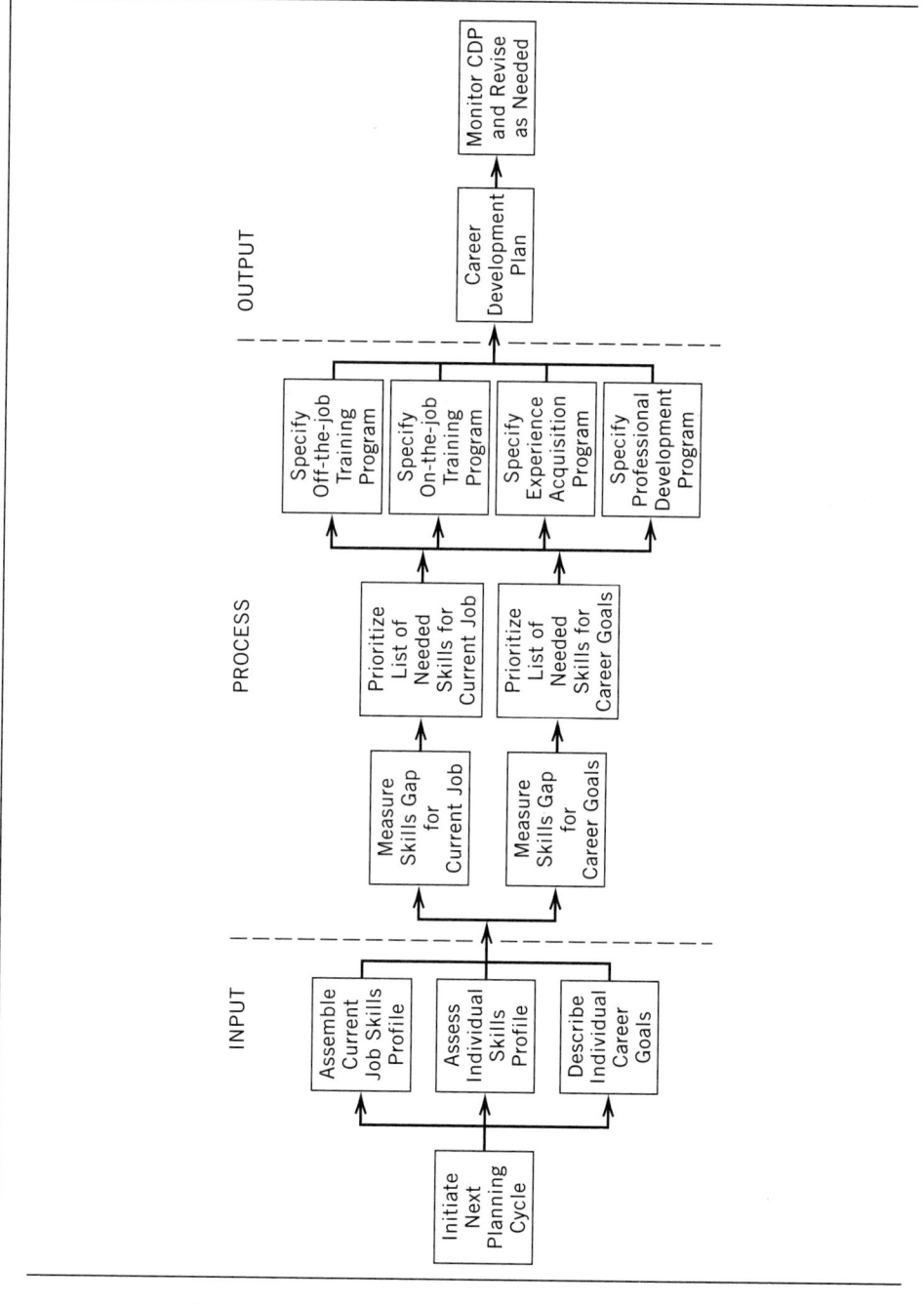

OUTPUT
- Monitor CDP and Revise as Needed
- Career Development Plan
- Specify Off-the-job Training Program
- Specify On-the-job Training Program
- Specify Experience Acquisition Program
- Specify Professional Development Program

PROCESS
- Prioritize List of Needed Skills for Current Job
- Prioritize List of Needed Skills for Career Goals
- Measure Skills Gap for Current Job
- Measure Skills Gap for Career Goals

INPUT
- Assemble Current Job Skills Profile
- Assess Individual Skills Profile
- Describe Individual Career Goals
- Initiate Next Planning Cycle

process. Recall that the company owns the individual's job and the individual owns one's career. This means that at the job level both manager and subordinate should have the same objectives, but at the career level the manager and the subordinate are likely to have differing views. This creates an interesting dynamic at career planning time. The worst case is that the individual's short-term interests may be somewhat in conflict with the manager's. If this gap is large enough, there is reason for the individual to look elsewhere for employment. If they are somewhat out of sync, the individual will be challenged to find opportunities within his current job responsibilities to further his career. For the individual this may mean stepping outside the current job responsibilities and volunteering for other assignments. There will be such opportunities but they may require going beyond the manager's expectations to take advantage of them. There should be no problem with this strategy as long as the individual can demonstrate added value for the business unit and the enterprise.

Developing the Career Development Plan

Let us turn now to a discussion of the process itself. There are three inputs. The job skills profile and individual's skill profile are the responsibility of the manager. The individual career goals are the responsibility of the individual. The process phase begins by documenting two different skills gaps. The skills gap for the current job will be the difference between the skills required to perform the job and the skills possessed by the individual. The skills gap for the career goals will be the difference between the skills possessed by the individual and the skills required to perform the tasks of the intended career. Using Bloom's Taxonomy these will be numerical values. They can both be prioritized.

For the manager the priorities will be based on the performance requirements of the current or planned job tasks. For the individual the priorities will be based on the career path and the skills required for the next career step. Once the priorities are determined, both manager and individual can draft the specific parts of the CDP. This may be done individually and negotiated. The deliverable is the CDP, which details, to the level available, exactly what will be done over the planning period. Generally the planning period covers one year. The process repeats itself for succeeding years.

Maintaining the Career Development Plan

Expect the CDP to change. Market conditions change. The enterprise responds appropriately. Jobs change. Training and development needs are revised. The process remains collaborative as manager and subordinate determine the impact on the CDP and agree to a revision that meets the needs of both parties. In some cases it may be necessary to temporarily suspend career development in favor of job requirements, but this too must be negotiated.

◆ ENTERPRISEWIDE CONSIDERATIONS

As organizations continue to grapple with the sweeping changes brought on by the information age, none are more challenging than maintaining a skilled workforce. The removal of several layers of management, the reduction of the workforce, a focus on customer service through process structures rather than functional structures, and empowerment of the worker all impact on the human resource equation. There are several questions to be answered among which we include the following:

Professional Level

- How should workers plan and manage their career?
- How does one find mentors and build a professional network?
- What is the role of the worker in career planning and development?
- How can workers find opportunities for advancing toward defined goals?
- What tools are needed and available to help individuals take charge of their careers?

Manager Level

- What is the role of the manager in the staff's career planning and development?
- What is the role of the HR manager in information-enabled professional development?
- What is the role of the training manager in information-enabled professional development?
- How can an on-the-job training program be used effectively in professional development?
- What tools are needed and available to help managers meet their respective responsibilities?

Corporate Level

- How should the enterprise plan for information technology skills development?
- How should the enterprise manage the skills gap of information-age professionals?
- What can be done to empower staff to accept responsibility for their career development?
- What tools are needed and available to assist organizations with workforce preparedness?
- What are the critical success factors for an effective professional development environment?

We leave the answers to these questions to a companion book we are currently writing and use this space for a few closing comments on this most critical issue.

Staff Planning

It is absolutely essential that senior management take a close look at how it invests in its human capital. The simple solution is to hire rather than retrain and redeploy. While that may seem to solve the immediate problem, it has other serious defects. There is always risk associated with a new hire. Such concerns as cultural fit, work ethic, ability to work on teams, and interpersonal relations are frequent problems with new hires. These are transferable skills that are difficult to assess during the interview process. They are a moot point with existing staff, however. The new hire does not have the enterprise knowledge that the current staff have acquired. This is a problem in organizations that have had repeated staff reductions. The higher salaried and more experienced staff are generally the ones who leave while the junior, less experienced staff remain.

The enterprise is then at risk when the more difficult issues—ones generally resolved by senior staff—cannot be resolved by junior staff. The problem is further exacerbated because, while staff have been reduced, the workload has not. We have, in fact, experienced situations where those who were laid off felt they were more fortunate than those who remained. At least they had an opportunity to redirect their careers where others were trapped in difficult situations with fewer options to consider.

Planning the Corporate Training Program

The need for training in the downsized organization is greater than it was before the downsizing took place. The survivors of the downsizing find that they have more responsibilities and more work than before. The workload did not decrease in proportion to the staff reductions. The result is that many workers will now be responsible for tasks for which they are not appropriately skilled. The problem is not easily solved for two reasons: It is difficult to find the time to be trained and training budgets are strained under the need for more training.

A new training paradigm is needed. Trainers and managers need to look inside the enterprise for training opportunities. Options such as working alongside someone who knows the skill and learning in a master/apprentice mode, observing the skill being practiced, reading programs, and reviewing how such skills were used, are a few possibilities. The notion that training requires a plane ticket and a stay in a hotel is not the only model to consider. The cooperation of management is needed, as is a little creativity.

Role of the IEMgmt Team

To assure a workforce that has the proper information-related skills, the IEMgmt team will have to take a more proactive role. As a group they have the best view of the enterprise's use of and need for technology skills. They will be aware of the many opportunities for on-site training whether it is off the job or on the job. That information needs to be collected and shared across appropriate parts of the enterprise. This approach will allow those needing the skills training to avail themselves of opportunities. In addition, the skills training needs across the enterprise must be aggregated and reported to the corporate training function. When the numbers to be trained in each skill area are known, decisions can be made to develop an in-house course, to contract with training providers, to send the staff to publicly offered programs, or to use on-site opportunities to observe, support, and practice the skills.

Reflections

GENERAL CONCEPTS

1. Have you ever thought about having a mentor? This will be some professional in whom you can confide your personal feelings regarding the current job, your future, career decisions, and other professionally related situations that may occur from time to time. They are "safe harbor." Whatever you tell them will remain confidential. Usually this is a person who has attained the kind of career you are seeking, but others can also serve the role equally well. The main ingredient is that they are someone to whom you can turn for whatever reason makes sense to you.
    a. Identify the characteristics and expertise of the person who could serve as your mentor. Identify one or more persons who have the desired characteristics.
    b. Try to begin building a relationship with that person. A good way to start would be to seek his or her advice on some area of interest to you. At this point it is not advisable to ask this person to be your mentor. In fact, that request usually isn't made. It just happens.

2. Write your personal mission statement. Be specific by stating general goals supported by operational objectives.
    a. Is it consistent or in conflict with the organization?
    b. Does it matter, especially in these days of repositioning due to downsizing?

3. Develop your long-range Career Development Plan. In order to do this, you must have some idea of where you want to go. Explore several possible directions and then identify training and education requirements and experience needed to reach them. Some type of tradeoff analysis will reveal the more probable directions from among the possibles.
    a. Identify the gap between what you have and what you need.
    b. After a tradeoff analysis, select the best career direction for the long term.

4. Develop a plan of activities (specific and detailed list of action items) over the next 12 months that will move you toward your career goals. Prioritize and schedule the activities and get started!

Reflections

ISI CASE STUDY

Human Resources

Thus far, attention has been focused on processes, activities, methodologies, philosophies, and forecasting. People generate the ideas behind them and when the enterprise makes the changes, people are the implementers. ISI has little or no professional development. Both the organization and the people are not information enabled. Without this dilemma resolved, ISI cannot move forward with any type of new venture. In fact, it is buried in crisis management and meeting current obligations. One approach to the people problem is to take the time to describe tasks, people, and skill requirements for the new ISI.

Deliverables

1. Identify tasks, people, and skill requirements.
2. Place people on the project management charts.
3. Take a skills inventory of all personnel and prepare a retraining program.
4. Identify and prioritize the skills needed for ISI to progress into the next decade.
5. Promote the concept that people have to take charge of their own career.
6. Incorporate information technology expertise in the training program.
7. Establish a collaborative program (management and staff) for career development.
8. Begin to think in terms of outsourcing: people, services, information technology.
9. Include human resource planning in the corporate master plan and support it with consistent project management techniques and the process flow of career planning (Exhibit 9–11).

Chapter 10

The Service Role of Information Technology

◆ ◆ ◆

Although it is undeniably important to ensure the integration of business and technical goals at the highest corporate levels, the information systems (IS) manager who only acts as integrator is little more than a consultant. In fact, the IS manager faces a broader challenge: In addition to consolidating the IS executive relationship, the IS manager must command a thorough knowledge of the IS department itself—the services it can provide, the means of delivering these services, and the general role of the department in advancing corporate goals.

For some IS managers, keeping in mind this difference in orientation—corporate versus departmental—is difficult. The challenge does not reduce simply to developing objectives at the corporate level and then directing the department to carry them out. Rather, the challenge is to maintain a dual or "stereo" vision of corporate opportunities and needs in tandem with departmental capabilities.

This chapter begins by looking at this triple role in more detail followed by a discussion of certain external and internal influences on the IS department. We then move to an examination of the department's functional responsibilities, which are broadly characterized as technical, futuristic, and innovative. The chapter ends with a look at compromise and consistency as the twin demands felt by modern IS departments.

◆ THE TRIPLE ROLE

One way of looking at the role of the IS department is to consider (1) situations where they take the leading role in suggesting technologies and applications, (2) situations where they are purely supportive and strive to meet requested demands, and (3) situations where they can be effective only by working in collaboration with their customers. We will also point out the seeming dilemma that exists between the proactive and reactive roles. Each role is described in terms of the responsibilities that characterize it.

Reactive Role

This role has persisted throughout most of the history of information systems in organizations. The obvious mission of the IS department is to perform the technical duties required by others—that is, to act as a service department responsible for meeting the needs of other business units.

Over the years, this role has evolved from one in which the user was totally dependent on the IS department to meet its every request. Initially that request was for applications development, operations support, and systems maintenance. In time, as users began to take on some of the responsibility for meeting their computing needs, education, and training were added to the list of reactive responsibilities. Later, as users began developing their own applications, consulting on systems design and development became an added reactive responsibility. Today the reactive role of the IS department still retains some of its earlier responsibilities but has turned more toward providing and maintaining the hardware, software, and data infrastructure required by the user community.

Proactive Role

The IS department is responsible for the organization's appropriate and strategic use of technology; it must lead efforts to maximize returns on technical investments. The observant student will have noted that the reactive and proactive roles can be in conflict with one another. In some cases, meeting corporate obligations may mean undermining commitments to supporting certain users' wishes. In other cases, the need to support technology that is easy and popular with users may involve a temporary lapse in corporate-level duties. Although user and corporate needs often can be simultaneously satisfied with creative compromises, the real challenge to the IS manager is to consistently satisfy end users through the use of a combination of leadership and service postures.

This proactive role of the IS department has had an interesting evolution over the years. At the time when computing first became an operational-level tool, it was the initiative of the IS department to provide the leadership to identify and develop accounting-related applications. The computer was beyond the reach of the user departments at that time. As the tools became more sophisticated and users began assuming some responsibilities for their computing activities, the proactive role moved from operations to tactical to strategic level involvements. Today, the IS department is significantly challenged to take a leadership role in identifying strategic opportunities made possible by the technology. The role is extremely difficult and accounts for much of the brief half-life of the CIO. While the proactive role will not disappear, organizations will find it necessary to let it further evolve into the collaborative version described in the next section.

Exhibit 10-1 Typical Reactive, Proactive, and Collaborative Responses at Various Levels

LEVEL	PROACTIVE	REACTIVE
External	Establish vendor program Target technical opportunities Promote activity in professional societies	Evaluate announcements of new technology React to competitors' uses of competitive technology
Corporate	Participate in strategic planning Provide executive training	Take budget-reduction action Justify staffing levels
User	Monitor user service levels Provide user education and orientation programs	Investigate complaints about system performance Act on maintenance requests
Internal	Institute increased controls and measurement Institute internal cross-training program	Respond to turnover problem with improved benefits Undertake emergency equipment repairs

Collaborative Role

This hybrid role is becoming more the rule than the exception. The emergence of the IEMgmt team will tend to further promote this collaboration among midlevel managers. The highly competitive business world is forcing a collaboration between the IS manager and the user manager. That collaboration includes the IEMgr(Tp), IEMgr(TP), and IEMgr(tP). First observe that they each have at least a minimal fluency in both the technology and the business process and that gives them a basis for communication. Through the IEMgr(TP), they are linked at a high level of technology expertise. That linkage allows them to collaborate at the strategic level both for the provision of technology to meet corporate needs and to meet specific business process needs. The collaborative effort is responsible for identifying breakthrough uses of technology; building the business case for acquiring the technology; and designing, developing, implementing, and maintaining the strategic applications portfolio that follows.

Exhibit 10-1 summarizes, by way of example, some of the differences among the reactive, proactive, and collaborative roles.

◆ CHANGING FUNCTIONS OF INFORMATION SYSTEMS

The functional responsibilities of the IS department are both diverse and extensive, much more so than has traditionally been assumed or perceived by the organization and the user areas. As the various dimensions of the department's functional responsibilities are evaluated, it is appropriate to consider the levels of proficiency required of the IS manager and selected managerial subordinates. By now the student should recognize that those levels of proficiency are constantly changing. For the IS manager to become the IEMgr(Tp), the emphasis must be on developing a minimal level of expertise in both business process and function, as well as collateral skills in creative problem solving, negotiations, consensus building, meeting management, project management, interpersonal relations, and others.

In this time of transition the functions of the IS department are principally guidance, training, and consulting. The traditional technical responsibilities must all be consistent with these three functions.

Systems and Programming

The IS group responsible for building elaborate structures that respond to user needs is the systems and programming group. This group must be able to respond to specific requests for support or to analyze a problem situation to determine possible hardware/software solutions. Like any builder, this group is required to display inventiveness in solving problems but cannot let its creativity eclipse the goal of constructing products that satisfy needs. Elegant, unused solutions are a failure; the customer may not always be right but the customer must be satisfied.

Because this same group is responsible for systems changes, it will try to identify or anticipate them in the systems design. Changes or extensions to a system can be made easier if the original blueprints allow for them. However, systems and programming's first goal is to meet immediate objectives within schedule and budget.

We need to clarify the boundaries of applications development responsibility between the IS department and the business units. Corporatewide applications systems design, development, and maintenance are the responsibility of the IS department. Business function or process applications systems are at a minimum a shared responsibility but in many cases will be the responsibility of the business unit with the IS department assuming a consultative role on the project team. We will have more to say on this topic in Part III.

Operations

The days of operators in white lab coats tending to the central computer operations facility are disappearing. In many companies the central operations facility is a server, a corporate data warehouse, and elaborate switches to route data transmissions across a variety of networks. Few people are to be found in these facilities. They appear in order to check the status of the network or handle a routine maintenance chore. The equipment is very reliable and seldom fails. It is becoming transparent to the user community. With much of the computing taking place over a network the user community handles their input and output needs without operations staff intervention or direct support. Computer services, much like telephone services, is provided on demand wherever and whenever the user requires it. The role of the IS manager is simply to make sure that it is available on demand.

Technical and Network Services

The building and operating of systems both have the advantage of being visible and readily understood activities. Users generally see the benefits inherent in these tasks. What they sometimes lose sight of, however, is the fact that systems rest on complex technology, and behind the scenes someone must keep that technology in working order. The group responsible for this in the IS department is technical support. This group's duties are broad and affect systems and programming and operations in various ways. The technical support staff selects the hardware, software, and communications technology with which applications systems are built. They guide the ways in which the systems will be used by advising analysts, programmers, and IEMgrs(TP) on design and programming alternatives that take advantage of the hardware and software on which applications will run. Technical support staff are also responsible for ensuring that the technology is maintained in proper order and performs well. This means that technical support is concerned with how efficiently systems and programming designs the system as well as how operations runs it. Technical support wants to be allowed to maintain the technology in top working order. Naturally, the operations group may have some difficulty with the many changes that might affect it; thus, another conflict may arise. The challenges to the technical support unit are manifold and always changing.

Corporate Database Access

This support function has come under close scrutiny of late. The bottom-line issue is the strategic value of the data resource. To realize this value involves first the creation of an enterprisewide data model, then assigning responsibility for its maintenance, then determining access privileges, and, finally, defining and implementing applications development policy and procedures. We discuss procedures for accomplishing this in Chapter 12. Here our concern is for the role of the IS department regarding the corporate database. That role includes facilitating the design of the database, and keeping the data safe and accessible—nothing more! While it may seem presumptuous, we place the responsibility for creation, editing, and updating squarely in the hands of the business units.

The IS department is the custodian, not the owner, of the corporate database. Within that custodial responsibility are included selecting data structures, providing for data integrity, and assuring data security.

Selecting Data Structures

The database administrator (DBA) decides on the best way to organize the data. This decision is based on extensive business unit input regarding data entities, data attributes, source, scope, level of summarization, time period of interest, volatility, mode of usage, frequency of use, ownership, and accuracy.

Providing for Data Integrity

This responsibility belongs to the user community. Part of the exercise in building a corporate data model is to identify the business unit responsible for each data item. In most cases the responsibility for creating the data item is held by a single department, while the responsibility for maintaining it may be vested in several departments. Whatever decisions are made as to who has responsibility for what, those decisions must be communicated to the user community.

Training and Education

As business units become more independent of the IS department and as technology continues to change, the need for training and education grows in importance. The role for the IS department is both proactive and reactive in training provision. On the proactive side is the offering of training on supported shrinkwrap products. As we discuss in Part III, users should not be forced to use any particular products, but the IS department may only provide training for the standard products. Those standards will have been negotiated with the business units. In many cases training will become partially decentralized. Since the business units can choose their own software, they will also have to make provisions for training for the use of that software. Depending on the specific training needs, that training may be either contracted out or developed in-house.

The practice of having internal training resources is viewed by many as a luxury and as a result the training function may involve no more than managing a cadre of outside contractors. In some organizations, trainers may serve rotating terms.

Help Desks

The IS manager should negotiate service-level agreements with the business units. Part of the service-level agreement will cover the Help Desk. The concern here is the scope and depth of help to be offered.

Technology Gatekeepers

This is an interesting service in that it was once the sole province of the IS department but now is clearly vested in the IEMgmt team. This has always been a team effort, but the team is no longer made up of just the technical support staff from the IS department. It now includes technology-savvy professionals from the business units, specifically the IEMgrs(TP). The scope of the technology gatekeepers is no longer just at the enterprise level but now moves down to the function and process level. For it is there that the enterprise should be looking for opportunities to exploit technology for the benefit of a single business process.

Standards

The IS department is still responsible for establishing and enforcing standards. That responsibility cannot be delegated to the business units. However, both the establishment and the enforcement are collaborative efforts between the IS department and the business units. This approach assures buy-in and commitment and improves the likelihood of successful enforcement.

◆ ISLANDS OF TECHNOLOGY

The term *islands of technology* is frequently used to describe the establishment, usually in isolation, of a specialized solution for a particular area or problem. Several factors have accelerated the trend toward islands of technology. Technology itself has opened the door, first with micro and minicomputers (which can be devoted to a selected user) and later with specialized software and devices to meet singular needs. The push toward decentralization and entrepreneurship in organizations has helped move computer acquisition decisions to user departments, allowing them to acquire standalone solutions sometimes without the knowledge or approval of the IS department. Competitive needs have dictated much of this trend.

Finally, users have developed their skills for readiness to assimilate necessary new technology. No longer easily intimidated, users are increasingly computer literate, aggressive professionals who know their needs and are no longer satisfied with inadequate or no solutions. For them, islands of technology are a highly positive new development.

Following are some examples of islands of technology. After briefly explaining each we turn to the more important, and sometimes controversial, topic of the role of the IS department in the management of islands of technology.

Office Automation

From its simple beginnings in word processing, office automation has expanded to become a complex part of the modern office environment. It can include:

- Word processing (standalone, shared logic, or networked)
- Copy/image/document management and/or transmission

- Records management
- Integrated voice communications
- Video conferencing
- *Miscellaneous* automated functions (e.g., travel services, room and equipment reservation, public access network applications)

It is instructive to consider the differences between automated systems and what we think of as traditional information systems. The former must be simpler and less complicated to use but, in the case of word processing, more responsive. Access in many cases is more casual and sporadic but available to a much larger clientele. Originally, integration of the many elements was not as important as simplifying systems access to standard and easily used equipment. Recently, integration of various elements—word processing and electronic mail, for instance—has become more important now that the separate elements have established themselves. Other disparities between office automation systems and IS include some differences in vendors, dissimilar work procedures and measurements, different job types, and different business roles.

In pioneering office automation, many industry experts note statistics which indicate that equipment investments per person in office environments are vastly less than those per worker in agriculture and blue-collar environments (where productivity is measurably higher). Productivity comparisons are complicated, but what seems to be clear is that capital investments for white-collar workers are catching up to those of blue-collar workers.

One difficulty in achieving office automation is that it belongs, in a sense, to everyone; no single department typically cost-justifies or installs it. Because it usually applies to the company at large, ownership (including maintenance and administration of the system) can be hard to determine.

Computer-Integrated Manufacturing

Computer-integrated manufacturing (CIM) is another island of technology. Unlike office automation, ownership of this application is usually more focused. Moreover, CIM is a very visible and high-payback application, concentrated as it is on a high-cost and critical part of the organization. CIM itself is an accumulation of smaller units of automation. Some of the elements of CIM include:

- Work-flow control (bar codes, laser scanning, etc.)
- Material control (automated material handling systems, robots, etc.)
- Process control (numerical machine control)
- Production planning and scheduling
- Computer-aided design/computer-aided manufacturing (CAD/CAM)

These and other elements of CIM require special knowledge of manufacturing, material handling, distribution, and so on. For this reason, and because CIM applications are very nonstandardized, CIM systems usually are heavily sponsored by an internal engineering group or rely heavily on outside specialized consulting. Many vendors can be involved, and integrating them is a real challenge, since there is no clearly accepted standard such as the manufacturing automation protocol (MAP). One important integration challenge that must be faced is how to include mainframe data and transactions within the CIM environment.

Desktop Publishing

As laser printing and flexible software come together, the tools to prepare simple typeset and visually stimulating documents have become cheap enough to be acquired by many companies and even departments. In-house preparation of price lists, assembly instructions, newsletters, product documentation, and a variety of other materials is becoming cheaper, faster, and more versatile. Moreover, the multiple steps involved in typesetting are avoided and errors are reduced. Such tools as personal workstations are easily available and immediately useful for copywriters, layout artists, and even graphic artists. However, the average company still relies on outside services for sophisticated processes or products such as three-color printing, printing on nonstandard stock, die cuts, and perfect binding.

Imaging and Document Management

Document capture, storage, and retrieval has gone far beyond paper and filing cabinets. Organizations that are information-intensive have, out of necessity, turned to electronic media to manage the flow of information into and through their business units. Documents are scanned and stored in electronic form and made available online to the knowledge worker. The net effect has been to eliminate much of the time spent in someone's in-basket waiting for processing. Many business reengineering efforts have included this work group environment so as to reduce or eliminate non–value-added time in document processing.

Departments that utilize these document management systems generally operate independently from the IS department except in cases where their information is required outside department boundaries. Such information is usually stored on a server and available to the clients through the enterprise network.

Multimedia

Desktop and laptop PC hardware and software technology has advanced to the point where many professionals are using the systems for presentations that incorporate sound-and-motion video in addition to the more popular slide presentation features. This software tends to be very intuitive and does not require formal training to utilize effectively. The typical user is up and running with little effort.

Integration Options

The role of IS in the management of islands of technology is by no means clear. In some environments, because of past opposition or perceived lack of expertise, the IS department is not even responsible for the strategic identification of such efforts. Even where the department has been an early champion, the degree to which it guides and leads an independent automation effort is controversial, pitting IS technicians against user technical experts and even executive against executive. On the one hand, the IS department's leadership and input can provide much help to users. Important issues such as data protection, documentation, procedures, and testing have been pioneered by IS. Also, the department can make sure that technology, systems, and data are capable of being integrated—if not immediately, then down the road. On the other hand, all these helpful guidelines tend to be seen as restrictions by those who ultimately own the systems. Users increasingly lobby for more autonomy, freedom from compliance with corporate standards, less emphasis on future integration, and more emphasis on current effectiveness. For these reasons, many sponsors of islands of technology have opted for low or no integration, freedom to pick any vendor, and minimal interference.

Users' reactions are largely justified, in light of the IS department's past tendency to want to control rather than assist where possible. The challenge for the IS department is to overcome the image (and sometimes the fact) of being unreasonably dominating and to be perceived as a facilitator of users' best interests. Then the department can guide user behavior or integration efforts, directing them toward the best interests of the company at large.

Certain issues of responsibility must be addressed before investing in islands of technology. If additional jobs are generated, where should they report and what types of jobs should they be—user or IS oriented? Where will security be handled? Who will plan disaster recovery and documentation control? Will data management and network management be handled as an IS responsibility? Will hardware and software be acquired using standardized acquisition procedures? Where will the equipment physically reside? Each of these questions must be answered in such a way as to ensure efficiency, protect the organization, and aid user progress.

It should be apparent that the IS department can share heavy responsibility for an island of technology without actually owning the application portion. A more sensitive responsibility, one defined more in practice than through formal procedures, is planning and migration. The user undoubtedly has ambitions for the future application of a particular type of automation. Helping the user to realize these ambitions and introducing other corporate opportunities are clearly tasks that fall within the IS department's scope of responsibility. However, they must be accomplished by involving others—and the department's and users' perceptions of when the timing is right for integration may be very different.

◆ ORGANIZING FOR CONTROL OF INFORMATION

Information is a corporate asset. In its more primitive data form it is protected by standards developed in collaboration by those who use it and is under the stewardship of the IS department. Access, security, and backup are the responsibility of the IS department. The generation of the data and the creation of information from the data is the responsibility of the user community.

Command and Control Structures

In the old command and control functional structures there were major obstacles to the creation of information and to its sharing across the enterprise. Functional business units tended to create data according to their own definitions (even when the same data existed elsewhere but was unknown to them) and to produce reports for their consumption only. The enterprise was not aware of the value pent up in their data and information and was therefore unable to take advantage of it.

Nonhierarchical Structures

The breakdown of the hierarchical structures and the emergence of a variety of other organizational structures have greatly facilitated the use of data and information across the enterprise. Next we briefly examine three nonhierarchical structures.

Task Forces

Worker empowerment naturally leads to the formation of task forces. Usually, these units are temporary (produce a specific deliverable) and may arise because the workers decide to create them or they may be established by management directive. With the evolution of the enterprise away from function and toward process structures, task forces are mostly cross-functional. To call them a team in the true sense of the word is probably an overstatement in most cases. Each member of the task force has specific responsibilities. Task forces always have someone appointed as leader. Task forces will often call on outside resources when such resources are needed and are not included within the span of control of the task force members. Deliverables often take the form of research reports with recommendations for action.

Project Teams

The project team is a modified form of task force. It has a specific deliverable with time and resource constraints. The team has both core members (assigned to the project from start to finish, although not necessarily on a full-time basis) and contracted members (assigned to the project only during the time when their specific contribution is needed, although not necessarily on a full-time basis). The core and contracted team members possess all of the resources needed to complete the project. Project teams are temporary structures which disband at the completion of the project but which may reform for a later project. Their projects tend to be of longer duration than those of the task force.

Self-Directed Work Teams

In a sense, the self-directed work team (SDWT) is a logical extension of the empowered worker and the project team. SDWTs differ from the above in that they are permanent, totally self-contained, do not have a leader (or pass the responsibility from team member to team member) and generally have a coordinator (responsible for the logistics of team meetings, agenda preparation, distribution of team documents, and other administrative details). Some SDWTs are vested with hiring, firing, and profit and loss responsibility. They do not report to a manager in the technical sense but often have a coach/facilitator, whose responsibility is to enable the team to meet its responsibilities. The SDWT is responsible for a core or support process or some part of one.

◆ MANAGING ORGANIZATIONAL CHANGE

It is not our purpose here to offer a definitive study of change management but to merely point out a few areas of interest as they relate to information management across the organization. First, it is important to note, as we have already done, that we are in the midst of a total metamorphosis regarding the role and value of information to the business of the enterprise. While we understand that rapid change is taking place, we do not understand exactly how to cope or how to best take advantage of the opportunities that are surely present. In fact, we cannot even imagine what opportunities are available. The information age is not fully understood by the business community!

Our best advice is to first empower individuals. Give them the latitude to investigate creative and innovative ways to improve the core and support processes in which they work. Reengineering casts a large shadow of pending job loss and delayering. Individuals must know that continued employment is a function of their ability to add value to the organization. All that they have the right to ask is the opportunity to add value and then it is up to them to do so.

Reflections

GENERAL CONCEPTS

1. If the future of information technology is changing so rapidly, why take a proactive role and risk being wrong? Why not just be reactive and wait until you have to act? With the accelerated changes taking place now (software becomes obsolete in a matter of months), information systems planning seems unnecessary.

2. What are the problems of "collaborating?" What are the differences among collaborating, negotiating, coordinating, getting consensus, voting, declaring, and communicating?

3. Islands of technology have arisen due to the advancement of microcomputing, distributed computing, and the fact that end-user departments have found their own solutions with menu-driven and friendly software.
   a. What are the problems and solutions associated with end-users building their own islands?
   b. How would you organize for control of information technology, understanding that some centralization is necessary for the computing infrastructure and that end users will continue to want (demand) local processing power?

Reflections

ISI CASE STUDY

Return to ISI Applications Portfolio—Service Role of IT

The triple role of the IEMgr is important to the success of ISI. The IEMgr must know what services it can provide (be up-to-date on the advances of IT), the means of delivering those services (options for end-user involvement, outsourcing, local processing flexibility, overall control of planning and budgeting), and the general role of the department in advancing corporate goals (strategic and operational master plans, including IT support). Now that ISI has been examined for process and people, information technology must be addressed. Traditional systems development practices (analysis, design, and implementation) may not be appropriate. If too much analysis is undertaken, the company will fold. If too little planning is conducted, none of the pieces will fit the big picture and inefficient operations will continue. Some type of information technology infrastructure must be envisioned in order to come close to desired outcomes (final award-winning bid by vendor to meet requirements).

One way to narrow the gap between future expectations and current operations is to hire consultants to help ISI move toward a total solution. These consultants should be IEMgrs. It may even be a good move to hire one or more IEMgrs on a permanent basis to manage the consultants. Some form of in-house expertise is needed to facilitate the process, provide leadership with top-level executives, and suggest measures to improve overall quality in all areas.

Integrating All Electronic Processing

Clearly, ISI's manual database system (card file) is one of the first application areas which needs attention. It must be automated. Other application areas (sales order processing, purchasing, distribution, financial processing, and human resources) must be analyzed for priority and scheduling. Programming languages, commercially available software, outsourcing capability, and communication infrastructure are all part of the planning process and must be integrated for effective use of limited resources. Small companies like ISI are caught in the middle—they must have automation sophisticated enough to provide timely and accurate information for customer retention and acquisition, but they may not have the funds to purchase the capability.

Deliverables

1. Examine the application areas, starting with the inventory of products.
2. Devise a scheme to prioritize them, perhaps with criteria and weighting functions.
3. Commence interrogation of vendors to enlist their help in configuration design.
4. Commence negotiation with vendors (if competitive bid, meet with each vendor separately to see what preliminary solutions each of them proposes).
5. In evaluating vendor preliminary bids, question them on:
   a. State-of-the-art technology
   b. Configuration diagram for hardware and software
   c. Their design for meeting your requirements
   d. Consistency with concepts suggested by your hired consultants
   e. Database conversion, access, integrity, standards, and other factors (Exhibit 6–2)

PART III

♦ ♦ ♦

Enabling Business Functions

We have seen how the transition to a process-oriented structure allows an organization to focus and measure its effectiveness in relating to its customers. In this part, we examine in more detail how the infrastructure has changed. Of particular importance will be the impact at the business function level. Specifically, what relationship between the information system department and the IEMgmt team must be created to service the processes and support their staff to serve the customer?

In Chapter 11, we lay the foundation of the relationship between the information systems function and the business functions and include an examination of the systems tools in use by the business units. In Chapter 12, systems development methods are reviewed with particular reference to those methods which involve the end-user as project team member or manager. The trend toward user-developed systems is established. Exactly how the IEMgmt team participates in those projects is the topic of Chapter 13. Finally in Chapter 14, we conclude our discussion at the business function level by examining the evolved roles and responsibilities of the IEMgmt team and end users in the development of applications systems. ♦

Chapter 11

Linking Information Technology to Business Functions

◆ ◆ ◆

The world has become more complex due to massive political changes, instant global communication systems, more customer demand for quality products and services, and the accelerated use of micro- and/or client server computer systems. In the two previous parts of the text, we discussed enabling the enterprise (business, government, or education) with information technology in an effort to use this technology effectively for personal and organizational productivity. In addition, business process reengineering has emerged as a significant factor in response to those changes. Now it is time to enable business functions and, in this chapter, link the new process orientation to business functions. We will explore organizational complexity, the impact of these new competitive forces on the decision-making process, and finally, support of decision makers with perspectives and techniques (business simulation methods) brought to the scene by information technology.

◆ DECISION-MAKING

Decision and Executive Support Systems

The more complex the world with more variables (known and unknown), external factors, and abundance of information (relevant and irrelevant), the more difficult it becomes to make decisions. There are too many options to process efficiently and effectively. There is less time available to make tougher decisions. At the same time, new worker empowerment and quality initiatives demand more time to reach consensus. Change will not diminish; it will continue to increase. Decision-makers must change their behaviors and adapt to work environments which are much more flexible and democratic than the command and control approaches of the past. Practitioners and educators will have to learn how to deal with a more diverse workforce. There will be more need to consider the impact of their decisions on the organization and other colleagues before enacting them. Information technology can be helpful in supporting the decision-making process.

In order to make a decision, you have to make sure that you have identified the right problem to solve, or better yet, prevent the problem, or symptom of the problem, from surfacing in the first place. In earlier chapters, divergent-thinking skills (higher-order skills) were discussed and will play an important part in this "problem-finding" stage. The major questions are:

What is the decision-making process?
Who makes what decisions?
What is the basis for decision making?
How are decisions made and what "styles" dominate the process?
What are the time and sequence of steps for making decisions?

Decision-Making Process

The decision-making process will depend on the nature of the enterprise, its marketing niche and how progressive it is in grasping new opportunities, its philosophy on conducting business at all management levels, and its effective use of information technology. Often, the process is not obvious and is not formally documented. If it is documented, the informal system very well may account for the major portion of decision making. Some type of framework is necessary to place *Decision Support Systems* (DSS) within our concept of managing information across the enterprise. Exhibit 11-1 depicts an arrangement of decision-making activity, the elements of which will be introduced as the questions posed in the previous subsection are addressed.

The outside segment of the chart (Decision-Making I) is a manual system derived from unprocessed data and informal data capture. For centuries, people have identified and solved problems and made intuitive and rational and irrational decisions without computer assistance. In some cases, this process continues. The next segment of the chart (Decision-Making II) identifies information systems as an integral part of the decision-making process for individuals working at various functional levels of the organization. Usually, a DSS is an interactive and computer-based system designed to assist managers to solve problems where some historical data is available for building predictive models. Turban [1993] adds a more sophisticated attribute, the use of DSS directly by end users in an iterative way for all phases of decision-making, including a knowledge base. A knowledge base is a collection of facts, procedures, and perhaps even decision rules which is brought to bear on a problem. More information on knowledge bases will be introduced later in the chapter as related to artificial intelligence systems. This concept of end-user data and model management (including direct dialog with software) is depicted in Exhibit 11-1 by the segment Decision-Making III.

Exhibit 11-1: Decision-Making Relationships in the Enterprise

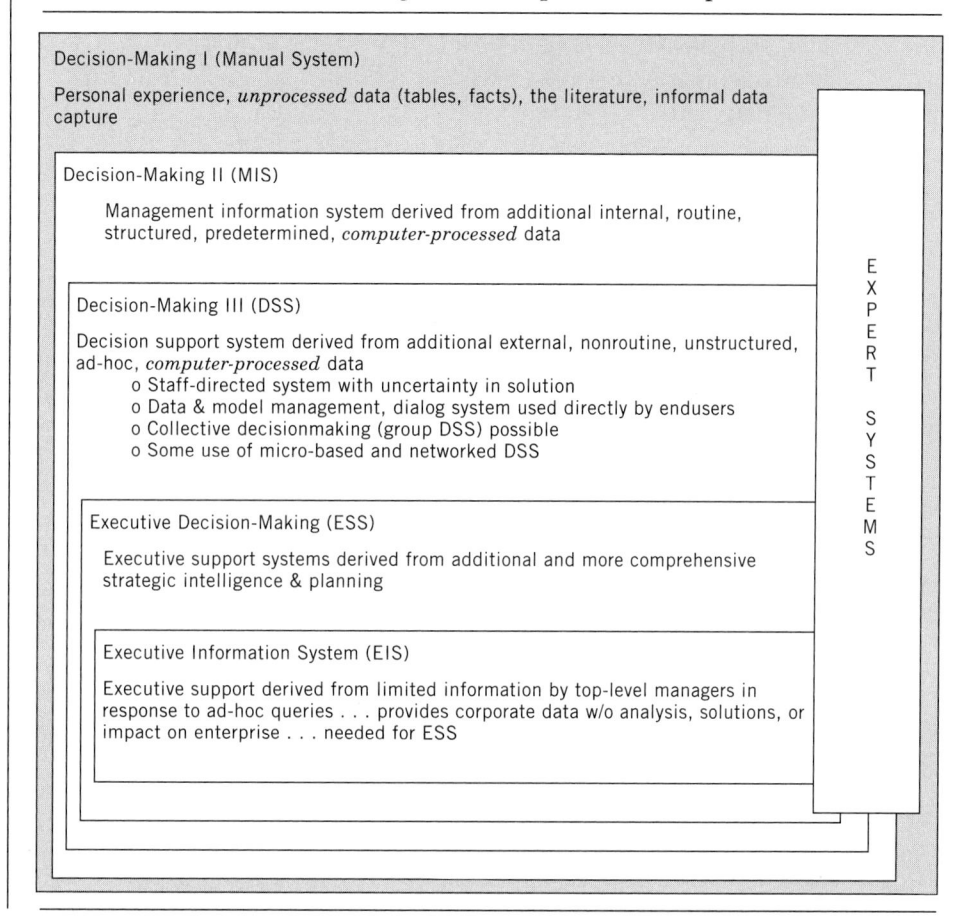

Decision-Making I (Manual System)

Personal experience, *unprocessed* data (tables, facts), the literature, informal data capture

Decision-Making II (MIS)

Management information system derived from additional internal, routine, structured, predetermined, *computer-processed* data

Decision-Making III (DSS)

Decision support system derived from additional external, nonroutine, unstructured, ad-hoc, *computer-processed* data
- o Staff-directed system with uncertainty in solution
- o Data & model management, dialog system used directly by endusers
- o Collective decisionmaking (group DSS) possible
- o Some use of micro-based and networked DSS

Executive Decision-Making (ESS)

Executive support systems derived from additional and more comprehensive strategic intelligence & planning

Executive Information System (EIS)

Executive support derived from limited information by top-level managers in response to ad-hoc queries . . . provides corporate data w/o analysis, solutions, or impact on enterprise . . . needed for ESS

EXPERT SYSTEMS

For example, DSS software can be used to examine plant capacity for meeting new product demands with different combinations of people, raw materials, production scheduling, finished goods distribution sites, and market destinations. Banks use them for producing financial statement summaries for top-level administrators. The insurance industry uses software to evaluate customer risk or assess real estate properties. Education systems can use DSS software for financial forecasting, for faculty, course, and room utilization efficiency, and for physical plant construction to be consistent with long-range institutional planning. Government agencies use such systems to assist in local voting district reorganizations, to conduct international war game scenarios, or to evaluate the cost/benefit impact of microcomputing versus clientserver technology.

Within DSS, two additional levels of decision-making for executives are noted on the chart. At a high level, *executive support systems* (ESS) focus on use of internal and external data processed by networked computer systems of all sizes. Turban [1993] suggests that the integration of DSS and the innermost segment, *executive information systems* (EIS), produces the ESS. For that reason, the ESS is portrayed as between DSS and EIS. Files are downloaded from the microcomputer at the EIS level (no analysis, no solutions) and uploaded to the DSS level where unstructured and ad-hoc queries can put the data to work. In practical terms, organizations have not exploited executive support systems because of unclear justification criteria. What is the return on investment for an ESS which deals with uncertainty, unknown variables, vision statements, and unknown results? The cost is more measurable because the hardware, software, and training reveal funding requirements. What is needed is a top-level executive (champion) willing to take the risk of gaining no competitive advantage for the cost. Some companies, such as Phillips Petroleum, Dun and Bradstreet, Coca Cola, and Lockheed [Sprague & Watson, 1993], have enjoyed some success with this concept. The benefits for the Lockheed-Georgia system appear to far outweigh the costs, namely, faster response, easier access to more detailed information, more integrated internal and external data, reduced maintenance, graphical display of information in a variety of flexible formats, and shared executive information.

The remaining segment of expert systems may consist of one or more parts of the decision-making process. Expert systems are those which extract data and information from "experts" so that their expertise can be captured for automation. The extraction of expertise from a human is conducted with the expectation that a computer program can be designed to emulate that behavior to solve new real-world problems. In the medical field, one might picture sitting at a computer terminal, which might be connected to a database containing all one's health information, and after inputting some symptoms on a menu-driven touch screen, one could be provided with some preliminary information about the next steps. Behind the scenes, one or more doctors were interrogated on the relationship of symptoms to more probable illnesses and their expertise was converted to the interactive computer session. In this way, some factual information is captured and screened, relieving the medical staff of recording routine questions and answers. A more detailed and separate discussion on expert systems and its impact on decision making will be addressed at the end of this chapter.

Who Makes What Decisions?

In the age of empowerment, self-directed work teams, and information-enabled managers at all levels (end users and information systems professionals), it is particularly important to identify the decision makers. Here, the linkage between information technology and business functions must be addressed. Currently, workers serve functional roles even though those roles will change dramatically toward process orientation during the next decade. Functions of a business (corporate planning, marketing and sales, accounting and finance, production and operations, and human resources) cut across enterprise processes and have certain responsibilities and accountabilities in each of their domains. In order to make decisions within these domains, the organizational infrastructure must distinguish functional decision making from process decision making.

During the period of transition from function to process, workers are apt to be confused not only by loyalties (department or process team), but also by decisional authority (within the department and within the team). In some cases, because of the need for fast response with or without complete information, authority conflicts cannot be resolved immediately. When this situation occurs, the element of risk enters. Is it worth it to delay the decision until the real decision maker emerges, or is it worth the risk to make a decision and be held accountable for the consequences, good or bad?

With more information immediately accessible to the information-enabled manager, the risk can be assessed more easily. With more accessible information, more information sharing is possible and can provide more effective communication (e-mail, groupware, internet, video-conferencing, graphical representation, user-friendly application systems). The question of who makes the decisions, under what circumstances, and with what authority will continue to plague the manager struggling to meet operational commitments, develop current budgets, spend resources prudently, and concurrently find time to direct staff for decision support or to make one's own executive decisions based on the integration of DSS and executive information systems (EIS).

What Is the Basis for Decision-Making?

The single most important criterion for making decisions is the integrity of the information upon which the decision is based. How much faith do you have in the facts, conversations, data dumps, logic statements imbedded within the DSS software, assumptions and constraints in using the DSS software (what it does not provide), and assessment of the situation? Are you in the information "overload" or "underload" condition as you react to a crisis? Whatever the situation, you need specific criteria for making decisions:

a. Purpose—goals (strategic statements) and operational objectives
b. Timeliness—short or long-range implications, or both
c. Certainty—known and unknown variables, confidence that the decision is the right one
d. Cost and Value—investment of resources (time, funds) for return (business value)
e. Reliability and Integrity—faith in information sources for completeness, accuracy
f. Precision—degree to which the information may be in error
g. Currency—timeliness of data
h. Weight of Criteria—value of importance of each criterion relative to others

The computer cannot be helpful in identifying purpose (item a), but it can provide assistance in all other categories. Your tool kit is full of techniques and methods (computer based or not); assessing these criteria and finding the right tool for the right situation can help you make the right decisions at the right time for the right reasons.

How Are Decisions Made?

A comprehensive discussion on managerial decision-making "styles" is not appropriate here; however, there is a relationship of such styles to information systems analysis, the subject of the next chapter, and therefore the concept will be introduced at this time. The general systems development stages of analysis, design, and implementation and the demand for less preliminary analysis and more responsiveness (prototype the system in a few months, place it online, and then modify it several times until it meets requirements) suggest that one's decision-making style is important to the process. If you are more action-oriented rather than reflective, a prototyping approach may be more appealing to you. If you are at the other extreme and would like to reflect on various aspects of the problem before making a decision, then you would be more patient in the analysis stage of the development methodology. In this latter case, you might want to make numerous DSS runs of what-if scenarios to better understand the relationships among the known variables and perhaps uncover additional variables needed for the process.

The nature of the organization will affect your decision-making style. If the organization is concerned with quality more than quantity in its products or services and is focused on long-term objectives (obtaining and keeping customers), you must make decisions accordingly. Your promises to the client will be tracked for responsiveness and completeness over time; decision making requires much thoughtfulness and reflection before action is taken by you or your staff.

For example, if you work for a vendor and meet client specifications in price, performance, and service but are unsure of being awarded the bid for your software product, you must make a major decision during the final bid negotiation process. Do you stand firm with your proposal and risk losing the contract, or do you lessen the profit margin in the hope that once the contract is awarded to you, you will have more opportunities for business? If the software vendor is a mail-order business, service to customer (other than prompt delivery and some technical assistance) may be quite different from a consulting firm offering the product as one of many products at its disposal. In this latter case, continued on-site presence is very important for continuing the client relationship. In fact, clients will be looking for more long-term relationships and alliances with vendors so that they can deal more effectively with the myriad options and with technology obsolescence issues [Davidow & Malone, 1992]. In other words, your decision-making style needs to be synchronized with the philosophy of the organization.

Time and Frequency Constraints

If a crisis is occurring or is imminent, the criteria and basis for decision making will not allow any in-depth analysis. Executive leadership on the corporate battlefield sometimes requires immediate action with the realization that all the relevant information may not be available. However, if a fully implemented DSS-EIS program is available for executive decision support, in situations of corporate mergers, acquisitions, or sales the impact of making adjustments can complement the intuitive and other nonquantitative factors involved in the decision. Most companies wait until the crisis situation emerges and then respond with the usual flurry of activity in a desperate search for relevant and available information, mostly stored in separate databases and file cabinets. Response must be immediate because the frequency of such situations will increase. Time-critical situations will continue to increase and will demand more attention to integrated executive support systems.

◆ BUSINESS SIMULATION FOR BUSINESS FUNCTIONS

The next step after considering an overall view of decision-making with a strong emphasis on computer-based systems support and on executive support systems is a more in-depth treatment of business simulation methods applied to business functions. One major concern of current and future business ventures is competitive advantage. In the early years, technology emphasis was on cost reduction and better information for decision making. Automation will always be expected to reduce staff needs, avoid unnecessary growth, and control inventory. For such "transaction-based" operations, it was easy to quantify. As we progressed to the use of information technology for higher-order (unstructured, ad-hoc, complex, cross-functional) decision making, a different array of questions arose: Can technology improve or protect market share? Will technology provide better customer relationships? Does technology expand offerings or suggest new products or services?

These questions are predictive in nature. Historical data will help to form a base from which extrapolations and inferences may be drawn, but in order to be predictive, business functions have to use business simulation techniques. These techniques are the underpinnings of the decision-support software systems described in the previous section. Some awareness of simulations of all types is necessary for the IEMgr to be productive throughout his or her career. The IEMgr holds the key to use of decision and executive support systems for effective decision making. The IEMgr bridges the gap between information technology and management of the enterprise.

Expectations

It is not reasonable to expect that a top-level manager will be able to utilize a business simulation package without some knowledge of the business, information technology in general, and computer-based decision-support systems in particular. Every business is different and each business may have a different array of decision-support products to address the many queries that arise from day to day. Using a simulation model, even if it is not automated, can be a new experience for some managers.

The concept of working on a team dedicated to certain goals and objectives and capturing and sharing information can be a meaningful manual and experiential exercise. It is not unlike athletic activities where one practices for an upcoming real event. War games at facilities like the Naval War College in Newport, Rhode Island have offered realistic scenarios to international groups for the past hundred years. Although warfare tactics are crisis situations, the games can be designed to avoid war or to plan strategies for building defensive strengths. Every year, one-week exercises are carefully planned and conducted with some information technology input. At Nellis Airforce Base in Nevada, pilots simulate foreign aircraft and engage in air combat maneuvers. In these examples, expectations of instructors and participants are identified at the outset.

In business scenarios, the same precautions are needed. The scope, limitations, and assumptions of the simulation exercise require examination before the software product is implemented. Once computer printouts are produced, or color graphical displays are projected on a wide-view screen in real-time, it is easy to become too absorbed in the output and not spend enough time reflecting on those constraints and assumptions. Management games complemented with computer-based and multimedia presentation can be captivating. Once the exercise is completed, another phenomenon occurs. Everyone is so exhausted by the execution of the simulation that their attention during a debriefing session is lacking. It is necessary that attention be paid to proper review of the exercise, because that is the time to repeat the limitations and assumptions of the model used in the exercise.

Simulation Model Design: A Manager's Perspective

The real value of simulation is the approach itself. Regardless of the outcome of conducting one or more sessions on computer-based models (DSS or otherwise), the experience provides a keen awareness of the situation and its effect on the organization. Downsizing means fewer people. How do you determine which categories of people to let go? Within the category, who goes? How many people might be dismissed? The immediate impact of fewer staff is cost containing. But suppose that the next year produces a market demand for a new type of product which requires the expertise of the personnel now employed elsewhere. At the time of downsizing, stockholders were happy. One year later, they are complaining about the lack of responsiveness to new opportunities, which is now impossible because the right people with the right skills are no longer available to make it happen. In addition, the smaller and busier remaining workforce is not apt to enter into the world of risk, especially after the last layoff. They are overburdened with more work (production quotas remained the same, with fewer workers to meet them), close to burnout, and are not receptive (even though empowered) to new ventures.

A simulation exercise could have examined numerous scenarios of staff displacement, retraining, and upsizing the individual [Johansen & Swigart, 1994] rather than dismissal. Additional factors could be a part of the scenario in addition to length of time with company, age, nearness of retirement, position, and immediate business value. Some other factors could have been the impact of corporate strategies for the next few years, merger opportunities, options for continuance of workers on a contract basis, temporary leave without pay, and delaying other new acquisitions and/or programs. Some of these factors would retain worker expertise, the most important asset. Again, the model may not provide the definitive solution, but it can provide some feasible solutions for further examination by management.

It is easy for model design to focus on numbers which are either discrete (succeed or fail) or continuous (follow uniform or normal distribution). Perhaps there is no theoretical expression to represent them, such as *random market sampling*. In any event, these quantitative factors are complemented with logic statements, procedure linkages (some executed before others), information flows, known variable declarations, and numerical methods designed to produce one or more solutions. A simulation is not reality but a representation of reality. It is designed to mimic reality based on information given to it by humans and is descriptive in nature. It formulates a solution with given information and predicts outcomes on that basis. Usually, simulations are used for very complex circumstances. Complex circumstances are those encumbered by so many related variables that the human mind cannot process them rapidly and frequently. Computers are better at following complex decision trees rapidly and frequently.

When the objective is to find satisfactory solutions to complex problems, a less procedural and more probing approach to searching for, learning about, and finding a solution is described as *heuristic*. Feedback loops iterate the process until *some* conditions are met, thereby producing less-than-satisfactory results. This approach is user oriented, promotes creative thinking for problem solving, and takes less computer time but gives somewhat unreliable results.

Simulations can be designed by an in-house team of end users and information systems professionals; however, there are numerous forecasting tools and commercially available software packages which can be customized. Is the data available for building or using the simulation package? How precise and reliable is it? What are the costs for acquisition, training, number of stations, maintenance, and modifications? How long will it take to conduct real scenarios with live data? Is it easy to use? How memory intensive is it? How many stations can use it concurrently? Is it compatible with microcomputer-based applications software (database, spreadsheet, graphics, word processing)?

In model design, the objectives of the simulation must be clearly stated. It is easy to define a few objectives, build the model, use the model to predict outcomes, and repeat this process until a best solution emerges. The process can be very efficient as long as the scope, assumptions, and limitations determined by the scenario fit within the framework of the model. But how effective are the results? Many business forecasting methods fail because the models are so large and complex that validation of input data and output reports is difficult, or because the models are so simple that they are unrealistic and perhaps even meaningless. Somewhere in the continuum of realistic simulation, there is an approach commensurate with the expected return for the investment of time and funding. The more top-level managers and other functional end users participate in the design specifications for the model, the more successful it will be.

The Simulation Process

Another way of examining the use of simulation methods in the enterprise is to track the process from idea to implementation (Exhibit 11-2). This five-step framework applies to any type of decision support system (DSS) and its related computer-based simulation. Types of DSS [Mallach, 1994] range from highly structured problems (suggestion systems) to those with very little structure (file drawer systems). Suggestion systems attempt to mimic the human mind and try to respond with solutions that the human "expert" would make. At the other extreme, file drawer systems usually refer to simple retrieving of data elements from a database so that the decision maker can act immediately (purchase a sale item with a credit card, make airline reservations, buy a ticket to a musical show). In between the two extremes, varying amounts of data manipulation occur among databases according to predetermined rules and constraints.

Integrated software packages with spreadsheets and databases allow easy manipulation of data by desktop computers with or without downloading of files. When uncertainty enters into the simulation, representational models are used to respond to inputs and logic statements in forecasting future events based on historical data. When various decision alternatives are produced by the simulation, especially if the basis for the solutions is mathematical, the program can "optimize" the process and select the best solution. The sequence of activities from idea to implementation (Exhibit 11-2) can be helpful to upper-level managers in discussing the approach, or type of simulation, to meet enterprise objectives.

In Step 1, an idea emerges. In Step 2, enthusiastic and divergent thinking skills (open and free association of concepts, issues, and ideas) allow simulation builders to include almost everything in the model until Step 3 forces convergence on the problem because of real constraints and resources necessary to build and/or buy the package. Someone has to champion the project, collect a team and resources, and assess the probability of full implementation of the model for actual decision making. Everyone is not an enthusiast of computer-based decision support systems, or simulations. Some managers prefer to make decisions in the most flexible and politically correct manner, a method which

Exhibit 11-2

Simulation: Idea to Implementation
---

1. IDEA!

motivators:
personal or organizational tragedy (crisis)
good experience for the career
productivity push by employer

2. WILD ENTHUSIASM

looking for right relationships is interesting
seeing some light at end of tunnel for complex problems
communication with other professionals
rush to include everything; all ideas are good
opportunity to depart from routine work
reality check: cannot include everything

3. CAREFUL CONTAINMENT

who is going to do the work? when? how?
will it be done in addition to everything else?
what is the risk of not doing it, or not completing it?
what is the return on the resource investment?

4. FOCUSED CREATIVITY

approach: intelligence, design, choice
(analysis, design, and implementation)
application of the simulation model: who, why?
prototype model: assumptions, constraints

5. THE PRODUCT

scope, limitations, user-friendliness, impact on decisions
machine and person: numbers and judgments
validity, acceptance, implementation

---

relies on personal and individual attention and on not sharing information and alternatives with others. Once creativity is focused (Step 4) and consensus is obtained to move forward with the venture, the model is designed and placed online (Step 5). If the project was properly designed to add business value to the enterprise when implemented, simulations can be effective in streamlining present operations, providing decisions for the best use of resources, and forecasting for the grasping of new opportunities.

For a more process-oriented discussion of the simulation process (Exhibit 11-3), a different set of activities trace the evolution of a simulation scenario.

Exhibit 11-3

Simulation: A Process Perspective

1. PROBLEM SCENARIO
purpose of simulation, expected outcomes
symptoms, problems, issues, parameters, scope
process team, general approach

2. MODEL DESIGN
specific approach, type of model, customization
assumptions, hypotheses, components
relationships among variables
constraints, accuracy, precision
creative thinking and systems analysis/synthesis

3. VALIDATION
testing simulation model with real world data
robustness (realism) of model
machine vs. people relationship
judgment added: impact of nonmodel factors

4. USE OF THE MODEL
realistic enterprise outcome predictions
learning the process further by building/applying the model
flexibility and modification of model
end-user execution, ease of use, sensitivity of variables

5. INTERPRETATION
detailed knowledge of assumptions and limitations
semantic analysis of output (what it means)
inferences and/or deductions
implications for further modification of model

Traditional systems design methodology (analysis, design, implementation) is applied to produce a five-step process.

In the first step, a detailed analysis of the decision-support system is conducted to uncover the real problems, address the issues from every conceivable direction, and converge on only those topics which will become the basis for Step 2, model design. Some of the results of the discussions using Exhibit 11-2 (Idea to Implementation) apply here as well. A complete set of end-user specifications should be produced much the same way that any other hardware, software, or services procurement would be undertaken (see Chapter 6 for a detailed account of how to develop the design specifications and address the make/buy decision). Validation of the model is always difficult (Step 3). Data may not be readily available from internal or external sources or may be too outdated to be useful. If the analysis and design steps were properly conducted, the source of input data to test the model would have been identified at the outset. Perhaps one set of data was used in building the model and a second set saved for testing or validating model design.

In addition to providing input data to the model, additional data on outcomes are necessary so that the validation process truly examines the model for its ability to depict realism. Once the model is built and validated, it is time to put the model to work and apply it to new situations (Step 5). New data sets and selection of assumption, constraint, and scope options allow the model to be tested further in the real world. As new experiences are tested, modifications are made to the simulation model to include new logic statements, additional variables, and other options such as user-friendly menus, graphics displays, and/or sensitivity measures. Sensitivity measures, also called scenario analyses, allow one to explore the impact of one or more variables on simulation results by conducting several "what-if" scenarios. In other words, how does the decision (or policy choices) reflect the assumptions, constraints, and nature of the outside real world? In this way, a plethora of policy alternatives are possible under a wide array of situations to assist in finding the best solution with some degree of confidence.

Artificial Intelligence and Expert Systems

Artificial intelligence (AI) is not a commercial product; it is a science to be applied to the marketplace and not a commercially available product. It is a part of computer science dedicated to mimicking human (real) intelligence. Turban's [1993] text devotes several chapters to the topic of artificial intelligence and its technologies (expert systems, natural language processing, speech understanding, robotics, computer vision, and intelligent computer-aided instruction). The field of artificial intelligence has had mixed reviews over the years because of the high expectations of the commercial world and high goal aspirations of the academic community. In the latter case, building software to learn from experience, sort out the semantic differences in language, apply models built on old data to new and different situations, make rational inferences, and "think" like a human are goals which are noteworthy but certainly are not attainable completely, accurately, and in a timely way. Conventional programming methods which focus on procedures, rules, and sequences according to some algorithm for solving the problem are quite different from AI methods.

AI software is symbolic (letter, word, number) and deals with objects, processes, and relationships. A *knowledge base* is created with related objects (things, events, facts) which are manipulated to provide solutions to problems. The major approach is to try to match patterns that satisfy the criteria, thus giving the impression that the machine is thinking. AI programming languages, such as PROLOG, can be used to build the model, or other software system "shells" can accelerate the process with a more user-friendly and menu-driven process rather than typical command-driven languages.

Expert systems is one of the categories of applied AI, which is itself a subsystem of DSS, that focus on duplicating the reasoning power of the mechanic. These humans, or experts, are interrogated in depth to extract the inputs, logic, and outputs of the reasoning process of the mind in an effort to capture this knowledge for replication by machine. Automobiles use expert systems for diagnostic tools; the car is connected electronically to a machine which replicates the reasoning power of numerous mechanics in locating problems and suggesting solutions. In medical diagnosis, computer screens display a sequence of options leading the human with the illness to clarify the symptoms, enter the data into the expert system (not given in person to the doctor), and await a further meeting with the doctor. In the meantime, the doctor will have reviewed the preliminary analysis provided by the expert system and together with other data brought on the screen in the form of windows (X rays, previous medical history, medications, and other laboratory information) will integrate the various sources of information and make a prognosis as to the cause of the illness. In addition, expert systems could recommend medication and suggest other medications that should not be used by this patient due to allergies or drug interactions.

Expert systems *shells* are commercially available products which allow end-users with no or little programming knowledge to communicate system requirements directly into them. Although the number of conditions, or rules, may be limiting, it is possible to use these shells on microcomputers to link factors together to solve large and complex problems. Some expert systems development efforts can be extensive (thousands of rules, costing millions of dollars) or can be very focused on specialized problems (less than fifty rules, costing thousands of dollars). Systems can take from a few weeks to several years to develop. One such expert system development package, 1stClass, can be learned by novice end users in a matter of days from online tutorials. Information capture from experts may take a few weeks, including translation of the interview into formal decision rules for entry into the shell. Within a matter of months, a working expert system can be placed online. From a learning standpoint, the overall concept of simulation can be introduced quickly and then used to demonstrate the unleashed power of the technique. The method can be very helpful in developing knowledge engineers from the end-user community.

Other knowledge engineering environments, such as KEE, work through frames to uncover the facts (not judgments) and design expert systems which relate objects (semantic networks) or which contain modules (objects) with both data and programming statements as an integral part of the object structure. Again, programming languages like PROLOG for semantic networks and C++ for object-oriented programs are applicable. In both cases, in-depth knowledge of the languages is necessary to build the models. For those situations where the facts and variables are known, it is a matter of assembling the program to search the network of possibilities for a solution, or for alternative solutions. When there is an ample supply of "experts" for extraction of wisdom and experience, the rules emerge and expert systems are built. When there are many examples of events, mostly unexplained, a different approach is needed. The world of "fuzziness" and neural nets are methodologies which try to take imprecise and/or random knowledge and make something of it.

The Brain, Neural Nets, and Fuzzy Logic

There is one clear difference between people and machines: people can take precise output from a machine and find ways of making it imprecise. The assumptions are invalid, it is too constrained, the variable list is incomplete or inaccurate, or the logic statements are more than a yes/no. For example, the last comment regarding yes/no situations is the basis for machine computation in the form of bits (binary digits, 1 or 0). The yes/no situations account for many of the logic statements in DSS or expert systems applications. We are conditioned to think in terms of such black/white, yes/no definitive logic in everyday life and work. People are rewarded for making decisions and providing leadership which is demonstrated by action. Except for politicians, who have mastered the technique of avoiding definitive answers, the rest of us round up and round down to a yes or no in almost all decision-making activity. Often, either too much or not enough information is available to assist in making a decision. The brain and its fuzzy-thinking processing power can handle the maybes, somewhats, or intuitions quite well. *Quite well* is somewhere between *well* and *very well*. Traditional approaches to problem-solving would force the issue: very well or not? Expert systems methods would attempt to handle various degrees of "wellness" all at the same time and not follow a contrived sequence of decision statements from very well to not well.

Billions of brain cells (neurons) and their interconnections (trillions of connections) fire simultaneously to produce or reproduce images. Machines cannot recognize a face (if at all) as fast as a human. Computer-based neural networks simulate living nervous systems [Nelson & Illingworth, 1991]. The methodology and the promise of neural networks are not new; however, in recent years, running computer processors in parallel instead of in sequence, hardware and software advancements, and opportunity to use easily accessible and convenient desktop computers have been factors encouraging and promoting neural network application development. Europe's neural network effort, ESPRIT II, took five years, eight countries, and several hundred worker-years of effort to build [Nelson & Illingworth, 1991]. Applications include speech understanding, robot control, and medicine. The U.S. Government through DARPA (Defense Advanced Research Projects Agency) has directed funds to technological research in this area.

In addition to a movement toward neural network computing, another methodology has emerged in the past decade which focuses on the imprecise, namely *fuzzy logic*. In the words of Bart Kosko [1993], fuzziness is grayness. Everything is a matter of degree. He continued the concept of Lotfi Zadeh, who published a 1965 paper on fuzzy sets which confronted and angered most modern scientists at the time and thereafter. The government would not recognize anything "fuzzy" and academe in general did not encourage researchers to pursue the topic. Without going into the details of the concepts, which are articulated in set theory by Kosko, it is instructive for IEMgrs to be aware of the potential for applications development; fuzzy logic is not a fad.

Are you satisfied with your federal government? If you were to raise this question to a random group of people in any environmental setting, some of them would raise their hands high, some not raise their hands at all, and some would raise their hands a little. Others would require more explanation before they would commit. What do you mean by "satisfied?" It is a matter of degree. Ten percent of the time, yes, perhaps. If it is necessary to qualify the question with additional information, the procedure becomes more precise but the "fuzziness" increases because we are taking into account more degrees of satisfaction along the continuum between not-satisfied and yes-satisfied. Expert systems based on fuzzy logic can store thousands of such fuzzy rules on a chip and execute them simultaneously in a millionth of a second. This reasoning speed is measured in FLIPS, or *fuzzy logical inferences per second*.

These systems are smart. These systems are not merely the wave of the future; they exist now. Since rule fuzziness is acceptable, the applications accept and tend to smooth out the fuzziness because they are programmed to do so. Anything which senses an operation and corrects it accordingly lends itself to a good application, such as smart missiles, smart traffic control, smart robots, and smart cruise controls in automobiles. Some of these systems are adaptive and learn their own rules the more they are used. Kosko [1993] suggests that neural networks can help to search for better fuzzy rules emanating from sensed behavior. As new data enters the system, the expert system analyzes it for new patterns and, upon finding them, automatically converts them into new rules. The program "corrects" itself as it is used, much like a human experiencing and processing new data for better decision making. Adaptive fuzzy systems are like connected logic statements except that they form an approximation of the set of conditions all at once.

The Japanese have embraced the fuzzy concept with enthusiasm. Matsushita eliminated camcorder image jerks caused by shaky hands; they smoothed out the process with fuzzy logic. Their fuzzy washing machines have an on/off switch without other settings; the machine sensors check dirtiness of the water, fabric type, size of load, and amount of water to dispense soap and activate other wash commands. Scientists and companies adhering to traditional systems development methods and procedure-based software development hamper development of the application of fuzzy concepts to hundreds of commercial products which could accommodate this technique for consumer benefit.

◆ BUSINESS APPLICATIONS AND INFORMATION TECHNOLOGY

Now that we have covered the nature and scope of simulations and expert systems, we turn our attention to the business functions for which they were developed. Some of the products and services were mentioned in previous sections of this chapter; at this time, we will discuss traditional business functions and indicate how information technology can enable them for improved organizational competitiveness.

Corporate Planning

It is essential to have long-range enterprise planning consistent with short-term operations, otherwise the more immediate operational activities will dominate and submerge any long-range planning effort. In addition, information systems planning (long-range and short-term) must be developed concurrently and in integrated fashion with the business plan. Corporate planning functions typically address these types of questions:

> What is the best corporatewide system for initiating and implementing strategic initiatives?
> How will the accelerated global changes affect our market share today and tomorrow?
> What new products and services should we develop to meet new opportunities?
> How should we be organized to respond to customers, retain them, and gain new ones?
> What are the critical success factors for competitive advantage in the long and near terms?
> How does the enterprise keep and hire employees who add the most value?
> Is reengineering the corporation a viable action? What are the impacts?

The best approach in deciding where to start is to address the first question in depth. The remaining questions will evolve from the discussion. Without a systematic way of getting the best initiatives from the right people, the organization will be reactive to change and most likely will always be too late in its response. Certainly in this scenario, there would be little time to find and grasp new opportunities. With a planned, formal, and continuous approach to this function, initiatives can arise from any management level, any department, any process team, or any individual. Strategic thinking, tactical thinking, and operational thinking should not be delegated to individuals positioned in the corporation according to their management level. In process-oriented and self-directed action teams it is common for different types of individuals to demonstrate creativity that transcends status and position. If an open-ended system nurturing the free and open exchange of ideas is encouraged, the corporate planning function can set the vision and require that business be conducted toward that vision.

There are four areas of concern for developing an integrated corporate planning system: product and/or service line for current and future markets; capacity planning; financial planning; and human resource planning. The enterprise must have the vision, have products and services aimed at that vision, have enough capacity at the right time to deliver those products and services, have the funding to support the effort, and have the right people with the right expertise for current operations and future growth. Managers at all levels participate, initiatives are documented in project management fashion (to provide continuity of information flow and communication on progress), and potential problems and issues are addressed before they become a burden.

Information technology is essential to achieve the vision. DSS and expert systems approaches and software are commercially available to assist the corporate planning process. Although financial forecasting packages tend to be an important driving force for the planning effort, numbers alone are not sufficient to justify action plans. Managers should avail themselves of financial planning systems, such as Excel, and IFPS (interactive financial planning system) from Execucom Systems Corporation of Austin, Texas. IFPS has existed for two decades and produces many numbers. Also, it performs risk analyses, performs goal-seeking scenarios (what-if question formats), and consolidates models and data files. A microcomputer version is available and enables the manager to use natural-language format in communicating with the machine. NOMAD, a product of MUST Software of Norwalk, Connecticut, is an integrated DSS package. There are several hundred management science packages commercially available that cover a wide range of planning activity, including project management, business simulation, and optimization routines. There exist numerous statistical packages, especially for microcomputers, which are useful in predictive efforts. Other typical planning models are designed for budgeting, marketing decision making, profit margin analysis, new venture planning, materials resource planning, and mergers and acquisitions analyses.

Marketing

The major components of the marketing subsystem are sales forecasting, research, advertising, sales order processing, and distribution of the product or service. For this business function, it is necessary to gather external information and ensure that it is integrated with enterprise planning activity. Information technology *cannot initiate* the creative thinking process. It can only take those marketing initiatives and analyze them for information technology enablement.

Once the initiatives are identified, it is possible to rank them so that the most valuable options are pursued. Computerized approaches for planning marketing strategy require input on market share, product quality, and research expenditures. Given this starting point, the company can use a simulation model to provide leads to other what-if questions and issues such as current cost for a particular strategy and its projected economic impact. For fast-moving products, there is a connection between the marketing system and finished goods inventory. It is important not only to check inventory levels of all items, but to monitor the change of the inventory for certain items. Marketing campaigns vary with fast or slow items, product availability, and the capacity of the corporation to accelerate production to meet demands.

The main point is that there is a chain of events which can be set in motion by the marketing effort or the lack of it. For this reason, an integrated approach to planning is mandatory or each subsystem micromanages for efficiency as the corporation fails to meet operational commitments determined by all the systems.

Mathematical models can be effective in sales forecasting (extrapolating the trends depicted by historical data to predictions of future sales) and venture analysis (new products for new markets). Linear programming models have existed for decades and are applicable for analyzing the effect of one or more independent variables on a dependent variable, or objective function. If the objective is to maximize profit and enough information is available on relationships of the objective to each of the dependent variables, an optimal solution can be derived by the technique. For example, if profit is to be maximized and is related mathematically to cost of production, plant capacities, market limitations as to the number and nature of certain products, and other constraints, then these linear expressions can be inputted to the model for optimization of the objective function (profit). This type of software is commercially available.

If there are several major marketing campaigns underway, their planning and progress can be controlled by project management tools and techniques. The *program evaluation and review technique* (PERT) is helpful in documenting the proper sequence of activities for new products to find their way to market. Such software tracks the process and the individuals accountable for meeting major milestones. If plant capacity falls behind, marketing resources can be shifted to other products which may be in high demand and are available.

In order to move into venture analysis, external information on the potential customers is needed. Computer simulations can aid in producing a profitability picture considering risk and uncertainty factors. For more mundane manipulation of data, microcomputer-based software is available for survey data gathering, statistical analysis, spreadsheet tabulations and calculations, graphical display, and presentation using multimedia techniques. These features are particularly important to the marketing function because of its close relationship to clients. For more sophisticated statistical routines, such as those for examining data from many variables for predicting some desired outcome through multivariate regression analysis, a more compute-intensive machine may be necessary.

For the advertising segment of marketing, the situation in some ways is more complicated. How do you determine what mix of media to use? How can information technology be used in this application? The simulation model can provide an extensive list of variables, some of which may have more importance than others depending on the situation. The nature of the product, funds available, target audience, and so on will be some of these variables. The model performs the statistical routines transparent to the user and with additional data produces several options for review.

Manufacturing, Production Scheduling, Inventory

The topics of inventory level and capacity planning were discussed in the previous section on marketing. There is a three-step sequence in the manufacturing process: purchase raw materials, produce the goods, and move them to inventory for sales. Moving from marketing backwards, they need the product to sell (most of the time), products may be backordered for production, the plant must have the capacity (plant and people resources) to produce the goods or lose business opportunities, and there must be enough raw materials on-hand for production. If we add product design and quality control functions to the list, a totally integrated system emerges. Software to control all of these processes is available on microcomputers (PC-MRP, or PC-based software for *materials requirements planning*) and its counterpart on very large computing systems. Some companies, such as Sikorsky Aircraft Division of United Technologies Corporation, control the entire process with a massive and sophisticated MRP program. The cost of this type of software can range from a few thousand dollars (microcomputers) to millions (mainframes). In addition to the purchase cost of such software, there are added costs for maintenance, data input, database control, software execution by production experts, and modification of the program as corporate requirements, products, and directions change. In the situation of mergers with other companies with different and perhaps incompatible computer systems, the cost of information technology conversion may be prohibitive.

Mathematical and simulation models enable managers to purchase the raw materials from the best vendors, schedule personnel and equipment to meet current and future production demands, and provide for distribution of the finished goods. In terms of product design, information technology can digitally store and retrieve blueprints, solve several complicated and interrelated mathematical formulas using numerical techniques, portray solutions in three-dimensional diagrams, allow for modification of design online and in real time directly from digitizing tablets (Computer-Aided Design/Computer-Aided Manufacturing, or CAD/CAM), and monitor quality standards and tolerances. During a recent business-academe total quality management action team activity for Sikorsky Aircraft, the finished goods quality inspection process was examined to streamline the process, compress the time for cross-functional activities, indicate new methods for assembly inspections, and increase the use of programming applications for tolerance testing of parts and assemblies.

For the purchasing of raw materials, factors other than low inventory are examined. Although selection of vendors has been discussed in considerable detail for computer-related activity, the same principles indicated in Chapter 6 apply here. In addition, vendor performance should be evaluated in some standardized way, especially for large numbers of vendors for a large number of items. *Electronic Data Interchange* (EDI) methods allow for companies to order electronically from suppliers. The catalog of items is available on the system, the buyer selects the items (cost and discount given by the system to that buyer), the order is placed, goods are shipped, and invoices may or may not follow. Electronic signatures are used by buyers and sellers. The need for salespeople visits and intervention is reduced, except for nonstandard purchases. For more expensive and complicated purchases, an elaborate and automatic screening program could assess which vendors have demonstrated the best past performance (quality materials, on time delivery, and discount) and other factors in arriving at a preliminary list of potential candidates for the sale.

One dynamic simulation software package, Ithink of High Performance Systems, Inc. in Hanover, New Hampshire, is an excellent visual thinking tool for building and conducting simulations for applications involving "systems thinking." The systems methodology is not a new approach and provides a conceptual framework to examine all factors and their interrelationships to portray an operational view of decision making. The Ithink simulation model (for Macintosh) with all of its icons for connecting objects and information flows allows the user to build the process much like a wiring or piping diagram. The software requires a considerable amount of training; however, once mastered, the modeling package can be applied to almost any application area. In manufacturing, the sales ordering process and its relationship to inventory, backorders, and future demands could be programmed to display by tables and graphics the variables for sensitivity analysis. Sensitivity is tested by looking at corrective measures for inventory discrepancies through ordering. Several scenarios of product demand could be introduced to see if supplier lead time is a sensitive parameter. It is not surprising to see the total quality management movement emphasize more long-term relationships with suppliers so that lead time is reduced and production cost is reduced.

Accounting and Finance

Clearly, in order to be competitive one must have a very good handle on monetary functions. It is not instructive to delineate the thousands of transactions in major corporations. In terms of transactions produced by the accounting and finance functions, there are only financial statements and sources of funds. Typical financial transactions are handled by microcomputer and/or mainframe software which has been developed in-house, is commercially available, or a full service for transaction processing is contracted to an outside firm. For the more elaborate information processing activities, such as financial forecasting, return on investment analysis, production of business plan scenarios, portfolio updates, stock management, overhead variance analysis, and other control type activity, an integrated system must be in place to provide the data for computer/statistical models to run.

In the area of ad-hoc, complex exception reports, unlike predetermined and structured reports, it is necessary to use simulation modeling software. Usually, the user is not sure of the questions to ask or the area to investigate. Expert, or "suggestive" systems, are helpful in directing the manager through the maze of alternatives until a path is suggested. The direction may be leading to more cash on hand, or improved collection of accounts receivable, or taking advantage of accounts payable discounts by quick payment. Projected cash flows, capital investments, and the economic consequences of mergers are likely candidates for simulation software.

The Ithink software package works equally well for financial applications. Traditional electronic spreadsheets are useful in dealing with rows and columns of numbers and their manipulation to form totals. In addition, logic statements can be applied to perform some static and rudimentary what-if scenarios for later output review by humans. However, when you are interested in dynamic interdependencies, you must go beyond the spreadsheet and let the software reflect on the numbers in a decision-support manner. The manuals for Ithink are tutorial and take considerable time to master, but they do explain the use of the simulation technique for present value analysis, receivables and payables, financial statement analysis, and cash flow optimization.

In higher education, this software package can be helpful in preparing long-range financial plans. The variables are known. Data values for them will change depending on the number of students entering the system, the number of faculty, facilities available and/or needed, and other costs associated with educational operations. Preliminary decisions can be made which outline the long-range vision and short-term objectives consistent with that vision. For example, the percentage of available revenues used for financial aid is set for certain conditions; tuition and faculty salaries will increase 3 percent per year for five years; no new facilities will be built for two years; and there will be only one new major academic program for this period. Armed with that information and using other data on revenues and expected expenditures (from past performance), a model could be constructed to show the financial picture over that five-year period. Better yet, the model can change values and/or variables to see how those changes affect the financial status of the institution.

For this scenario and others to be effective, the variable list must be complete and accurate. For higher education planning, a major issue centers around the priorities of the initiatives in the simulation. Some weighted-averaging system would be helpful in arriving at a rank ordering of initiatives and their effect on the variables. When this information is entered into the simulation, the results have more integrity. This simulation model (Ithink) is best used when model experts team with managers to ensure that each party understands the power, limitations, and possibilities of simulation in supporting decision making at all levels.

Human Resources

It has often been said that people are the most important resource of a company. Over the past decade, the quality imperative has been foremost in corporate vision. Not only does it apply to products and services, but also to the workforce. How can the enterprise keep its most valuable employees, train and retrain them to meet current and future requirements, and motivate them for excellence and at the same time be mindful of financial statements requiring cost containment (including downsizing)? Traditionally, the matching process between worker abilities and organization needs has been informal, random, and related more to being in the right place at the right time than to some systematic matching process. Want ads are posted; workers read them, perform their own self-assessment, and apply for the position.

Now that there is a dramatic shift away from the typical job, or position, and toward a more open view of "work" for an enterprise [Bridges, 1991; & 1994], the old matching process becomes even more informal and random. Human resource functions of the future no longer will have volumes of position descriptions. The federal government, other government agencies, and higher education will be forced to make adjustments in the way they hire individuals. The business sector is leading the way with total quality management efforts, one aspect of which is for the increased view of business processes and self-directed work teams.

The emphasis on these two concepts changes the way that human resource staffs, together with operating business managers, seek and retain employees. Although there will remain some discipline-specific and experience standards necessary for employment, more focus will be required on interpersonal skills, written and oral presentation capability, leadership, project management, creative and innovative thinking, individual responsibility and accountability, and information enablement. This organizational metamorphosis regarding relationships between employees and management suggests that not only should the organization reengineer itself, but also workers should reengineer themselves. Continued service is contingent on their ability to add value to the organization. Workers must take charge of their own career. The human resource function must adapt to this new setting and assist individuals and the organization to match capability to need through collaboration [Marshall, 1995], both in short-term immediate productivity and in long-term career growth.

Computerized human resource management systems are available to meet all types of enterprises (business, government, and education). Many of them are inexpensive and provide a substantial return for the investment. Personnel databases act as a source of data for other functions, such as payroll, merit and service promotions, membership on team projects, and other collateral duties within the enterprise. When the database, or manipulation of the database, moves into the realm of worker attributes and/or skills, whether or not they pertain directly to the worker's current role, a much more extensive application is indicated. The rationale for capturing the data would be to match electronically current and future organizational needs with worker placement. Once resource loading characteristics and availabilities of workers become input to an automated system, it is possible to create numerous scenarios through simulation to maximize worker performance. Workers would be automatically placed in possible positions for the mutual benefit of the organization and themselves.

Then, judgment would prevail regarding other nonspecific factors (i.e., worker interest and motivation, lateral movement within a function, relocation of family, impact on education of children, working spouse situation). It is clear that software packages cannot provide a total solution, particularly in light of "job shift" [Bridges, 1994].

Software for human resource functions has another challenge in that it must be a multiuser system. Most of the time, queries are made about individual records without the need to modify them. Some of the time, such as in the case of airline reservations, the record must be up-to-date, accessible, and modifiable for flights, meals, and seats. Microcomputers are not well suited for managing large database systems; however, they are valuable for downloading segments of the database for further manipulation.

Workforce simulations are mathematical models to develop personnel plans. In the past, these simulations provided end-of-year data on employees to management. In the future, the simulations will be run on a continuous basis throughout the year in order to monitor individuals on self-directed work teams and/or to provide aggregate information on gains, losses, and displacements. Changes in corporate vision statements, mergers with other enterprises, product demand changes, and other factors have an impact on human resource simulations. For example, the number of workers for night shifts may change dramatically or the number of workers in certain categories may change (permanent employees, part-timers, contracted workers). Such changes also impact financial systems because of new qualifications for benefits and union constraints. The increased demand for ad-hoc and immediate reporting in this very competitive and global marketplace means that human resource systems may very well be the most important part of the enterprise.

Reflections

GENERAL CONCEPTS

1. Investigate a local enterprise (business, government agency, or institution of higher education) and analyze the environment for the decision-making process:
   a. Who makes decisions and under what conditions?
   b. What is the organizational "culture" for decision-making? Is there an open and free exchange of ideas for problem solving and do they carry over to the decision process?
   c. Do individual managers' styles predominate in the way they make decisions or do they make them in accordance with corporate policy? Are these approaches in conflict? Under what conditions?
   d. Are business simulations used? For what application areas? Have the expectations of end users been met? Why or why not?
   e. How much credence is placed on simulation methods? If they are used, to what extent does human judgment

prevail over simulation predetermined reports? How flexible are the simulations? Can you define the parameters, limitations, and reliability of the simulation?

f. Looking ahead to expert systems and neural nets, are there any application areas ripe for use of these techniques? If yes, prescribe a plan for implementing the concept for one such application of limited scope and practicality.

2. Examine a DSS or expert systems software package at a local business, such as NOMAD, FOCUS, IMPACT, and others identified in a current DSS text (such as Turban, 1993), and report on it to the class. Most of these packages are complex and expensive, and cannot be learned in only a few weeks; you can see one demonstrated, discuss its attributes, and explain its relationship to Exhibits 11-2 and 11-3.

Reflections

STEP MODEL

1. The STEP Model depicts the dimensions of technology (T), business process (P), and staff (S) in a three-dimensional graph format. The ideal situation for the enterprise is to have coordinates with high use of T, P, and S. Other combinations of these dimensions show where most organizations are placed; the idea is for the organization to move to the ideal location by using effectively information-enabled people in an information-enabled organization.

    a. How do simulation techniques help the enterprise to identify the right path, to move on that path in the most effective way, and to synergize its workforce to achieve progress in that direction?

    b. Are there any downsides to that approach? Can simulation make errors?

    c. How many resources are "enough" for the developing simulation expertise? What are the hidden costs? How do you conduct an ROI analysis on simulation applications?

    d. Devise a plan to ensure that all factors are considered in use of simulation techniques for a specific application area (marketing, etc.).

Reflections

ETHICS

Scene: MILITARY GAMES

This exercise divides the class into two groups for separate discussion of the issues. Students could adopt "roles" to represent perspectives from the end-user (group A) or from the IS staff (group B). Once the issues are discussed separately, all students could be present for a general discussion.

Sub-Group A: Department of Defense (DOD) Enthusiasts (End-Users)

Your department within the DOD wants to accelerate the development of the use of computerized war games. You have just read about the wonderful development process of prototyping with expert systems and can see many advantages to developing models for decision making by high-level military leaders. The games are international in nature and focus on success determined by kills, kill rates, destructive maneuvers on land, sea, and air, and in some cases, conflict avoidance.

The target areas could be anywhere in the world, including the United States. Extensive use of computer graphics is contemplated so that debriefing sessions can be conducted at the conclusion of the exercise.

Develop a list of system requirements and benefits for Information Systems staff to review for feasibility of development. Indicate purpose and scope of simulation model building, including one specific scenario example with objectives, desired outputs, constraints, assumptions, and so on.

Sub-Group B: Concerned and Hesitant Information Systems Staff

- Computerized command and control?
- Machines making judgments?
- Need for standardization of decision-making?
- Probability of success?
- If we are required to develop this high degree of decision-support systems, we will leak it to the papers . . . and refuse to do it. Current programs are adequate to handle training requirements.

Reflections

ISI CASE STUDY

Linking IT to Business Functions

Decision-making decision support systems (software used to assist in making decisions at all levels), executive support systems (derived from more comprehensive strategic intelligence), and executive information systems (providing corporate data needed for executive support systems) are intertwined in using information technology to competitive advantage. In this chapter, specific criteria are noted for making decisions and form the framework for obtaining just the right amount of information at the right time for managers to make the right decisions for effective planning and conducting efficient business operations.

The ISI case study includes traditional business functions, the process of moving product from sales order through distribution, and the many managers in need of information technology enablement (processing and forecasting). In addition, ISI needs a master plan which integrates corporate goals and objectives with strategies for information technology infrastructure and processing. Thus far in the case, the approach has been to emphasize computer systems requirements (end users and selection team) as well as managing projects with some attention paid to general computer systems design (consultant to ISI and/or vendor preliminary bids).

The next step is to move into higher-level decision-making activity with an evaluation of expert system and simulation techniques which very well may be applied to business applications. One question related to this activity is whether or not the software should be made or bought. ISI either has to contract (outsource) for this service separately or include software requirements within the specifications of the RFP.

Deliverables

1. All groups: Investigate the various commercially available DSS packages and assess their applicability to ISI.
2. End users: Review the concepts of outsourcing (Chapter 6) and perhaps include this option within the contract specifications.
3. Commence conducting more formal sessions between end users/selection team and vendors to evaluate each vendor's bid for meeting or not meeting specifications of the RFP.
4. Continue to formally evaluate vendor performance in the negotiation process.
5. Require vendors to demonstrate DSS packages appropriate for use at ISI; ensure that their implementation is practicable for end users.
6. Armed with sales forecasting methods, should ISI consider increasing its target markets beyond the region? Will the proposed configuration allow for expansion of services?
7. What other business functions at ISI should be reviewed for improved decision making at strategic and operational planning levels?

Chapter 12

Systems Development Methodology

◆ ◆ ◆

*A*long with all of the enterprise changes that we have discussed, there are equally dramatic changes taking place in the systems development arena. No longer are we operating in an environment where the information systems department is singly responsible for systems development. The responsibility is now shared and the methodologies changed in accordance with the shared responsibilities. In this chapter, we begin our study of systems development from the perspective of the information systems department. Later in this part, we discuss systems development from the perspective of the end user.

The construction of information systems initially rested in the hands of a few clever specialists who, like other artisans, possessed high levels of inventiveness and craftsmanship. Their task was eased by the fact that these builders were responsible for determining the content as well as the functionality of information systems.

But things have changed, and the IS professionals no longer determine the functionality of users' systems. Indeed, the complexity of modern systems makes it difficult for individual professionals to construct systems on their own. Today's systems are neither self-contained nor isolated. They must be integrated with surrounding systems and must also incorporate data and features from earlier predecessor systems.

The result has been a growth of development methodologies allowing an individual (or, more likely, a team) to construct a system properly by following guidelines tested over the years in many different systems development projects. A popular analogy comes from the building trade. Whereas in the past a craftsman could build a house by relying chiefly on intuition, modern home builders are teams of specialists who come together to do different tasks and who together can build many different houses. For this to happen, the chief builder (project manager) follows similar procedures (such as blueprints and financing plans) for each house. Along the way there are reviews and approvals to refine the house and to limit risk. The chief builder, although probably familiar with the technology of the trade, is mainly responsible for ensuring that each house is built on schedule, within budget, *and* according to specifications. *To do this, the chief builder must spell out clear rules and see that they are followed. The rules encourage early design decisions; subsequent decisions can then be made based on a sure foundation.*

Although there are many ways to build a house, it is the similarities in contemporary house-building methods that are most pronounced. This is true of the development of traditional computer systems as well. All go through a similar life cycle, as shown in Exhibit 12-1. All system development methodologies, even those that look different, are ways of describing and controlling this same cycle. Some will parallel it step by step (or phase by phase, to use popular systems development terminology); others will combine several events into one phase or even deconstruct one event into several measurable activities.

To illustrate the diversity of methodologies and to give you a flavor of the popular variety, in this chapter we will discuss an assortment of system development methodologies, all of which will refer to the process outlined in Exhibit 12-1.

System development methodologies have evolved to make contemporary systems more productive, and continuing changes in both production and management methods will be forthcoming. It is up to the IS manager to anticipate the type and timing of these changes. As more sophisticated software is used, as more integration is required, as more turnkey products are installed, and as fewer technically skilled professionals are needed to perform systems and programming duties, carefully tailored management techniques must be in place to support this evolution.

In this chapter we look first at system design methodological issues and then, more broadly, at system development projects themselves. We start with the goals of systems development methodologies (SDMs) and the relationship of SDMs and corporate priorities. Next, we consider means of incorporating standardized design methods into customized SDMs. The possible phases of an SDM are our next concern; from there, we launch into various development techniques and data conversion strategies.

Next, we turn to the actual systems development projects within which SDMs are practiced: large, traditional, maintenance projects, and other irregular or emergency projects. We discuss the functional objectives of most systems development projects and then examine issues of project initiation—an important step, as it happens—and scheduling concerns. We conclude with a look at important project management issues.

◆ TRADITIONAL PERSPECTIVE

Most SDMs have many aims, some of which seem in conflict, yet all of which must be kept in balance. The following sections discuss the goals and benefits of SDMs.

Exhibit 12-1

The Systems Life Cycle

Inception
   Preliminary

Feasibility study
   Existing procedures
   Alternative systems
   Cost estimates

Systems analysis
   Details of present procedures
   Collection of data on volumes, input/output files

Design
   Ideal system unconstrained
   Revisions to make ideal acceptable

Specification
   Processing logic
   File design
   Input/output
   Programming requirements
   Manual procedures

Programming

Testing
   Unit tests
   Combined module tests
   Acceptance tests

Training

Conversation and installation

Operations
   Maintenance
   Enhancements

Efficiency

As Exhibit 12-2 indicates, a certain degree of guidance and direction can definitely improve efficiency. However, it is also clear that rules and regulations can be overdone. Lengthy rule books or massive paperwork requirements may provide comprehensive constraints but will hardly allow systems development projects to be completed in a timely, efficient manner. If efficiency is a primary objective, some happy medium must be struck by the SDM. The task of finding this point is complicated by several factors. Fourth-generation languages, for example, do not require all the guidance and restrictions required by older languages, such as COBOL. A data-dictionary coordination step is undertaken automatically by some new languages and is therefore redundant or detrimental if carried over intact from previous SDMs. The most recent additions to the development toolkit—Lotus Notes, Visual Basic, Visible Analyst, Powerbuilder, Microsoft

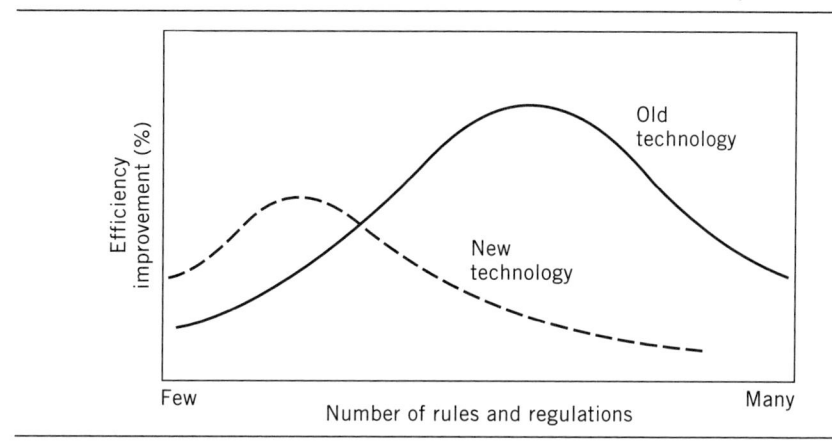

Exhibit 12-2

Systems Development Methodologies and Efficiency

[Graph: Efficiency improvement (%) vs Number of rules and regulations (Few to Many). Two curves shown: "Old technology" (solid curve peaking toward the right) and "New technology" (dashed curve peaking toward the left).]

Access, and others—have put powerful tools into the hands of IEMgrs(TP) allowing them to take on more responsibilities for applications development. What this means is that the steps of the traditional SDM are disappearing as they become imbedded in the development tools. On the positive side, this increases productivity but on the negative side it reduces the checks and balances found in the more traditional approaches. At the same time, because the ease of use of new technology makes it (in theory) more productive, additional efficiencies to be gained through regimented procedures are more limited.

Communications

An SDM usually designates specific moments during a project at which certain facts are to be communicated to others. This communication could involve both specific members of the project team, the customer or end user of the deliverables, and outside parties. Although there are a multitude of concerned participants and functions in any systems development project, all can be grouped as management, users, or technicians. Obviously, each is concerned with different aspects of the project and each has different communications needs. Managers look for cost and schedule information, users for developments that affect their specifications, and technicians for design information. Those persons who fall into more than one category typically have to balance several communications interests. The SDM must facilitate a steady, reliable information flow among all parties.

Control

Controls can entail acquiring permission to proceed with a project (e.g., approvals for a spending plan) or being told how to proceed (e.g., users specifying a preferred online dialog). Although a liberal use of controls can instill a feeling of involvement and confidence and might prevent missteps, too-heavy controls can have negative effects on the project schedule, costs, and content.

In most projects, the scarcest resource is the most heavily controlled. Thus, in cost-conscious environments, budget variance reports may be heavily used; in schedule-conscious settings, reports on time expenditures will be frequently issued. The most difficult challenge for the project manager is to manage in such a way as to satisfy two or more control constraints. Achieving either budget or schedule performance goals is easier than satisfying them both.

Documentation

A byproduct of communications, documents are important enough to become separate SDM goals. Like blueprints, documents are used to guide the construction of a product and ultimately become archival in nature. Indeed, many documents are designed with a future use as standing documentation in mind. Documentation can include users' manuals, systems overview information, operator instructions, maintenance programmer background information, restart and error recovery instructions, and more.

Role Definition

An SDM serves to define the roles of everyone in the system development project. By spelling out "who does what to whom," SDMs help reduce anxiety, minimize arguments over duties, and discourage inefficient, superfluous activity. Role definition does not come without costs, however. It may not be appropriate to keep roles static from project to project, and some flexibility and latitude is beneficial. Nevertheless, many development tasks are easily defined and lend themselves to repetition, and specifying these in an SDM saves much effort.

Consistency

One important reason for using a readily repeated process to build information systems is to ensure that the results are consistent. Consistency introduces operational efficiencies, such as faster run times and better response times to new systems. It also ensures that current or future integration can occur. Finally, it discourages any confusing variety. The SDM channels project activity through appropriate existing corporate processes such as data management, spending approvals, work assignments, and other typical organizational practices. A consistent SDM improves on the learning curve for future projects, allows comparisons of performance across projects, and assists in future project planning.

◆ SYSTEMS DEVELOPMENT CONSIDERATIONS FOR THE IEMGT TEAM

Each of the foregoing goals can be achieved, to a greater or lesser degree, by a thorough SDM. However, because some of these goals (efficiency and control, for instance) have contradictory components, the IEMgrs must answer some difficult questions in choosing the right SDM.

The first question to be answered concerns the priorities of the corporate environment. An SDM cannot accomplish everything, but it can be slanted toward specific organizational priorities and objectives. One way to begin is to identify the target beneficiaries of a planned system, along with attendant SDM features (see Exhibit 12-3). Emphases in one area can, however, be perceived as negligence in other areas. Exhibit 12-4 lists the tradeoffs of an IS-dominated system development life cycle as compared with one that heavily favors users.

Another related way to begin is to identify corporate or other institutional factors necessitating tradeoffs. Exhibit 12-5 illustrates two basic tradeoff dilemmas. For instance, existing rules may give project team members the authority to adjust the development process and permission to make many decisions themselves. Approval of the network manager might be required only if, in the

Exhibit 12-3

Target Beneficiaries of a New System and Areas of Emphasis

TARGET BENEFICIARY	AREA OF EMPHASIS
Project manager	Project management tools
	Schedules
	Action plans
	Step-by-step procedures
Management	Escalation procedures
	Approval points
	Project reporting requirements
	Postevaluation reviews
Technical professional	Hardware determination
	Software determination
	Structured walkthroughs
	Detailed design reviews
	Performance testing
User	General design review and approval
	User testing/acceptance criteria
	User documentation
	Training

Exhibit 12-4

Two Systems-Development Emphases and Possible Implications

IS-DOMINATED DEVELOPMENT LIFE CYCLE	USER-DOMINATED DEVELOPMENT LIFE CYCLE
Too much emphasis on database hygiene	Too much emphasis on problem focus
No recent new supplier or new distinct services (too busy with maintenance)	IS says out of control
New systems always must fit data structure of existing system	Explosive growth in number of new systems and supporting staff
All requests for service require system study with benefit identification	Multiple suppliers delivering services and frequent change in supplier of specific service
Standardization dominates; few exceptions	Lack of standardization and control over data hygiene and system
IS designs/constructs everything	Hard evidence of benefits nonexistent
Benefits of user control over development discussed but never implemented	Soft evidence of benefits nonexistent
Study always shows construction costs less than outside purchase	Few measurements/objectives for new system
Head count of distributed minis and development staff growing, but surreptitiously	Technical advice of IS not sought or, if received, considered irrelevant
IS specializing in technical frontiers, not user-oriented markets	User buying design, construction, maintenance, and even operations services from outside
IS spending 80% on maintenance, 20% on development	User building networks to meet own needs (not corporate needs)
IS thinks it is in control of all	Some users growing rapidly in experience: other users feel nothing is relevant because they do not understand
Users express unhappiness	No coordinated effort for technology transfer or learning from experience
Portfolio of development opportunities firmly under IS control	Growth in duplication of technical skills
General management is not involved but concerned	Communications costs rising dramatically through redundancy

SOURCE: Reprinted by permission of Richard D. Irwin, Inc. An exhibit from *Corporate Information Systems Management* by F.W. McFarlan and J.L. Kenney. copyright © 1983 by Richard D. Irwin, Inc.

Exhibit 12-5 — Basic Systems Development Tradeoff Dilemmas

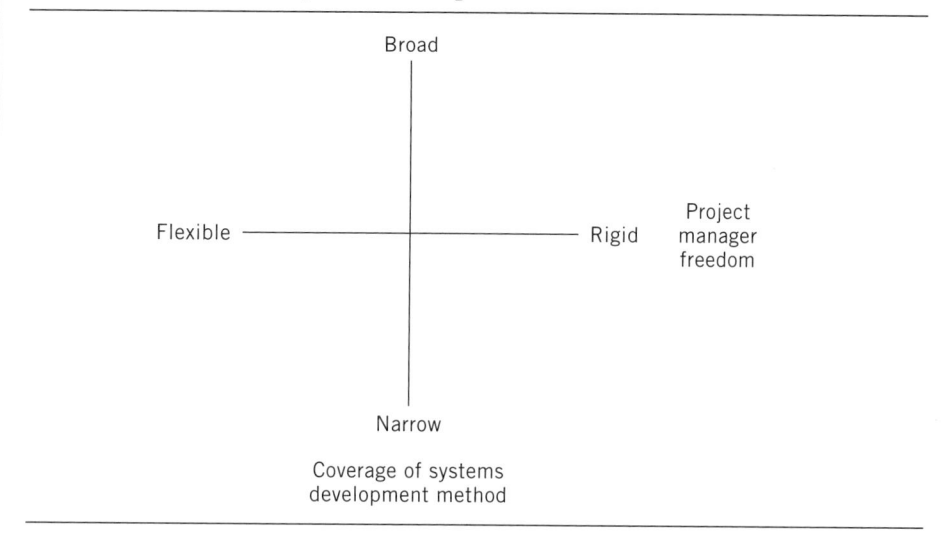

```
                        Broad
                          |
                          |
                          |
    Flexible  ————————————+———————————— Rigid     Project manager
                          |                       freedom
                          |
                          |
                          |
                        Narrow
                  Coverage of systems
                  development method
```

judgment of the project manager, significant changes to the network environment are planned. Making the rules more rigid would mean consistently requiring the network manager's approval, so that this person would, in effect, become the arbiter of "significant changes." An SDM can be written to be completely comprehensive, covering every project phase and every kind of project, or it can be restricted in its area of coverage to major or typical areas.

A final question concerns support of the corporate IS strategy. It is difficult to follow general, high-level guidance from above and simultaneously listen to and satisfy user needs from the bottom of the organization. An SDM must keep top-down planning and bottom-up design in balance and must also allow for constructive ways to resolve conflict. Exhibit 12-6 illustrates this dichotomy and indicates where cross-checks in the design process are necessary.

Regardless of the philosophy underlying it, every SDM has similar elements. Although some differences between phases may occur, radical inconsistencies or discontinuities should be avoided.

In building SDMs, IEMgrs(Tp) have two options. The first is the option of purchasing flexible but predefined methodologies. Several products, complete with integrated automated productivity components, are on the market. In some instances the productivity tools, such as CASE products, can be purchased separately and integrated into an existing, home-grown SDM. If such systems fit predefined needs, their purchase will save much time, provide a more comprehensive system, and save "reinventing the wheel" in several areas. These systems typically come with considerable help and advice on their use.

The other option is to incorporate standardized design methods and analytical techniques into the customized SDM. This might be one of the multitude of

Exhibit 12-6

Top-down Planning and Bottom-up Design

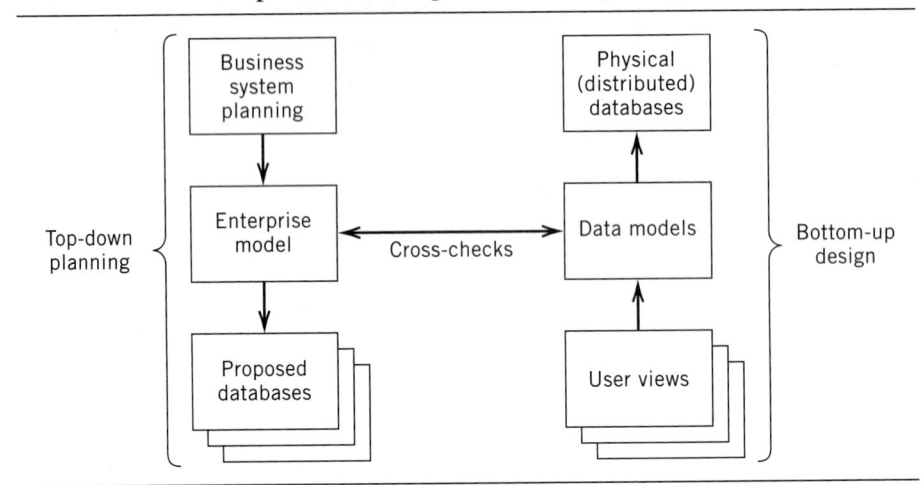

Top-down planning: Business system planning → Enterprise model → Proposed databases

Bottom-up design: Physical (distributed) databases ← Data models ← User views

Cross-checks between Enterprise model and Data models.

SOURCE: Fred R. McFadden and Jeffrey A. Hoffer, *Data Base Management,* Menlo Park, CA: Benjamin/Cummings, 1985, p. 60.

structured programming techniques, data diagramming methods, top-down design techniques, or object-oriented technologies. Although many of these require considerable degrees of precision, each is purported to yield advantages in product integrity and work efficiencies. Many allow key areas, such as data flow, to be emphasized. In some cases, a popular method or technique will be familiar to new and existing employees as a result of academic training or previous experience.

Although there are many software development methodologies with from three or four phases up to as many as twelve phases, the differences among them are largely fine points of emphasis and procedural variations. Even within this common framework, however, some important choices remain. For example, one SDM might contain the following phases:

- Phase I   Problem definition
- Phase II   Feasibility study
- Phase III   Alternative selection
- Phase IV   Logical design
- Phase V   Physical design
- Phase VI   Implementation
- Phase VII   Postaudit

In contrast, another method might use a more limited but flexible approach consisting of these phases:

- Phase I   Feasibility study
- Phase II   General and detail system design
- Phase III Programming and procedures
- Phase IV   System acceptance
- Phase V   Implementation and support

The latter approach is likely to have simplified checkpoints and to entail less administrative overhead, at least in the beginning. Although it might be quite versatile in handling certain projects, it is less likely to be comprehensive in the types of projects it can easily handle. In contrast, the former method would involve a more disciplined approach to analyzing multiple options. Some IEMgrs(Tp) that highly value activities such as training might see both approaches as flawed for imbedding this element within the larger phases and failing to give it explicit visibility.

Enterprisewide Strategies for Applications Development

As systems development methodologies have evolved, many productive techniques have been used by creative IEMgrs(Tp). The following two alternatives have strong proponents. Of course, like other techniques, they will continue to be refined.

Prototyping

Prototyping is a "trial balloon" approach. There are several variations within the methodology, but fundamentally prototyping puts some version of a system in place for the user to experience and from that experience be able to define additional functions and features for the next version of the system. The process continues this cyclical pattern until a fully functional system is in place or the effort abandoned because it fails to converge to an acceptable solution. Because it is associated with other experimental approaches, it will be covered more thoroughly later in this part. However, the following list of characteristics developed by A. Milton Jenkins [1983] should serve to highlight prototyping's strengths:

- It provides the ability to try out ideas without incurring large costs.
- Its overall development cost is lower than that of many other approaches.
- It provides the ability to quickly place a functioning system in the hands of users.
- It effectively divides labor between users and IS professionals.
- It greatly reduces development time.
- It provides for effective utilization of scarce people resources.

Although the concept of prototyping is appealing (and many feel the overall value is incontrovertible), it is still not clear how our systems development methods, project management methods, management control, and so on must adjust to accommodate this new approach. Elimination of some procedures and overhead would seem to be in keeping with the economy of prototyping; however, a set of checks and balances is clearly in order.

Computer-Aided Software Engineering

Computer-aided software engineering (CASE) is a term applied to a group of tools used by IS professionals in the systems development process to more quickly and accurately design, display, integrate, and elaborate on technical products. Howard W. Miller [1988] describes CASE this way:

- It offers support for the common development life cycles, with built-in audit capabilities that ensure compliance.
- It is an information repository for storing the elements of the software engineering process including specifications, designs, graphics, and pseudocode.
- It offers a graphics interface for drawing structured diagrams, data flow diagrams, and data structures.
- It comprises a highly integrated set of tools to automate every phase of the development life cycle.
- It automates code and dictionary generation from design specifications.
- It allows for prototyping of new designs and reverse engineering (i.e., converting existing software back into design specifications for modification and software regeneration).

These tools are more than just aids to productivity; they are redefining major portions of the software development process by collapsing activities (such as testing), introducing new flexibilities and integration, and facilitating communication. CASE has been an important strategic initiative because it affects both the efficiency and effectiveness of the SDM. Reducing the time between initiation and implementation of a system can result in significant strategic benefits.

Unfortunately, CASE has not lived up to its expectations. This in no way lessens its importance to the IS community. Developers are watching and waiting for the cost benefits to appear. Until then, little more is expected in the way of CASE tool implementation.

Alternative Development Techniques

Michael Treacy [1988] has observed that traditional systems development techniques are appropriate in situations where there is a clear understanding of systems-related needs and those needs are reasonably complex. Traditional methodologies stress accuracy and controls; and they permit a more top-down development of system features. Where the need is not well understood but

Exhibit 12-7

Appropriate Systems Design Cycles

	Complexity of design: Low	Complexity of design: High
Initial understanding of the need: Low	Evolutionary design cycle	Innovative design cycle
Initial understanding of the need: High	Simple project management cycle	Systems development life cycle

SOURCE: Michael Treacy, "Strategic Sales and Marketing Systems: A Development Approach," *The Consultant Forum*, vol. 5, no. 1, Digital Equipment Corporation, Nashua, NH, 1988, p. 6. Reprinted with permission of the author.

potential complexity is reasonably limited, Treacy suggests that an evolutionary approach such as prototyping is useful in a trial-and-error mode. He goes on to point out, however, that this approach will not work where the need is poorly understood and the design will be highly complex, as indicated in Exhibit 12-7. For this situation, an approach called Innovative Systems Life Cycle is appropriate (see Exhibit 12-8). This more methodical way of constructing a system relies on the same process used by marketers to introduce new products. The idea is to develop the system in steps culminating in an IS product that has been adjusted to meet the requirements of the environment into which it is introduced. A similar approach described in Chapter 14 addresses the larger question of when end-user computing is appropriate.

From Enterprise to Process to Function Levels

The systems development effort spans the entire organization. At the enterprise level, we encounter systems such as payroll, accounts receivable, accounts payable, billing, and so on. The responsibility for development and maintenance of these systems lies at the enterprise level through the information systems department. Also found at this level are major systems development efforts that span several business processes and/or business functions.

Next in complexity are systems that span the functional areas that comprise a single business process. In the absence of a process owner, such issues as who manages the development effort, where responsibility for its maintenance and further enhancement lies, and who owns it are critical. Many of these problems are solved by having a permanent team assigned to the project. Team members will come from the functional areas that are part of the process as well as any

Exhibit 12-8: Innovative Systems Life Cycle

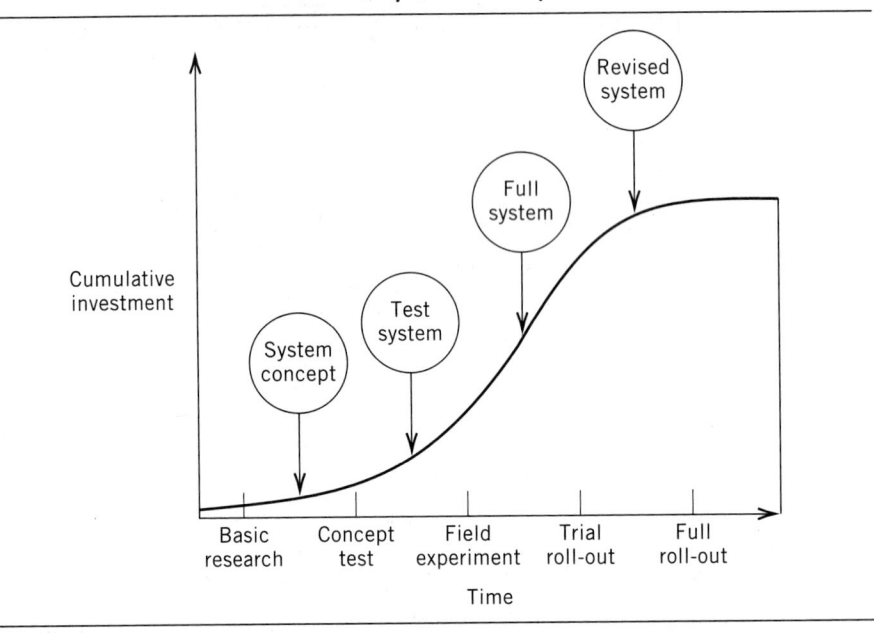

A curve showing cumulative investment over time, with the following stages marked along the time axis: Basic research, Concept test, Field experiment, Trial roll-out, Full roll-out. Callouts along the curve identify: System concept, Test system, Full system, and Revised system.

SOURCE: Michael Treacy, "Strategic Sales and Marketing Systems: A Development Approach," *The Consultant Forum,* vol. 5, no. 1, Digital Equipment Corporation, Nashua, NH, 1988, p. 6. Reprinted with permission of the author.

business units (i.e., information systems) that support the business process. Clearly, there are leadership roles for IEMgrs(TP) in such development efforts.

The functional levels provide another set of circumstances that are both simplifying and confusing at the same time. Issues of ownership are not present. There are fewer interactions to incorporate in the design as compared to enterprise- or process-level efforts. The complicating issue is who develops the system. In those organizations where information systems have not been used strategically, systems development may still be the province of the information systems department. In such cases, the problem reduces to one of effective communication between requestor and provider. On the other hand, enlightened organizations will have moved the responsibility of applications development to the process owners through their IEMgrs(TP). Control of the development effort becomes the issue. If the IEMgr(TP) is aligned with the information systems department, the systems development effort will follow established convention. On the other hand, if the IEMgr(TP) is aligned with the process and is not an experienced information systems professional, then there may be control problems regarding the SDM in use at the process level. This can be a major sticking point in the systems development effort and we return to the topic in Chapter 14.

Application Partnerships

Regardless of whether the systems development effort is aligned at the enterprise, process, or function level, there is a common thread linking all such efforts. Every systems development effort must be based on a partnership between the information systems department and the business unit for whom the system is being developed. In some cases, the information systems department will take a leadership role (enterprise-level applications and major systems efforts) while in others, it may take a more passive role (consultant or monitoring and oversight of compliance to agreed-upon standards). The partnership may be between a few departments, in which case they may share responsibility for project management. When this becomes unwieldy, the information systems department may assume project management responsibility of a cross-functional project team. In either case it is advised that, at a minimum, the information systems department facilitate the project planning sessions and function in a standards-compliance and quality-control role.

◆ TAXONOMY FOR DEVELOPMENT

Most SDMs are designed for and apply easily to major systems development projects with large scope, substantial resources, and complex activities. Such projects can easily bear the administrative overhead cost of the SDM process. However, not all SDMs are flexible enough to address other types of projects, such as those efforts elaborated next.

Maintenance Projects

For the support or maintenance request, which is smaller and more limited than the major project, different procedures apply. Small size of the project usually exempts it from the detailed planning that accompanies development projects as well as associated management reporting. Similarly, its lesser importance status usually means that a broad and thorough design review is either unnecessary or not worth the effort. And the maintenance request may have alternative approval cycles. For instance, the IS department traditionally exerts additional influence on the approval and solution process for maintenance efforts, as the department is usually well-versed in the hidden risks and long-term efficiencies of either postponements or superficial repairs.

Martin Buss [1981] warns of three risks encountered by firms that allow software to lapse into an outmoded condition.

1. Old software is risky. It creates unnecessary dependence on increasingly scarce personnel, hardware, and software support. Breakdowns become more likely. Moreover, obscure software is difficult to manage.

2. Outdated software helps the competition. If customers are lost, it may be impossible to attract new customers when software-based services are obsolete. If competitors have better support software, catching up becomes difficult.
3. Outmoded software is not cost effective. The costs for users to operate it, for programmers to support it, and for hardware to run it are all higher. Inadequate software can even forment personnel turnover, which is itself quite costly.

Despite the fact that it is sensible not to fall behind on software repair and correction, maintenance activity has a dangerous tendency to steal time away from IS development. The following are five approaches to avoiding maintenance where possible:

1. *First-Time Accuracy.* If attention is paid to the accuracy and appropriateness of specifications at project definition time, many inconvenient changes can be avoided.
2. *User-Flexible Systems.* New technologies that allow users to take over elements such as report generation or even simple applications development can help systems and programming staff get out of the business of performing necessary but trivial tasks.
3. *Ignoring Maintenance Requests.* This approach can be heartless but is often justified, as many requests are not of overwhelming business importance. Care must be exercised so that the occasional essential requirements are not overlooked.
4. *System Replacement.* Although no single change is crucial, collective changes point to software that has outlived its usefulness. Careful monitoring of deterioration can lead to a decision not to continue patching the product but rather to replace it altogether. This can be planned through a technique known as "piggybacking" [Martin, 1987], where a replacement system is initiated while the old system is still healthy, so that the new one will be ready when deterioration accelerates (see Exhibit 12-9).
5. *Rationing Maintenance Resources.* A compromise solution that does not entirely ignore the need for occasional change but also does not permit wholesale commitment of systems and programming resources is to severely (and often arbitrarily) limit the amount of repair attention that a given system receives by restricting the personnel and hardware resources that are applied to it.

Systems Upgrade Projects

Systems upgrade projects fall in between maintenance requests and new system development. Where one leaves off and the other begins is often a judgment call by the IS manager. Oftentimes the choice is made solely on the amount of effort,

Exhibit 12-9

Piggybacking

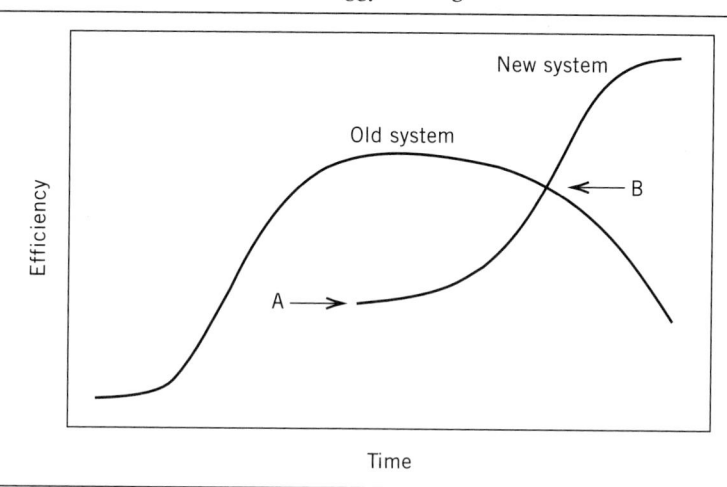

[Graph showing Efficiency vs Time with two S-curves: "Old system" curve rising then declining, labeled A on its rising portion; "New system" curve rising later and crossing the old system curve at point B]

SOURCE: Merle P. Martin, "The Human Connection in Systems Design—Part VI: Designing Systems for Change," *Journal of Systems Management,* July 1987, p. 15. Copyright *Journal of Systems Management* 1987.

risk, business value, complexity, or some other measurable criteria required to execute the upgrade. As used here, a system upgrade falls into the category of a project and therefore requires that some or all of the standard project management methodology be used. The extent to which the project management methodology is used is determined by the extent of the upgrade. See Chapter 8 for more details on project classifications.

New Applications Development

A precise statement of what the new system should contain is a critical element of any systems development project. One of the major responsibilities of the project manager is to see that such a statement is developed. When the project will be completed and degree of detail presented will have significant implications for the approval, support, and management of the project—not to mention its final content. Specifying too much detail too early can discourage constructive improvements or can result in committing extensive resources to work that is later discarded. But postponing specification of system details can leave projects in an aimless or misdirected state. While somewhat simplistic, the statement "How do you know when you get there if you don't know where you are going?" summarizes the thought precisely.

If we had to pick one area where systems development projects run into trouble it would be at the very beginning. For some reason, people have a difficult time understanding what they are saying to one another. How often we

Exhibit 12-10 — Establishing Conditions of Satisfaction

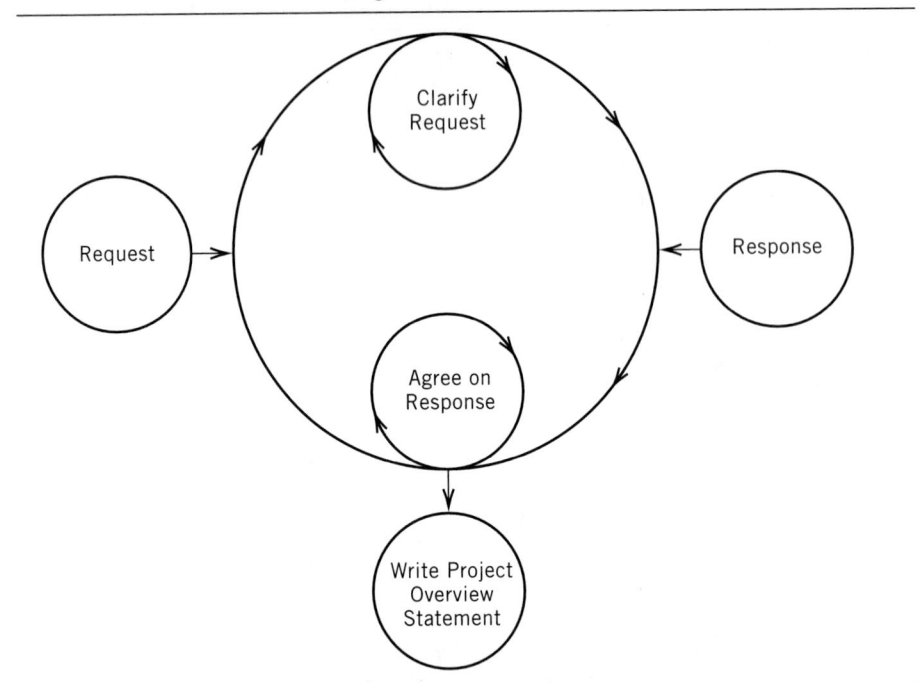

Diagram: A "Request" circle feeds into a large cycle containing "Clarify Request" and "Agree on Response"; a "Response" circle feeds into the same cycle. The cycle leads downward to "Write Project Overview Statement."

find ourselves thinking about what we are going to say while the other party is saying their piece. If you are going to be a successful project manager, you must put a stop to that kind of behavior. A critical skill for you is good listening skills.

There are several dimensions to the conversations and negotiations that eventually lead to agreed-upon "Conditions of Satisfaction" [Wysocki et al., 1995]. Exhibit 12-10 is a graphical depiction of the Conditions of Satisfaction.

What the Requestor Wants

A request is made; the provider explains what he or she heard as the request. A clear understanding of the request is established by both parties. This part of the process usually proceeds quickly. The step is actually completed when the requestor is satisfied that the provider understands what is being asked.

What the Provider Can Deliver

The provider then states what he or she is willing to do to satisfy the request. The requestor then restates what he or she understands that the provider will provide. Again a clear understanding of the response is established by both parties. At this point in the process both parties are ready to begin reaching agreement on what will actually be provided.

Negotiating the Deliverables

Expecting that there will not be agreement on the first pass, this process repeats itself until there is an agreed-upon request that is satisfied by an agreed-upon response. Accompanying the agreement is a quantitative statement of when the request will have been satisfied. It is important that the statement be very specific. Do not leave to someone's interpretation whether or not conditions have been met. An ideal statement will have only two outcomes—the criteria were met or the criteria were not met. There can be no in-between answer here. This so-called "doneness criteria" will become part of the Project Overview Statement. The result is documented as the Conditions of Satisfaction and becomes input to the Project Overview Statement.

We stress again the importance of this early step. It is especially difficult to do a thorough job when everyone is anxious to get on with the work of the project. It is also painful. People will get impatient; tempers may flair. Remember, pain me now or pain me later. You choose what you are willing to live with.

Monitoring Conditions of Satisfaction

The Conditions of Satisfaction is not a static document to be written and then filed. *It is a dynamic document that must become part of the continual project monitoring process.* Situations change and so will the needs of the customer. That means that Conditions of Satisfaction will change. At every major project status review or milestone event, review the Conditions of Satisfaction. Do they still make sense? If not, change them and change the project plan accordingly. This will be especially important in those projects that are for external customers. Market conditions change so frequently that what may have been a well-thought-out plan last month may no longer make sense this month. The situation will also arise in those projects whose requirements could not be completely defined or in projects that utilize breakthrough technologies. In other words, for any project that may be unstable for any number of reasons, the Conditions of Satisfaction will change.

◆ INCORPORATING A PROJECT MANAGEMENT METHODOLOGY

Good systems development requires the use of a sound project management methodology. In Chapter 8 we presented a robust five-phase project management life cycle. All good project management methodologies will contain variants of each of the features discussed. In this section, we further expand on that life cycle and discuss specific applications to the systems development life cycle.

Exhibit 12-11

Project Classification

CLASS	DURATION	RISK	COMPLEXITY	TECHNOLOGY
Type A	> 18 months	High	High	Breakthrough problems certain
Type B	9–18 months	Medium	Medium	Current problems likely
Type C	3–9 months	Low	Low	Best of breed; some problems
Type D	< 3 months	Very low	Very low	Practical; no problems

Sizing the Project

The variation of systems development projects that arise suggests that a one-size-fits-all mentality for the methodology to be used does not make good sense. Rather, we suggest that the IEMgmt team define a classification of systems development requests such that a project's classification determines the project management methodology to be used. An example of such a classification is given in Exhibit 12-11.

Class A systems development projects require that the full methodology be used. As we move from Class A to Class B, then C and D, less of the methodology is required—making more of it optional. We advise systems development project managers to decide for themselves whether any of the optional parts offer added value to their ability to manage the project. Each organization will have to determine its own criteria for defining project classes. The important point is to always consider the cost/benefit of the part of the project. In this case, cost will be project team time.

Establishing Project Scope and Detailed Project Planning

Once the project scope has been developed from the Conditions of Satisfaction and preliminary approval has been given, it is time to do the detailed planning. Only after the planning is completed can we say that the project scope is finally determined. As part of the detailed planning, the customer and/or the project team may find sufficient cause to revise project scope.

The actual planning itself is conducted in a *Joint Project Planning* (JPP) Session. These are not unlike Joint requirements planning (JRP) or joint applications design (JAD) sessions. The participants are a facilitator, the project manager, key technical specialists, a customer representative, resource managers, the project champion, and a recorder. We strongly advise this participative approach. It has many benefits, among which are customer buy-in, the beginnings of team formation, familiarity with the project work and schedule, the opportunity to make a public commitment and show of support for the effort, and others.

JPP sessions are run on consecutive days until completed. Two to three days is typical. The deliverables are the work breakdown structure, the project network schedule, and the resources required to complete the project. All of this documentation is assembled into a project proposal and submitted to senior management (both IS and the customer) for approval. Approval at this point is approval to do the project.

Monitoring and Controlling Project Work

Once project work commences, the project moves into the monitoring and control stage. Despite the best efforts of the customer and the project team, the plan will not happen as expected. Changing market conditions, random acts of nature, staff turnover, changing business priorities, and myriad other factors will affect the plan. The systems development team must expect these changes and be prepared to respond. Well-documented and understood problem resolution and change management processes are indispensable. Treat every request as potentially a major request. It is not uncommon to reconvene the JPP session to prepare a response to a customer request or problem situation.

◆ SYSTEMS DEVELOPMENT

Systems development has changed its focus in the last 10 to 15 years. Prior to the introduction of the microcomputer, many of the decisions to build or buy new systems were based more on technological considerations than they were on business decisions. With the advent of the microcomputer and end-user-oriented development tools, the decisions became more business-focused. The use of technology could be measured more in terms of business value and hence viewed more from a strategic perspective.

A Strategic Approach

"Infomate," is a term coined to simply say that the enterprise must find ways to:

- Add an information component and hence value to the product.
- Use information to develop new and unique products.
- Sell or broker information.

We see ample evidence of this concept already. The Internet, for example, has made it possible for enterprises to exist in virtual state only; for enterprises to link themselves electronically with their suppliers, distributors, and customers; and for information to be delivered immediately to their markets.

Product/service positioning, quick response, mass customization, customer service focus, and quality imperatives are some of the major areas that can be affected by technology. The enterprise must establish a strategy, enable it with technology, and constantly monitor the results. The choices are bewildering. There are so many technologies emerging and at such a rapid pace, that it is impossible for any organization to monitor them all. Choices must be made, and often under high-risk conditions with incomplete information.

Design and Development Strategies

The methodologies to support the information-age enterprise are available. However, implementation is problematic. Delayering and downsizing have had a major impact on the way people work. We are all faced with a heavier workload. While positions disappeared, the work remained; there are now fewer people to do more work. What this means is that time has become a binding constraint for many organizations. Face-to-face meetings of four or more people are very difficult to schedule. Much of our interaction is now carried out through workgroup software (Notes, cc:mail, etc). Despite the fact that we know that collaboration and user involvement are critical success factors, we can't seem to meet the challenges. Everybody is busy and reluctant to free their time for three-day JAD, JRP, or JPP sessions. Despite the logistics problems, a way must be found to take advantage of a powerful toolset. We turn now to a brief discussion of these tools.

Environmental Scans

Before launching headlong into a systems development effort, most organizations seek a solution they can *acquire* rather than develop in-house. In larger organizations, this scan might be internal. Is there anyone in another of our divisions or business units that might have an applications system that we can use and/or adapt to the problem at hand? Next, we look outside the organization, perhaps at our competitors, but most likely at other businesses. What do they have that we can use? The obvious strategy here is to buy/modify/adapt before deciding that to build is the best approach.

Benchmarking for Best of Breed

Another approach common in quality initiatives is to look at the competition or some other business that is recognized as the leader in that area that relates to our problem. L.L. Bean is a clear leader in catalog sales. How do they do it? What is their model? Can we take the best of it and apply it to our problem?

Joint Applications Design

Simply put, a *joint applications design* (JAD) session involves customers and developers coming together for one or more intense sessions in which the functions and features are discussed in terms of how customers will interact with the system and how developers will develop the system. For details on how this is actually done the student should consult Wood and Silver [1989].

Design Walkthroughs

The design walkthrough is an opportunity for the analyst to share his or her thoughts with peers and other qualified professionals. All that is involved is to present the systems design to a panel of qualified observers. Their role is to look for problems and alternatives that might improve the flow of the system, its open design, maintainability, adaptability, usability, and so on. "Test my thinking" is the basic idea behind these sessions. In addition to the IEMgrs(Tp), the IEMgrs(TP) from other function or process units might be invited.

Multiple Release Strategies

Because time to market has become another of the critical success factors, a multiple release strategy is often advised. This can take many forms. For example, if product functions and features can be prioritized, say, those that we must have, those that we would like to have, and those that are merely the wish list, then we might introduce version 1 with the must-have features and functions, then version 2 with the would-like-to-have features and functions, and then, even later, version 3 with the wish list. There are several advantages to this strategy:

- Get to market sooner.
- Reformulate the need for later features and functions.
- Learn from customer experience.

These releases can be concurrently developed, developed in series, or developed in some combination of the two. In all cases, reducing time to market is the objective.

Rapid Application Development and Prototyping

All of the simple systems have been developed. We no longer write payroll or accounts receivable systems. What we are developing are systems that have strategic value and these systems are often only vaguely defined. Requestor and provider have an idea of what is needed but are not able to define the exact systems requirements or how customers will interact with the system. In such cases prototyping is a development strategy. It allows both requestor and developer to get something running that may only have some of the known features and functions. Often it is written using tools that create "cardboard versions," not "production versions," of the system requested. By learning from these prototypes what is really needed, and only then developing the production version, development time can be significantly reduced.

Phase Reviews

Just because the system was approved for development based on some business value criteria, there is no assurance that the justification remains valid throughout the development effort. It has become quite commonplace for the enterprise to revisit the business case at every major project milestone. This inspection should include a revisit of the Conditions of Satisfaction. Very few project plans and deliverables definitions remain static. There are too many market changes, competitor product announcements, technology changes, and resource availabilities that can occur to render a project obsolete. These changes give rise not only to significant scope creep, but also to project abandonment, even at very late stages of the project life cycle.

Testing

To assure that the system does what it is supposed to do, testing must be conducted. The responsibility lies with both parties. The provider must test code logic, error recovery, and throughput under heavy transaction volume, and otherwise assure expected performance. The requestor must assure that all functions and features work as expected; that the user interface is intuitive. In short, they try to break the system. The final acceptance of the deliverables should be based on requestor-generated test data. These are called Acceptance Test Procedures and should be written by the requestor.

Deployment Strategies

The actual implementation of the new system basically takes one of three forms as discussed below.

Cut-Over

This is the riskiest but quickest and simplest of the three conversion strategies. It simply involves unplugging the old system and plugging in the new system. While not advised, sometimes there is no alternative. The physical facility may not be able to accommodate two separate hardware systems at one time. Staffing limitations may be such that only one system can be maintained.

Phased

Staff limitations may necessitate implementation being done over a period of time. The new system is introduced one department, location, or business unit at a time. This is done in the chronological order in which processes or functions are executed in the organization.

Parallel

This is the least risky but most expensive conversion strategy. The old and the new system both exist in a production environment. Until the complete business cycle represented by the new system has been checked against the old system and all variances accounted for, the old system is not unplugged. Obviously the physical facility and staffing complement must be available. In some cases, temporary help may be engaged during the parallel conversion.

Postdeployment Audits

Postdeployment Audits are greeted with the same enthusiasm as writing system documentation. Some of the questions to be answered by this type of audit are:

- Was the projected business value realized?
- How did our methodology work?
- How well did we follow our methodology?
- What were the lessons learned?

The reasons for not conducting the audit are many and include such excuses as: We have too much work in the backlog and can't afford the time; I'm not really interested; the project is over and I can't do anything about it anyway; and, it's not billable time. The obstacles to conducting the audit do not diminish its importance.

◆ DATA MANAGEMENT

As the enterprise moves away from the centralized mainframe environment toward a client/server architecture with computing dispersed throughout the enterprise, the lack of a data model becomes a bottleneck. One of the first problems facing the IS manager is how to take a wide assortment of user-built databases with redundant and poorly defined data elements and create an enterprise data model that meets all its users' needs. It is clear that building an enterprise data model is a major undertaking. In the past two decades, most installed information systems were implemented in reaction to crises with little regard to data integration [Forcht, 1994]. As we move into the next century, we cannot adopt this posture; we must use database management systems effectively to reduce data redundancy, improve data integrity, be more responsive and flexible, and be able to access, modify, and protect data. In this section, we explore the enterprise data model—its definition, development, and use.

The Corporate Data Model: Access, Security

Ideally, the enterprise would like to have every data element stored once, have one department responsible for its creation and maintenance, and have it read-only accessible to authorized personnel, anywhere and any time. If only life could be that simple. In fact, it may be advantageous to have copies stored in several places (perhaps under different names) and maintained by several authorized personnel (with appropriate audit trails). The shift away from the ideal situation has been evident for several years as various business units look for quick response to customer inquiries and for ways to improve customer service. Wetherbe [Wetherbe & Vitalare, 1994] looks at an information systems architecture based on the layered approach. The layers are presentation, application, input/output, network, and database. The database layer is the most important layer because we need access to the right data at the right time by the right (authorized) people. Now that the computing landscape has a network of intelligent terminals (microcomputers) with great local processing capability and connectivity to client/server systems, managing the data is even more important. The process involves all end users (multidisciplinary), is very complex (easy access versus security dichotomy), and is a team effort (perhaps even a self-directed development team).

Distributed Data

Wetherbe's [1994] network layer is another complex undertaking for most large organizations because the information technology infrastructure establishes what can and cannot be accomplished on the distributed system. Many computers and stations exist at several locations, the local control of which may vary from organization to organization. Some end-user departments may only query the system for data observation without entry responsibilities. Others may make online entries (airline reservation systems) which depend on accurate and complete information upon inquiry. There may be several updates simultaneously occurring and in some cases, these must occur without lockout. Lockout refers to the capability for many users to concurrently update and not be "locked out" of system use. There are network standards to be met and the system must have open architecture, or *open system interoperability* (OSI), to ensure that business operations such as electronic data interchange (EDI) is possible. EDI allows sales orders to be placed electronically by the client directly to the supplier without catalogs, sales staff, or visits to product distribution centers. As more systems move toward connectivity, file compatibility, and direct access and retrieval, and they move closer to end-user personnel, data security measures and database integration become even more important.

One way to achieve integration is to describe all data in one centralized, consolidated data dictionary [Martin et al., 1994]. In this way, only one definition exists in the data dictionary, or data directory, for each data element, even though the elements may be stored in several databases. Actual physical location of the data elements is transparent to users; in the long term, these separate databases in the distributed system should be managed on one standardized database system.

One of the goals of data resource management is to separate the dependence of data from the applications. In this perspective, data is treated like items in inventory, like a warehouse. In fact, the concept brings forth the term *data warehousing*. Data is retrieved from the warehouse when needed, updated and manipulated, and restored for use at some later time. This central repository is available for any application program. The concept is quite the opposite from the trend toward imbedded data within the application in the object-oriented analysis and design approach (OOAD). In this latter case, all processing takes place within self-contained "objects" which house the data, data relationships, and processing logic. As new applications are developed, this approach allows adding objects which can interact with those already placed online. The idea here is to acquaint you with some approaches in data modeling so that you can appreciate the enormous task facing all enterprises, namely, How should the data be managed for producing the right information for the right people in a timely, complete, secure, and accurate way? In this age of networks, easy access, and optical fibers (allowing very-high-speed and concurrent transmission of data, images, sound, and text), it is important to pay attention to the data resource.

Data Security

Because it sets up access to most software and systems, technical support often ends up with security responsibilities by default. Because security can mean data access, application or function access, or network access, the technical support staff are in a good position to orchestrate all three areas. It is often difficult, however, for a highly skilled function such as technical support to take over a very procedural, even clerical, duty such as security.

Of course, there are more substantial aspects of this duty. Often, providing completely flexible control over data access is too sophisticated a task for many security environments and some compromises must be struck. Also, a continuing challenge is to not let security procedures or systems overhead get in the way of user-friendly efficient systems use. This is particularly difficult in today's end-user community (EUC) environment. Access requests may arise spontaneously; access needs may be onetime and are more individual than departmental; intended use may not be clearly known, and access needs may even extend into the personal files of others. This does not even consider the nonsecurity issues of maintaining data currency and ensuring proper data definition. Security in such a setting can be very complicated.

One helpful capability is the provision of granular security, which allows access to less confidential portions of the database without jeopardizing the confidentiality of sensitive portions. For example, a department manager could access the personnel records of people in that department without being able to see similar records of those not in the department. This access could be restricted to appropriate portions of the record without disclosing personal data. Granular security allows access to summary data (such as average salary of all corporate employees at a certain level) without giving any specific information on any individual. Such a system requires even more security management efforts but conforms more closely to the growing needs of modern corporate computing.

Another difficult tradeoff that must be determined when managing security is how much protection is worth the investment. There are clear costs to installing, operating, and maintaining data security that must be kept commensurate with the risks of loss or compromise of important information. Determining the value of information and the degree to which protection is necessary is ultimately a management responsibility. In administering a data security program, the IS department is often put in the unfortunate position of independently deciding on security measures due to company indifference or compromising with resistant users at inappropriate levels.

Data Architecture Alternatives

One of the database administrator's important duties is determining how data should be organized. Obviously, a critical time for doing this is at the point when a database management system (DBMS) is selected; here, the needs for hierarchical, relational, or other structures can be assessed. Even after this event, however, decisions must periodically be made as to how data relationships should be represented under the chosen structures or whether certain data belongs under such a structure at all. Moreover, the database administrator (DBA) may see the need for alternative structures to meet selected needs or as a platform for migration. Thus, a relational database may be chosen to supplement a traditional data structure in order to support some EUC functions and for future applications.

Whatever the technology, the DBA role cannot be overemphasized, for it subtly determines the usability of data. Even those organizations astute enough to appreciate the significance of data structure issues cannot afford to frequently fund complex and disruptive data-restructuring projects. Mistakes made in one instance will be paid for repeatedly.

In a like manner, the meaningfulness of data is strongly affected by decisions regarding how data elements are related, defined, and maintained. Moreover, data accuracy and renovation responsibilities must be regularly fulfilled. Many of these assignments and decisions rightly occur in systems and programming projects, which means the project managers, analysts, and even programmers are instrumental in deciding issues of data integrity. The DBA must make sure that technical support retains responsibility for guidelines and standards in this area as well as selected review responsibility. The days where this could be enforced through necessary control of centralized software are gone!

Relational Data Structures

Today, relational databases are replacing the more traditional database management systems of mainframes. Vendors of microcomputing software make claims and counterclaims about their products and their relational attributes. Gone are the days of single "flat files" where a single table of rows and columns represents the entities (records) and attributes. A student record can contain data elements, or attributes, such as Social Security number, course listings this semester, and cumulative grade point average. The file of records can be sorted by microcomputer software, such as dBASE III+, with simple one-line commands to immediately produce only the complete records for students taking only three courses, one of which is information systems. The list of selected conditions can be created, modified, accessed, and manipulated easily because it is one table (flat file) with no information required about other data from other files. Once information is needed from several files, which therefore have to be linked table-to-table, relational processing is needed.

This logical arrangement of records from file to file or database to database requires an analysis of entities, attributes, and relationships derived from data-gathering techniques. In the subsequent, more detailed phase of data modeling, we employ prototyping, or heuristic, trial-and-error methods to provide the database layer and ensure that it is an integral part of the grand design of information technology infrastructure. The local processing power of the microcomputer with all its commercially available database software (e.g., dBASE III+, Paradox, Access, Foxbase, and Foxpro), some of which products are truly relational, can provide the predetermined and ad-hoc reports needed for decision making at all levels.

Corporate database information can be downloaded and manipulated without the need of mainframe processing. In order to query data from different relational databases, the American National Standards Institute (ANSI) has developed a standard query language (SQL). This language allows various databases to communicate and share data across applications.

Entity Relationship Model

During the data-gathering process, information and work flow (data flow diagrams), systems architecture (system structure charts), and decision-making logic (decision tables) provide enough information for a general design of one or more application areas. This process was described in earlier sections of this chapter. For the data modeling segment of this process, it is necessary to explore in depth the meaning of the data to ensure that there is no ambiguity in data representation. If ambiguity exists in data definition and relationships among data elements, managing the data becomes impossible. The wrong data items will be retrieved for manipulation. *Extended entity-relationship* (EER) diagramming methods can help to avoid this situation. The notation uses four special symbols to track relationships among entities (with a specific name for a person, event, place, or thing) which may have one or more subclass types. For example, the notation can help track a system by identifying the events taking place, which departments are involved in the transactions, and what actions occur among the events. For specific examples of this comprehensive methodology, we refer you to Martin, et al. [1994].

From a management perspective, the approach provides complete documentation of entities, their primary keys (the mechanism to access the data, such as Social Security number), and more importantly, relationships and rules. The result is a cross-functional listing of entities used for the database so that data redundancy is reduced, data capture is efficient and has integrity, processing is efficient and effective, standards are upheld, and operational activity is coordinated. It is documented for flexibility and the enterprise model structure ensures integration.

◆ EMERGENCE OF OBJECT TECHNOLOGY

In a previous section on distributed data, the trend toward object-oriented analysis and design was introduced as yet another alternative for managing data. In recent years, an increasing number of businesses, including the vendor community, are beginning to take object technology more seriously. In addition, there are several other factors which require that we take a closer look at this technology [Guttman and Matthews, 1995]:

1. Many large businesses are at a point where they have to decide whether or not modify or change completely their legacy information systems developed over a decade or two ago.
2. Any such change requires a strategic business perspective taking into account local reengineering ventures, probable or possible mergers with other similar or dissimilar businesses, global electronic mail and electronic data interchange (EDI), information system adaptation to rapidly changing business conditions (new rules for decision-making, new opportunities), and much more time spent on new development rather than the maintenance effort.
3. A recent survey by the object management group (OMG) of a representative sampling of IS professionals and end users indicates that 80 percent of them think that object technology will become the basis for business computing systems.
4. It is clear that reusable and transportable computer code will be even more needed as we progress into the next century as interenterprise computing will continue to emerge.
5. Object technology encompasses business strategies and operations in all aspects of analysis, design, and implementation of information systems; it is more than just object-oriented programming.
6. If an enterprise is to adopt object-oriented concepts, a formal and comprehensive transition plan developed by all types of IEMgrs can place the organization in a most competitive posture, not only for today but also for tomorrow.

What exactly is object technology? An object is a reusable, self-contained, mutually exclusive event, person, place, thing, or concept [Watson, 1996]. It is a "record" data item but has the added feature of its ability to act independently. Because of this ability to act, procedural languages and relational databases are not designed to store and/or manipulate this data structure. In fact, traditional programming thinking must be completely replaced in order to capture the essence of objects and their more encompassing capability to handle multimedia, economic forecasting models, and other complex structures.

Different types of languages (e.g., SIMULA, C++, Smalltalk, Visual Basic) are necessary to assemble and use objects. The objects contain all instructions (methods) for the data as well as the data itself. The objects have classes, such as a student object class, which is a part of a teacher's grading system. They communicate with each other through "message passing"; however, objects don't change other objects. These self-contained objects, much like entities in data modeling, can be used for many different programs. The idea is to spend a considerable amount of time up-front in organizing the classes in the most general way so that they can be reused for a variety of applications. These reusable modular components will replace traditional custom-written code. In fact, it is easy to imagine new companies dedicated to building a library of objects and selling them to one or more customers.

Object-oriented database management systems (OODBMS) store objects and provide direct linkage to object-oriented programming languages (OOPLs). If the technique is so advantageous, why isn't it used throughout the industry? Although IS managers agree that object orientation is the best solution in the long run, they don't want to be vendor dependent. In most cases, the change would be time consuming, their staff may not have the motivation or expertise to move in this direction, and there are not standards. For those reasons, relational systems will continued to dominate for the next few years. Watson [1996] suggests that a hybrid object/relational model may emerge.

Reflections

GENERAL CONCEPTS

1. Why must systems development efforts for an application be integrated with other applications?
   a. If it is a self-contained (closed) system and perhaps a standalone microcomputer solution with commercially available software, why is it necessary to be concerned about enterprisewide data management and other corporate issues?
   b. Why not just "prototype" the application and get it online within weeks?
2. What are some of the factors involved in developing a systems methodology for an enterprise?

a. Examine a local enterprise (business, government agency, or educational institution) for its existing (formally documented) SDM.
   - Does everyone follow it or is there in place an informal way of doing it?
   - If not, why not? If yes, how would you improve it?
   - Does it allow for changing conditions and fast response to new demands?
   - How much end-user involvement is there? What are the policies for end users?
   - Is there an information technology infrastructure plan? Is it integrative?
   - What are the control issues, such as priority of applications development?
   - What roles do IEMgrs play in developing and implementing the SDM?
   - Are CASE tools and techniques used?

3. What are the issues involved in software upgrades?
   a. Under what conditions does the organization step back and reflect on major software changes (new software for major application areas, expensive upgrades, requirements for modification, etc.)?

4. If the systems development methodology has been implemented with "success" for the past decade, why try to fix it?
   a. What is "success?"
   b. Why even take the time and expense to evaluate it if it works?
   c. If you did decide to evaluate it, would you use a consultant to do it? Why or why not?

Reflections

STEP MODEL

1. Although the subject of project management has been covered in detail in Chapter 8, the topic is reintroduced in this chapter. In addition, the STEP Model is based on the movement of the enterprise toward the maximum use of technology (T), process (P), and staff (S), which activity has a direct relationship to SDM.
   a. Explain how project management is related to the STEP Model.
   b. Why is it important to keep an eye on a STEP Model pathway throughout the SDM process?

Reflections

ETHICS

Scene: Body Parts Management

Inventory management is an important part of information systems curricula. Database systems management is indispensable in the systems analysis, design, and implementation of all computer-based business applications. Typical applications, such as those described in the ISI in Chapter 6, are sales order processing and distribution systems for wholesale and retail operations and for stock levels of purchased materials for manufacturing environments. Other small businesses keep track of video availabilities and rentals. Accountants working at home keep track of client accounts and perform mail/merge operations to distribute bills.

There is an increasing need to react to emergency conditions for people with requirements for liver and heart transplants and for other parts of the body. There are people willing to donate their organs and body parts upon death or near death. Often, time is crucial and numerous telephone calls, information collection, permissions, legalities, ethical dilemmas, and moral questions are not conducive to efficient and effective decision-making. Rational and irrational thoughts prevail, emotions are high, and the process is not always delineated.

Computer technologists, doctors and medical staff (knowledge experts), and systems analysts are eager to address this problem. The technology and expertise to use that technology are immediately available. Funding can be obtained through matching corporate and federal and state government grants. The resources to complete the project can be obtained, although a cost/benefit analysis may not have been conducted to ascertain the feasibility of the project. Other parties have serious reservations about the project.

More information must be collected and a comprehensive analysis must be conducted by persons other than the technological "designers" of the model in order to draft a comprehensive solution to the problem of matching needed and available body parts. With this brief introduction to the scenario, develop it further and identify the major issues.

As separate groups in independent discussion, define the scope of the problem and produce a "process" which would lead to project (applications development and implementation) adoption or cancellation. Examine the hypothesis that there is no truly correct answer and deal with (accept) it.

Reflections
ISI CASE STUDY

Systems Development

Because ISI does not have full in-house expertise beyond consultants on retainer and some recent hires of IEMgrs, it is necessary to build a systems development capability to maintain the installed system and to adapt to changing market demands and opportunities. The three- to five-year master plan will provide some direction to ISI in establishing its place in the competition. However, the plan is itself a dynamic entity and will require continuous modification.

The process of automating ISI has proceeded to the final negotiation stages where technical, economic, operational, and political feasibility concerns have been addressed.

Deliverables

1. At this point, the following documents should have been prepared and presented:
   a. RFP: All specifications for ISI requirements for today and the next three- to five-year period; although the expectation is that ISI will continue beyond that period, there must be some timeframe which defines the bid evaluation process (perhaps five years) so that vendors' bids can be compared on the same basis.
   b. Selection Process: criteria and specific system for evaluating vendor bids.
   c. Vendor Bids: complete and confidential document with technical and economic segments; as part of the bid, a plan for systems development beyond installation must be included (technical and economic considerations).

2. Some type of overall point system for rating vendors should be executed. The RFP should have mandatory and desirable requirements not only for hardware, but also for software and services. The mandatory requirements would be a small list of items necessary for ISI to conduct business in an effective way; the desirable requirements would be a much longer list of items, some of which ISI may not procure or may defer to a later time. In any event, some type of evaluation system is needed to ensure that all vendors are evaluated on the same basis.

3. System upgrades: How are modifications to the applications software to be made? Maintenance contracts will ensure that current systems remain online. Because of the changing nature of business, it is clear that the system will require modification to adapt to new and different ad-hoc reports from new managers with different decision-making styles.

4. Measurement of success: How will success be determined? Is it enough that the promised system is installed and operational? Once the system is accepted and operational for several months, how effective is it and will it meet the upcoming requirements? What are the performance measures?

Chapter 13

Information Technology at the End-User Level

♦ ♦ ♦

W*e have clearly established that the enterprise has entered a phase in its use of computers and data where further competitive advantage cannot occur without the leadership of both the information technology professionals and the business process and function professionals. We have already discussed the proactive role of the IEMgr(Tp) and the collaborative role of the IEMgmt team. Recall that the discussion followed first from a business process perspective (in Part II) and then from a business function perspective (in Chapter 11). In this chapter we take yet another view of the enterprise's use of computing—from the end-user perspective. In our treatment of the topic we will see that there has been a role reversal. The IEMgr(Tp) and IS department assume a reactive role while the IEMgr(TP), IEMgr(tp), IEMgr(tP), and the rest of the end-user community assume a proactive role.*

The astute student should begin to see that a trend has been developing over the last 20 years. That trend has the IS department moving from a systems developer to systems supporter role while the user community has moved from a systems user to a systems developer role. Underlying these role changes we see that both groups have had to become multidisciplined. The IEMgmt team is the embodiment of that multidisciplinary trend. The result is that we have created a more collaborative role for both groups and hence a development environment that can, at last, begin to exploit the information technologies for business advantage.

We begin our discussion by understanding the end-user community. This raises a number of management concerns that must be addressed. We then consider how changes in technology and the focus on business processes rather than business functions have changed the way workers interact. Finally, we offer a number of strategies to organize and support end-user computing.

◆ TYPES OF END USERS

In the broadest sense, anyone (secretary, accounting clerk, financial analyst, supervisor, manager, president) who uses a computer can be called an *end user*. Panko and Sprague [1984] identify two types of end users:

1. Type I: An "information worker" who is told what to accomplish and the steps to accomplish it.
2. Type II: An "information worker" who must understand general goals and then figure out how to attain them.

The kind of work that each type performs helps distinguish them, as Exhibit 13-1 shows.

Type III End Users

The executive is emerging as another type of end user, one whose needs are very different from those of the Type I and Type II end users defined by Sprague and McNurlin [1986]. Exhibit 13-2 represents a revision of their original two categories into a new three-category scheme proposed by Wysocki and Young [1990]. Their Type II and Type III users are an outgrowth of the original Sprague and McNurlin Type II end user.

The Type III user is rather different from the other two, and his or her needs will be met in ways that are very different. This end user typically spends very

Exhibit 13-1 Two Types of Information Work

TYPE I	TYPE II
High volume of transactions	Low volume of transactions
Low cost (value) per transaction	High value (cost) per transaction
Well-structured procedures	Ill-structured procedures
Output measures defined	Output measures less defined
Focus on process	Focus on problems and goals
Focus on efficiency	Focus on effectiveness
Handling of "data"	Handling of concepts
Predominantly clerical workers	Managers and professionals
Examples:	Examples:
"Back office"	Loan department
Mortgage services	Asset/liability management
Payroll processing	Planning department
Check processing	Corporate banking

SOURCE: McNurlin, Barbara C. and Ralph H. Sprague, Jr., *Information Systems Management in Practice*. Englewood Cliffs, NJ: Prentice-Hall, 1986, p. 10.

little time with the technology, uses a variety of simple but highly integrated tools, and views graphical displays of highly aggregated forecasted and historical data. This user's objective is to form general judgments and to develop strategic initiatives; therefore tools and data must be readily available and easy to use in very unstructured and nonrepetitive sessions. Clearly, this type of end-user requires services, support, and systems that are totally different from any of those that the IS manager had to provide in the past. The tools that the IS department will need in order to accomplish this task are natural language interfaces, expert systems, and artificial intelligence.

The strategy for designing systems for Type III users will involve examining corporate critical success factors (CSFs) to identify areas of interest chiefly to the executive. Using these CSFs, the IS department will be able to store highly aggregated extracts of the corporate database and a variety of reporting options in a front-end processor to bring very sophisticated data modeling down to a few simple keystrokes. This major challenge has not yet been met.

Even with the addition of the Type III end users, this typology tends to oversimplify the complex management issues related to end-user computing (EUC). A better approach is to define end users from the standpoint of the computing skills they offer and to intersect these skills with the types of

Exhibit 13-2

Future Trends in End-user Types

TYPE I	TYPE II	TYPE III
Clerical workers	Professionals and middle managers	Senior managers
High volume of transactions	Moderate volume of transactions	Low volume of transactions
Frequent use	Little use	Very little use
Low value per transaction	Moderate value per transaction	High value per transaction
Routine and repetitive	Somewhat structured and repetitive	Unstructured and used once
Specific output	Control/analysis/report output	General directives, judgments, and initiative outputs
Efficiency focus	Effectiveness focus	Innovation and differentiation focus
Individual records	Summary of internal historical data	Highly aggregated and integrated internal and external data
Use of a single tool	Multiple tools with some integration	Large variety of highly integrated tools
Rote training	Somewhat structured and self-paced	Unstructured training with direct payoff

information these workers process. John Rockart and L. Flannery [1983], following such an approach, identify six types of end users: nonprogramming, command-level, and programming-level end users, and functional-support personnel, EUC support personnel, and data processing programmers. Their model still is valid today even though the tools each type uses have changed radically.

Nonprogramming End Users

This type of end user uses applications systems developed by others. The developers may be personnel from their own department [IEMgr(TP) or IEMgr(tp)] or from the IS department (i.e., data processing programmers). The nonprogramming end user uses the computer by responding to a series of menus and/or prompts for very specific information. He or she needs little understanding of the computer beyond routine interactions with the system. Airline reservation clerks and department store cashiers are typical representatives of this end-user category. This end user is clearly a Type I information worker as defined by Panko and Sprague. Nonprogramming end users were the earliest and, for a long time, the only type of end user that the traditional IS department anticipated serving. That view changed with the availability of fourth-generation tools designed for end users.

Command-Level End Users

This user differs from the nonprogramming end user in that the system is partially or totally command driven, hence more under individual control. This type of system is clearly more powerful than the menu-driven system in the sense that the user has more flexibility in interacting with it. To use it, the user must form a query statement that the system then interprets and executes. The information retrieved may be a single record or a summary of data from a subset of records meeting conditions specified by the user. The user must have a working knowledge of the command-driven language which usually is part of the database management system. Some applications may require porting retrieved data to a word processing or graphics package for further manipulation and reporting. In some cases, the procedure that was followed to retrieve and report the data can be stored in the computer as a macro for further use. Thus, this user may need an elementary knowledge of operating systems too.

As new software becomes available, the command-level end user will make more sophisticated use of computers. Financial analysts and marketing researchers are typical representatives of this category of end-user. The tools available to these end-users have become so sophisticated and intuitive that it is difficult to distinguish their results from those of the next category of end user.

Programming-Level End Users

A typical user in this category has the ability to design and write programs in compiler or interpreter languages and to produce custom-designed analyses and reports. Often the systems this user develops will be used by nonprogramming or command-level end users. Programming-level end users are usually attached to a single business unit [(IEMgr(tp) and IEMgr(TP), for example] and are not part of the IS department. They tend to develop exceptional skills in one or two application packages and will frequently have more expertise with the package than do the personnel in the IS department who are assigned to support users of the package. The obvious danger in this situation is that the end user becomes a solution looking for a problem. These users may try to use their knowledge of one or two packages to solve every problem that comes their way.

The term "power user" is sometimes applied to these end users. As we will see later, these information technology gatekeepers will prove to be a valuable resource for the IS department in providing EUC support services. Much of those users' development efforts are for their own purposes, although they will often provide informal support to others in their department. Power users are often found in IEMgr(TP) positions and less often in IEMgr(tp) positions.

Functional-Support Personnel

This group of end users is almost always found in the functional departments or business processes. These users are technically skilled but view themselves as function or process based rather than IS-department based. They can write programs in compiler-based languages but seldom use anything other than end-user languages. They often serve as liaison with the IS department and represent their unit on systems development projects. These users typically develop systems for use by others. Clearly all IEMgrs(TP) and some IEMgrs(tp) fall in this category.

End-User Computing Support Personnel

These users are usually assigned to an information center and are specialists in one or more end-user programming packages. They offer general support to new nonprogramming and command-level end users. Training at the introductory and advanced levels with a specific package is their main responsibility; they are usually weak in function-specific applications. They also offer support to command-level and programming-level end users in data extraction and package choice, as well as occasional systems-development advice.

They may also be assigned to the IS department and function as IEMgrs(TP) for a specific business unit. In this case they will have expertise in a specific business functional area or process.

Data Processing Programmers

This is the most frequently overlooked of the end-user groups. These users are exactly like COBOL programmers except that they program in end-user languages at a high skill level. Their needs are very different from those of the other types.

Productivity training and automated software design, code generators, and related technologies are their principal areas of need. They are the real experts in end-user languages but frequently lack a functional business orientation. Large companies often set up information centers, or development centers, to meet the needs of this group.

◆ IMPORTANCE OF END-USER COMPUTING

Managers generally agree that end-user computing (EUC) is an important variable in the total computing equation of the enterprise. The enterprise's competitive position is strengthened when individual efficiency is improved. Technology that helps reduce the labor intensity of routine and repetitive tasks will improve overall worker effectiveness. The use of sophisticated applications and software packages designed to improve management's decision-making ability will impact competitive position.

The resulting productivity gains also favorably affect the value chain in areas that have strategic payoff. For example, the use of a database management package to track and analyze sales by lead source can lead to a revision of shipping schedules that in turn will result in both faster service to more active accounts and service differentiation from the other competitors—a strategic gain for the company. Although this chain of events is not strictly causal, it is clear that EUC has strategic value.

At the senior management, IS, and end-user levels of a business, the planning process must integrate EUC as a strategic weapon in the corporate arsenal. This is easier said than done; EUC is generally an ad-hoc activity and hence difficult to budget. For budget planning purposes, it needs to be viewed in much the same light as a typical research and development function where some benefits are intangible and/or not immediately measureable.

◆ MANAGEMENT CONCERNS

For both the organization and its managers, it is crucial that the strategic potential of EUC be realized. However, although senior, IS, and end user managers all have a vested interest in accomplishing this goal, they do not share identical concerns about EUC. Consider the following set of managerial questions:

Senior Managers

- Have we identified areas of strategic opportunity for EUC?
- Are we taking full advantage, across the organization, of our EUC efforts?
- Have we identified the targeted benefits?

- Does the planning process incorporate EUC as a strategic option?
- Is the organization configured to support EUC?
- Are enough resources being allocated to EUC?

IS Management

- Have the developers followed accepted analysis, design, and programming standards?
- Are EUC systems appropriately documented?
- Have user managers made provisions for the maintenance of their systems?
- Have any strategic opportunities been missed by not consulting with the IS department?
- Should any of the users' systems be part of the corporate systems portfolio?
- Have users taken advantage of existing corporate data or developed their own?

User Management

- Are appropriate design standards in place, and are control methods satisfactory?
- Are established systems development methods being followed?
- Are the benefits of EUC being fully realized?

In addition, senior management is concerned with fostering an organizational culture and managerial environment conducive to EUC. This suggests placing the justification for EUC with the end-user manager. In that way, various value-added criteria can be used as valid measures for the justification and prioritization of end-user-developed applications. An entrepreneurial environment structured along the lines of projects, tasks forces, and strategic business units encourages EUC.

For IS management the challenge is to allow end-user units sufficient autonomy, but not at the expense of the necessary controls, standards, and policies needed to ensure that EUC complements other corporate activity. And for user managers, the challenge is fourfold:

- To maintain a corporate perspective in managing the EUC activity in their unit
- To ensure proper compliance with IS departmental practices
- To ensure that hardware/software acquisitions are compatible with corporate standards and supportable by the IS department
- To provide appropriate planning and support for EUC in their units

Exhibit 13-3

The Relationships Among Managers in an EUC Environment

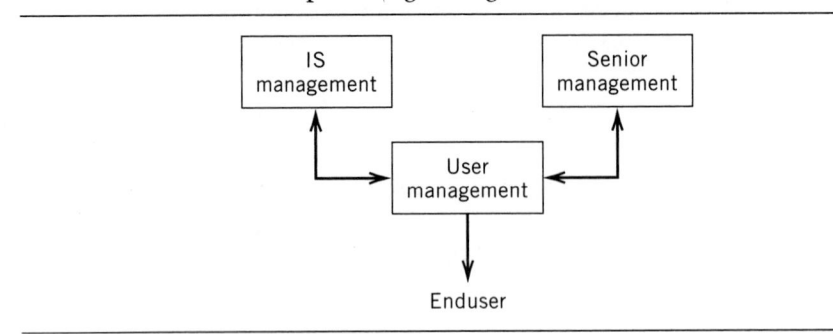

```
   IS              Senior
management       management
    ↑                ↑
    ↓                ↓
         User
       management
           ↓
        Enduser
```

The ultimate success of EUC depends heavily on user management. The relationships of the three elements are shown in Exhibit 13-3, which emphasizes the critical role of the user manager in ensuring successful EUC activity.

IEMgmt Team

To the extent that some of the above are in fact members of the IEMgmt team, we have already commented on their concerns. There are, however, a few points that apply specifically to the IEMgmt team that are worth citing separately. Some of their concerns are listed below.

- Is the IEMgmt team fully effective as a team?
- Is the IEMgr(TP) from each business unit adequately representing his or her area to the other team members?
- Does the information systems planning process incorporate the IEMgmt team both proactively as a team and reactively as individuals representing a business unit?

Thus far in this chapter, we have addressed specific concerns between user managers and IS professionals for effective team efforts within the organization. Information-enabled managers throughout the enterprise must work together toward business goals and objectives. Before we examine further the issues, problems, and alternative solutions addressed by the IEMgmt team, or "work group," we must think more divergently and venture outside the confines, assumptions, and constraints of the enterprise for a more global view of the marketplace and the role of information technology in that perspective.

◆ GLOBALIZATION AND INFORMATION TECHNOLOGY

It is clear that the impact of our shrinking world is being felt in small towns and cities throughout the world. Global competitiveness is pervasive. According to

Rosabeth Moss Kanter of the Harvard Business School [1996], who has researched this topic comprehensively during the past few years, communities must open their connections to the world and be more "cosmopolitan" in their outlook. Her book on how to be a "world class" business is very insightful, visionary, and practical. She suggests that success in the global economy goes beyond setting and meeting standards and emphasizes strong relationships and partnerships in joint ventures. Her grassroots approach places the burden on local communities to examine their foreign policy strategies, and infrastructure for collaboration to attract and use resources effectively, and to provide specific action items to embrace new world-ready opportunities.

The globalization phenomenon certainly has heralded the disappearance of the "lifetime job" throughout the world. The cosmopolitan community and worker of tomorrow must have portable skills and be ready to apply them wherever and whenever they are needed. We are facing the prospect of a bold new world [Knoke, 1996] and not everyone is prepared to deal with it. Knoke's age of everything-everywhere represents a major shift from tenure-secure jobs of the past to the more insecure work of the future. By 2025, his "placeless society" of workers will supply only 5 percent of all manufacturing needs, will change careers three or four times during a lifetime, and will experience more redeployment than unemployment.

Information technology has created this world of instant and global response. During the past decade advances in hardware, software, and services have moved organizations to more dynamic and less bureaucratic structures and have motivated the workforce to be more aware of growth areas in automation. Managing information across the enterprise and across the world requires effective use of information technology as data transactions will increasingly occur across national borders. Each day, $600 billion is converted from one type of currency to another; Citicorp has 20 million customer accounts in eighty-nine countries; and electronic data systems can handle the most complex transactions in less than an hour [Knoke, 1996].

Workers' jobs (including information workers) are at risk unless they understand that they are in the age of service and it will continue into the twenty-first century. In the Placeless Society of Knoke, electronic fingerpoints are everywhere and information on each of us will be available before purchases are made. Databases will continue to enlarge, sometimes without proper privacy and surveillance measures in place. The World Wide Web exacerbates the situation by opening this new frontier to anyone with electronic access to the network. Information technology is blurring geographic lines of demarcation. It is incumbent on the worker to understand and work with others who may well have different cultures, value systems, and/or religious beliefs. In the next sections, we discuss this need for workers to perform in groups and to extend that performance to better customer response through electronic commerce application.

◆ WORK GROUP COMPUTING

The migration to client/server architectures and the availability of software tools have created an electronic workplace connecting workers regardless of their organizational placement and have made it possible for the enterprise to move to a higher level of productivity. Also, it has facilitated realigning the organization along business processes rather than limiting it to traditional functional units. As we have already discussed, that migration has given impetus to improved customer service in a variety of contexts. Let us look at this developing work environment.

Intradepartmental and Interdepartmental Relationships

As the enterprise continues to move toward a business process orientation, the boundaries between the functional areas will continue to disappear. In time the "boundaryless" organization envisioned by Jack Welch, Chairman of General Electric (see Tichy and Sherman [1993] for an excellent account of the evolution of GE under Welch's leadership) will be embraced as the structure of choice. Organizations are in transition at this writing and from a technology standpoint are operating with systems that are contained within departments and that span departments.

People must collaborate to perform work. Groups of workers make decisions; the traditional command/control structures for unilateral decision making have been replaced by self-directed work teams and empowered task forces. The more complex a decision, the more information from diverse individuals is necessary to converge on timely, complete, and practical solutions. In order to be successful in work group activity, it is important to realize certain benefits [Turban, McLean & Wetherbe, 1996]:

1. Groups are better than individuals at uncovering and understanding problems.
2. If empowered, people can be held accountable for decisions in which they participate.
3. Groups are less likely to make major errors in judgment.
4. More alternatives arise from groups.
5. Quality of a group is larger than the sum of what is produced by independent individuals.
6. Work groups can motivate individuals to share needed information toward defined business objectives.
7. If the work group has designed a new process and is empowered to implement it, the process has a good chance of success.

The authors have extensive national and international experience with work groups at all levels of the government, business, and education enterprises. Certainly, work group dysfunctions arise [Turban, 1993], but they can be reduced or eliminated with careful planning. In addition, it is wise to identify a team leader who has facilitation skills and is able to:

1. Focus the team on predetermined objectives.
2. Select diverse team members.

3. Lead the team with patient and coordinated progress.
4. Manage the team using appropriate project planning and control measures.

Facilitation of a group can be enhanced with automation. The latter two items of leading and managing can make good use of project management tools and techniques such as Microsoft Project. Activities are identified, relationships among activities are displayed a number of ways on various charts, and resources (including people) are allocated for maximum utilization. In this way, schedules are produced, resources are used prudently, and all team members are apprised of progress continuously. Human communication is improved, coordination is ensured, and milestones are met. More elaborate decision-support software for groups (groupware) is available and may be effective in idea generation. The Decision Support Center at the University of Northern Colorado, uses a comprehensive local area network software product, Gp. Systems V, which allows many team members to communicate electronically through the many phases of group decision making. Lotus Notes is another, more limited product for team facilitation.

An example of the use of groupware involves the drafting of a bid in response to a formal request for proposal (RFP) for consulting services. The RFP describes the services to be performed, milestones, and deliverables at each milestone. In response, the consulting firm is required to state its overall approach to solving the problems specified by the RFP, to identify the methodology and success criteria, and to provide all technical, economic, and operational data to support that approach. In gathering information for the proposal, the consulting firm needs several different types of information from different individuals, perhaps located throughout the world.

Usually, the response time is a matter of weeks and although the prospective account manager can be assigned immediately, other resources for the project must be determined (e.g., available project workers with technical expertise for this particular venture, billing and other financial data, contractual support for complex terms and conditions, and special software needed to monitor progress for client applications). Groupware allows several individuals to work independently and concurrently on one electronic document (response to the request for proposal) and come to closure more effectively (meet client requirements) and efficiently (on time). The same groupware could have been used by the originator of the RFP to assemble information from several departments and produce the solicitation document. Such software allows for differing points of view and strategies upfront and culminates with the best solution for the given timeframe. If both provider and supplier are connected electronically by some predetermined formal arrangement, the same groupware would be more beneficial to both parties.

◆ ELECTRONIC COMMERCE

A more simplified version of a multiple-access communication system for all individuals with the access mechanism, and perhaps with no particular formal task in mind, is electronic-mail (e-mail). Senders can mail information to receivers, who can reply or forward it to other receivers. E-mail systems existed for many years in central computing environments with mainframe computers and/or timesharing services. With the advent of distributed systems, local area networks using simple network structures or more complex client/server systems extend e-mail beyond the local area to other internal and external computer systems. Text, image, color, and sound transmission over telephone and satellite links is commonplace and reaches into the home through personal computing hardware and software.

The World Wide Web (WWW) is the newest addition to this network of networks (Internet) which facilitates the easy sharing of information [McKeown & Watson, 1996]. The "hypertext" concept of pages on the Web is a method which links related documents through keywords. The user can bring a document on the screen, click on a predetermined link, or keyword, and navigate to the next and more definitive document on that topic. The documents, or Web pages, have unique addresses, for example, http://whitehouse.gov, is the address of the server for the White House [McKeown & Watson, 1996]. There are many ways to access information on the Web; however, Mosaic and Netscape Navigator are the most popular "browsers" on the market. A browser is a piece of software which contains visual buttons which you can click to access a Web page. The Internet server computers, which hold the Web pages, are Web "sites." The sites hold the "home page," from which other Web pages can be accessed.

Now that some terminology has been introduced, we are ready to exploit this new information technology medium for business purposes. The global marketplace demands that we place importance on electronic communication. Business reengineering efforts and the advent of self-directed work teams demonstrate that work-group computing is a major force in quality business performance and will require electronic communication in order to be responsive and, therefore, competitive.

Why should businesses use the Web? McKeown and Watson [1996] suggest that *not* to use it increases risk. If the business wants to address demand, innovation, and/or inefficiency, then it can reduce the risk by using the Web. How can it use the Web? It is an inexpensive way of advertising products and services to millions of Web users throughout the world. Like most computer images, the ads can be edited and updated easily, making this an excellent marketing device. Simply by browsing the Web, one may think of other ways to market, or other products to provide, or new customers to approach. Sales orders can be placed electronically, eliminating some costs of conducting business. Rooms and airline seats can be reserved. Leisure activities can be planned. Information is abundant—the trick is to access only what you need, when you need it. New jobs are created by the Web. Experts are emerging on interface programming languages (HTML, Visual C++, Visual BASIC, JAVA). Internet operations require new skills to use e-mail, File Transfer Protocol (FTP), Telnet, and Gopher. Electronic commerce is at the beginning of a new era in global business marketing, production, and distribution.

◆ CONTROL VERSUS AUTONOMY

Now that we have digressed to cover global issues, workgroups computing, and electronic commerce, it is necessary to converge our thinking and return to the internal operations of the enterprise and address further the control and support issues involved in attaining the cosmopolitan posture needed for the future. To be effective in supporting EUC, the organizational structure must take into account the two opposing objectives of control versus autonomy. The control objective is to develop appropriate policies and procedures to ensure that users' systems development activities are consistent and compatible with the corporate IS function.

Meeting the control objective entails developing a staff to help the end user consider feasible options and alternatives. The role is not new. More than 10 years ago Henry Lucas [1986] suggested that the end user assume the role of project manager even for those development projects where systems and programming staff does the analysis, design, and programming. When first proposed, Lucas's idea was met with skepticism and mistrust. It was a process that could easily be abused, so that the end user would be merely a figurehead and not really a principal player on the development team. However, Lucas's notion has turned out to be a very effective strategy.

The second objective relates to end-user autonomy. The organizational structure must allow the end-user to have control over the entire systems development process, including the creative part of the process—for it is here that the user first has an opportunity to buy into the system. Empirical studies of factors that lead to implementation success identify user ownership as an essential ingredient. Getting users involved early and keeping them in control is the best way to generate that sense of ownership. Along with that sense of ownership comes a vested interest in the success of the project.

An Anthology of End-User Computing Support Strategies

As EUC first emerged on the corporate scene, IS managers tended to ignore these new users, reasoning that their interest was a fad and would be shortlived. It was relatively easy for the IS department to isolate these users and not worry about them. Even if they did not go away, they would not be able to make a serious contribution to the computing activities of the organization. Many IS managers also thought that the new users would soon become frustrated with trying to use the new tools and would go back to their old ways. Remember, the end user had little experience in systems development and few had any expertise in programming. However, vendors came to the rescue with training, "user friendly" software, and enhanced capability and functionality in microcomputer hardware. Yet even when users seemed to be enjoying some success, many IS managers still resisted and ignored them. That, as it turns out, was a big mistake. This "laissez-faire approach" was definitely the wrong one to adopt.

Other IS managers adopted a totally different strategy—one that has the characteristics of a defensive posture. Their objective was tight control. They insisted on policies and procedures that made it impossible for the end user to do anything. The user community was forced into a particular hardware/software environment with not much thought as to whether such choices were best for the users. This was not a covert action but rather one that IS managers thought was in the best interest of the organization. After all, the IS department was charged with the integrity of the data and systems that supported the business activities of the organization. This "monopolistic approach" was adopted as a protection against accidental or uncontrollable user actions. Clearly, the focus was risk avoidance, not user support.

The emergence of "user friendly" software changed the face of EUC. Since the user community was now able to "do their own thing," the IS manager had no choice but to step in and provide support. At least the IS manager would be aware of end-user applications development efforts and could provide some guidance and structure in those efforts. The information center emerged as that support organization. Its mission was to help the end user become self-sufficient in the appropriate applications of the technology. That approach meant collaborating with end-users in the establishment of standards and procedures and in the mutual enforcement of those standards. At first, the information center was little more than a fancy name for a training department. Activities were pretty much limited to helping the users become familiar with shrinkwrapped software and how to access the corporate database.

The information center approach served its purpose well into the 1980s until Thomas Gerrity and John Rockart [1986] proposed a management structure called the "managed free economy." Their objective was to take advantage of the benefits of the information center approach and, at the same time, strike a balance between the extremes of the laissez-faire and monopolistic approaches. Their controls are designed not to create barriers to end-user development activities but rather to provide a structure for those activities. By adhering to mutually agreed-upon guidelines, users will receive maximum support when they need it, will be able to tie into the corporate data and systems portfolio, and will be able to take advantage of any expertise that may have been developed in other user departments or within the IS staff itself. The *managed free economy approach* has five components as follows.

1. Articulating an End-User Strategy

It is important that users understand the computing environment in which they have to work. Part of that environment consists of the hardware and software support that they receive from the IS department. By having the IS department specify the computing strategy, the user is better able to design systems consistent with that strategy. Another important part of the environment is the organization's strategic technological direction; again, helping users understand this direction better equips them to plan for the future.

2. Defining the User/Information Systems Working Relationship

A working partnership arises when the IEMgmt team develops a set of policies and procedures that define the computing environment. This represents a radical departure from the days when the IS department told users what the rules of the game were going to be—an approach that was destined for failure. It has become clear, from experiences involving users in the systems development process, that a sense of ownership is critical to implementation success. The same is true with regard to giving the user an equal role and responsibility in policy and procedure specification.

3. Developing Critical End-User Systems and Applications

The responsibility for bringing new technologies to end-user applications and systems has traditionally belonged to the IS department. In this new partnership, IS technical experts (both the IEMgr(Tp) and the IEMgr(TP)) disseminate information on new and emerging technologies that have relevance to the critical needs of the end user. These critical needs are defined as part of the exercise of identifying corporate and departmental critical success factors within the context of forming the strategic plan. Dissemination of information takes place as part of the environmental analysis step in the integrated strategic planning process. The "white papers" that are part of the initial corporate and departmental planning process are the vehicle for providing that information.

Armed with technology updates, the IEMgr(TP) and the IEMgr(tP) must seek out opportunities for individual or departmental efficiency, effectiveness, or innovation that may lead to competitive advantage. Although this multifaceted process identifies only certain application projects, at least it provides some input for the strategic plan.

4. Integrating the Support Organization

It is essential that a separate organizational entity, devoted exclusively to end-user support, be established. The users must be absolutely convinced that they are not second-class citizens in the eyes of the IS department, and anything short of a separate support function would risk causing that perception. The traditional information center is not sufficient. The solution must go beyond that, focusing rather on the type of support given and the fact that users are continuing to expand their skills in applications development, are working with a more sophisticated tool kit, and are gradually taking over the responsibility for applications development. Above all, this support organization must be adaptive and must anticipate the evolving needs of the user community.

5. Emphasizing Education

The support personnel must be technically competent. More importantly, they must understand that they are dealing with a range of user expertise that runs from novice through expert. Education becomes a shared responsibility. Some education will be the responsibility of the IS department and some will be the responsibility of the end-user departments.

◆ ORGANIZING FOR END-USER SUPPORT

A model suggested by Watson and Carr [1987] seems to have transcended the technological advances of the last decade and is still appropriate today. They suggest a three-tiered organizational structure for supporting EUC (see Exhibit 13-4). It seems to work well with the ideas put forth by Gerrity and Rockart. Watson and Carr's structure has three units or groups: the corporate model unit, the decision support systems (DSS) unit, and the information center unit.

The Corporate Model Unit

The corporate model unit enhances the corporate plan through a planning exercise specifically designed to support EUC. This exercise includes a definition of the needs by the end user and an examination of existing data and systems by the manager of the corporate model unit. Solutions to specific user problems are then identified and additional opportunities that the new application may create for others are also noted. The process also includes planning for the integration of the end user's application into the corporate systems portfolio.

Exhibit 13-4 An Organizational Structure for Supporting EUC

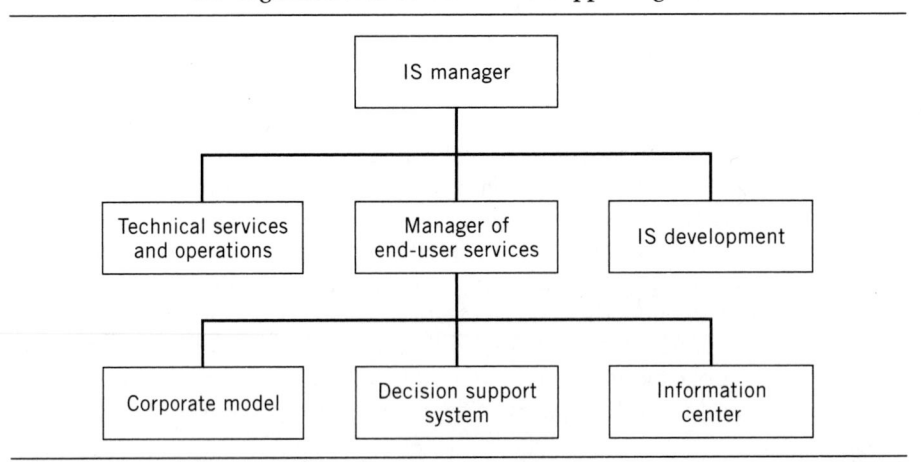

```
                    IS manager
                        |
        _____|_____
        |               |                |
  Technical       Manager of          IS
  services        end-user         development
  and operations  services
                        |
        _____|_____
        |               |                |
   Corporate       Decision          Information
   model           support           center
                   system
```

SOURCE: Reprinted by permission. Adapted from Hugh J. Watson and Houston H. Carr, "Organizing for Decision Support Systems: The End-User Services Alternative." *Journal of Management Information Systems*, vol. 4, no. 1, Summer 1987, p. 91.

While it is not part of Watson and Carr's approach, we suggest a critical role here for the IEMgr(TP). That role has two parts. The first is to define the business unit's request at the level of a systems requirements document. This is clearly within the responsibility of IEMgrs(TP) and appropriate given their level of technical expertise. The second is to have a high-level technical discussion with the IS department for the fit of the proposed system to the existing development applications portfolio.

In the absence of the IEMgr(TP), as in prior years, this discussion could not have taken place. While we admit that in some settings there will be a synergistic effect resulting from brainstorming sessions between the technical expert and the business unit expert that will lead to acceptable solutions, *there really is no substitute for individuals possessing both technical and business unit expertise.* The IEMgr(TP) is uniquely positioned to deliver best-of-breed solutions. That solution means competitive advantage in the final analysis. There is a process of discovery that can take place that is not likely under the two-person scenario which results because the discussion can take place at a technical level not otherwise possible. To the extent that the IEMgr(Tp) can increase his or her knowledge of the business unit, that discussion is even more likely to produce exciting results.

The Decision Support Systems Unit

The decision support systems (DSS) group works closely with the user in the development of systems that utilize appropriate corporate computing and information resources. Just as the corporate model unit is the planning function for EUC, the DSS group is its implementation function. With this unit, Watson and Carr recommend development support rather than training in the use of development tools; the unit thus represents an extension of traditional end-user support services. Carrying the Watson and Carr model to the next step we see a variety of contributions that the IEMgmt team can make.

The Information Center Unit

In the Watson and Carr structure, the information center unit offers typical microcomputer support services but does not include development services. Its chief responsibilities are training in software use and answering questions. It also assists end users with their data acquisition problems and needs. The information center provides maximum freedom for the user along with expert advice and development support consistent with the strategic direction of the enterprise.

As users have become more sophisticated and knowledgeable in their use of information technology, the role of the information center unit will similarly become more sophisticated. Some of the recent support needs will naturally be met by experts in the user's business unit. Here we see a local support role being provided by both the IEMgr(TP) and the IEMgr(tp). In cases where higher levels of support are needed, the managers can be referred to the information center unit.

Reflections

GENERAL CONCEPTS

1. The text to this point has made the case that competitive advantage cannot occur without the leadership of both information technology personnel and business process professionals. In addition, there are role reversals in that the more technical IEMgrs(Tp) assume a more reactive stance and other managers become more demanding and proactive in the use of information technology.
   a. Do you agree with this phenomenon? Why or why not?
   b. Conduct a brief literature search to develop your view and/or justify your comments.

2. End-user computing (EUC) has been in existence from the first day of handling information using electronic means. During the past decade, the types of end users have changed, the topic of EUC has grown in importance, and the issue remains a hotly debated one (between IS professionals and business managers).
   a. Why is it a hotly debated issue?
   b. What strategy would you adopt to resolve the conflict? Use a specific scenario.
   c. How would you implement a plan for collaboration and consensus?
   d. What major factors should be addressed at the outset?

3. Compare and contrast the training and support needs for each type of end user. What would you identify as the major challenge to IS management in providing the training?

4. How would you implement controls and standards for an EUC applications development procedure?

Reflections

STEP MODEL

1. For EUC to be effective, support by top-level management is important. All members of the IEMgmt team need to be proactive in the process and justify that support. Explain how the IEMgmt team could accomplish this objective. Illustrate your comments with examples from a selected enterprise and certain issues particularly relevant to strategic decision making.

Reflections

ETHICS

Scene: END-USER END RUNS

The managed free economy approach (articulating an end-user strategy, defining the user/IS relationship, developing critical applications, establishing support, and emphasizing education) provides a framework for examining a local area network for an organizational element. The element could be the contracting department of a company (purchasing raw materials for manufacturing), a computer science department of a university (server containing all server applications software), or perhaps the planning function of a federal agency (several departments accessing the same software for brainstorming and defining strategic initiatives).

The installation of software for a local area network carries with it the usual technical and economic problems of feasibility. The technology is available but how much will it cost, for whom, and for what applications? In addition, who will maintain it, make the modifications as stations are added, and supervise not only the physical setup, but also the database of software and its access?

Select a scenario from one of the above mentioned examples and deliberate further on the ethical issues:

a. Your friend, who is not formally affiliated on the LAN site but is a member of your organization, wants to use an installed software application for his department. The LAN cannot be accessed electronically from his or her location (purposely excluded from access from other departments because of the confidentiality issue dealing with competitive contracting). Do you let your friend use the system from your office with your access code on your account?
- If yes, should you be present? If no, what other alternatives are possible?
- Whether yes or no, how does the managed free economy approach relate to the unauthorized use of a LAN?

b. Another friend of the vendor community is interested in selling a groupware software package to your organization for the LAN. The package will enable your department to work as a group on the same document concurrently. This procedure will allow individuals to make contributions with the full knowledge of others involved in the process.
- Why not use a system which facilitates the process and produces a final document?
- Should you provide information to your friend for better definition of end-user requirements? Any ethical issues here?

Reflections

ISI CASE STUDY

End Users and IT

Before the contract is awarded, one more issue has to be addressed: How will end users be involved in the development and implementation of the proposed system? It is important to be aware of the various types of end users and their information technology fluency before any conclusions are reached. ISI personnel require extensive training and retraining in order to be responsive to the effective use of information technology. They are knowledgeable of business operations, but are not knowledgeable of the possibilities of advanced information technology. The ISI negotiation sessions should have served to raise the level of knowledge in integrating people with technology for better decision making.

Deliverables

1. Include a discussion of end-user computing (EUC) in the negotiations and address:
   a. Importance with regard to value chain productivity areas
   b. Realization of EUC advantages, especially for ISI operations
   c. Formal arrangements between end users (all levels) and IS staff
   d. Who, how, and when EUC can be conducted; implementation policies
   e. Control of acquisition and allocation of computer resources
   f. Maintenance and certification of EUC efforts, including data administration
   g. IEMgmt team roles, responsibilities, and accountabilities
   h. Workgroup computing: need, system, applicability
   i. Educational implications of EUC: costs, categories of training, timing

2. These issues already may have been addressed in RFP development. They are included here to ensure that they have been discussed (or reviewed) for inclusion in the contract. EUC will continue to be a major force in the use of information technology.

3. Do you agree with the statement that the IEMgr(Tp), an information-enabled manager with high technical and low business process expertise, will adopt a reactive role while the other categories of end users (TP, tP, and tp) will adopt proactive roles?

Chapter 14

The Support Role of Information Technology

◆ ◆ ◆

All four types of IEMgrs have a support role in helping the business units take full advantage of information technology. The division of these responsibilities should be carefully delineated by the IEMgrs. In this chapter, we examine exactly how the support responsibilities are apportioned to the IEMgrs.

◆ DEVELOPING A SUPPORT SERVICE LEVEL AGREEMENT

It would be inappropriate for the IS manager to simply issue an edict outlining the service level agreement when it comes to supporting the end user. We have reached a point in the evolution of computer use where there are experts in every quarter. It would be foolish to have a service level agreement that was based on the assumption that the IS department was the single source for support. Users might get help from their colleague in the next cubicle rather than seek it out from the IS department. Furthermore, all four types of IEMgrs are quite capable of answering many questions without the need for a formal process of request and follow-up. For all of these reasons, it is highly recommended that the service level agreement be a joint effort. It is sufficient to have a representative number from each group draft a document and circulate it for comment. Once the document is revised, it will have a much better chance of being useful.

Some of the items to be considered in drawing up this service level agreement are:

- What types of support will be offered?
- What levels of support will be offered?
- Who should offer the support?
- How will requests be escalated?
- How will requests be prioritized?

◆ ROLES AND RESPONSIBILITIES

As we delineate the roles and responsibilities, note that the environment is one of shared responsibility. The notion of a fixed set of responsibilities from which no deviations are made makes no sense in the team-oriented organizations that dominate the business landscape. Rather, the strategy should be one in which individuals eagerly provide service and support whenever the occasion calls for their expertise. Let us see how that might work in each of the major areas where the IS department interacts with its user community.

Setting Corporate Policy and Standards

At the corporate level, policies that govern all aspects of computing—including privacy, security, access privileges, and the ethical use of computing resources—must be established. In addition, standards must be established in such areas as hardware, software, data definition, data communications, systems analysis and design, and documentation. This is not easily accomplished. Standards are guidelines and their purpose is not to constrain the end user, but rather to create an environment in which users can be more productive and effective in systems development efforts. If the end user is truly convinced of this, the problem of standards enforcement will be significantly reduced. Therefore, end user management should be involved in the development of standards and must agree to them. The actual exercise will be one of compromise between control and autonomy. The IEMgrs(TP) are the appropriate representative body to collaborate with the IS department in drafting the policy and procedures statement. IEMgrs(tP) are the final authority for approvement of the standards and procedures because they will be responsible for enforcement in their business unit.

Standards should not be applied unilaterally across the organization or without regard to specific situations. The IS department must be sensitive to whether the system to be developed has short-term or long-term business or strategic implications. For the short term, some variance from standards might be allowed; for the long term, a more rigid enforcement may be in order. In many cases, a system may have strategic value only if it can be quickly implemented. In these cases, some variances might be allowed so that opportunities are not missed simply because of delays in imposing a development methodology. Exhibit 14-1 is an example of standards as they might be developed for the end-user systems development life cycle.

Data Administration

Clearly, the IS department is responsible for defining the corporate data structure as well as providing the environment in which that data can be maintained and made accessible to the organization. The data architecture must be appropriate

Exhibit 14-1: Standards for the End-user Systems Development Life Cycle

STEPS IN THE SYSTEMS DEVELOPMENT LIFE CYCLE	END-USER CONTROL
Problem definition	Problem statement is reviewed by IS for possible integrations with existing systems portfolio
Feasibility study	IS reviews the design for a better alternative using existing technology
Systems design	Design walkthrough with appropriate IS staff Data definition and database design review
Implementation	Consulting available to assist user
Testing	IS creates test data and signs off on valid test completion
Documentation	IS accepts documentation for systems portfolio

for the needs of the organization, and decisions regarding its structure should involve the IEMgr(TP). IEMgrs(TP) are critical to such definition. They understand the data structure, contents, and accessibility needs of their business unit. When more in-depth expertise is required than they possess, they will consult the IEMgr(Tp) for help and advice with regard to data design for their current and future systems.

The notion of who owns the data has evolved over the years. In the old command and control stovepipe organizations, ownership was decentralized into the business units. There was little need for cross-departmental uses of data. When the situation arose in which one department needed information "owned" by another, they went to that department asking for and justifying their need for the data. Now organizational barriers are disappearing, and there is more cross-functional and process structure in place where data ownership has become a meaningless concept. Rather, data is owned by the organization. The responsibility for keeping it current and correct seems to have remained decentralized. In such organizations, the parties responsible for creating and maintaining each data element will have been determined. In summary, data and information are corporate assets, accessible to anyone with a need to know.

Communications

By defining the hardware and software alternatives within which users must operate, the IS department makes it possible for data communications to take place across the organization. Anything short of this approach creates a barrier to the truly strategic use of information and systems by others in the organization. One of the major problem areas for the IS department is the creation of a "seamless" data environment for the user. As data becomes more distributed across the network, it is important to remove as many barriers to data communications as possible.

Technology Research

The ideal strategic planning process is business driven, but without the participation of IEMgrs(tP) and their IEMgrs(TP) the planning process is severely handicapped. A technology-driven process is not the answer. It is the responsibility of the IS department to keep the organization informed of the latest technologies as they presently or might someday apply at the enterprise or business-unit level. Since their knowledge of specific applications at the business-unit level may be somewhat limited, they share technology research responsibilities with the IEMgrs(TP). Since they have business-unit expertise, they are best qualified for keeping abreast of the latest technologies as applied to their respective business units. At the same time, the IS department should establish an R&D effort, in conjunction with the appropriate business-unit IEMgrs(TP), to investigate and try out new information technologies. A proactive partnership with the business units can significantly diminish the likelihood of missing strategic opportunities.

Training and Education

Managers and users always have a need for training and education that can best be provided by a centralized unit. Typically, current end-user needs are for education in all aspects of the systems development life cycle, including documentation, testing, and maintenance. These are areas that the end user has traditionally overlooked, largely because of ignorance of their value for the entire development effort. Much of the process and procedure of IS-developed systems are inappropriate for user-developed systems and for systems developed with fourth-generation tools.

◆ END-USER MANAGEMENT RESPONSIBILITIES

Approximately 25% of all application systems are developed by the end user [IDG, 1995]. By assuming responsibility for their own application development and report generation, user departments also become responsible for a number of other computing activities that traditionally have been undertaken by the IS department. Often, this is recognized too late. With authority to control systems also comes the responsibility to support them, which the following sections delineate.

Applications Management: Implementation Strategies

Decisions regarding which applications to develop, and what the priorities of the application development portfolio should be, are the responsibility of the end-user manager. In those business units that have one, this responsibility can be vested in the IEMgr(TP). As with decentralized applications development, having the user assume this responsibility confers certain benefits. Better allocation of personnel and other resources is possible, and cost/benefit analysis is easier. The actual policies and procedures used by the business units can be tailored to meet the specific needs of that department. However, applications development cannot be totally divorced from corporate policy and procedure. Where the application involves other departments, systems development needs to take place in accordance with policy and procedure established at the corporate level. The issue of who is in charge of cross-departmental development projects is not easily resolved. Systems designed and projects managed by committee are not the solution.

The implementation phase of systems development is the responsibility of the end-user business unit. If the system is to be used by several people in the unit, the developer's unit is responsible for systems design and testing, documentation, and training. Again, this process will not take place independent of established policy and procedure. For example, design reviews and/or walkthroughs may be jointly conducted by the IS department and the user business unit. The IS department may also assume some responsibility for signing off on the system test phase. Once the system is put into production, the user-developer also assumes responsibility for ongoing support. This support takes the form of software maintenance, additional training for new hires, perhaps a user group, systems changes in response to new report requests, and so on. The IS department can play an important role in the initial training of user-developers in the complete systems development life cycle.

Perhaps the most difficult responsibility for the end user involves areas not visible to the typical user, including backup procedures, error detection and correction, file maintenance, and quality assurance. Left to their own devices, end users usually realize the importance of these operational responsibilities only after suffering the consequences of not fulfilling them. Losing a large data file or application program for which there was no backup is a common problem—and a hard way to learn the lesson. The IS department should be responsible for educating the end user in all aspects of applications management, including operational activities.

◆ IMPLEMENTATION POLICIES AND PROCEDURES

Allan Sewell [1987] discusses the shift in responsibility for policy and procedure from the IS department to the business units. Although the IS department is clearly responsible for the development of policy and procedure, Sewell maintains, and we concur, that it is not responsible for its implementation. That is definitely an end-user responsibility. Because policy and procedure are developed in concert with end-user management, it should be straightforward for user managers to assume responsibility for implementation. They will have been educated as to the value and benefit of meaningful policy and procedure and should be willing participants in their implementation, particularly in light of the fact that policy and procedure can be tailored to the specific needs of their unit.

When applications systems cross departmental or business, unit lines, implementing policy and procedure can become more complex. However, user management can nonetheless ensure conformance with corporate policy and procedure so as to preserve the integrity of the system. The IS department's responsibilities thus end with integrating data and systems among business units and establishing uniform corporate policies, procedures, and communication.

Sewell provides some guidelines that will facilitate this transfer of responsibility:

1. An open communications link must be established between the IS department and systems personnel in the user department. This link will help resolve questions of procedure.
2. Procedures must exist to update corporate data so that user-derived data will be up to date.
3. One person in each user area must be given responsibility for operations, for maintenance of critical data, and for communicating procedural matters.
4. The IS department should establish a small liaison staff to be responsible for communicating with user business units. Ideally, the notion of "one-stop-shopping" for the user business units should be established. A help desk is one possibility.

John Rockart [1987] advocates that line management must take the lead in systems development with the IS department moving into a support role. (We see a definite role for the IEMgr(TP) to take that lead position.) He bases his argument on the fact that the IS manager cannot know enough about each functional area and its strategies to design appropriate systems. The functional manager must learn enough about the technology to recognize and seize strategic opportunities. For this to happen, a partnership between functional and IS managers is needed in order to integrate strategic systems across organizational boundaries. Rockart calls the result a "Wired Society" and concludes that achieving it requires transforming not only the way we do business but also the organizational structure itself.

We submit that the transformation is taking place and the IEMgr concept lies at the core of the transformation. Rather than continuing to depend on the mutual support and cooperative relationship between IS manager and business-unit manager, we see the cloning of their skills in the form of the IEMgr. That, we believe, is the only practical way for technology to really make the impact on business that is needed to promote a world-class operation.

The Life Cycle of End-User Systems Development

Applications development has moved away from transactions-oriented systems and into control or strategic systems at the middle and senior management levels.

Many systems needs at this level are not well defined. The user manager often has only a vague description of the system and what it needs to do, is often unsure of exactly how the decision process works, and is therefore not able to write a statement of the problem, as the traditional systems development life cycle would require.

Hard and Soft Controls

Whatever development process the end user might use, a well-defined set of controls and standards is necessary. These are developed under the direction of the IS department with the full cooperation and collaboration of user management. As we have seen with respect to policy and procedure, by having user management participate in the definition process, the IS department can be sure that the controls and standards developed will be acceptable, workable, and enforceable.

Controls and standards are needed to protect the interests of the organization as a whole. At the same time, it is important not to stifle the interest, enthusiasm, and creative processes of the end user. Furthermore, because there are several classes of users to consider, it is very likely that one set of standards and controls will not be appropriate for all. Add to this the possibility that the application type may determine the type of controls and standards needed, and the problem becomes quite complex.

Richard Ball [1987] describes a model for developing a set of controls and standards. His model is based on the premise that appropriate controls and standards are a function of system complexity and risk. Ball classifies application traits as data attributes, application attributes, and project attributes. Data attributes include volume considerations, scope (individual, departmental, or corporate), retention requirements, and use (normal business functions or critical decisions). Application attributes include the technology used by the application, be it a single-user or multiuser system, and whether its use is scheduled or as needed. Project attributes are basically sizing characteristics, such as development time.

Another dimension Ball considers is risk. He defines three risk categories: A (low-risk, small applications for personal use), B (medium-risk, departmental or corporate-level computing), and C (high-risk, large end-user development efforts that have strategic impact). Attributes and risk categories can be arrayed in a matrix, as shown in Exhibit 14-2.

An application is placed in the risk category corresponding to its highest ranking on any of the attributes. The standards vary dramatically from class A to class C applications; this takes into account the fact that users developing class A applications are likely to be relatively unsophisticated as compared to users developing class C applications. The needs of each user type will be very different. For example, a user developing a class C application may not be acquainted with the various control, cost, and feasibility analyses that are required. Obviously, the IS department has a responsibility to see that this end

Exhibit 14–2   The Application Matrix

	CLASS A	CLASS B	CLASS C
Data attributes	"Personal" Nonstrategic Low volume Independent	Departmental High volume Used by other programs	Strategic or sensitive Used to update corporate database
Application attributes	"Personal" Standalone Low complexity	"Corporate" Used by more than one person	Complex "Yellow" or "red" technology
Project attributes	One to five workdays No formal project management warranted	Six to 20 workdays Some project approval, project management warranted	Twenty-one to 40 workdays Formal project approval, project management More than 40 workdays—use system development standards

	GENERAL STANDARDS	CLASS A STANDARDS PLUS	CLASS B STANDARDS PLUS
Associated standards	Use passwords Back up data Use common sense Label	Controls analysis recommended Must document Must register with end-user computing applications library Label	Controls analysis required Feasibility and cost-benefit analysis Database administrator's approval to update corporate database Label
Examples	Electronic mail Word processing Database query Simple spreadsheet	Spreadsheet used on a scheduled basis Database reporting program used by more than one person	Micro DBMS application Complex spreadsheet Simple spreadsheet, used for critical decision support

SOURCE: Copyright by CW Publishing Inc., Framingham, MA 01701—reprinted from *Computerworld*.

user has the tools needed to implement such a set of standards. It is also responsible for seeing that these standards are widely accepted and enforced. For this to happen, end users and their managers will have to cooperate in the development of the standards.

Compliance with these standards will occur only when they have broad support. Ball [1987] gives some suggestions for ensuring that compliance. He urges that user managers can be made responsible for ensuring compliance. He also suggests that EDP internal auditors be made aware of these standards and assist in checking for compliance. More recently, we are aware of companies setting up quality assurance offices as well as project offices. These offices could be made responsible for compliance checking.

Hard controls are necessary in the areas of hardware, software, and communications. Soft controls, in contrast, create the necessary bonding between the IS department and the end-user business units. J. Daniel Couger [1987] lists a number of these soft controls.

Maintenance

The IS department can encourage users to pick from among a specified number of hardware and software alternatives by offering to maintain only those devices on the approved list. In extreme cases, perhaps only one family of devices or one vendor's equipment is listed. Of course, the department needs to take into account varying user needs in determining this list. Being too conservative will constrain users and encourage noncompliance; being too liberal will place an undue burden on the IS department with regard to hardware and software maintenance. Here is a good place for the IEMgmt team to take a leadership role.

Centralized Purchasing

By centralizing the purchasing function, the IS department can negotiate quantity discounts that can be passed on to the user. There may also be some leverages that accrue to the purchaser simply because of the larger orders placed. Being a volume customer can only help in dealing with current or potential vendors. Lower prices will certainly be an inducement to user managers on a tight budget or with large quantities to purchase.

Training

By providing training on a selected collection of software products, the IS department can encourage users to work within that set. This training will also create user groups for each of the major software products. Users will still have a need for specialized software not widely used in the organization, but with good planning, a major part of the organization's software needs can be met by a relatively small collection of products. Users, especially those not technologically sophisticated, will find comfort in knowing that specialized help is available if they need it. For those packages that are not supported by the IS department, the IEMgr(TP) may be able to offer specialized help.

Shared Data

To develop strategic systems, the user will eventually need to access and share data from different functional areas of the organization. The IS department can anticipate this need and step forward with appropriate file-sharing software. If the IS department is successful in creating a "seamless environment," users will be encouraged to develop systems that will be compatible across user departments.

Centralized Software Control

The IS department should maintain the current release of all supported software and keep users up to date with the latest versions. This preserves software compatibility and consistency across user areas and also makes it easier to maintain the software.

Systems Development Training

Most users have no background in applications development methods. Feasibility studies, logical design, database design, data dictionaries, and so forth are new concepts to most users. They are going to develop their own applications regardless of what the IS department does to help or hinder them. The shrinkwrapped software available to them hides much of the methodology behind pick-and-choose or click-and-drag commands. Applications can be developed without using good development practices but the price will be paid later when it is time for maintenance and updating. Too often we have seen users adapting the one package they know to every problem they encounter.

The IS department can help users acquire good systems development habits by providing extensive training in applications development. This gives the department an opportunity to instill corporate policies and procedures regarding applications development, which in turn will leave users better equipped to manage their own future development projects. The IS department also benefits in those cases where maintenance of the system may come under their jurisdiction at some later point. The IEMgr(TP) will be key to seeing that users receive timely training and will provide support after the training to see that good habits have been instilled and are practiced.

Communications

The IS department should do whatever it can to create a reliable communications system among its users. Electronic mail services should be provided to PC users just as they have been provided to mainframe users. Product-specific user groups can also be effective in encouraging compliance with supported software packages. The user's peer group is very influential for decision making; the new user may well decide to follow peer group advice and go with a supported package if it offers an apparent value or benefit.

Soft controls are initiatives taken by the IS department to convince users that conformance to policy and procedures is in their best interest. If these controls are properly used, the user will feel drawn, not forced, to conform.

Certifying User-Developed Systems

The IS department will want to certify that a user-developed system meets standards for several reasons:

- To ensure compatibility with existing and planned applications portfolios
- To see that the system conforms to corporate data architecture
- To see that the system can be integrated with existing systems for strategic benefit
- To ensure that appropriate system and user documentation is in place
- To see that the system can be maintained by the IS department if necessary

Although the systems development process is well defined for third-generation-based systems, the same cannot be said for fourth-generation-based systems. End-user software has reached a level of sophistication such that the user has little more to do than define a collection of data tables, load data, invoke a report generator, and produce a variety of summary reports. All of this may be done through a menu-driven system so that the user never considers alternative solutions, data definition, data modeling, choice of software, system flows, and so on. Because the user's main objective is to get a system up and running quickly, many traditional systems development practices appear to contradict this objective and are bypassed by users who either do not know about them or choose to ignore them. This situation may be addressed by educating users about the systems development life cycle. User management will help ensure compliance to standards. As a final check, the IS department must verify that the system does meet established standards and can be put in the corporate portfolio.

There are three levels of certification to consider. The first involves areas that have been defined as personal computing; they are mentioned here for the sake of completeness, but in fact there is no need for standards at this level. Even if standards were contemplated, there would be no way to enforce them or to certify compliance. The situation is one where individuals find their own approach or short-cut that helps them be more productive. It may be of no value to anyone else because of different work habits, and preferences.

The second level of certification concerns user-developed systems that are for the benefit of a single department; these may be required to meet only those standards specified by the manager of that department, who is responsible for the proper use of resources and the accomplishment of departmental goals and objectives. For these systems the IEMgr(TP) will play a coordinating and liaison role, assuring the IS department of conformance and assisting the user with proper execution of the systems development procedures.

The third level of certification concerns those systems which have use outside the department in which they were developed. Information reported from the data and system developed in one department and used by another must be correct. Departments benefiting from other users' systems may not have the luxury of verifying the integrity and correctness of data that produced the information on which they will make decisions and take action. It is therefore essential that such systems be certified by the IS department.

As Robert Peterson [1987] notes, the certification of a system involves both the product of the system and the process that was used to create the system. Product certification involves verifying that data is correctly defined and retrieved, calculations are correct and consistent with corporate practices, and information is correctly reported from those calculations. Process certification compares the development procedures in use against established development procedures and notes any variances. Once a system has been certified, it is cataloged into the corporate libraries and follows the same life cycle as would any other IS-developed system. The accepted maintenance procedures that apply to IS-developed systems also apply to certified end-user-developed systems. EDP auditors will apply the same scrutiny as well.

Peterson notes a few exceptions. If the certified system is seldom used, certification is no longer necessary. Responsibility for making and communicating changes lies with the user department, which should approve and manage all changes. In these cases the role of the IS department is custodial.

Peterson also lists four requirements for a successful certification program. There must be a well-defined set of policies, procedures, and standards that users have agreed to follow. A portfolio of certified systems must be published, and it should contain information to help the user decide whether an existing system can be used in place of the one contemplated. The incentive for users to seek certification must be known. Finally, user managers must actively support the program not only by promoting it, but also by acting as "gatekeepers" in their departments. That responsibility would actually be vested in the IEMgr(TP) in that business unit. The IEMgr(TP) can be the link between the IS department and the end-user with respect to ensuring compliance with standards.

Reflections

GENERAL CONCEPTS

1. Centralized purchasing of hardware, software, and services has advantages and disadvantages depending on your point of view (IS professional or business manager). Discuss this issue from both perspectives.
    a. What specific "rules" would you adopt so that procedures would allow some flexibility of purchase with responsibility and accountability This approach would require rules for IS professionals as well as end users.
    b. What complexities do client-server systems introduce to such purchasing agreements?
    c. How would vendors be handled? Would you have a "script" for negotiating contracts?
    d. Shared data is important. What are the issues with regard to decentralized control of computer system procurements?
    e. How would you certify that any new software purchases are effective? Who will conduct the audit, the centralized control organization?
2. What financial planning and budgetary concerns are involved in the issue of support level agreements between IS staff and business managers? Examine an enterprise for financial planning and discuss its implications for control considerations for support of information technology.
3. Ideas for supporting information technology abound in many organizations. Many of them do not have the creative initiatives that accompany innovative action plans. If implementation planning has been conducted, often it is ineffective. If it can be agreed that information technology must be an integral part of the competitive advantage process, why are not the actions consistent with the ideas?
4. Discuss the transitional problems associated with any new procedure for supporting information technology. Individuals may have to change behaviors. The enterprise may have to change the way it conducts business, make strategic decisions, and look for new opportunities. Transitions are disruptive, especially if business operations currently are flourishing and stockholders are happy. Discuss these transitional issues for staff (all types) and customers (current and future).

Reflections

ETHICS

Scene: IEMgrs ARISE

One major theme of the text is that we cannot rely solely on a cooperative relationship and business managers to information-enable the enterprise effectively during the next decade and beyond. Numerous legacy computer systems still exist and will be analyzed extensively for upgrade and/or change to new client/server system configurations. Master computer resource planning is important in orchestrating the change with the players positioning themselves to retain or gain control of information technology across the enterprise. Information systems professionals will continue to disperse to operating business functions and end users will continue to be information technology fluent. The IEMgr (those managers from areas of both technology and management) will emerge as a major force in planning, distribution, and control of information technology.

From each perspective, describe how your group (business managers, information systems staff) would handle the following scenarios:

Scenario #1: The University Campus (Admissions)

It has been suggested by the Information System staff of the University that a commercially available, computerized service be implemented to track student applications to other colleges and universities. This procedure would be helpful for identifying early admissions candidates and tracking them as well as other inquiries and applications. You have seen the package demonstrated and it appears to be acceptable by other universities for obtaining the best qualified students.

In preparation for your upcoming small group discussions, interview the Director of Admissions of the University. Prepare an organized semistructured interview. Document the opening questions for examining the main issues. Consider not only the systems development life cycle procedures, but also socioethical issues in deciding whether to pursue applications development. Consider these comments/questions in opening the discussion within each group:

a. Technical and economic solutions are not enough to come to a conclusion.

b. The main purpose of this application: Track students with more than one early admission and eliminate those students from the early admission pool.

c. Who determines the requirements? Who makes the decision?

Scenario #2: The Local House of Worship

Your consulting group has been contacted to convert the current manual system of processing information for donation accountability and related activities (information inquiry, bookkeeping, word processing, etc.) to a computerized system. In addition, you are to consider the feasibility of fund collection using Master Card, American Express, and/or Visa. Consider electronic transfer of funds directly from the bank account each month.

Each group is to interview the President of the Parish Lay Group, which acts as advisor to the church, the head of the church, and a consultant who may or may not be interested in the account. Some isues are:

a. What church officials want as compared with church requirements

b. "Big brother" concerns over technology's invasion of the church

c. Vendor's obligations ... good business practice versus ethics

Reflections

Scenario #3: Athletics

Subgroup A: The coaching staff (end users or business managers)
You are the football coach (business manager or end user). You have just heard of this marvelous technological breakthrough for inserting microchips in the helmet of the quarterback. In this way, you could communicate with him without intricate hand signals and, furthermore, you could integrate information from your assistants (online) and provide the best options for plays.

Playback monitors already have been provided on the sidelines for continuous viewing by the coaches and players. The scouting report data, as well as current game data, are available. Your coaching staff wants this data integrated with computer graphics to produce an online simulation perhaps a play or two ahead of the current game, so appropriate adjustments could be made either to make the simulation happen (our team advantage), or prevent unfavorable situations from occurring.

Arrange for an immediate interview with information systems staff after filing the appropriate request for serivce. You have contacted the Alumni Association and they are behind you 100 percent. The Director of Athletics is an ex-football coach and supports the concept. His endorsement will aid your request to move to the head of the line for applications development.

The football program will provide some resource support through funds for software and hardware. Prepare your presentation to the Users Group, which group considers each quarter the applications portfolio, progress of projects underway, and perhaps reprioritization of projects as they impact the effectiveness of the organization.

Subgroup B: The Information Systems Users Group
Think about all the reasons why this request should or should not be considered. Some issues are as follows:

a. Robotic behavior of individuals (losing human identity).

b. What degree of automation is acceptable? Who decides?

c. The ends justify the means ... more money for the university.

Epilog

Positioning the Enterprise for the Future through People and Technology

◆ ◆ ◆

In our prologue, we commenced this text with the notion that the business world is not what you think. We painted a picture of the placement of information technology in that business world with all its successes and failures. The scope of our study of information technology extended beyond the business sector to include government agencies at the national, regional, and local levels and institutions of higher education in the United States, hence the use of the word "enterprise" throughout the text. It is clear from our discussion that advances in information technology will continue to test our patience as we try to catch up with the technology and harness its capabilities in our work and life.

With enterprises and individuals placing more importance on quality products and services, customers, and timeliness in a global marketplace, and on the need for the workplace and workers to be information enabled in order to be productive, *information technology, business process, and staff* must be fully integrated in order to compete successfully. These three entities (T, P, and S, respectively) are the basis for our STEP (*S*trategies for *T*echnology *E*nablement through *P*eople) Model presented in Chapter 1 (Exhibit 1–3). If any one of the entities are missing, the enterprise will not be able to position itself for the future. Other combinations of technology, process, and staff provide the enterprise with a starting point (corners of the cube) to move in the direction of the optimum situation (T, P, S). In brief, the three-dimensional view shows movement from one of the other seven corners to the ideal coordinate (T, P, S) along some path determined by the enterprise. The pathways were discussed in detail in the first part of the book.

Here, suffice it to say that some path toward information enablement must be identified by the enterprise. It may very well take the form of a visionary statement followed by specific actions which will enable the organization to use information technologies to streamline current operations, train and use its people effectively, and grasp new opportunities. Strategic initiatives, action plans, and action will dictate the path, how fast the organization moves along the path, and how effective and efficient it is in following the path. Stagnation in any of the three dimensions will adversely affect the outcome.

In Part I of this text, the need for strategic thinking is indicated, with the STEP Model illuminating the paths ahead. The IEMgr is a powerful force in this movement toward the ideal mix of business, process, and technology. Higher-order thinking skills, such as creative problem solving, must prevail across the enterprise in order to gain any momentum on the path. People create the momentum. Armed with the concept that an individual's technology or business sense, taken separately, is not enough to propel the enterprise along the path, the enterprise can proceed competitively with current operations and future aspirations. A new look at strategic opportunities, at information as a support umbrella for other business functions and proper deployment of information processing, and at a comprehensive approach to managing computing across the enterprise makes the trip easier to define and navigate.

In Part II, the business process dimension is fully examined. The new and challenging mechanisms for responding to accelerating global change require that some of the old department/discipline walls come down and be replaced with more intensive measures focused on processes. In this way, the service role of information technology can emerge in a timely and effective manner. People can improve their personal productivity; the enterprise can move toward the ideal condition of high and equal levels of technology, process, and staff.

In Part III, information technology is linked to business functions in order to indicate the ways in which the pathway can be traversed. How do information systems professionals and end users, representing all of the various types of IEMgrs in the enterprise, work in collaboration to bring information technology into appropriate areas of the enterprise? This part of the text examines several approaches to enabling business functions to move in concert toward enterprise goals and objectives.

Clearly, the paths have inherent flaws that impede travel, such as worker resistance, legacy bureaucratic organizational structures, legacy computer systems, societal pressures, crisis management practices, authoritarian decision-making styles, and the inability of teams to act responsively and to be accountable. Our text addresses these and other issues so that the reader will be more aware of the changing landscape of the business, government, and education sectors and will have the necessary tools to increase productivity and effectiveness in this world of change.

Appendix A.1

Information-Enabled Management (IEMgmt) Curriculum

◆ ◆ ◆

A.1.1. LEARNING OBJECTIVES FOR THE INFORMATION-ENABLED MANAGER (IEMgr)

In an effort to present a specific curriculum, it is necessary to begin with an overview of the IEMgr concept, which is discussed in-depth in Chapter 2. A summary of the four types of managers is depicted in Exhibit A.1–1.

In addition, other major concepts derived from Chapters 1 and 2 are summarized, as follows:

a. *Control systems:* In the new business environment, more control is passed to individuals at lower management levels with more localized accountability.
b. *Changing nature of enterprise:* To a workplace that is a faster, more complex, global and electronics-influenced environment.
c. *Virtual organizations:* Time and space compression creates the need to ensure quality with quick response, and customer service for "virtual," or customized, products and/or services.
d. *Changing roles of business professionals:* Effective use of technology by people; organizational expectations and worker aspirations (career planning).
e. *Emergence of a new breed of information-age professional (IEMgr):* A taxonomy for managing information across the enterprise, changing boundaries of information systems, and the learning organization.
f. *Education and training of the IEMgr:* Business outcome model with new learning objectives.

The ultimate goal is to introduce a specific "learning curriculum" developed over the past decade by the authors and presented at the DPMA INFOTECH

Appendix A.1

Exhibit A.1–1 — Types of IEMgrs in the IEMgmt Team: Technology vs. Process

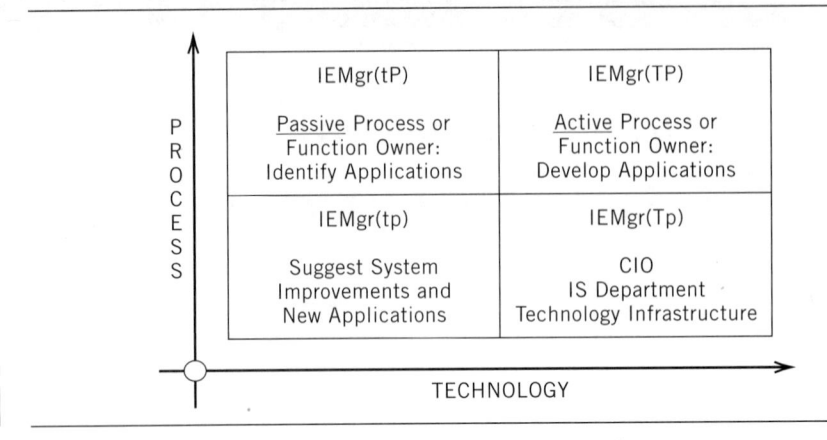

PROCESS ↑	IEMgr(tP) — Passive Process or Function Owner: Identify Applications	IEMgr(TP) — Active Process or Function Owner: Develop Applications
	IEMgr(tp) — Suggest System Improvements and New Applications	IEMgr(Tp) — CIO IS Department Technology Infrastructure

TECHNOLOGY →

Management Conference and Exposition [Wysocki & DeMichiell, 1991]. The content and delivery of this methodology was met with enthusiastic response by a large audience of educators and practitioners participating in this half-day professional development program. In order to design a comprehensive curriculum, a listing of learning objectives is provided in Exhibit A.1–2.

The IEMgmt program should not extend too far either in the management direction (ignoring the need for knowledge, comprehension, and application of information technology) or in the area of technology (without business sense, practicality of solution, and planning strategy). Management, technology, and more importantly, management of information technology, are necessary for enterprise effectiveness.

A.1.2. CURRICULA GUIDELINES AND TRENDS

The ACM, ASM, and DPMA collaborated and produced an information systems curriculum [Longenecker, et al., 1995]. This DPMA95 IS curriculum starts with desired characteristics for IS '95 graduates and learning units needed to provide those attributes and culminates with ten IS courses contained within five curricula areas. The academic program is designed for a small segment of information systems majors. Undergraduate IS programs throughout the country select aspects of the guidelines to be consistent with unique university requirements and limited faculty and computer resource constraints. For those IS-specific programs, there is a trend toward the middle of the continuum between technology-based courses and management-based courses [DeMichiell & Katz, *Interface*, 1992] summarized in Exhibit A.1–3.

Exhibit A.1-2

Learning Objectives for the IEMgr

Management and Conceptual Skills
- Have world view of enterprise, competitive markets, and changing role of manager
- Ability to balance competing objectives with resources and priorities
- Provide "relational" leadership to individuals and cross-functional teams
- Facilitate activity, gain consensus for decisions, and make decisions
- Be visionary and strategic in outlook; facilitate implementation of strategies
- Be enabled with information technology for personal productivity
- Flexible for adaptation to change; create and welcome change
- Ability to think creatively, critically, and entrepreneurially for innovative solutions
- Be a "systems thinker" and focus on interrelationships among problems and issues
- Ability to work with others in developing mission-critical and quality programs

Human Factors
- Commitment to organizational goals and objectives; accountable for actions
- Ability to develop practical and realistic alternative solutions
- Adopt a human-centered approach to the use of information technology
- Be aware and sensitive to the needs of other colleagues
- Be aware of the impact of other cultures and value systems on the enterprise
- Communicate openly and share information vital to productivity
- Incorporate ethical, social, legal, and political factors in problem solving
- Be proactive, reflective, and patient in approaches with colleagues

Technical and Analytical Skills
- Build and/or use various management and computer models
- Apply analytical and computation skills in analyzing and solving problems
- Ability to synthesize complex information in presenting alternative solutions
- Apply discipline-specific and multidisciplinary concepts to new situations
- Gathering data and information for conversion to general oral and written reports

Information-Enabling Skills
- Knowledge of information technology hardware, software, and services
- IS development methodology; analysis and design techniques
- Algorithmic design, programmatic problem solving, and data modeling
- Decision support and expert systems
- Telecommunications and networks
- Word processing, spreadsheets, presentation, database, project management, statistical software
- Direct work with business, government, or education on real, major projects

*Non-IS majors and minors would have only an exposure to these topics; the IEMgr would experience a program which would include many of these topics as an integral part of the liberally based, business program.

Exhibit A.1-3

Future Distribution of IS Undergraduate Programs

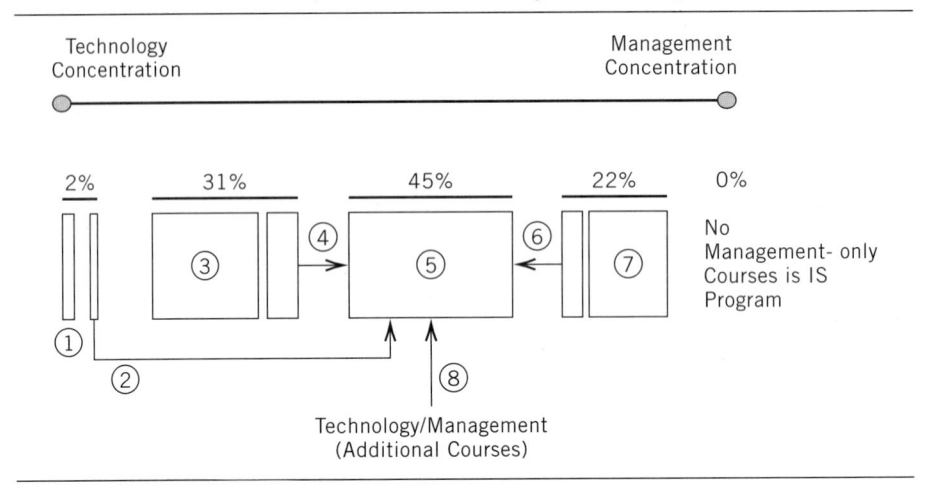

Technology Concentration ○————————————————○ Management Concentration

2% | 31% | 45% | 22% | 0%

① ② ③ ④ ⑤ ⑥ ⑦ ⑧

No Management-only Courses is IS Program

Technology/Management (Additional Courses)

A.1.3 BUSINESS OUTCOMES MODEL

Although the research and results of the DPMA effort are commendable, the other 30 courses of the 40-course university experience are not within the scope of that study. For IS professionals headed for technical systems positions in information systems departments that are shrinking due to decentralization of the IS function, certainly the DPMA academic program is appropriate. For the larger body of managers who are more a part of enterprise operating functions and more importantly, of "processes" in the form of cross-functional project teams, a different type of curriculum is needed. We suggest a total systems approach be applied to curricular design for students who will manage information across the enterprise and fill the large gap between the pure IS technologist (with no managerial skills) and the manager generalist (with no enablement in information technology). The link between what business wants and what academe can deliver is noted by Exhibit A.1-4.

A.1.4 BUSINESS CORE AND SUPPORT "STREAMS"

The framework for our curriculum is division of content into support and core "business streams," provided by Exhibits A.1-5 and A.1-6. The streams capture the multidisciplinary nature of our concept which permeates the entire program design. In addition to the content areas of the streams, it is expected that interactive and experiential methods (case study, simulation, and other student-driven activity) will dominate the teaching/learning scenario. Content and deliv-

Exhibit A.1-4 — Business Outcome Model

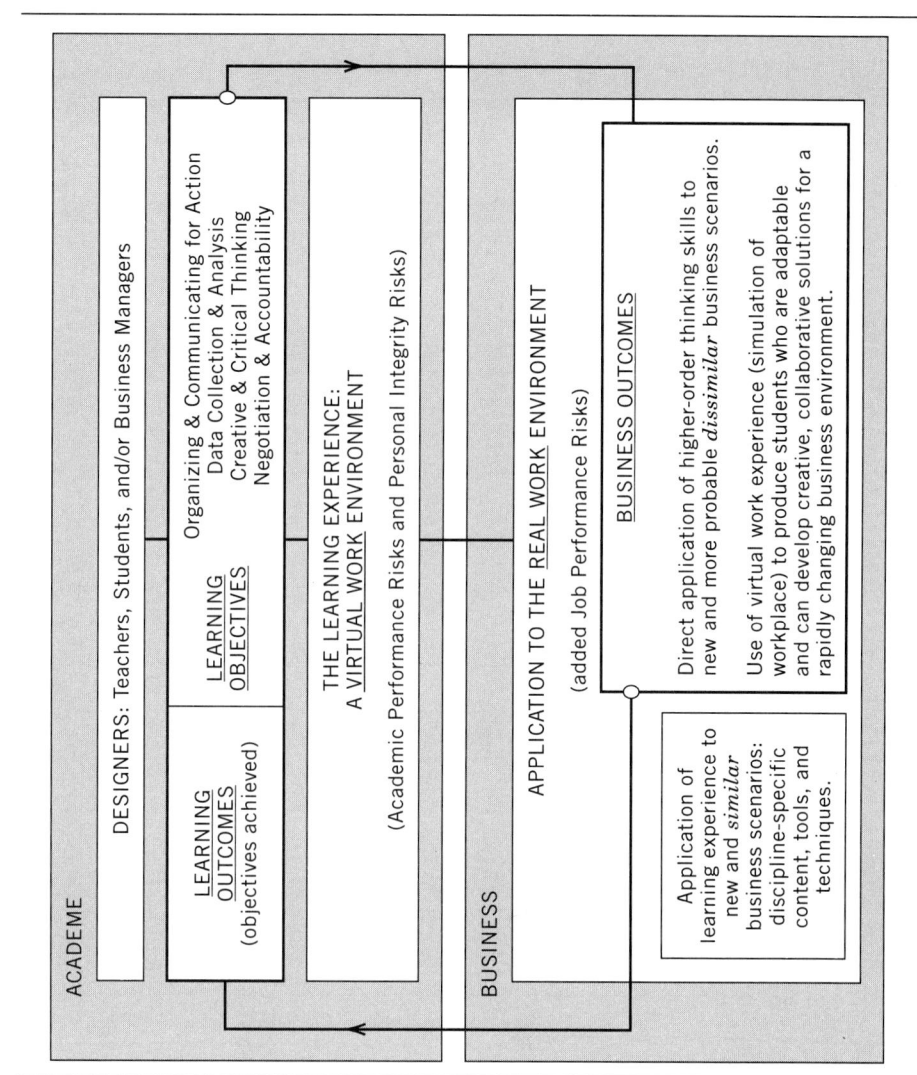

ery systems go hand in hand if the program is to achieve the explicit and comprehensive learning objectives.

A.1.5 CURRICULUM 2000

The final step is a specific set of courses for the comprehensive curriculum (not just Information Systems courses) depicted in Exhibit A.1–7.

Appendix A.1

Exhibit A.1–5

General Concepts for Information-Enabled Management (IEMgmt)

Business & Management ←— integration of core and support streams —→ Information Technology

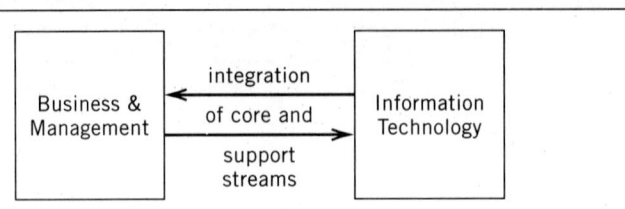

Exhibit A.1–6

General Educational Program

Support Streams

LIBERAL ARTS

English	History
Literature	Government
Fine Arts	Psychology
Philosophy	Languages
Sociology	Social Science

CREATIVE PROBLEM-SOLVING & HUMAN COMMUNICATIONS

SCIENCE, MATHEMATICS, AND ECONOMICS

Sciences, Logic, Statistics, Economics

Core Streams

BUSINESS SYSTEMS

Organizational Behavior, Management
Accounting Principles and Application
Politics, Ethics, Law
International Studies

MANAGING INFORMATION ACROSS THE ENTERPRISE

Information Systems in Society, Organizations, Individuals
Marketing Information Systems
Manufacturing Information Systems
Financial Information Systems

INFORMATION TECHNOLOGY

Computer Systems, Systems Analysis and Design
Telecommunications and Networks
Data Modeling, Decision Support and Expert Systems
Business Applications Projects

Exhibit A.1–7

Curriculum 2000
Traditional Four-year Undergraduate & Three-year Part-time Graduate Version

Full Time
Academic Environment
Undergraduate

Yr.	FALL TERM		SPRING TERM	
1	English History Language Economics Free Elective	Math(Logic) Introduction to IS Math(Stat) Accounting I	English History Language Economics	Math(Calc) Business Systems Psychology
2	Creativity & Problem Solving Management of Information Literature/Arts Mgmt & Science Behavior		Literature/Arts Government Philosophy Science	Accounting II
3	Human Comms Information Systems Analysis	Manufacturing IS	Sociology Information Systems Design International Business	Marketing IS
4	Social Science IS/Mgmt Elective Data Modeling	Business Law Financial IS	Business Ethics Decision Support Systems IS Elective Business Project Internship	

Part Time
Integrating Academic and Work Environments
Graduate

Yr.				
4,5	Managing Change Project Mgmt Marketing Management Competitive Forces	Financial Mgmt	Modeling & Logistics Value Chain Analysis Telecommunications Business Policies & Strategic Planning	Expert Systems
6,7	Business Internship (2-course equivalent)		Business Systems Project: Internship	

This proposal for the education of an IEMgr over a seven-year period culminating in a Master's Degree shows an arrangement of courses based on enterprise outcome and learning objectives for the learning organization. Other arrangements in content and scheduling are possible. The one selected for presentation here is chosen because it is the one most used by students/graduates. Certainly, there are inherent problems with Curriculum 2000 and its integrated approach, such as:

a. Discipline-specific faculty not interested in team teaching or facilitating student teams
b. Absence of texts for multidisciplinary courses (e.g., Marketing Information Systems)
c. Organizational complexity in designing courses, faculty workloads, and prerequisites
d. Organizational inertia against change; if agreeable, too long to implement program
e. Inclusion of all stakeholders in process; requires much added effort for everyone
f. Career implications of employability and promotability not formalized

If we wait for all the problems to be fully analyzed before the first step is taken, progress will be delayed. The authors have been involved in undergraduate and graduate higher education for over thirty years with complementary extensive experience in business and government. After researching the literature, teaching some portions of this program over the past decade, and listening to hundreds of students and workers at all levels, we have verified the soundness and practicality of this quality program for work and life in the year 2000 and beyond.

Appendix A.2

Case Study Data for Computer Resource Management Model (CRMM)

◆ ◆ ◆

STAGE I: ASSESSMENT

Management of Organization

Case #1. Religous organization. General administrative procedures, information work flow, data processing. Parish, shrine, and support groups.
[detailed analysis over several months]

Case #2. Computer consulting company. Client tracking system, medium-size company with branch offices in Washington and New England.
[general interviews only over several months]

Case #3. Security company. General administrative audit. Branch offices networked with diversified responsibilities and clients.
[preliminary analysis over several days]

Perception of Automation

Case #4. Cooperative Municipal Electric Company. Requirements analysis for diversified regional client base and internal user group. Broker of electrical energy.
[very detailed analysis; numerous interviews over two years]

Case #5. High-technology company. Special micro-based application of retirement planning model with connectivity to corporate computer.
[detailed analysis; limited interviews over several months]

Case #6. Food retail store for national chain. Requirements analysis for major upgrade of information technology. Expanded applications portfolio.
[detailed analysis over several months]

Case #7. State agency. Data from educational and business organizations on implementation strategies for programs on information technology.
[detailed analysis primarily from documentation over one year]

Planning

Cases #8–#13. Six colleges or universities in New England. Strategic initiatives focused on development of master computer resource plans. Management issues.
[detailed analysis; hundreds of interviews; follow-up data collected over five years]

Case #14. Advertising agency. Preliminary analysis of requirements needed for major changes in the use of information technology.
[limited interviews over a few weeks]

Case #15. Construction company. Large operation in commercial sector. Needs analysis for conversion to fully integrated administrative and proposal writing systems.

STAGE II: ACQUISITION

No case study data apply to this stage of the process. Data for Stage II are collected and analyzed for a separate research effort.

STAGE III: ALLOCATION

Case #16. Wholesale industrial supplies company. Large regional distributor with five branches. Expansion from a few independent microcomputer stations to several stations networked across five branch offices and warehouses.
[detailed analysis of numerous in-depth interviews over two years]

Case #17. Securities investment branch office. Office automation and presentation applications.
[analysis of a few interviews over several days]

Case #18. Insurance company accounting department. Training needs assessment for measurement of end-user computer literacy.
[limited interviews over a few days]

Case #19. Credit collection company. Expansion of information technology from independent station to network.
[preliminary analysis from limited interviews over several months]

Case #20. Federal government agency. High-level administrative office with special needs for electronic messaging.
[analysis from limited interviews over two months]

References

Adair, Charlene B. and Bruce A. Murray. 1994. *Breakthrough Process Redesign*. New York: Amacom. (ISBN 0-8144-5150-0)

Alter, Steven. 1996. *Information Systems: A Management Perspective,* 2nd edition. Manlo Park, CA: Benjamin/Cumings (ISBN 0-8053-2430-5)

Andrews, Dorine C. and Susan K. Stalick. 1994. *Business Reengineering: The Survival Guide*. Englewood Cliffs, NJ: Yourdon Press. (ISBN 0-13-014853-9)

Araoz, Daniel L. And William S. Sutton. 1994. *Reengineering Yourself: A Blueprint for Professional Success in the New Corporate Culture*. Holbrook, MA: Bob Adams.

Ball, Richard 1987. "Harnessing End-User Computing Without Hindering It," *Computerworld* (October 26), pp. 91–100.

Benjamin, Robert I., John F. Rockart, Michael S. Scott-Morton, and John Wyman. 1984. "Information Technology: A Strategic Opportunity," *Sloan Management Review,* 25, 3 (Spring): pp. 3–10.

Boisjoy, R. and R. DeMichiell. 1995. "A Business Outcome Model With an International Component: A New Workplace Dictates New Learning Experiences," *World Association for Case Method and Research Application International Conference Proceedings,* Switzerland, June.

Boone, Mary E. 1993. *Leadership and the Computer: Top Executives Reveal How They Personally Use Computers to Communicate, Coach, Convince, and Compete*. Rocklin, CA: Prima Publishing. (ISBN 1-5598858-323-1)

Branscomb, Anne Wells. 1994. *Who Owns Information? From Privacy to Public Access*. New York: Basic Books, HarperCollins.

Bridges, William. 1991. *Managing Transitions: Making the Most of Change*. Reading, MA: Addison-Wesley. (ISBN 0-201-55073-3)

Bridges, William. 1994. *JobShift: How to Prosper in a Workplace Without Jobs*. Reading, MA: Addison-Wesley. (ISBN 0-201-62667-5)

Buchanan, Jack R. and Richard G. Linowes. 1980. "Making Distributed Data Processing Work," *Harvard Business Review,* **58**, 5 (September–October): pp. 143–161.

Burgelman, Robert A., Modesto Maidique, and Steven C. Wheelwright. 1996. *Strategic Management of Technology and Innovation*. Chicago: Irwin. (ISBN 0-256-09128-5)

Burrus, Daniel with Roger Gittines. 1993. *Technotrends: How to Use Technology to Go Beyond Your Competition*. New York: HarperCollins. (ISBN 0-88730-627-6)

Buss, Martin D. J. 1981. "Penny-Wise Approach to Data Processing," *Harvard Business Review,* **59**, 4 (July–August): pp. 111–117.

Byham, William C., PhD. with Jeff Cox. 1988. *Zapp! The Lightning of Empowerment*. New York: Fawcett Columbine, Ballantine Books.

Champy, James. 1995. *Reengineering Management: The Mandate for New Leadership*. New York: HarperCollins. (ISBN 0-88730-698-5)

Cheney, Theodore R. 1989. "The Power of Irrelevant Thinking." Unpublished work, *Fairfield University Working Paper*, February 4.

Christensen, C. Roland et al., eds. 1991. *Education for Judgment: The Artistry of Discussion Leadership*. Boston: Harvard Business School. (ISBN 0-87584-255-0)

Churchland, Paul M. 1995. *The Engine of Reason, the Seat of the Soul: A Philosophical Journey into the Brain*. Cambridge, MA: MIT Press. (ISBN 0-262-03224-4)

Cleland, David I., *Strategic Management of Teams*, 1996. New York: John Wiley & Sons. (ISBN 0-471-12058-8)

Couger, J. Daniel. 1987. "End-User Computing: Investing for High Returns," *Computerworld* (May 25): pp. 67–72.

Couger, J. Daniel. 1996. *Creativity and Innovation in Information Systems Organizations*. New York: Boyd & Fraser. (ISBN 0-7895-0109-0)

Davenport, Thomas H. 1993. *Process Innovation: Reengineering Work through Information Technology*. Boston: Harvard Business School Press. (ISBN 0-87584-366-265)

Davidow, William H. and Michael S. Malone. 1992. *The Virtual Corporation*. New York: HarperBusiness. (ISBN 0-88730-593-8)

Davidson, Mike. 1995. *The Transformation of Management*. London: MacMillan. (ISBN 0-333-65083-2)

Davis, R. and T. Davenport. 1994. *2020 Vision*. New York: Simon and Schuster.

Dejoie, Roy, George Fowler, and David Paradice, eds. 1991. *Ethical Issues in Information Systems*. Boston: Boyd & Fraser. (ISBN 0-87835-562-6)

De Michiell, Robert. 1990. "Information Technology Transfer Between Educators and Practitioners: Management Strategies for Success," *Journal of Research on Computing in Education* (Summer 1990).

DeMichiell, R. and A. Katz. 1992. "Trends in Information Systems Curricula: Technology and Management-Driven Aspects," *Interface,* Spring.

DeMichiell, R. and E. Pavlock. 1994. "Performance Measurement of Student Accountability in Case Study Analysis," *World Association for Case Method and Research Application International Conference Proceedings,* Montreal, June.

DeMichiell, R. and R. Wysocki. 1991. "Facilitating Change with Cases Emphasizing Creativity," *World Association for Case Method Research and Application (WACRA) Annual International Conference Proceedings,* Berlin, July.

DeMichiell, R. and Wysocki, R. 1990. "Czechoslovakia in Transition: Developing Strategic Initiatives with Case Study Methodologies." *World Association for Case Method Research and Application Symposium,* Prague, 1990.

Dent, Harry S., Jr. 1995. *Job Shock*. New York: St. Martin's Press.

References

Dimancescu, Dan. 1992. *The Seamless Enterprise: Making Cross Functional Management Work*. New York: HarperCollins. (ISBN 0-88730-544-X)

Dobkin, Bruce H., M.D. 1986. *Brain Matters: Stories of a Neurologist and His Patients*. New York: Crown. (ISBN 0-51755983-8)

Drucker, Peter F. 1992. *Managing for the Future: The 1990s and Beyond*. New York: Truman Talley Books/Plume. (ISBN 0-452-26984-9)

Emshoff, James R. with Teri E. Denlinger. 1991. *The New Rules of the Game*. New York: Harper Business. (ISBN 0-88730-507-5)

Forcht, Karen A. 1994. *Computer Security Management*. Danvers, MA: Boyd & Fraser. (ISBN 0-87835-881-1)

Forester, Thomas. 1992. "Megatrends or Megamistakes? Whatever Happened to the Information Society?" *Computers and Society: Journal of ACM Special Interest Group* **22** (1,2,3,4).

Fried, Louis. 1995. *Managing Information Technology in Turbulent Times*. New York: Wiley. (ISBN 0-471-04742-2)

Gattiker, Urs E., ed. 1992. *Technology-Mediated Communication*. Berlin: Walter de Gruyter. (ISBN 3-11-0134195-5)

Garson, G. David. 1995. *Computer Technology and Social Issues*. Harrisburg, PA: Idea Group. (ISBN 1-878289-28-4)

Gerrity, T. P. and J. F. Rockart. 1986. "End-User Cumputing: Are You a Leader or a Laggard?" *Sloan Management Review*, **27**,4 (Summer): pp. 25–34.

Grover, Varun and William J. Kettinger. 1995. *Business Process Change: Concepts, Methods and Technologies*. Harrisburg, PA: Idea Group. (ISBN 1-878289-29-2)

Guinta, Lawrence R. and Nancy C. Praizler. 1995. *The QFD Book: The Team Approach to Solving Problems and Satisfying Customers Through Quality Function Deployment*. New York: Amacom. (ISBN 0-814405139-X)

Guttman, Michael and Jason R. Matthews. 1995. *The Object Technology Revolution*. New York: Wiley. (ISBN 0-471-60679-0)

Hafner, Katie and John Markoff. 1991. *Cyberpunk*. New York: Simon and Schuster. (ISBN 0671-68322-5)

Hammer, Michael and James Champy. 1993. *Reengineering the Corporation*. New York: Harper Business.

Hammer, Michael and Steven A. Stanton. 1995. *The Reengineering Revolution: A Handbook*. New York: HarperCollins. (ISBN 0-88730-736-1)

Hanna, Mary. 1993. "Attention to Process: UPS Software Quality." *Software Magazine* (December).

Hardaker, Maurice and Bryan K. Ward. 1987. "How to Make a Team Work," *Harvard Business Review*, **65**, 6 (November–December): pp. 112–117.

Harrington, H. James. 1991. *Business Process Improvement: The Breakthrough Strategy for Total Quality, Productivity, and Competitiveness*. New York: McGraw-Hill. (ISBN 0-07-026768-5)

Hogan, Rex. 1990. *A Practical Guide to Data Base Design*. Englewood Cliffs, NJ: Prentice-Hall. (ISBN 0-13-690967-1)

Johansen, Robert and Rob Swigart. 1994. *Upsizing the Individual in the Downsized Organization: Managing in the Wake of Reengineering, Globalization, and Overwhelming Technological Change*. Reading, MA: Addison-Wesley. (ISBN 0-201-62712-4)

Johnson, Deborah G. 1985. *Computer Ethics*. Engelwood Cliffs, NJ: Prentice-Hall. (ISBN 0-13-164005-4)

Johnson, Deborah G. and John W. Snapper. 1985. *Ethical Issues in the Use of Computers*. Belmont, CA: Wadsworth. (ISBN 0-534-04257-0).

Kallman, Ernest and John Grillo. *Ethical Decision-making and Information Technology*. New York: McGraw-Hill. (ISBN 0-07-033884-1)

Kanter, Rosabeth Moss. 1989. *When Giants Learn to Dance*. New York: Touchstone, Simon & Schuster. (ISBN 0-0671-61733-8)

Kanter, Rosabeth Moss. 1995. *World Class: Thriving Locally in the Global Economy*. New York: Simon and Schuster. (ISBN 0-684-81129-4)

Kao, John J. 1991. *The Entrepreneurial Organization*. Englewood Cliffs, NJ: Prentice Hall. (ISBN 0-13-282328-4)

Kaplan, Robert E. with Wilfred H. Darth and Joan R. Kofodimos. 1991. *Beyond Ambition: How Driven Managers Can Lead Better and Live Better*. San Francisco, CA: Jossey-Bass. (ISBN 1-55542-315-9)

Keen, Peter G. W. 1991. *Shaping the Future: Business Design Through Information Technology*. Cambridge, MA: Harvard Business School Press.

Khosrowpour, Mehdi, ed. 1995a. *Managing Information & Communications in a Changing Global Environment: Proceedings of the 1995 Information Resources Management Association International Conference, May 21–24, 1995, Atlanta, GA USA*. Harrisburg, PA: Idea Group. (ISBN 1-878289-31-4)

King, W. R. 1978. "Strategic Planning for Management Information Systems," *MIS Quarterly,* **2**: pp. 27–37.

Klein, H., R. DeMichiell, and R. Wysocki, eds. 1990. *Czechoslovakia in Transition: Developing Strategic Initiatives with Case Study Methodologies*. WACRA Symposium Publication, October.

Knoke, William. 1996. *Bold New World: The Essential Road Map to the 21st Century*. New York: Kodensha America. (ISBN 1-56836-095-4)

Kosko, Bart. 1993. *Fuzzy Thinking: The New Science of Fuzzy Logic*. New York: Hyperion. (ISBN 1-56282-839-8)

Lacity, Mary C. and Hirschheim, Rudy. 1995. *Beyond the Information Systems Outsourcing Bandwagon*. New York: Wiley. (ISBN 0-471-95822-0)

Larson, Richard W. and David J. Zimney. 1990. *The White-Collar Shuffle: Who Does What in Today's Computerized Workplace*. New York: Amacom. (ISBN 0-8144-5996-X)

Lasden, Martin. 1980. "Should MIS Report to the President?" *Computer Decisions* (August): pp. 54–65.

Leebaert, Derek, ed. 1991. *Technology 2001.* Cambridge, MA: MIT Press. (ISBN 0-262-12150-6)

Lucas, Henry C. 1986. *The Analysis, Design, and Implementation of Information Systems,* 2nd edition. New York: McGraw-Hill.

Madron, Thomas W. 1991. *Enterprise-Wide Computing: How to Implement and Manage LANs.* New York: Wiley. (ISBN 0-471-53297-5)

Mallach, Efrem G. 1994. *Understanding Decision Support Systems and Expert Systems.* Burr Ridge, IL: Richard D. Irwin. (ISBN 0-256-11896-5)

Malone, Thomas and John Rockart. 1991. "Computers, Networks, and the Corporation," *Scientific American,* **265**, 3.

Marion, Peller. 1993. *Crisis-Proof Your Career: Finding Job Security in an Insecure Time.* New York: Carol Publishing Group. (ISBN 1-55972-181-2)

Marshall, Edward M. 1995. *Transforming the Way We Work: The Power of the Collaborative Workplace.* New York: Amacom. (ISBN 0-8144-0255-0)

Martin, E. Wainright, Daniel W. DeHayes, Jeffrey A. Hoffer, and William C. Perkins. 1994. *Managing Information Technology: What Managers Need to Know.* Englewood Cliffs, NJ: Macmillan. (ISBN 0-02-376751-0)

Martin, Merle P. 1987. "The Human Connection in Systems Design—Part VI: Designing Systems for Change," *Journal of Systems Management* (July): p. 15.

Maynard, Herman Bryant, Jr. and Susan E. Mehrtens. 1993. *The Fourth Wave: Business in the 21st Century.* San Francisco, CA: Berrett-Koehler. (ISBN 1-881052-15-X)

McFarlan, F. W., and J. L. McKenney (1983). *Corporate Information Systems Management: The Issues Facing Senior Executives,* Homewood, IL.: Irwin.

McKeown, Patrick G. and Richard T. Watson. 1996. *Metamorphosis: A Guide to the World Wide Web and Electronic Commerce.* New York: Wiley. (ISBN 0-471-13689-1)

McLeod, Raymond, Jr. 1989. *Introduction to Information Systems. A Problem-solving Approach.* Chicago, IL: Science Research Associates. (ISBN 0-574-18745-6)

McLeon, Raymond, Jr. 1993. *Management Information Systems: A Study of Computer-based Information Systems.* New York: Macmillan. (ISBN 0-02–379481-X)

Mensching, James R. and Dennis A. Adams. 1991. *Managing an Information System.* Englewood Cliffs, NJ: Prentice Hall. (ISBN 0-13-552746-5)

Morris, Daniel and Joel Brandon. 1993. *Re-engineering Your Business.* New York: McGraw-Hill.

Morton, Michael S. Scott. 1991. *The Corporation of the 1990s: Information Technology and Organizational Transformation.* New York: Oxfort University Press. (ISBN 0-19-506358-9)

Mowshowitz, Abbe. 1976. *THe Conquest of Will: Information Processing in Human Affairs.* Reading, MA: Addison-Wesley. (ISBN 0-201-04930-9)

References

Naisbitt, John. 1994. *Global Paradox: The Bigger the World Economy, the More Powerful Its Smallest Players*. New York: Avon Books, Hearst Corporation. (ISBN 0-380-72489-8)

Naisbitt, John and Patricia Aburdene. 1985. *Re-inventing the Corporation: Transforming Your Job and Your Company for the New Information Society*. New York: Warner Books. (ISBN 0-446-51284-2)

Naisbitt, John and Patricia Aburdene. 1990. *Megatrends 2000: Ten New Directions for the 1990s*. New York: Avon Books, Hearst Corporation. (ISBN 0-830-70437-4)

Negroponte, Nicholas. 1995. *Being Digital*. New York: Knopf. (ISBN 0-679-43919-6)

Nelson, Marilyn McCord and W. T. Illingworh. 1991. *A Practical Guide to Neural Nets*. Reading, MA: Addison-Wesley. (ISBN 0-201-52376-0)

Neumann, Seev. 1994. *Strategic Information Systems*. New York: Macmillan. (ISBN 0-02-386690-X)

Nolan, Richard. 1979. "Managing the Crisis in Data Processing," *Harvard Business Review,* **57**, 3 (March–April): pp. 115–126.

Nolan, Richard L. and David C. Crosson. 1995. *Creative Destruction*. Boston, MA: Harvard Business School Press. (ISBN 0-87584-498-7)

Nolan, Richard L. and Cyrus F. Gibson. 1974. "Managing the Four Stages of EDP Growth," *Harvard Business Review,* **52**, 1 (January–February): pp. 76–78.

O'Brien, James A. 1995. *Introduction to Information Systems: An End User/Enterprise Perspective*. Chicago, IL: Richard D. Irwin. (ISBN 0-256-16221-2)

Oliva, Lawrence. 1992. *Partners, Not Competitors: The Age of Teamwork and Technology*. Harrisburg, PA: Idea Group. (ISBN 1-878289-09-8)

Owen, Darrell E. 1986. "Information Systems Organization: Keeping Pace with the Pressures," *Sloan Management Review,* **27**, 3 (Spring): p. 64.

Pagels, Heinz R. 1988. *The Dreams of Reason: The Computer and the Rise of the Sciences of Complexity*. New York: Bantam Doubleday Dell. (ISBN 0-553-34710-1)

Palvia, Shailendra, et al. 1992. *The Global Issues in Information Technology Management*. Harrisburg, PA: Idea Group. (ISBN 1-878289-10-1)

Panko, Raymond R. 1988. *End User Computing: Management, Applications, and Technology*. New York: Wiley. (ISBN 0-471-01102-9)

Parker, Marilyn M. and Robert J. Benson with H. E. Trainor. 1988. *Information Economics: Linking Business Performance to Information Technology*. Englewood Cliffs, NJ: Prentice Hall. (ISBN 0-13-464595-2)

Parsons, June Jamrich and Dana Oja. 1995. *New Perspectives on Computer Concepts*. Cambridge, MA: Course Technology. (ISBN 1-56527-164-5)

Penzias, Arno. 1989. *Ideas and Information: Managing in a High-Tech World*. New York: Simon & Schuster. (ISBN 0-671-69196-1)

References

Peters, Tom. 1992. *Liberation Management: Necessary Disorganization for the Nanosecond Nineties.* New York: Fawcett Columbine, Ballantine Books. (ISBN 0-4499-90888-7)

Petersen, John L. 1994. *The Road to 2015: Profiles of the Future.* Corte Madera, CA: Waite Group Press. (ISBN 1-878739-85-9)

Peterson, Robert. 1987. "Giving End-Users the MIS Seal of Good System Building," *Computerworld* (October 15): pp. 83ff.

Pigford, D. V. and Greg Bauer. 1995. *Expert Systems for Business: Concepts and Applications.* Danvers, MA: Boyd & Fraser. (ISBN 0-87709-127-7)

Porter, Michael E. 1980. *Competitive Strategy.* New York: Free Press.

Porter, Michael E. and Victor E. Millar. 1985. "How Information Gives You Competitive Advantage," *Harvard Business Review,* 63, 4 (July–August): pp. 149–160.

Restak, Richard M., M.D. 1979. *The Brain: The Last Frontier.* New York: Doubleday.

Rheingold, Howard. 1991. *Virtual Reality: The Revolutionary Technology of Computer-Generated Artificial Worlds and How It Promises to Transform Society.* New York: Simon & Schuster. (ISBN 0-671-69363-8)

Roberts, Lon. 1994. *Process Reengineering: The Key to Achieving Breakthrough Success.* Milwaukee, WI: ASQC Quality Press.

Rochester, Jack B. and John Rochester. 1994. *Computers for People,* 2nd edition. Burr Ridge, IL: Richard D. Irwin. (ISBN 0-256-10777-7)

Rockart, John F., and Adam D. Crescenzi. 1984. "Engaging Top Management in Information Technology," *Sloan Management Review,* vol. 25, no. 4 (Summer), pp. 3–16.

Rockart, John and Lauren Flannery. 1984. "The Management of End User Computing," in *The Rise of Managerial Computing,* Rockart, John and Christine Bullen, eds.

Rowan, Roy. 1986. *The Intuitive Manager.* New York: Berkley Publishing Group. (ISBN 0-425-13079-7)

Ruth, Christopher and Stephen Ruth. 1988. *Developing Expert Systems Using 1st Class.* Santa Cruz, CA: Mitchell. (ISBN 0-394-39275-2)

Rydz, John S. 1986. *Managing Innovation: From the Executive Suite to the Shop Floor.* Cambridge, MA: Ballinger. (ISBN 0-88730-028-6)

Saunders, Carol Stoak. 1986. "Impact of Information Technology on the Information Systems Department," *Journal of Systems Management* (April): pp. 18–24.

Senge, Peter M. 1990. *The Fifth Discipline: The Art & Practice of the Learning Organization.* New York: Doubleday/Currency. (ISBN 0-385-26094-6)

Sinclair, Stuart W. 1986. "The Three Domains of Information Systems Planning," *Journal of Information Systems Planning,* 3, 2 (Spring): pp. 8–16.

Sinetar, Marsha. 1991. *Developing a 21st Century Mind.* New York: Villard Books. (ISBN 0-679-40105-9)

Smith, Donna M. and David A. Kolb. 1986. *User's Guide for the Learning Styles Inventory.* Boston, MA: McBer and Company.

Sprague, Ralph H., Jr. and Barbara C. McNurlin. 1993. *Information Systems Management in Practice,* 3rd edition. Englewood Cliffs, NJ: Prentice Hall. (ISBN 0-13-465477-3)

Sprague, Ralph H., Jr. and Hugh J. Watson, eds. 1993. *Decision Support Systems: Putting Theory into Practice.* Englewood Cliffs, NJ: Prentice-Hall. (ISNBN -13-0366229-8)

Stack, Jack. (1992). *The Great Game of Business.* New York: Doubleday. (ISBN 0-385-47525-X)

Stoner, James, A. F. 1982. *Management,* 2nd ed. Englewood Cliffs, NJ: Prentice-Hall. (ISBN 0-13-549667-55)

Straus, Susaan. 1992. "Thinking Styles and Organizational Effectiveness." *European Business Report,* (October–November).

Talbott, Stephen. 1995. *The Future Does Not Compute.* Sebastopol, CA: O'Reilly and Associates. (ISBN 1-56592-085-6)

Thierauf, Robert J. 1987. *Effective Management Information Systems: Accent on Current Practices.* Columbus, OH: Merrill. (ISBN 0-675-20745-2)

Thompson, Arthur A., Jr. and A. J. Strickland, III. 1992. *Strategic Management: Concepts and Cases.* Homewood, IL: Richard D. Irwin. (ISBN 0-256-09698-8)

Tom, Paul. 1987. *Managing Information as a Corporate Resource.* Glenview, IL: Scott, Foresman.

Tomasko, Robert M. 1993. *Rethinking the Corporation: The Architecture of Change.* New York: American Management Association. (ISBN 0-8144-5022-9)

Turban, Efraim. 1993. *Decision Support and Expert Systems: Management Support Systems.* New York: Macmillan. (ISBN 0-02-421691-7)

Turban, Efraim, Ephraim McLean, and James Wetherbe. 1996. *Information Technology for Management.* New York: Wiley. (ISBN 0-471-58059-7)

von Oech, Roger. 1990. *A Whack on the Side of the Head.* New York: Warner. (ISBN 0-446-39-158-1)

Wang, Charles B. 1994. *TechnoVision: The Executive's Survival Guide to Understanding and Managing Information Technology.* NewYork: McGraw-Hill. (ISBN 0-07-068155-4)

Watson, Hugh J. and Houston H. Carr. 1987. "Organizing for Decision Support System Support: The End-User Services Alternative," *Journal of Management Information Systems,* **4**, 1: pp. 83–95.

Wetherbe, James C. and Nicholas Vitalari. 1994. *Systems Analysis and Design: Best Practices.* New York: West. (ISBN 0-314-02697-7)

Wood, Jane and Denise Silver. 1989. *Joint Application Design: How to Design Quality Systems in 40% Less Time.* New York: Wiley.

Wysocki, Robert K. 1990a. "On Chauffers, Hybrids, and Corporate Citizens," *CIS Educator Forum,* **2**, 2 (Winter): pp. 26–28.

Wysocki, Robert K. 1990b. "On Educating the Technomanager," *CIS Educator Forum,* **2**, 3 (Spring): pp. 22–24.

Wysocki, Robert K. and James Young. 1990. *Information Systems: Management Principles in Action.* New York: Wiley. (ISBN 0-471-60302-3)

Wysocki, Robert K., Robert Beck, Jr., and David B. Crane. 1995. *Effective Project Management: How to Plan, Manage, and Deliver Projects on Time and within Budget.* New York: Wiley. (ISBN 0-471-11521-5)

Zahedi, Fatemeh. 1995. *Quality Information Systems.* Danvers, MA: Boyd & Fraser. (ISBN 0-7895-0061-2)

Zuboff, Soshana. 1988. *In the Age of the Smart Machine: The Future of Work and Power.* New York: Basic Books.

Index

Accounting and finance, 269–270
Artificial intelligence (AI), 261–262
  See also Expert systems

Benefit/beneficiary matrix, 50–52
Bloom's Taxonomy
  application of, 213
  components of, 210–212
Business
  information technology in, 17–19
  as a matrix, 150–151
  as set of processes, 150
  trends in international, 26–27
Business functions
  See also Accounting and finance; Corporate planning; Human resources; Manufacturing; Marketing
  information technology applied to, 265–272
  simulation, 255–264
Business outcome model, 36–37
Business process
  See also Process quality management
  benefits of using, 152
  boundaries between, 151–152
  core process, 150–151, 154–156
  defined, 150
  design, 155–156
  identification, 184–185
  implementing new, 186
  redesign hierarchy, 180–182
  redesign process flow model, 187–188
  roles in, 156–157
  support processes, 150–151, 154–156
Business process redesign
  See also Business process reengineering
  hierarchy of change, 180
  process flow model, 187

Business process reengineering
  definitions, 180–181
  IEMgmt team in, 181–182, 186
  lessons learned, 158–160
  methodologies, 182–186
Business simulation
  model design, 256–258
  process of, 258–261
  uses for, 255–256
Business systems planning (BSP) methodology, 88–91

Career development
  information-enabled professionals, 207–223
  planning, 16–17, 223–225
  plans, 225–228
Career interests profile, 212
Centralization
  of IS department, 101–102
  organizational operations, 103–104
Chief executive officer (CEO), 117–118
Chief information officer (CIO)
  See also Information systems (IS) manager
  changing nature of, 59–61
  responsibilities, 40
Client/server architecture, 61, 103, 106–108
Competitive strategy
  IEMgmt team responsibility for, 53
  role of information technology in, 66–69
Complexity, 72
Component design, 155–156
Computer-aided software engineering (CASE), 286
Computer-integrated manufacturing (CIM), 240–241
Computer Resource Management Model (CRMM)
  components, 126–127, 132
  implementation of, 128–132

Computer systems
  computer resource management model, 126–141
  factors in development, 122
Computing
  end user, 314–315
  work group, 109–110, 317–319
Concurrent engineering, 155–156
Continuous quality improvement, 182, 192–193
Contract negotiation
  managing, 140
  in procurement process, 134–135
Corporate data model, 299–300
Corporate planning
  areas of concern, 266
  questions related to, 265
Creativity, 15, 70–74
Critical success factors (CSFs)
  defined, 82
  examples of, 83
  sources of, 82
Customer value integration concept, 166
Customer value profile, 166

Data
  enterprise data model, 84
  management, 299–304
  object technology, 304–305
  security, 301–302
Database management
  integrated, 300–301
  object-oriented systems, 305
Databases
  enterprise, 103
  relational, 302–304
Data processing, six stages model, 43
Data processing (DP) unit, 42
Data warehousing, 301
Decentralization
  of IS department, 102
  IS department push toward, 109
  of organizational control and operations, 4–5, 103–105
Decision-making
  decision support systems, 249–252
  executive support systems, 249–252
  introduction of information technology, 68–69

Decision-making systems (DSS)
  artificial intelligence in, 262
  software packages, 26
Decision support systems (DSS), 249–252
Desktop publishing, 241
Documentation, 165

EDI. *See* Electronic data interchange (EDI)
Educational delivery requirements, 73
EER. *See* Extended entity-relationship (EER)
Effectiveness, 53–54
Efficiency, 53–54
Electronic data interchange (EDI), 7, 9–10, 300
Electronic data processing (EDP), 44–45
Electronic mail (e-mail), 320
Elevation gap, 107
End user community (EUC), 301–302
End user computing (EUC)
  factors in effective support for, 321
  management concerns related to, 314–315
  support strategies, 321–324
End users
  management responsibilities, 332–334
  relation to information work, 310–314
  systems development life cycle, 334–340
Engineering, concurrent, 155–156
Enterprise
  decision-making relationships in, 250–255
  future, 27–28
  responsibilities of IEMgmt team in, 52–57
  strategic grid, 47–50
Enterprise database
  design of, 103
  server as, 103
Enterprise data model, 61, 84
EUC. *See* End user community (EUC); End user computing (EUC)
Executive information systems (EIS), 252
Executive support systems (ESS), 249–253
Expert systems, 261–263
  based on fuzzy logic, 264
  shells, 262
Extended entity-relationship (EER), 303

Fuzzy logic, 264

Index

Globalization, 316–317
Graphical user interfaces (GUIs), 7
Groupware, 319

Hardware architecture
  client/server, 61
  data, 61
Hardware infrastructure, 108
Human resources
  as business function, 270–272
  computerized management systems, 271–272
Hypertext, 320

IEMgmt team
  in business process, 157
  considerations in systems development, 281–289
  defined, 33
  evolution of, 57
  growth and maturation of, 47
  in process quality management, 182
  responsibilities of, 52–57
  role at end user level, 316
  role in continuous quality improvement, 192–193
  role in human resource development, 230–231
  role in process quality management, 192
  role in reengineering, 181–182
IEMgrs
  collaborative strategies for, 136–137
  defined, 30–31
  education and training, 33–37
  evolution in corporation, 42–47
  learning objectives, 349
  relationships among, 62
  role in project management, 201–203
IEMgr (TP), 32
  as bridge, 157
  in developing information systems department, 46
  role in reengineering, 181
  support function, 157
IEMgr (Tp), 31–32
  emergence, 107
  at enterprise level, 156–157
  relation to IEMgmt team, 52–53
  role in reengineering, 181
  support function, 157
IEMgr (tP), 33
  beginnings of, 46
  responsibility of, 157
  role in reengineering, 181
  role in technology acquisition, 157
IEMgr (tp), 33
  beginnings of, 46
  relation to IEMgr (tP), 157
Imaging and document management, 241
Information
  as corporate resource, 46
  management across enterprise, 17–19
  organizing for control of, 243–244
Information enabled professions database (IEPD), 208–209
Information function
  deployment alternatives, 100–108
  evolution within an organization, 97–100
Information systems (IS)
  benefit/beneficiary matrix, 50–52
  domains of IEMgmt team, 53–55
  management of islands of technology, 242
  new applications, 291–293
  product classification, 85–87
  responsibility for, 40–41
  six stages hypothesis, 42–47
  strategic grid model, 47–50
  in support function, 55–57
  trends in organization of, 97–100
  upgrade projects, 290–291
Information systems (IS) department
  alternative organizational structures, 110–114
  centralized or decentralized, 101–106
  changing functions of, 235–239
  combining centralized and decentralized elements, 103
  controls and standards, 335–340
  corporate responsibility of, 53–54
  functional areas of, 107–108
  organizational structures, 110–114
  proactive, reactive, and collaborative roles, 233–235
  push toward decentralization, 109
  reporting alternatives, 116–118
  role in work group computing, 109–110

Information systems (IS) department—(*Continued*)
  in six stages model, 46
  as support organization, 114–116
Information systems (IS) manager
  certification of end user systems, 339–340
  as IEMgr (Tp), 107
  investment portfolio of, 85–88
  reach in organization, 107–108
  reporting to CEO, 117–118
  reporting to steering committee, 116–117
  roles and responsibilities, 330–332
  service level agreement, 329
  in six stages model, 47
Information systems (IS) planning
  business systems planning, 88–91
  integrated strategic, 91–94
  methods, 80–84
Information systems portfolio, 85–87
Information technology
  applied to business function, 265–272
  in business, 17–19
  in business process redesign, 181
  business value of, 40
  in corporate planning, 266
  effect of, 5–13
  exploitation of, 6, 60–61
  factors in effective management, 14
  with globalization, 316–317
  planning for, 74–80
  in strategic grid model, 47–50
Innovation, 15, 70–74
Internet, 6–7, 320
Investment portfolio, 85–86
Islands of technology
  definition, 239
  examples, 239
  information systems management of, 242

Job analysis, 219–223
Joint applications design (JAD), 296–297
Joint project planning (JPP), 294–295

Knowledge base, 261
Knowledge engineering environments, 262
Knowledge worker, 11

Learning corporation, 27–28, 70
Learning styles inventory (LSI)
  components of, 214–217
  individual data, 218
Learning styles profile, 212
Legacy systems, 61–62

Mainframe architecture, 106–108
Management
  See also Information systems (IS) manager; Project management
  information systems portfolio, 85–88
  obsolete structures of, 76
Management information systems (MIS)
  in six stages model, 45–46
Manufacturing, 268–269
Marketing, 266–268
Market test, 155–156
Multimedia, 241

Neural networks (neural nets), computer-based, 263–264

Object technology, 304–305
Office automation, 239–240
Open system inoperability (OSI), 300
Opportunity assessment, 163
Organizations
  restructuring, 70–74
  role in worker development, 15–16
  structures of, 110–114
Outsourcing
  advantages and disadvantages, 128, 130
  issues, 118–119, 123–126
  process, 128–141
  selective, 126–128

Planning
  See also Information systems (IS) planning
  business systems planning methodology, 88–91
  dynamic nature of, 69–70
  for information systems, 80–84
  information technology, 74–80
  for information technology, 78–80
  integrated strategic information systems, 91–94
  methods for information systems, 80–84

Index

Process quality management (PQM), 182, 187–188, 192
Procurement process
    computer resource management model (CRMM), 126–127
    overview of, 130, 131
    recommendations for general, 135
Product development, new, 154–156
Productivity, 162
Product test and release, 155–156
Professionals
    development, 33–37
    development of IEMgr, 33–37
    information system and non-information system, 29–37
    new information age, 17–19, 29, 41–42
Professionals, information-enabled
    defined, 5
    development, 207–223
Programming languages
    interface, 320
    object-oriented, 305
Project
    defined, 197–198
    parameters, 198–199
    project management life cycle, 199–201
    project team, 243–244
    role of IEMgr, 201–203
Project management
    components of, 193–195
    functions and tasks, 195–198
    in information systems development, 293–295
    life cycle, 199–201
    parameters, 198–199
    role of IEMgr, 201–203
Project planning, joint, 294

Quality
    See also Total quality management (TQM)
    achieving, 157–160
    continuous quality improvement, 182, 192–193
    defined, 161
    quality-level expectations, 170–171
Quality function deployment (QFD)
    application, 173–176
    stages of, 164–169
    for total quality management, 163–164
Quality impact matrix, 191

Reengineering. *See* Business process reengineering
Request for Proposal (RFP), 134–139, 319
Return on investment (ROI), 168–169
RFP. *See* Request for Proposal (RFP)
Risk
    computing applications, 335–339
    in management of change, 63–64

Self-assessments, 212
Self-directed work teams, 244
Server, 103
Simulations
    business functions, 255–264
    software for, 269–270
    workforce, 272
Six stages model (Nolan), 42–47
Skills
    rethinking, 16–17
    skill levels using Bloom's Taxonomy, 210–212
Skills gap, 208–209
    definition, 219
    measurement of, 221–222
    prioritizing, 222–223
Software
    browsers, 320
    computer-aided software engineering, 286
    in evolving information systems, 106–108
    for human resource functions, 271–272
    intuitive, 6
    problems of outmoded, 289–290
    simulation packages, 269–270
SQL. *See* Standard query language (SQL)
Staff skills profile database (SSPD), 208–210
Standard query language (SQL), 303
Steering committee, 116–117
STEP model
    components of, 153–154
    explained, 19–23
Strategic grid model, 47–50
Strategic success factors. *See* Critical success factors (CSFs)
Strategy
    defined, 161
    individual's future work-related, 179
Success
    critical success factors, 189–191
    measurement of, 171–172

SWOT analysis, 128
System development methodologies (SDMs)
    goals, 277–280
Systems development methodologies (SDMs)
    choosing, 281–289
    life cycle, 278
Systems development project classification, 294

Technology gap, 6
Total quality management (TQM), 163–164

Value-added, 161, 169
Value-added assessment
    analysis, 169–170
    in reengineering, 161

Value chain theory, 67–68
Value creation, 166–167
Vendor relationships, 131–134
Virtual work environment
    in business outcome model, 36–37
    defined, 36
Vision, 161

Work, information-related, 310–314
Workforce simulations, 272
Work groups
    computing, 109–110, 317–320
    formation of, 109
World Wide Web (the Web, WWW), 6, 320